Oracle Press™

D1551079

Hands-On Oracle Database 10g Express Edition for Windows

Compliments of

PITT-Greensburg

Bookstore

ORACLE®   *Oracle Press*™

Hands-On Oracle Database 10g Express Edition for Windows

Steve Bobrowski

McGraw-Hill

New York   Chicago   San Francisco
Lisbon   London   Madrid   Mexico City   Milan
New Delhi   San Juan   Seoul   Singapore   Sydney   Toronto

McGraw-Hill books are available at special quantity discounts to use as premiums and sales promotions, or for use in corporate training programs. For more information, please write to the Director of Special Sales, Professional Publishing, McGraw-Hill, Two Penn Plaza, New York, NY 10121-2298. Or contact your local bookstore.

Hands-On Oracle Database 10*g* Express Edition for Windows

1234567890 CUS CUS 019876

Book p/n 0-07-226332-6 and CD p/n 0-07-226333-4
parts of
ISBN 0-07-226331-8

Sponsoring Editor	**Proofreader**
Lisa McClain	Susie Elkind
Editorial Supervisor	**Indexer**
Janet Walden	Valerie Robbins
Acquisitions Coordinator	**Production Supervisor**
Alex McDonald	James Kussow
Technical Editors	**Composition**
Tom Kyte	International Typesetting
Chris Beck	and Composition
Copy Editor	**Illustration**
William McManus	International Typesetting
	and Composition

For Tesia

About the Author

Steve Bobrowski is the CEO of 4SKWare Technologies, Inc., which operates the popular web service The Database Domain (www.dbdomain.com), an information hub dedicated to teaching people all about high-end database management systems such as Oracle. The site has recently launched training specifically for users of Oracle XE. In addition to writing for several leading industry publications such as *Oracle Magazine*, Steve is also the author of the award-winning book, *Mastering Oracle7 & Client/Server Computing* (Sybex; 1994, 1996), and of Oracle Press's (McGraw-Hill) *Oracle8 Architecture* (1997), *Oracle8i for Windows NT Starter Kit* (2000), *Oracle8i for Linux Starter Kit* (2000), and *Hands-On Oracle Database 10g Express Edition for Linux* (2006). Steve has also presented at industry events such as Oracle OpenWorld, and provides contract database administration, application development, and performance-tuning services for Fortune 1000 businesses and major government institutions. Previously, Steve worked for Oracle Corporation, where he assisted in the development of Oracle and wrote more than 1500 pages of Oracle's own documentation for Oracle7 and Oracle8.

Contents at a Glance

Contents

PART I
Getting Started

PART III
Database Administration

Foreword

n 1987 I was just graduating from college and starting my career as a software developer. I started as a PL/I programmer on IBM mainframes using two databases: SQL/DS on VM/CMS and DB2 on MVS. I became familiar with SQL, but was limited as to what I could do on these production environments.

One day while reading a magazine, *Dr. Dobbs Journal*, I noticed an advertisement for a relational database that ran on DOS—simple PCs. It was a product named "Oracle." I clipped out the coupon, filled it in, and ordered this relational database for $99. About two weeks later, a dozen or so 5-1/4" floppy disks showed up in my mailbox and I had Oracle version 5.1.5c and all of the development tools I needed to start playing, learning, and exploring with. I was hooked.

That was then, this is now—and now, you have the ability to do in 10 minutes for free what took me weeks and $99 ($166 in 2006 dollars!) in 1987 to accomplish. With the introduction of Oracle Database 10g Express Edition, you can download, develop, deploy, and distribute your applications for free.

The book you are looking at now is the roadmap to exploiting this free software offering, the guide you need to successfully learn the ins and outs of this thing called Oracle. When I first started in 1987, all I had was the software and documentation to go on (and much slower computers). Today you have access to not only the software and documentation (as well as discussion forums), but also the roadmap and guide you need to be successful and productive with Oracle Database XE in hours or days—not the weeks and months it took in the past.

Steve Bobrowski has written the definitive guide on getting started with Oracle Database XE and you have it in your hands right now. I like things that are simple, easy to understand, easy to read—all of that is present in this book.

Steve starts with a quick introduction to databases and Oracle in general. After this very quick overview, we get into the meat of the book with the installation and getting started with Oracle Database XE. Installation is quick and easy, and within minutes, you'll be on your way to the rest of the book.

The remainder of the book is logically broken into two main components. The first part is geared towards application development (my favorite topic). Steve builds up from using simple SQL, to implementing with PL/SQL, and finally building true applications with Oracle Database XE's Application Express tool, the web-based development/administration tool that comes with Oracle Database XE. Steve uses both the character mode, command-line tool SQL*Plus (an invaluable tool everyone should be familiar with) and the graphical environment built with Application Express, interchanging between the two environments to provide a comprehensive overview of both. After you are done with this section, you will be able to not only get into Oracle Database XE and play around, but also build "real" applications that can be deployed to a large group simply by advertising a URL.

The next section contains the technical background you need to administer, secure, and tune your database and applications. Steve covers everything from access control to how to run and interpret Statspack reports in a step-by-step tutorial fashion. Everything is covered here—from how to read and understand the Statspack reports (a report showing how the "system" is performing, the work it is doing), to how to install it and get your first reports generated. Nothing is left out.

Every chapter is full of examples, *concrete* examples. The examples are well thought out and demonstrate the key concepts Steve is trying to get across. A friend of mine ends his e-mails with the Latin quote "nullius in verba," or "nothing in words;" another way of saying "don't trust just words." This book exemplifies that trait and takes pains to prove out time and time again that what is written here is true.

If you are just beginning Oracle, whether you are an experienced SQL developer coming from another database, as I was in 1987, or a complete "newbie" to this database thing, you will find this book truly useful in getting started—quickly and easily.

Tom Kyte
asktom.oracle.com

Acknowledgments

Typically, the author of a book gets all or most of the credit for writing the masterpiece itself. Think about it—how many of you can name Stephen King's editor? However, what most people do not understand is that producing a book is the collective effort of several people working toward a common goal. The words that follow are an attempt to thank formally the many people who have helped me write, edit, and print this book. Hopefully, our work has produced a publication that helps you accomplish your own personal goals in working with Oracle XE.

First of all, I'd like to thank my family and friends for tolerating how many times I had to say "I can't do it, I'm behind on a deadline." There were way too many early mornings, late nights, and long weekend days spent alone in front of a computer, apart from my significant others, producing this book. I greatly appreciate the breathing space that everyone gave to me so that I could accomplish this task.

Next, I'd like to thank the two technical editors who contributed to this book: Tom Kyte and Chris Beck. The outstanding technical expertise and reviews of these Oracle professionals were instrumental in making this book a comprehensive and accurate guide to Oracle XE. I'd also like to extend an extra special thanks to Tom Kyte for writing the Foreword for this book.

There are countless other people that, through the years, have knowingly or unknowingly contributed to my Oracle knowledge. While it would be difficult to identify and thank them all, I'd like to extend a special thanks to the person that I will always consider as my mentor in the context of Oracle: Ken Jacobs. The unabridged knowledge that Ken possesses about Oracle, SQL, and database systems is nothing less than amazing. While working with Ken during my tenure at Oracle Corporation, his enthusiasm for Oracle was contagious and forever changed the direction of my professional career. Thanks Ken.

The folks at McGraw-Hill also deserve many thanks for publishing this book. Specifically, I'd like to thank Lisa McClain and Alex McDonald, who demonstrated enormous patience as the pages of this book trickled in. Project editor Janet Walden kept things on track and copy editor Bill McManus did an outstanding job spotting and correcting all my grammatical faux pas—thanks very much.

Also, this book would not have been possible without the help of coffee.

Introduction

his book is a hands-on, intermediate-level introduction to the installation, configuration, and use of Oracle Database 10*g* Express Edition (Oracle XE). For your convenience, this book also includes a CD with a copy of Oracle XE. Once you install Oracle XE on your computer, you can complete the practice exercises in each chapter to quickly learn, with a hands-on approach, the most typically used features of Oracle XE. The following sections explain important additional information that you should understand before beginning to read the body of this book.

This Book Covers...

This book teaches you the concepts of Oracle XE and then provides you with hands-on exercises so that you can quickly learn the skills necessary to work with Oracle XE. Whether you want to develop and maintain database applications with Oracle XE or simply want to understand more about how Oracle functions, this book is for you. Oracle is a sophisticated database management product that is challenging to master, no matter what background you have with computers, software, or information management technology. After reading this book, you will have a tremendous perspective of everything Oracle, including the structure of Oracle databases, how Oracle's software architecture manages access to shared databases, and other concepts about Oracle.

This book is not meant to be a complete guide for Oracle Database 10*g* Express Edition or Oracle. Rather, this book's primary goal is to get you started with Oracle XE quickly and give you the confidence to pursue more advanced studies with Oracle XE (and, perhaps, other editions of Oracle).

This Book Assumes...

This book assumes that you are new to Oracle XE and want to learn something about its features and functionality in some depth. However, given the intended scope of this book, it also assumes that you have a general knowledge of database systems, especially relational database systems. Because Oracle XE is a relational database management system, some general experience with relational database systems will most certainly make this book easier to read. For example, if you already understand some of the basic concepts of a relational database system such as tables and views, you will simply have to focus on how Oracle XE implements the relational database model. If you have no background with database systems, I suggest you read the classic work, *An Introduction to Database Systems, Eighth Edition* (Addison Wesley, 2003), written by one of the founders of the relational database model, C. J. Date.

Conventions Used Throughout This Book

Throughout this book's hands-on exercises, you'll be interacting with Oracle XE using SQL commands—for introductory information about SQL, see Chapters 1 and 3. This section explains the conventions that this book uses when presenting SQL command syntax listings and examples.

Except in clauses that contain case-sensitive conditional tests, Oracle ignores the case of letters throughout SQL commands. However, as you read this book, you'll notice that SQL command examples include a mix of uppercase and lowercase keywords and variables. For clarity, all SQL keywords are listed in uppercase letters, and all command variables (command components that are not actually part of the SQL language) are listed in lowercase letters. For example, consider the following example of the SQL command CREATE TABLE:

```
CREATE TABLE salesreps (
      id  INTEGER,
      lastname  VARCHAR2(100),
      firstname  VARCHAR2(50),
      commission  NUMBER(38)
     );
```

This book also includes syntax listings for many SQL commands so that you know how to structure corresponding SQL statements. For example, the following is an abbreviated syntax listing for the SQL command ALTER TABLE:

```
ALTER TABLE [schema.]table
     ADD [CONSTRAINT constraint]
       { {UNIQUE|PRIMARY KEY} (column [, column] ... )
       | FOREIGN KEY (column [, column] ... )
```

```
     REFERENCES [schema.]table [(column [, column] ... )]
     [ON DELETE {CASCADE|SET NULL}]
  | CHECK (condition)   }
```

Note the following about this syntax:

- All SQL keywords appear in uppercase letters (for example, ALTER TABLE, ADD).

- All command variables appear in lowercase italic letters (for example, *schema, table, constraint*).

- All optional command components appear between brackets, [ ]. *Do not enter brackets when building a command.*

- All required command components appear between braces, { }. *Do not enter braces when building a command.*

- A vertical bar (|) indicates an option in a list of an optional or required command component. *Do not enter a vertical bar when building a command.*

- Unless otherwise stated, all parentheses, commas, operators (for example, =, :=), and other symbols are part of the command itself and must be entered when building a command.

- Ellipses (...) indicate that the preceding command component can be repeated. *Do not enter ellipses when building a command.*

Errata

If you find a mistake in this book, please do not hesitate to send an e-mail to me at handsonxe@dbdomain.com. I will be glad to do my best to fix the problem in the next revision of the book. An ongoing list of confirmed errata for this book is maintained at www.oraclepressbooks.com.

Onward

Now that you know where this book will take you and how it will present information, you are ready to begin learning all about Oracle XE and how you can use it to manage information.

PART I

Getting Started

CHAPTER
1

Introduction to
Databases and Oracle

ost everyone has heard the cliché, "information is power." And is this ever true. When you think about it, one of the most important assets of any institution is its information. For example, a typical business must keep track of its customers, orders, product inventory, and employee information, for obvious reasons. Additionally, the analysis of pertinent business information can help make a company more competitive. For example, a sales analyst can use current and historical sales data to forecast future sales and identify trends that might help to improve overall business profitability.

This chapter provides you with a brief introduction to the following topics:

- Databases

- Database management systems

- Database applications

- Oracle Database 10*g*

- Oracle database instances

- Tables

- SQL

- Oracle Application Express

Information Management

In today's world of high technology, computers manage most information because they make it easy to organize, store, and protect valuable data. The proliferation of powerful personal computers and networks has made it possible for all businesses, large and small alike, to quickly and safely make information readily available to people that require access to it. This section introduces the basic concepts of a database, database management systems, database applications, and Oracle.

Databases

Computers typically store and organize large amounts of information within a database. A *database*, whether or not a computer manages it, is nothing more than an orderly collection of related information. A database is a tool that you can use to safely store information and properly organize it for fast retrieval. For example, a business can use a database to store tables of customer records, corresponding sales orders, product parts, and employee lists. Various workers can then use the database to efficiently perform their jobs. For example, salespeople can quickly enter or look up sales orders, advertising executives can study and forecast product sales, and warehouse personnel can efficiently manage product inventories.

Databases come in many varieties. *Inverted list*, *hierarchic*, and *network* database models are older types of database systems designed primarily for prescribed transactions that input data; they are not suitable for dynamic environments in which interactive data analysis is critical.

The very weaknesses of these earlier systems are exactly why *relational* databases now dominate newer information management systems. Relational databases are easy to understand, design, and build. Relational databases store and present all information in tables, an easily understood concept. Furthermore, relational databases hide the complexities of data access from the user, making application development relatively simple when compared to other types of database systems.

Database Management Systems

A *database management system (DBMS)* is computer software that manages access to databases. A typical multiuser DBMS performs the following tasks, and more:

- A DBMS safely manages shared access to a single database among multiple concurrent users. For example, a DBMS locks data as users add and update information so that users do not destructively interfere with one another's work.

- A DBMS uses computer resources wisely so that a large number of application users can access the database and perform work with fast response times for maximum productivity.

- A DBMS protects database information in such a way that it can reconstruct work lost due to anything from a simple power outage, to a disk failure, to even a complete site disaster in some cases.

You can purchase any one of several commercially available DBMSs to build and manage databases. The market-leading DBMS in use today is Oracle Corporation's Oracle Database, also known simply as *Oracle*. The latest version of Oracle is Oracle Database 10*g*. Two goals of this book are to teach you how Oracle works and provide you with hands-on experience using the software's most typically used features.

Database Applications

Oracle Database 10*g*'s many features make it a potent database server for all types of common database applications, including:

- **Online transaction processing (OLTP)** Applications that process many small update transactions, such as banking, reservation, and order-entry systems

- **Decision support systems (DSSs)** Applications that query targeted information from a database for the purposes of data analysis

- **Data warehousing** Applications that access large, read-only databases that are specifically optimized for fast access to even the most esoteric bits of information

For example, consider the databases that a large online retailer might use to manage its business. When you go to the company's online store to browse and order products, you are using the company's OLTP database system. When you request information about your sales invoices and recommendations for future purchases that match your profile, you are using the company's DSS. Internally, the company offloads and transforms transactional information from its OLTP system into a read-only data warehouse so that it can analyze sales trends and make wise choices about future product offerings and marketing campaigns.

Oracle Database 10*g*

Oracle Database 10*g* is available in several different license formats:

- **Oracle Database 10*g* Standard Edition One** An entry-level version of Oracle that includes the most commonly used options and features available with Oracle and supports two-processor systems.

- **Oracle Database 10*g* Standard Edition** Similar to Standard Edition One, except this version supports four-processor systems.

- **Oracle Database 10*g* Enterprise Edition** The complete version of Oracle that provides multiuser access to all features, including features for high-end database processing, data warehousing, and large, multiprocessor systems.

- **Oracle Database 10*g* Personal Edition** A single-user development database license that provides access to most of the Oracle Database 10*g* Enterprise Edition features.

- **Oracle Database 10*g* Lite**   An Oracle-compatible database designed for use in mobile computing environments. Oracle Lite is not discussed in this book.

- **Oracle Database 10*g* Express Edition**   A free version of Oracle that supports most popular Oracle database features. Also called and henceforth referred to in this book as Oracle XE, you can use Express Edition to design, build, deploy, and support Oracle-based applications that run on one-processor systems with databases of 4 gigabytes (GB) or less. Oracle XE is very easy to install and automatically includes powerful application development tools that you can use to begin using Oracle quickly. This book's CD contains a free copy of Oracle XE, but you can always download the latest version from Oracle's website.

The various editions of Oracle Database 10*g* are available on most popular operating systems such as Microsoft Windows, Linux, and various Unix platforms. In this book, you will use Oracle XE to get started using Oracle while it operates on top of one of the most popular server operating systems in use today, Microsoft Windows. This book teaches you about the operating system–independent features of Oracle, as well as several Oracle features available only with Microsoft Windows.

NOTE
For the most part, Oracle operates the same way no matter what operating system or edition of Oracle that you choose. Therefore, the large majority of this book is useful, no matter what operating system or edition of Oracle you are using.

Oracle Fundamentals

Before proceeding to the next chapter to install Oracle XE for Microsoft Windows on your computer, you should understand some of the basic terms related to Oracle and relational database systems. If you already have experience working with Oracle, the following sections contain information that you might already know.

Databases and Instances

An *Oracle database* is a collection of related operating system files that Oracle uses to store and manage a set of related information. Structurally, an Oracle database has three primary types of files: data files, log files, and control files. Subsequent chapters of this book will explain more about the purpose and management of each type of database file.

NOTE
This book will also teach you about several other types of files that Oracle uses along with a database such as parameter files, an alert log, trace files, and a password file; however, these types of files are not actually part of a database's physical structure.

A *database instance* or *database server* is the Oracle software that manages physical database access. No one can use the data in an Oracle database until after you "start up" an instance. An instance's operating system processes and memory areas "mount" (associate) and "open" the physical database files to facilitate data access.

NOTE
Be aware that people commonly mix and match terms like database, instance, and DBMS that have different technical meanings.

Figure 1-1 is a simple illustration that identifies the relationship between a physical database and a database instance.

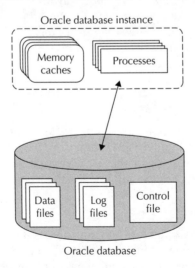

FIGURE 1-1. *An Oracle database instance provides access to the physical files that constitute a database. Together, a database instance and database make up an Oracle DBMS.*

For now, this is all that you need to understand about Oracle databases and instances. You'll learn more about databases and instances in the next chapter of this book.

Tables

Tables are the basic data structure in any relational database. A *table* is nothing more than an organized collection of *records*, or *rows*, that all have the same *attributes*, or *columns*. Figure 1-2 illustrates a typical CUSTOMERS table in a relational database. Notice that each customer record in the example CUSTOMERS table has the same attributes, including an ID, a company name, a last name, a first name, and so on.

For now, this is all that you need to understand about tables. Subsequent chapters will teach you more about building and using tables in an Oracle database.

SQL and Data Access

To work with a commercial relational database system, such as Oracle, applications use *Structured Query Language (SQL)* commands. SQL (pronounced both "sequel" and "ess-que-ell") is a simple command language that allows database administrators, developers, and application users to do the following:

■ Retrieve, enter, update, and delete database data

■ Create, alter, and drop database objects, such as tables

In fact, the only way that an application can interact with an Oracle database is to issue a SQL command. Easy-to-use graphical user interfaces (GUIs) might hide the complexities of SQL commands from users, but under the covers, an application always communicates with Oracle by using SQL.

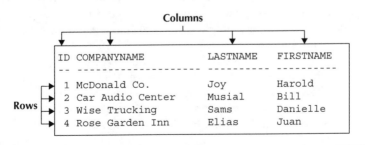

FIGURE 1-2. *A table is a set of records with the same attributes.*

If you currently do not have any experience with SQL, don't panic. SQL is a relatively simple language to learn because you build SQL commands by combining intuitive keywords and clauses that ask Oracle to perform specific tasks. For example, the following SQL statement is a simple query that retrieves specific columns of all rows in the PARTS table:

```
SELECT id, description, unitprice FROM parts;

        ID DESCRIPTION             UNITPRICE
--------- -------------------- ---------
         1 Fax Machine                 299
         2 Copy Machine               4895
         3 Laptop PC                   2100
         4 Desktop PC                  1200
         5 Scanner                       99
```

At this point, you do not need to know much more about SQL. In almost every other chapter of this book, you will use SQL statements to access Oracle and perform tasks. Chapter 3 provides you with a complete introduction to the basics of the most commonly used SQL commands.

Database Users and Sessions

Oracle is a DBMS that manages shared access to a database among one or more users. To provide database access to someone, you or an administrator must create a *database user account* for the person. To perform work with Oracle, you must start an application and establish a connection to Oracle using your account's username and password. A *database session* starts when you establish a connection to an Oracle database and ends when you disconnect.

You will learn more about database users and database security later in this book.

SQL*Plus

One type of application that you can use to enter SQL commands and interact with an Oracle database system is an *ad hoc query tool*, such as Oracle's SQL*Plus. *SQL*Plus* provides you with a very simple command-line interface that you can use to enter SQL statements and then view the results of each statement execution. In effect, SQL*Plus lets you talk with an Oracle database server so that you can either query the database for information or input, update, or delete data in the database. For example, the following commands demonstrate a simple SQL*Plus session that connects to an Oracle database, retrieves some data from the CUSTOMERS table, and then terminates the session by disconnecting from the database:

```
SQL> CONNECT hr/hr;
Connected.
SQL> SELECT job_title
```

```
  2    FROM jobs
  3    WHERE min_salary > 10000;

JOB_TITLE
------------------------------------
President
Administration Vice President

SQL> DISCONNECT;
Disconnected from Oracle Database 10g Express Edition
```

Many of the examples and practice exercises throughout the chapters in this book use SQL*Plus to communicate with Oracle.

Oracle Application Express

Oracle Application Express (formerly Oracle HTML DB) is a *rapid application development (RAD)* tool that you can use to design, develop, and deploy applications for Oracle. Even with minimal knowledge of SQL and other programming concepts, you can use Application Express to quickly build robust web browser–based applications. Application Express also contains a limited set of administration tools, including utilities for database system configuration, user management, data loading, and more. Application Express is a standard feature of Oracle that you can use for no additional cost. Subsequent chapters in this section of the book teach you how to quickly begin using Oracle Application Express.

Chapter Summary

Oracle XE is a powerful product that you will use to manage information. Now that you have a general idea of what Oracle XE is all about, the remaining chapters in this book present essential Oracle concepts and corresponding practice exercises so that you can quickly become proficient using Oracle XE on Microsoft Windows for information management.

CHAPTER
2

Install and Start Using Oracle Database 10g Express Edition

he installation of Oracle Database 10g Express Edition (Oracle XE) for Microsoft Windows is extremely easy and fast. Using the instructions in this chapter, you should be up and running in a matter of minutes.

This chapter first provides you an overview of the Oracle XE installation process, the system requirements to meet before attempting an installation, and what to expect after you install. Next, you will learn how to start and stop Oracle XE, start SQL*Plus and establish a database connection, and launch and become familiar with the Database Home Page database management tool. This chapter also explains how to troubleshoot some common problems that you might encounter, and the preparatory steps necessary to use the practice exercises in subsequent chapters of this book.

NOTE
After reading this chapter, it should take you no more than 30 minutes to install Oracle XE and complete the subsequent practice exercises in this chapter.

Installation Overview

The installation process for Oracle XE on Microsoft Windows creates many items, including the following:

- **Oracle base directory**   Henceforth referred to as *ORACLE_BASE*, this directory is the root of the Oracle directory tree. For example, a typical ORACLE_BASE for Oracle XE on Microsoft Windows is C:\oraclexe.

- **Oracle home directory**   Henceforth referred to as *ORACLE_HOME*, this is the working directory in which a particular version of Oracle software executes. For example, a typical ORACLE_HOME for Oracle XE on Microsoft Windows is C:\oraclexe\app\oracle\product\10.2.0\server.

- **A starter database (seed database)**   You can use this default database to get started working with Oracle. Typically, the name of the Oracle XE starter database is *XE* and its files are located in ORACLE_BASE\oradata\XE.

- **Several Microsoft Windows services**   You can use these services to control the availability of the starter database and other Oracle XE components.

- **Several keys in the Microsoft Windows registry**   These keys correspond to ORACLE_BASE, ORACLE_HOME, the starter database, Oracle-related services, etc.

■ **A local Microsoft Windows group named ORA_DBA** The installation process makes the user that installs Oracle Database 10*g* Express Edition a member of the ORA_DBA group. Members of the ORA_DBA group are authorized to control the availability of Oracle XE (and other installations of Oracle that might be on the same computer).

Database Server System Requirements

In this chapter, you'll learn how to install the Oracle XE database server, which includes the Oracle Database 10*g* software, a starter database, and client tools that you can use to interact with the database server. Before you get started, make sure that your computer meets the minimum system requirements to succeed. Tables 2-1 and 2-2 document the basic system requirements that your computer must meet in order to successfully install the Oracle XE database server for Microsoft Windows.

Notice in Table 2-1 that there are both minimum and recommended settings. For your best experience with Oracle XE, I advise that you meet the recommended settings.

 NOTE
If your computer does not have MSI 2.0 components or later, the installer will not run immediately. Instead, you will normally be presented a message box with a link asking you to install this Microsoft Windows component; if not, visit Microsoft's website, do a search for MSI, and download it.

EXERCISE 2.1: Check System Requirements

Complete this exercise to check that your computer meets the system requirements necessary to install Oracle XE for Microsoft Windows:

1. Choose Start | [All] Programs | Accessories | System Tools | System Information.

2. Click System Summary to display a summary of information that reveals your computer's processor, physical memory (RAM), and version of Microsoft Windows.

3. Under System Summary, expand Components, expand Network, and then click Protocol to reveal if TCP/IP is available.

4. Under Components, expand Storage, and then click Drives to check the amount of free space on your computer's hard drives.

5. Under System Summary, expand Software Environment, click Loaded Modules, and search for **msi** in the list of modules and check its version.

Hardware Component	Requirement
Processor	Intel x86
Disk space	1.6GB minimum 5GB recommended
RAM	256MB minimum 512MB or more recommended

TABLE 2-1. *Hardware Requirements for the Oracle Database 10*g* Express Edition Database Server on Microsoft Windows*

6. Under System Summary, expand Internet Settings, expand Internet Explorer, and then click Summary to check your version of Internet Explorer. If you plan to use a different web browser with Oracle XE, you can most likely check the version of that browser using its About feature on the Help menu.

7. When you are done with the System Information application, choose File | Exit.

Software Component	Requirement
Operating system	■ Microsoft Windows 2000 (32 bit) Service Pack 4 or later ■ Microsoft Windows Server 2003 (32 bit) ■ Microsoft Windows XP Professional (32 bit) Service Pack 1 or later
Network protocol	TCP/IP
Microsoft Windows Installer (MSI)	MSI version 2.0 or later
Web browser	Although not a requirement for installation of Oracle XE, a web browser is necessary to use many product features subsequent to installation. Your web browser, such as the following, should support JavaScript, HTML 4.0, and CSS 1.0 with support for cookies enabled: ■ Microsoft Internet Explorer 6.0 or later ■ Netscape Navigator 7.2 or later ■ Mozilla 1.7 or later ■ Firefox 1.0 or later

TABLE 2-2. *Software Requirements for Oracle Database 10*g* Express Edition on Microsoft Windows*

NOTE
This chapter teaches you how to install the Oracle XE database server. Once you install the database server on a computer, you can install the Oracle XE client on remote computers that must access your database server. The client consists of SQL*Plus and the libraries necessary to execute applications developed with the Oracle Call Interface (OCI), Oracle C++ Call Interface (OCCI), *and* Java Database Connectivity OCI (JDBC OCI) *application programming interfaces (APIs). Do not waste time trying to install both the Oracle XE database server and client on the same computer, because the database server already includes all of the client components.*

Additional Requirements for Application Development

Although not requirements to install Oracle XE, Table 2-3 documents additional requirements to consider for the optional application development environments that Oracle XE for Microsoft Windows supports. The reason they are mentioned here is that some requirements must be met *before* installing Oracle XE on Microsoft Windows; consider each requirement only when you plan to use the corresponding application development environment.

Application Development Environment	Requirements
Oracle Database Extensions for .NET Oracle Developer Tools for Visual Studio .NET	This book does not discuss these application development environments. See the *Oracle Database 10g Express Edition Installation Guide for Microsoft Windows* before installing any software related to Oracle XE. Also see www.oracle.com/technology/tech/dotnet/tools/index.html.
PHP	PHP (www.php.net) or Zend Core for Oracle (www.oracle.com/technology/tech/php/zendcore/index.html).

TABLE 2-3.   *Additional Software Requirements to Consider Before Installing Oracle Database 10g Express Edition on Microsoft Windows*

Oracle Database 10g Express Edition Software

For your convenience, this book ships with a CD that contains a copy of Oracle Database 10g Express Edition for Microsoft Windows. You can use this copy to install the product, or download a more recent copy of the product from the *Oracle Technology Network (OTN)* website www.oracle.com/technology/.

NOTE
Even if you do not download software from OTN initially, you will want to visit this valuable resource as you work with Oracle to read documentation, browse discussion forums, download software updates, and keep current with Oracle.

Installation

The hands-on exercises in this section teach you how to install Oracle XE for Microsoft Windows.

EXERCISE 2.2: Establish a Microsoft Windows Administrator Session

To prepare for installing Oracle XE, establish a Microsoft Windows Administrator session. To do this, you can use your own user account if it is a member of the Administrators group; otherwise, you can connect by using the default Administrator account.

NOTE
How can you tell if your account is a member of the Administrators group? On Microsoft Windows XP, choose Start | Control Panel | User Accounts. The User Accounts window should display summary information about all local accounts. If your account is a member of the Administrators group, it will be listed as a "Computer administrator." Use similar steps for other versions of Microsoft Windows.

EXERCISE 2.3: Install Oracle XE Step-by-Step

To install Oracle XE on your computer, follow the directions in this exercise that takes you step-by-step through the installation process.

The Oracle XE for Microsoft Windows installer is a user-friendly wizard that quickly guides you through the installation procedure.

NOTE
If you have previous experience installing Oracle, it is likely that you are familiar with Oracle's proprietary installer, the Oracle Universal Installer (OUI). *The OUI is a Java-based program that looks and operates the same no matter what operating system you happen to be using. Oracle Database 10g Express Edition does not use the OUI. Instead, the Oracle XE installer program is native to your computer's operating system. In the context of this book, a Microsoft Windows InstallShield Wizard guides you through the installation process.*

There are two different software packages to consider for character set support:

- If you want to install Oracle XE and a database that supports multibyte, universal character sets (UTF8), install using OracleXEUniv.exe. This package is the correct choice for users who want to build databases and applications that must support Brazilian Portuguese, Chinese (Simplified and Traditional), English, French, German, Italian, Japanese, Korean, and Spanish.

- If you want to install Oracle XE and a database that supports Western European character sets only, install using OracleXE.exe. This package is the correct choice for users who want to build databases that support single-byte character sets and applications that must support English only.

Once you establish a Microsoft Windows session using an account that is a member of the Administrators group, you can begin the installation procedure as follows:

1. Choose Start | Run.

2. Use Browse to find and run OracleXE.exe or OracleXEUniv.exe.

Once the installer starts, it prepares itself (see Figure 2-1) and then displays a Welcome page (see Figure 2-2).

After you read the Welcome page, click Next to continue with the installation and proceed to the License Agreement page (see Figure 2-3). Carefully read the license before you click Next to continue.

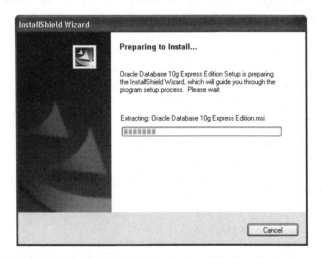

FIGURE 2-1. *The installer launches...*

Among other things, you need to understand the following about the Oracle Database 10*g* Express Edition license that you are agreeing to:

■ Oracle XE will only make use of the processing resources equivalent to a one-CPU computer, even when your computer has multiple processors (including dual-core processors).

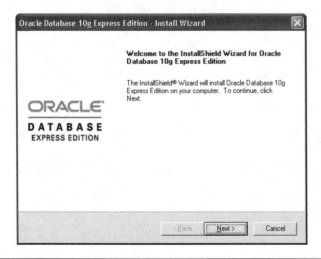

FIGURE 2-2. *...and then presents a Welcome page.*

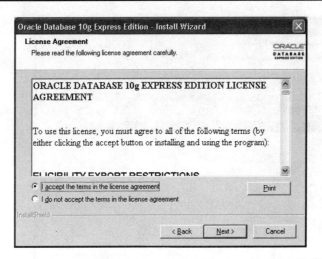

FIGURE 2-3. *You must acknowledge that you have read and understand the Oracle Database 10*g* Express Edition license agreement.*

- Oracle XE does not support more than one database instance of Oracle XE on the same computer. However, you can start an Oracle XE database on a computer that also has other licensed versions of Oracle database software in use.

- Oracle XE will not allow you to manage more than 4GB of user data, even when more disk space is available for you to allocate to Oracle.

- Oracle XE will not use more than 1GB of RAM, even if your computer has more.

NOTE
*If you require more resources than the Oracle XE license stipulates, consider using Oracle Database 10*g* Standard Edition One, Standard Edition, or Enterprise Edition. See Chapter 1 for more information about these editions of Oracle.*

The Choose Destination Location page of the installer (see Figure 2-4) lets you decide where you want to install the Oracle XE software. The installer will also use the location that you specify to create the default starter database.

If your computer has access to more than one disk drive that meets the system requirements, carefully consider your options. Disk I/O is costly in the context of database performance. An Oracle database typically performs better when you create its files on fast rather than slow storage devices.

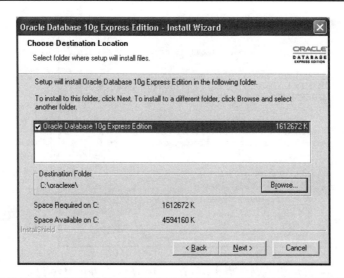

FIGURE 2-4. *Choose a file system location in which to install Oracle Database 10*g *Express Edition.*

Database protection and availability is another issue to consider when choosing the location for Oracle software and database files. If your computer has access to an array of disks that stripe and mirror the blocks of files (for example, a RAID 5 or RAID 10 array), consider installing Oracle XE in a storage location that can take advantage of its fault-protection benefits.

Click Browse to modify the location, if necessary, and then click Next to continue with the installation.

NOTE
At this point, you may be prompted to enter some TCP/IP port numbers, but only if your computer has software that is currently using any of the following ports: 1521, 2030, or 8080. If none of these port numbers are currently in use, then the installer assigns them to related components of Oracle XE without prompting you.

The subsequent Specify Database Passwords page (see Figure 2-5) requests an initial password to use for the default database administration accounts, SYS and

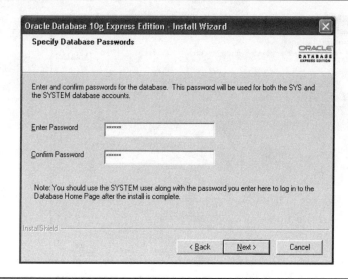

FIGURE 2-5.   *Enter an initial password for the SYS and SYSTEM database accounts.*

SYSTEM. Make a note of the password you plan to use, enter and confirm the password, and then click Next to continue.

Review the Summary page (see Figure 2-6) to make sure that all of your choices are correct. Pay special attention to the TCP/IP ports that the installer will use to configure services related to Oracle XE. If your computer has the Microsoft Windows XP firewall executing, take a moment to open these ports before you continue so that Oracle XE functions properly once installed; user-friendly firewalls such as ZoneAlarm will prompt you to open ports interactively during the installation procedure when the Oracle-related programs attempt to use the ports.

NOTE
Use the Microsoft Windows help system or visit the Microsoft Windows website for help using the Microsoft Windows firewall.

When you are ready, click Next to commence installation of Oracle Database 10*g* Express Edition. It usually takes no more than a few minutes for the installation to complete, although the time can vary depending on your computer's hardware resources (see Figure 2-7).

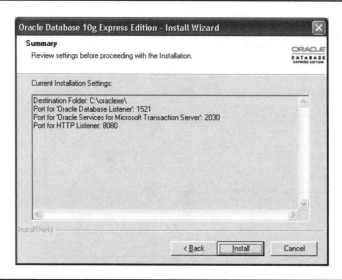

FIGURE 2-6. *Review the installation choices and note the ports that Oracle requires.*

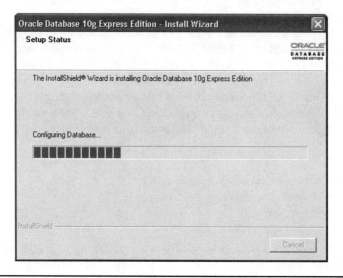

FIGURE 2-7. *The installation of Oracle Database 10g Express Edition should take no more than a few minutes.*

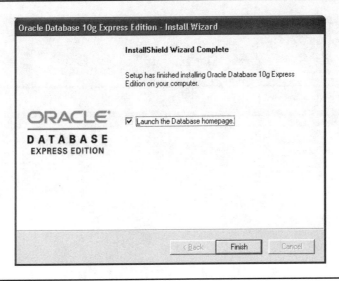

FIGURE 2-8. *Use the installer to launch the Database Home Page and confirm a successful installation.*

Once the installation completes, check the Launch The Database Homepage box, and then click Finish (see Figure 2-8) to confirm a successful installation.

After the installer exits, your default web browser should start and load the login screen for Oracle Application Express. Oracle Application Express is a web-based tool, automatically installed with Oracle XE, that includes features for database administration and application development. You will learn a lot about Oracle Application Express features in subsequent chapters of this book.

If the login screen for Oracle Application Express appears as Figure 2-9 shows, you can be sure that your installation completed successfully; if not, skip ahead to the "Troubleshooting Tips" section of this chapter for help diagnosing your problem.

NOTE
Several issues can cause an unsuccessful installation of Oracle Database 10g Express Edition for Microsoft Windows, or result in a configuration that does not function properly after successful software installation and database creation. To troubleshoot installation or configuration problems, you first need to learn some of the skills that subsequent exercises in this chapter introduce. Then read the "Troubleshooting Tips" section later in this chapter.

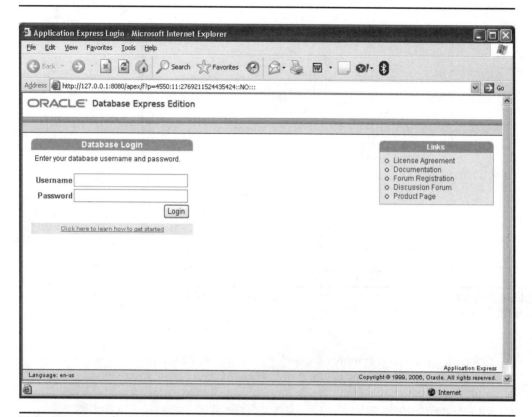

FIGURE 2-9.   *The login screen for Oracle Application Express appears in your web browser if your installation of Oracle Database 10g Express Edition is successful.*

Post-Installation Exercises

Although not required, the following exercises explain several tasks that you should understand before continuing with Oracle Database 10*g* Express Edition.

EXERCISE 2.4: Accessing the Documentation

You will no doubt need to reference the Oracle Database Documentation Library for Oracle XE (see Figure 2-10) as you work with the product. The Oracle XE documentation is available online at OTN. To quickly start a new browser window and view the online documentation, choose Start | [All] Programs | Oracle Database 10*g* Express Edition | Get Help | Read Documentation, or click Documentation in the Links menu of the login screen for Oracle Application Express (refer to Figure 2-9).

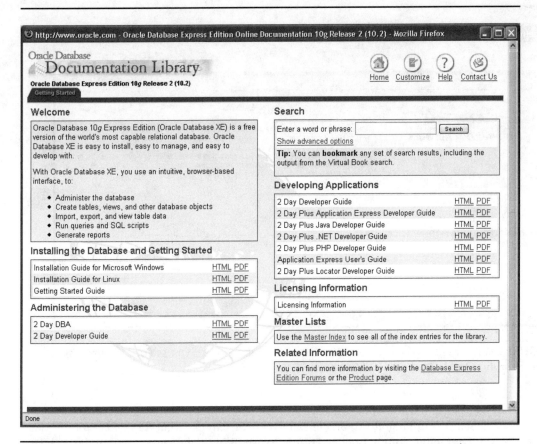

FIGURE 2-10.   *The online documentation for Oracle Database 10g Express Edition is available at the Oracle Technology Network.*

TIP
For faster access to the documentation that does not depend on Internet connectivity, consider creating local copies of PDF versions of selected titles on your computer.

EXERCISE 2.5: Registering for the Discussion Forum

Oracle Database 10g Express Edition is a free product for which Oracle Corporation does not provide official technical support. Instead, user community support is available at OTN via an Oracle Database 10g Express Edition Discussion Forum. Before you can access the support forum, you need to register yourself (see Figure 2-11). To register,

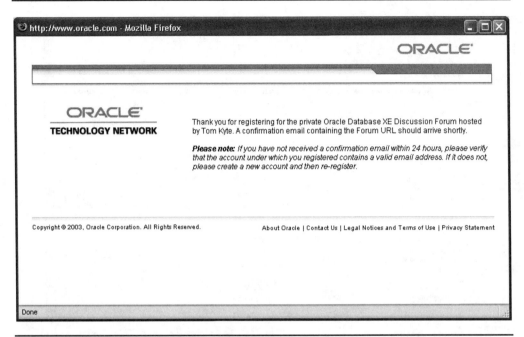

FIGURE 2-11.   *Register for access to the Oracle Database 10*g *Express Edition Discussion Forum at the Oracle Technology Network.*

choose Start | [All] Programs | Oracle Database 10*g* Express Edition | Get Help | Register For Online Forum, or click Forum Registration on the Links menu of the login screen for Oracle Application Express. Then follow the instructions that appear in a new browser window.

NOTE
*If you have an existing OTN account, you can use it to register for Oracle Database 10*g *Express Edition Discussion Forum access.*

EXERCISE 2.6: Accessing the Support Forum

To get support and share ideas with others using Oracle XE, go to the Discussion Forum at OTN (see Figure 2-12). Choose Start | [All] Programs | Oracle Database 10*g* Express Edition | Get Help | Go To Online Forum, or click Discussion Forum in the Links menu on the login screen for Oracle Application Express. You must enter your OTN username and password.

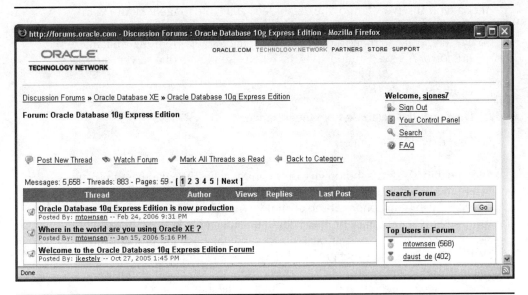

FIGURE 2-12. *Use the Oracle Database 10g Express Edition Discussion Forum at OTN for support issues and to collaborate with others.*

Basic Oracle XE Skills

Now that you have Oracle Database 10*g* Express Edition installed on your computer, you are ready to learn some fundamental database management procedures so that you can get started using Oracle XE and troubleshoot problems, if any exist.

Oracle Startup and Shutdown

Chapter 1 explains the fundamental concepts of Oracle databases, database instances, and their relationship to one another in a DBMS. Before anyone can work with an Oracle database, someone must *start up* the DBMS or database server. Database server startup is an ordered sequence of events that includes the following:

1. Start a database instance.

2. Mount (associate) the physical database to the instance.

3. Open the database.

After a typical server startup, the database is available for general use with applications.

Conversely, you can make a database unavailable by performing a database server *shutdown*. A server shutdown is the reverse sequence of a server startup:

1. Close the database.

2. Dismount the database from the instance.

3. Shut down the instance.

After a database server shutdown, users cannot access the database until after you restart the instance, mount and open the database.

A *server crash* is an abnormal server shutdown. For example, an unfortunate operating system operation or problem could unexpectedly kill one or more of Oracle's background processes. Consequently, the database server might crash. Oracle has built-in features that protect the work of all committed transactions, and automatically perform the necessary recovery from an instance that crashes. Subsequent chapters explain more about Oracle's database protection mechanisms.

EXERCISE 2.7: Check the Status of Oracle XE

The default installation of Oracle XE automatically configures a Microsoft Windows service to start up an Oracle database instance when you start the computer. One way to start and stop the Oracle database instance on your Microsoft Windows computer is to use the Services window to manage the corresponding database service. To start the Services window, choose Start | Control Panel | Administrative Tools and then double-click Services.

NOTE
You might need to be logged on as an administrator or a member of the Administrators group to launch the Services window.

The Services window, shown in Figure 2-13, includes a list of all the services installed on your computer, as well as their current status (for example, Started) and their Startup configuration (such as Manual, Automatic, or Disabled).

The service that corresponds to the database instance on your machine is the service with the name OracleService*name*, where *name* is the name of your starter database. By default, all Oracle XE installations create a starter database with the name XE; therefore, the service to look for is OracleServiceXE.

If the current status of OracleServiceXE is Started, then an Oracle instance is available to provide access to the starter database on your computer. However, if the current status of OracleServiceXE appears as null (as a blank space), an instance is not running and the starter database is not accessible.

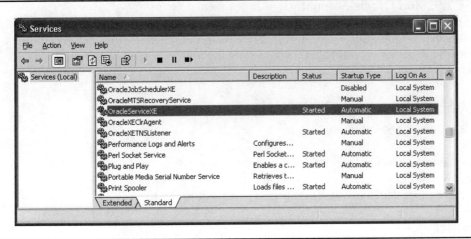

FIGURE 2-13. *The Microsoft Windows Services window*

EXERCISE 2.8: Start Oracle Manually

When the OracleServiceXE service is not running, you can start up an instance and make the starter database available for access by completing the following steps with the Microsoft Windows Services window:

1. Select the service OracleServiceXE.

2. Click the Start button.

After the database service starts, the status of OracleServiceXE should change to Started, which means that an instance is now started and mounted to the starter database, and the database is open for user access.

When you know that an instance is not running, you can avoid using the Services window and more quickly start up the database service by choosing Start | All Programs | Oracle Database 10g Express Edition | Start Database.

NOTE
You can also start up an Oracle instance and mount and open the database by using the STARTUP command of SQL*Plus. See your Oracle documentation for more information about this SQL*Plus command.

EXERCISE 2.9: Stop Oracle Manually

The procedure for shutting down the database service is similar to that of server startup. When OracleServiceXE is started, you can shut down the instance and make the starter database unavailable by completing the following steps with the Microsoft Windows Services window:

1. Select the service OracleServiceXE.

2. Click the Stop button.

When you know that an instance is running, you can avoid using the Services window and more quickly stop the database service by choosing Start | All Programs | Oracle Database 10g Express Edition | Stop Database.

NOTE
You can also shut down an Oracle database server by using the SHUTDOWN command of SQL*Plus. See your Oracle documentation for more information about this SQL*Plus command.

EXERCISE 2.10: Automate Oracle Startup

By default, the installer configures Microsoft Windows to automatically start the OracleServiceXE database service when Microsoft Windows starts. To control automated database service startup, complete the following steps with the Microsoft Windows Services window:

1. Click the OracleServiceXE service with your mouse's alternate button.

2. From the pop-up menu, click Properties.

3. Set the Startup Type options list of the Services window to your liking. Use the Automatic option to have Microsoft Windows automatically start the database service when the computer starts. Use the Manual option if you want Microsoft Windows to start up faster and require you to manually start the database service when necessary.

Database Connections

After Oracle XE is up and running, you can use a client application, tool, or utility to establish a database connection and perform work. Behind the scenes, the mechanisms of the database instance work to complete your requests and the requests of others that are using the same database instance. At the same time, Oracle XE automatically protects the work of all transactions while preserving the integrity of the shared database.

Local Database Connections

When the client application and database instance execute on the same computer, you can establish what is known as a *local database connection* or *bequeathed database connection*. When establishing a local database connection, a client application typically provides just a database username and password; the current setting of your session's ORACLE_SID environment variable determines the local database instance to target for the connection.

NOTE
*On Microsoft Windows, the default value for ORACLE_SID is set in the Microsoft Windows registry. If you have other instances of Oracle on your computer and want to use SQL*Plus to establish a local connection to the XE database, start a Command Prompt, use the Microsoft Windows command SET to set the ORACLE_SID environment variable to XE (e.g., SET ORACLE_SID=XE), and then start SQL*Plus with the **sqlplus** command.*

Oracle Net and Network Database Connections

When the client application and database instance execute on different computers, you must establish what is known as a *network database connection*. A network database connection request not only specifies a database username and password, but also a service name; for now, just think of a *service name* as an alias or shortcut that specifies how to connect to an Oracle database instance.

To support a network database connection, all computers involved in the connection must be able to communicate with each other using a network protocol, and each computer must use Oracle's networking software, *Oracle Net*. Oracle Net is available with support for the most common network protocols, including TCP/IP, TCP/IP with Secure Sockets Layer (SSL), Named Pipes, and the Sockets Direct Protocol (SDP) for InfiniBand.

NOTE
You can also establish a network connection between a local client and a database server simply by specifying a service name for the connection. Tools such as Application Express rely on network database connections rather than local database connections.

A *TNS Listener,* more simply called a *Listener,* is necessary to establish connections to an Oracle database via a network protocol such as TCP/IP. A Listener is a process that receives a connection request, resolves the network address of the destination, and establishes a connection to the destination. For example, consider what happens when you start SQL*Plus and specify a username, password, and service name for a connection to a database:

1. Your computer resolves the provided service name to the address of a Listener that is registered to handle connection requests for the target database. Your computer then forwards your connection request to the Listener.

2. The Listener determines the network address of the target database, and then forwards the address of the client and the connection request to the database server.

3. Oracle establishes a connection for your client application, SQL*Plus. The Listener no longer plays a role in the connection.

Figure 2-14 illustrates this sequence of events.

For your convenience, the Oracle XE installer configures a Microsoft Windows service named *OracleXETNSListener* for the Listener, and configures the service to

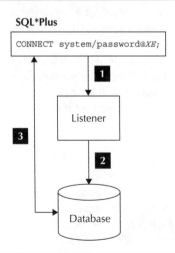

FIGURE 2-14. *The Listener resolves database connection requests that use network protocols.*

automatically start when the system reboots. As an optional exercise, you can check the status and control the availability of the Listener service using steps similar to those in Exercises 2.7, 2.8, and 2.9.

Now that you understand the basics of Oracle database connections, the exercises in this section teach you how to connect to and disconnect from Oracle XE using two different database tools, SQL*Plus and the Database Home Page. Subsequent chapters in this book explain more about service names, the Listener process, and Oracle Net configuration. The information that this chapter provides should be just enough for you to get started with Oracle XE, make sure that the system is functioning properly, and troubleshoot some simple database connection problems.

EXERCISE 2.11: Connect to Oracle with SQL*Plus

Once you have the Oracle XE database service started on your Microsoft Windows computer, you can start SQL*Plus, establish a database connection, and start working with the starter database. The easiest way to start SQL*Plus is to choose Start | All Programs | Oracle Database 10*g* Express Edition | Run SQL Command Line.

NOTE
*You can also start SQL*Plus on a Microsoft Windows computer by starting a Command Prompt window and entering the command **sqlplus**.*

If everything works properly, SQL*Plus will start and display a message similar to the following:

```
SQL*Plus: Release 10.2.0.1.0 - Production on xxx xxx xx xx:xx:xx xxxx
Copyright (c) 1982, 2006, Oracle.  All rights reserved.
SQL>
```

The blinking cursor after SQL> in the last line of the display is SQL*Plus's default command prompt. Here, you can interactively type SQL and SQL*Plus commands to perform work. The next chapter will provide you with a more thorough introduction to SQL and SQL*Plus commands.

At this point, you can use the SQL*Plus command CONNECT to establish your first Oracle database session. The abbreviated syntax of the CONNECT command is very simple:

```
CONNECT username
```

username is the case-insensitive name of the database user account that you want to use to establish a connection. To complete this basic exercise, enter a CONNECT command and use the username **SYSTEM**. When you enter the command, SQL*Plus then prompts you for a password. Enter the password that you assigned to the SYSTEM account during Oracle XE installation. SQL*Plus does not display the characters of the password as you enter them, to protect your password. If you enter the correct password, Oracle indicates that you are connected; otherwise, Oracle returns an error and you'll have to enter a new CONNECT command to try again. The expected transcript of the commands in this exercise should be similar to the following:

```
SQL> CONNECT system
Enter password:
Connected.
SQL>
```

NOTE
*When you start SQL*Plus from a command prompt using the **sqlplus** command without any arguments, SQL*Plus immediately prompts you to connect—you do not have to use a CONNECT statement unless you start SQL*Plus with the **/nolog** argument (i.e., **sqlplus /nolog**).*

Your current connection is a local or bequeathed database connection. Why? Your connection request with the previous CONNECT statement provided nothing more than a username (and password), which implies that you want to connect to the local database currently identified by your session's ORACLE_SID environment variable setting.

To confirm the availability and configuration of the local Listener, make sure that you can establish a network database connection to your XE database instance. To do so, enter the following CONNECT command:

```
CONNECT system@XE
```

Notice the @XE at the tail end of the command. The @ character precedes a subsequent service name specification. For your convenience, the installer creates the XE service name for your local XE database instance.

Once you respond to the prompt for the SYSTEM account password, Oracle XE establishes a network connection to the local XE database instance.

EXERCISE 2.12: Disconnect from Oracle and Exit SQL*Plus
After you are finished using SQL*Plus, disconnect from Oracle and exit SQL*Plus by entering the EXIT command (type **EXIT**) at the SQL*Plus prompt.

EXERCISE 2.13: Launch the Database Home Page

After a successful installation, the installer launches Oracle Application Express if you ask it to. If you did not request this, or have since closed this page, to launch the login screen again, choose Start | All Programs | Oracle Database 10g Express Edition | Go to Database Home Page. Your default web browser will start and load the login screen for Oracle Application Express, as Figure 2-15 shows.

NOTE
The default URL for Oracle Application Express is
http://127.0.0.1:8080/apex/.

To establish a database connection to your Oracle database service using Oracle Application Express, enter **SYSTEM** in the Username field and the

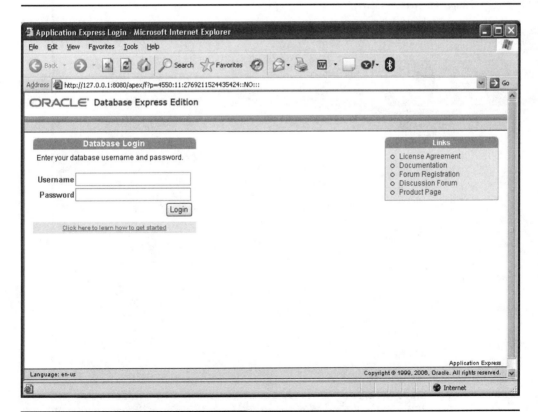

FIGURE 2-15.   *The login screen for Oracle Application Express*

corresponding password in the Password field, and then click Login. Once you establish a connection, Oracle Application Express presents the Database Home Page. The *Database Home Page* presents a number of icons with drop-down menus, and hyperlinks to external websites that you can use to perform work and learn more about Oracle XE, as Figure 2-16 shows.

Feel free to browse the Database Home Page user interface at this time. Subsequent chapters of this book explain how to use most of its features in the proper context. Once you are done, terminate your database session by clicking Logout.

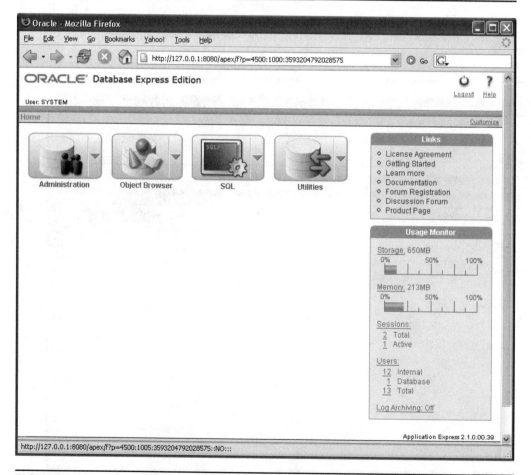

FIGURE 2-16. *The components of the Database Home Page provide access to database administration and application development tools and utilities.*

Troubleshooting Tips

At this point, you should have a good idea whether Oracle XE is working properly.
If you are having problems starting Oracle XE, connecting to Oracle with SQL*Plus,
or viewing the Database Home Page, the tips in this section should help.

Confirm Existence of Oracle XE Software and Database

To check the status of the Oracle XE software and database installation, complete
the following steps.

1. Choose Start | [All] Programs | Accessories | Windows Explorer.

2. Use Windows Explorer to confirm that ORACLE_BASE exists (e.g.,
   C:\oraclexe) with the subdirectories app and oradata.

3. Use Windows Explorer to confirm that ORACLE_HOME exists (e.g.,
   C:\oraclexe\app\oracle\product\10.2.0\server) along with a long list
   of subdirectories ranging from bin to xdk.

4. Use Windows Explorer to confirm that ORACLE_BASE\oradata\XE exists
   and includes the database files for the default starter database: control.dbf,
   sysaux.dbf, system.dbf, temp.dbf, undo.dbf, and users.dbf.

If some or all of the directories and files in the previous list do not exist, your
installation of Oracle XE was not successful. Most likely, the system does not meet
the requirements necessary for Oracle XE (refer to Exercise 2.1) or you tried to
install Oracle XE using a Microsoft Windows account that is not a member of the
Administrators group (refer to Exercise 2.2). Once you address all issues, try
reinstalling Oracle XE using Exercise 2.3.

If the ORACLE_BASE and ORACLE_HOME directories exist, but the default
starter database's files do not exist, examine the log files in ORACLE_HOME\
config\log to help troubleshoot the source of your problem. Once you resolve the
issue, you can either uninstall and reinstall Oracle XE, or open a Command Prompt
window and try running the ORACLE_BASE\config\scripts\XE.bat batch file to
create the default starter database. If database creation fails again, the output from
the batch file might include errors that help identify the cause of your problem.

Check Oracle-Related Services

To check Microsoft Windows services related to Oracle XE, use Exercise 2.7 to
check the status of OracleServiceXE and OracleXETNSListener. Then use Exercise
2.8 to start the OracleServiceXE and OracleXETNSListener if they are not already
"Started."

If you have trouble starting OracleXETNSListener with the Services window, open a Command Prompt window, enter the following command, and watch for any error messages:

```
net start OracleXETNSListener
```

If OracleXETNSListener starts but you have trouble starting OracleServiceXE with the Services window, open a Command Prompt window, enter the following command, and watch for any error messages:

```
net start OracleServiceXE
```

If you get error messages when executing either of these commands, search the Oracle XE Discussion Forum at OTN for postings that describe similar problems and resolutions.

Permit Network Access

Once you can successfully start both the OracleServiceXE and OracleXETNSListener services, confirm that you can connect to the database with SQL*Plus by using the steps in Exercise 2.11. Make sure that you try to establish both local and Oracle Net connections.

If you can establish a local connection to Oracle XE with SQL*Plus, but not an Oracle Net connection, the Listener is not receiving the connection request or cannot communicate using its configured ports. By default, the Listener listens for Oracle Net connection requests on TCP/IP port 1521. To confirm the Listener configuration, start a Command Prompt window and enter the following command:

```
lsnrctl status
```

The status report for the Listener displays a lot of information. The key section to focus on is the Listening Endpoints Summary section:

```
Listening Endpoints Summary...
   (DESCRIPTION=(ADDRESS=(PROTOCOL=ipc)(PIPENAME=\\.\pipe\
EXTPROC_FOR_XEipc)))
   (DESCRIPTION=(ADDRESS=(PROTOCOL=tcp)(HOST=myhost)(PORT=1521)))
   (DESCRIPTION=(ADDRESS=(PROTOCOL=tcp)(HOST=127.0.0.1)(PORT=8080))
     (Presentation=HTTP)(Session=RAW))
```

The preceding example output is representative of a default Listener configuration that listens on TCP/IP port 1521 for Oracle Net connection requests and TCP/IP port 8080 for HTTP connection requests.

Next, use the Microsoft Windows command **netstat** to display information about the active connections on your computer, including the network protocol, port number, and process ID (PID), that corresponds to each connection:

```
netstat -a -o
```

The report will most likely include several records of information, depending on what applications you currently have running. Focus on the records that correspond to the TCP/IP ports in your Listener configuration, shown in bold here:

```
Active Connections

  Proto  Local Address            Foreign Address        State           PID
  TCP    ALIDEV2:epmap            MYHOST:0               LISTENING       656
  TCP    ALIDEV2:microsoft-ds     MYHOST:0               LISTENING       4
  TCP    ALIDEV2:1079             MYHOST:0               LISTENING       3576
  TCP    ALIDEV2:1521             MYHOST:0               LISTENING       428
  TCP    ALIDEV2:2869             MYHOST:0               LISTENING       768
  TCP    ALIDEV2:1143             MYHOST:0               LISTENING       428
  TCP    ALIDEV2:2000             MYHOST:0               LISTENING       2448
  TCP    ALIDEV2:4444             MYHOST:0               LISTENING       2448
  TCP    ALIDEV2:8080             MYHOST:0               LISTENING       428
  . . .
```

In the preceding example report, process 428 is listening on ports 1521, 1143, and 8080. To map a process ID to a program, complete the following steps:

1. Press CTRL-ALT-DEL.

2. Click Task Manager if the Windows Task Manager does not immediately appear.

3. Click Processes.

4. If necessary, choose View | Select Columns and select PID to add process IDs to the current display.

If a process that is not the Listener is using some or all of the ports for which the Listener is configured, then you must complete several reconfiguration steps to support network connections with Oracle XE. See the Oracle XE documentation for more information.

If the Listener is in fact listening on the expected ports and you can establish a local connection to Oracle XE with SQL*Plus but cannot establish a network connection with SQL*Plus, the next most likely problem is that your computer has security software or a firewall enabled that is prohibiting necessary network communication. To check if this is the cause of your problem, complete the following steps:

1. To be safe, physically disconnect your computer from the network, especially if you are connected to the Internet.

2. Disable your firewall, security software, etc.

3. Use SQL*Plus to attempt another network connection to Oracle XE.

If you can now connect to Oracle XE, this confirms that your security software is blocking network connections with Oracle XE; you must configure your security software to allow network communication over the ports required by Oracle XE and the Listener. Consider searching the Oracle XE Discussion Forum at OTN for posts that explain what to do with whatever security software or firewall your computer uses.

NOTE
*Consider running another **netstat** report at this time and make note of all ports in use by the current Oracle XE connection.*

Web Browser Configuration

If you are having problems accessing the Database Home Page after using the previous troubleshooting tips to resolve other issues, and you are sure that your web browser meets the system requirements documented earlier in this chapter, it could be that your web browser requires some special configuration to allow access to the Database Home Page.

Microsoft Internet Explorer

Use the following steps to configure Microsoft Internet Explorer to work properly with Oracle Application Express and Oracle XE:

1. Choose Start | Control Panel | Internet Options.

2. Click the Security tab.

3. Select Local Intranet.

4. Click Sites.

5. Display the Advanced tab.

6. In the Add This Web Site To The Zone text box, enter the following site: **127.0.0.1**.

7. Click OK twice.

8. Display the Privacy tab.

9. Click Advanced.

10. Click the Accept radio button under First-Party Cookies.

11. Click OK twice.

Mozilla Firefox

Use the following steps to configure Mozilla Firefox to work properly with Oracle Application Express and Oracle XE:

1. Choose Tools | Options.

2. Display the General property sheet.

3. Click Connection Settings.

4. When using a proxy server, in the No Proxy For text box, enter the following site: **127.0.0.1**.

5. Click OK.

6. Display the Privacy property sheet.

7. Expand Cookies.

8. Click Exceptions.

9. In the Address Of Web Site text box, enter the following site: **127.0.0.1**.

10. Click Allow.

11. Click OK twice.

If after configuring your browser you still have problems accessing the Database Home Page, try a different browser. If that does not solve the problem, try searching the Oracle XE Discussion Forum for help with your specific issue.

Oracle Database 10*g* Express Edition Updates

Oracle Corporation plans to regularly release software updates for Oracle Database 10*g* Express Edition via the software downloads area of OTN. You should check this area frequently, download updates when available, and install them.

Depending on the type of update, the procedure that you undertake can vary. Simple software updates would most likely require that you just shut down Oracle XE, install the patch, and then restart Oracle XE. When a patch must update your database, the installer (or you) might run some command scripts to make the necessary changes to the database.

CAUTION
Before applying any Oracle XE software update,
always do two simple things: back up your database
to a location completely outside the scope of
ORACLE_BASE, and take the time to read the
documentation that comes with the update. Chapter 9
explains how to back up your database; taking
the time to read the update documentation is your
responsibility.

Using This Book's Support Files

All subsequent chapters in this book contain hands-on exercises that provide you with invaluable experience using Oracle XE. At the beginning of most chapters, a section called "Chapter Prerequisites" explains the steps necessary to prepare for the chapter's exercises. Typically, you'll be asked to use Oracle's SQL*Plus utility to run a SQL command script that builds a practice schema for the chapter, complete with a set of tables and other supporting database structures. Some scripts also set up custom display formats for the SQL*Plus session so that the results produced by the chapter's exercises are easy to read.

The support files and code examples for this book are present on the CD distributed with this book as an archive handsonxe_support.exe. Extract the contents of the file by using a tool such as WinZip. The file will extract itself and create the following subdirectories:

- **doc**   Contains a single file, readme.txt, that contains the latest information about the support files for this book.

- **sql**   Contains several SQL command scripts, named by chapter number, that support the corresponding chapters in this book. SQL command scripts are simple text files that contain SQL, PL/SQL, and SQL*Plus commands.

- **code**   Contains code examples from chapters in the book. Each file is a simple text file with SQL and PL/SQL commands.

When you start a new chapter, follow the directions in the "Chapter Prerequisites" section to prepare for the chapter's exercises. Unless otherwise indicated, after you successfully run a chapter's supporting SQL command script using SQL*Plus, do not exit the SQL*Plus session. You should use the SQL*Plus session to complete the exercises in the chapter, starting with the first exercise in the chapter, all the way through the final exercise in the chapter.

If you do not have time to complete all exercises in the chapter during one sitting, that's OK. When you have time to continue, simply restart SQL*Plus and rerun the chapter's SQL command script to refresh the necessary data and SQL*Plus display settings. Then repeat all exercises in the chapter, starting with the first exercise again. In fact, I encourage you to repeat a chapter's exercises as many times as necessary to make working with Oracle XE second nature.

Chapter Summary

This chapter has explained how to install Oracle XE for Microsoft Windows, as well as the basic concepts and procedures necessary to get started working with Oracle XE:

- An Oracle database is not available until after you start a database instance, mount and open the database.

- On Microsoft Windows, you can check the status of and control the availability of the default starter database by using the Services window to manage the OracleServiceXE service.

- To establish a local database connection to an Oracle database with SQL*Plus, you use the SQL*Plus command CONNECT along with a database username and password.

- To establish a network database connection to an Oracle database with SQL*Plus, you use the SQL*Plus command CONNECT along with a database username, password, and service name. The Listener is a process that forwards the network database connection request to the target database instance. On Microsoft Windows, you can check the status of and control the availability of the Listener by using the Services window to manage the OracleXETNSListener service.

- Oracle Application Express is a web-based tool that you can use to manage the Oracle Database 10*g* Express Edition starter database and develop applications. By default, Oracle Application Express is available at the URL http://127.0.0.1:8080/apex/.

PART

II

Fundamentals of Application Development

CHAPTER
3

Access Database
Data with SQL

o get work done, applications must communicate with Oracle to enter and retrieve data, and do so in a way that protects the integrity of the database's data. This chapter introduces the basic concepts of how applications use SQL statements and encompassing transactions to interact with an Oracle database system.

Chapter Prerequisites

To practice the hands-on exercises in this chapter, you need to start SQL*Plus as instructed in Exercise 2.11 and run the command script

```
location\handsonxe\sql\chap03.sql
```

where *location* is the file directory where you expanded the support archive that accompanies this book. For example, after starting SQL*Plus, you can run this chapter's SQL command script using the SQL*Plus command @, as in the following example (assuming that your chap03.sql file is in C:\temp\handsonxe\sql):

```
SQL> @C:\temp\handsonxe\sql\chap03.sql;
```

Once you reply to all of the prompts and the script completes successfully, leave the current SQL*Plus session open and use it to perform this chapter's exercises in the order that they appear.

What Is SQL?

To accomplish work with Oracle, applications must use *Structured Query Language (SQL)* commands. SQL (pronounced either as "sequel" or "ess-que-ell") is a relatively simple command language that database administrators, developers, and application users use to

- Retrieve, enter, update, and delete database data

- Create, alter, and drop database objects

- Restrict access to database data and system operations

The only way that an application can interact with an Oracle database server is to issue a SQL command. Easy-to-use graphical user interfaces (GUIs) might hide SQL commands from users and developers, but under the covers, an application always communicates with Oracle using SQL.

Types of SQL Commands

The following are the four primary categories of SQL commands:

■ **DML**   *Data manipulation* (or *modification*) *language (DML)* commands are SQL commands that retrieve, insert, update, and delete table rows in an Oracle database. The four basic DML commands are SELECT, INSERT, UPDATE, and DELETE. Subsequent sections of this chapter provide you with a thorough introduction to these four commands.

■ **Transaction control**   Applications that use SQL and relational databases perform work by using transactions. A *database transaction* is a unit of work accomplished by one or more related SQL statements. To preserve the integrity of information in a database, relational databases such as Oracle ensure that all work within each transaction either commits or rolls back. An application uses the *transaction control* SQL commands COMMIT and ROLLBACK to control the outcome of a database transaction. Subsequent sections of this chapter explain how to design transactions and use transaction control SQL commands.

■ **DDL**   *Data definition language (DDL)* commands create, alter, and drop database objects. Most types of database objects have corresponding CREATE, ALTER, and DROP commands. See Chapter 5 to learn more about DDL commands.

■ **DCL**   An administrative application uses *data control language (DCL)* commands to control user access to an Oracle database. The three most commonly used DCL commands are the GRANT, REVOKE, and SET ROLE commands. See Chapter 7 for more information about, and examples of, these DCL commands.

Application Portability and the ANSI/ISO SQL Standard

The *ANSI/ISO SQL standard* defines a generic specification for SQL. (For your information, ANSI is an acronym for *American National Standards Institute* and ISO is an acronym for *International Organization for Standardization.*) Most commercial relational database systems, including Oracle, support ANSI/ISO standard SQL. When a database supports the SQL standard and an application uses only standard SQL commands, the application's SQL is said to be *portable*. In other words, if you decide to substitute another database that supports the ANSI/ISO SQL standard, the syntax of the SQL commands that the application uses should continue to function unmodified.

The ANSI/ISO SQL:2003 standard has many different levels of compliance. To a large degree, Oracle complies with the core SQL:2003 standard and subsequent levels. For a detailed explanation of Oracle's SQL standard compliance, see the appendixes in the *Oracle Database SQL Reference*, available online at www.oracle .com/pls/db102/homepage.

Oracle also supports many extensions to the ANSI/ISO SQL:2003 standard. Such extensions greatly enhance the capabilities of Oracle and take advantage of unique, powerful features of Oracle. *SQL extensions* can take the form of nonstandard SQL commands or just nonstandard options for standard SQL commands. However, understand that when an application makes use of proprietary Oracle SQL extensions, corresponding SQL statements are not portable—most likely, you would need to modify and recompile the application before it would work with other database systems.

Ad Hoc SQL Tools

One type of application that you can use to enter SQL commands and interact with an Oracle database system is an ad hoc query tool, as explained in Chapter 1. This chapter introduces you to two ad hoc query tools available with Oracle XE: the Oracle Application Express Query Builder and SQL*Plus.

Now that you have a general understanding of SQL, the remaining sections in this chapter introduce you to the types of SQL commands that you will most often use to access an Oracle database: SELECT (a query), INSERT, UPDATE, DELETE, COMMIT, and ROLLBACK.

Retrieving Data with Queries

The most basic SQL statement is a query. A *query* is a SQL statement that uses the SELECT command to retrieve information from a database. A query's *result set* is the set of columns and rows that the query requests from a database server. For example, the following query retrieves all rows and columns from the ORDERS table:

```
SELECT * FROM orders;

        ID      C_ID ORDERDATE SHIPDATE  PAIDDATE  STATUS
--------- --------- --------- --------- --------- ------
        1         1 18-JUN-06 18-JUN-06 30-JUN-06 F
        2         2 18-JUN-06                     B
        3         3 18-JUN-06 18-JUN-06 21-JUN-06 F
        4         4 19-JUN-06 21-JUN-06 21-JUN-06 F
        5         5 19-JUN-06 19-JUN-06 28-JUN-06 F
        6         6 19-JUN-06 19-JUN-06           F
        7         7 19-JUN-06                     B
        8         8 20-JUN-06 20-JUN-06 20-JUN-06 F
        9         9 21-JUN-06                     B
       10         2 21-JUN-06 22-JUN-06 22-JUN-06 F
       11         4 22-JUN-06 22-JUN-06           F
       12         7 22-JUN-06 23-JUN-06 30-JUN-06 F
       13         4 22-JUN-06                     B
       14         1 23-JUN-06 25-JUN-06           F

14 rows selected.
```

NOTE
All relational database systems, including Oracle, do not guarantee the physical order of rows in a table; therefore, do not be surprised if the order of the rows in your result sets are not identical to the order of the rows in the example result sets in this book. Later in this chapter, you will learn how to explicitly sort the rows in a query's result set.

The Structure of a Query

Although the structure of a SELECT statement can vary, all queries have two basic components: a SELECT clause and a FROM clause.

A basic query's *SELECT clause* specifies a *column list* that identifies the columns that must appear in the query's result set. Each column that appears in the SELECT clause must correspond to one of the tables in the query's FROM clause.

A SELECT clause can also contain *expressions* that derive information from columns using functions and operators that manipulate table data, as well as simple literals like numbers, strings, etc. Subsequent sections of this chapter explain how to build expressions in a query's SELECT clause.

A query's *FROM clause* specifies the *row source* for the query to target. The FROM clause of a basic query specifies a list of one or more tables. Simple queries target just one table, while more advanced queries join information by targeting multiple related tables.

Besides tables, a FROM clause in a query can specify dynamic row sources that are built when the query executes. For example, a query's FROM clause can specify a *subquery* to build a specific set of rows as the row source for the main query; a subquery used in this context is known as an *inline view*. When you use a subquery in a query's FROM clause, SELECT clause expressions in the main query can refer to columns in the result set of the inline view.

NOTE
You can use subqueries in many parts of a SELECT statement. For example, the SELECT clause can use a scalar subquery, a subquery that returns a single value from a single row. Subsequent sections of this chapter explain more about subqueries.

To review, a basic query has the following syntax:

```
SELECT column or expression, column or expression, ...
    FROM row source, row source, ...
```

Building Basic Queries

The following set of hands-on exercises teaches you how to build basic queries and several related functions, including the following:

- How to retrieve all columns and rows from a table
- How to retrieve specific columns of all rows in a table
- How to "describe" the structure of a table
- How to specify an alias for a column in a query

EXERCISE 3.1: Retrieving All Columns and Rows

Using your current SQL*Plus session, enter the following query to retrieve all columns and rows from the ORDERS table:

```
SELECT * FROM orders;
```

The results of the query should be identical to the following:

```
       ID      C_ID ORDERDATE SHIPDATE  PAIDDATE  STATUS
--------- --------- --------- --------- --------- ------
        1         1 18-JUN-06 18-JUN-06 30-JUN-06 F
        2         2 18-JUN-06                     B
        3         3 18-JUN-06 18-JUN-06 21-JUN-06 F
        4         4 19-JUN-06 21-JUN-06 21-JUN-06 F
        5         5 19-JUN-06 19-JUN-06 28-JUN-06 F
        6         6 19-JUN-06 19-JUN-06           F
        7         7 19-JUN-06                     B
        8         8 20-JUN-06 20-JUN-06 20-JUN-06 F
        9         9 21-JUN-06                     B
       10         2 21-JUN-06 22-JUN-06 22-JUN-06 F
       11         4 22-JUN-06 22-JUN-06           F
       12         7 22-JUN-06 23-JUN-06 30-JUN-06 F
       13         4 22-JUN-06                     B
       14         1 23-JUN-06 25-JUN-06           F

14 rows selected.
```

The *wildcard asterisk character (*)* in the SELECT clause indicates that the query should retrieve all columns from the row sources listed in the FROM clause.

EXERCISE 3.2: Retrieving Specific Columns

To retrieve specific columns from all rows, a query's SELECT clause must explicitly specify the name of each column to retrieve. For example, enter the following statement to retrieve just the ID and ORDERDATE columns for all rows in the ORDERS table:

```
SELECT id, orderdate FROM orders;
```

The result set is as follows:

```
        ID ORDERDATE
---------- ---------
         1 18-JUN-06
         2 18-JUN-06
         3 18-JUN-06
         4 19-JUN-06
         5 19-JUN-06
         6 19-JUN-06
         7 19-JUN-06
         8 20-JUN-06
         9 21-JUN-06
        10 21-JUN-06
        11 22-JUN-06
        12 22-JUN-06
        13 22-JUN-06
        14 23-JUN-06
```

```
14 rows selected.
```

EXERCISE 3.3: Using the SQL*Plus DESCRIBE Command

If you are using SQL*Plus and you do not know the names of the columns in a table that you would like to query, use the special SQL*Plus command *DESCRIBE* to output the structure of the table. Enter the following DESCRIBE statement to display the column names of the ORDERS table (as well as additional information for each column):

```
DESCRIBE orders;
```

The results of the previous command should be similar to the following:

```
Name                                                  Null?    Type
----------------------------------------------------- -------- ----------
 ID                                                   NOT NULL NUMBER(38)
 C_ID                                                 NOT NULL NUMBER(38)
 ORDERDATE                                            NOT NULL DATE
 SHIPDATE                                                      DATE
 PAIDDATE                                                      DATE
 STATUS                                                        CHAR(1)
```

Subsequent sections in this book explain more about the Null and Type columns output by the DESCRIBE command. All things in good time.

EXERCISE 3.4: Specifying an Alias for a Column

To customize the names of the columns in a query's result set, you have the option of specifying a *column alias* (an alternate name) for each column (or expression) in the query's SELECT clause. To rename a column or expression in the SELECT clause, just specify a column alias after the list item.

NOTE
As this exercise demonstrates, you must delimit the column alias with double quotes if you want to specify the case, specify spacing, or include special characters in an alias.

To use a column alias, enter the following query, which specifies an alias (in bold) for the ONHAND column of the PARTS table. Notice that you must delimit the column alias with double quotes if you want to specify the case, specify spacing, or include special characters in an alias.

```
SELECT id, onhand AS "IN STOCK"
   FROM parts;
```

The result set is as follows:

```
       ID  IN STOCK
--------- ---------
        1       277
        2       143
        3      7631
        4      5903
        5       490
```

As this example demonstrates, you can precede a column alias with the optional keyword AS to make the alias specification more readable. Subsequent queries in this chapter provide many more examples of alias specifications.

Building Expressions in a Query's SELECT Clause

The SELECT clause of a query must always be a list of expressions. An *expression* evaluates to a value such as a character string, datetime, or numeric value, just to name a few. There are several different types of constructs that you can use to build expressions in a query's SELECT clause and return the resulting data in the query's result set, including column names, operators, SQL functions, and decoded expressions. The next few sections provide a brief introduction to some SELECT clause expressions that are more complex than just the simple column names used in the previous exercises of this chapter.

EXERCISE 3.5: Building SELECT Clause Expressions with the Concatenation String Operator

An *operator* transforms data and returns a result. For example, a simple way to build an expression in a SELECT clause is to use the *concatenation operator*—two solid vertical bars (||)—to concatenate character columns and/or string *literals* (explicit value).

Enter the following query, which includes a simple SELECT clause expression. For each record in the CUSTOMERS table, the expression (in bold) concatenates the LASTNAME field with a comma and a blank space (delimited by single quotes), and then the resulting string with the FIRSTNAME field. The expression also has a column alias to make its column heading in the result set more readable.

```
SELECT lastname || ', ' || firstname AS name
   FROM customers;
```

The result set is as follows:

```
NAME
--------------------
Ayers, Jack
Clay, Dorothy
Elias, Juan
Foss, Betty
Haagensen, Dave
Joy, Harold
Musial, Bill
Sams, Danielle
Schaub, Greg
Wiersbicki, Joseph

10 rows selected.
```

NOTE
The expressions on which an operator acts are called operands. The concatenation operator is an example of a binary operator—*an operator that takes two operands and creates a new result. An operand that creates a value from a single operand is called a* unary operator.

EXERCISE 3.6: Building SELECT Clause Expressions with Arithmetic Operators

Oracle's unary and binary arithmetic operators are listed in Table 3-1. An *arithmetic operator* accepts one or more numeric operands and produces a single numeric result.

Arithmetic Operator	Description
+x (unary)	Indicates that x is positive
–x (unary)	Indicates that x is negative
x + y (binary)	Adds x and y
x – y (binary)	Subtracts y from x
x * y (binary)	Multiplies x by y
x/y (binary)	Divides x by y

TABLE 3-1. *Arithmetic Operators Supported by Oracle Database 10g*

Table 3-1 is by no means a complete list of all operators that you can use with SQL; it's merely a quick reference to some of the more commonly used operators that you will see as you are getting started with Oracle XE. For complete information about operators, see the *Oracle Database SQL Reference.*

Now try a query that contains a SELECT clause expression that uses a binary arithmetic operator. Enter the following query, which uses an arithmetic expression (in bold) to determine how many of each part remain in inventory above the corresponding part's reorder threshold:

```
SELECT id, onhand - reorder AS threshold
    FROM parts;
```

The result set is as follows:

```
    ID THRESHOLD
--------- ---------
        1       227
        2       118
        3      6631
        4      4903
        5       290
```

EXERCISE 3.7: Building SELECT Clause Expressions with SQL Functions

You can also build an expression in a query's SELECT clause by using one or more of SQL's built-in functions. A *function* takes zero, one, or multiple arguments and returns a single value. There are two general types of SQL functions that you can use with queries: single-row functions and group functions.

A *single-row* (or *scalar*) *function* returns a value for every row that is part of a query's result set. Oracle supports many different categories of single-row SQL functions, including character, date, numeric, and conversion functions. For example, enter the following query, which uses the SQL functions UPPER and LOWER (in bold) in SELECT clause expressions to display the company name in uppercase letters for each customer record and the last name of each customer record in lowercase letters:

```
SELECT UPPER(companyname) AS companyname,
       LOWER(lastname) AS lastname
  FROM customers;
```

The result set is as follows:

```
COMPANYNAME                           LASTNAME
-----------------------------------   ---------------
MCDONALD CO.                          joy
CAR AUDIO CENTER                      musial
WISE TRUCKING                         sams
ROSE GARDEN INN                       elias
FOSS PHOTOGRAPHY                      foss
PAMPERED PETS                         schaub
KEY LOCKSMITH                         wiersbicki
PARK VIEW INSURANCE                   ayers
KENSER CORP.                          clay
DAVE'S TREE SERVICE                   haagensen

10 rows selected.
```

Now enter the following query, which uses two numeric single-row SQL functions in SELECT clause expressions, SQRT and LN (in bold), to display the square root of 49 and the natural logarithm of 10, respectively:

```
SELECT SQRT(49), LN(10)
  FROM DUAL;
```

The result set is as follows:

```
SQRT(49)    LN(10)
---------  ---------
        7 2.3025851
```

NOTE
The previous query targets a special table called DUAL that is present in every Oracle database. DUAL is a table consisting of one column and one row that you can use to satisfy the requirement for a row source in a query's FROM clause. DUAL is useful for queries that just perform arithmetic or use a SQL function to return a value.

A *group* (or *aggregate*) *function* returns an aggregate value for all rows that are part of a query's result set. For example, enter the following query, which uses the group SQL functions COUNT, MAX, MIN, and AVG (in bold) to return the number of records in the PARTS table, as well as the maximum, minimum, and average UNITPRICE for records in the PARTS table, respectively:

```
SELECT COUNT(id) AS count,
       MAX(unitprice) AS max_price,
       MIN(unitprice) AS min_price,
       AVG(unitprice) AS ave_price
   FROM parts;
```

The result set is as follows:

```
    COUNT MAX_PRICE MIN_PRICE AVE_PRICE
--------- --------- --------- ---------
        5      4895        99    1718.6
```

The example queries in this section have introduced just a few of the many SQL functions that are available with Oracle. For complete information about the many powerful SQL functions that you can use with Oracle XE, see the *Oracle Database SQL Reference.*

EXERCISE 3.8: Working with Nulls in SELECT Clause Expressions

A *null* indicates the absence of a value (think *unknown*). For example, the SHIPDATE field of a sales record in the ORDERS table is unknown (and thus null) until the order ships. When the order ships, you can replace the null with an actual date value.

Grasping the concept of nulls is very important when working with relational database systems like Oracle. When building queries, you must pay special attention to the possibility of nulls; otherwise, you might unintentionally obtain results that do not accurately reflect your question. In most cases, an expression that includes a null evaluates to null or UNKNOWN.

To explicitly handle nulls in expressions, you can use the special scalar SQL function *NVL* to return a value of your choice when a column is null. For example, enter the following query, which uses the NVL function (in bold) to substitute the string literal 'UNKNOWN' when the FAX field of a record in the CUSTOMERS table is null:

```
SELECT id, NVL(fax, 'UNKNOWN') AS fax
   FROM customers;
```

The result set is as follows (the bold text indicates nulls for which the NVL function substituted the literal 'UNKNOWN'):

```
        ID FAX
--------- ----------------------
         1 UNKNOWN
         2 775-859-2121
         3 203-955-9532
         4 214-907-3188
         5 215-543-9800
         6 602-617-7321
         7 718-445-8799
         8 UNKNOWN
         9 916-672-8753
        10 UNKNOWN

10 rows selected.
```

Please see the *Oracle Database SQL Reference* for more information about other SQL functions that you can use to address nulls, including NVL2, NULLIF, and COALESCE.

EXERCISE 3.9: Implementing Conditional Logic in SELECT Clause Expressions

The previous exercises have introduced some very simple types of expressions that you can use in a query. Now you are prepared to learn about two types of expressions that are a bit more advanced: case expressions and decoded expressions.

A *CASE expression* is a technique that you can use to implement IF-THEN-ELSE procedural logic in an expression. A CASE expression can use one of two forms: a simple or searched CASE expression.

A simple CASE expression is useful when you want to translate column values in a table that are codes or symbols that represent values:

```
CASE expression
      WHEN value THEN return_value
      WHEN value THEN return_value
      [ ... ]
      ELSE default_return_value
END
```

As the preceding syntax listing indicates, a simple CASE expression compares the result of a source expression to a value and, if they match, returns the corresponding return value; if they do not match, Oracle evaluates the next WHEN clause in the same manner and continues until it finds a match. If Oracle does not find a match, the CASE expression returns the default return value; when you omit a default return value, Oracle returns null.

For example, enter the following query, which includes a simple CASE expression (in bold) to convert the codes F and B of the STATUS column in the

ORDERS table to the corresponding string literals FILLED and BACKORDERED, respectively:

```
SELECT id,
       CASE status
          WHEN 'F' THEN 'FILLED'
          WHEN 'B' THEN 'BACKORDERED'
          ELSE 'OTHER'
       END AS status
  FROM orders;
```

The result set is as follows:

```
   ID STATUS
--------- ---------------
    1 FILLED
    2 BACKORDERED
    3 FILLED
    4 FILLED
    5 FILLED
    6 FILLED
    7 BACKORDERED
    8 FILLED
    9 BACKORDERED
   10 FILLED
   11 FILLED
   12 FILLED
   13 BACKORDERED
   14 FILLED

14 rows selected.
```

A simple CASE expression is relatively new SQL decoding syntax. Because Oracle applications have traditionally used a *decoded expression* for this purpose, it's likely that you will run across a decoded expression and will need to understand this alternative to a simple CASE expression. A decoded expression uses the SQL function DECODE, which takes three parameters. The first parameter is the expression to be evaluated, which can be as simple as a column in a table. The second parameter is a comma-separated list of key-value pairs; for each possible key, specify a corresponding display value. The final parameter, which is optional, is a default display value for all expression values that are not specified in the second parameter's list of key-value pairs. To become familiar with decoded expressions (in bold), enter the following query, which is functionality equivalent to the query in the previous exercise:

```
SELECT id,
       DECODE (
          status,
```

```
            'F','FILLED', 'B','BACKORDERED',
            'OTHER' ) AS status
    FROM orders;
```

Retrieving Specific Rows from Tables

So far, all of the example queries in this chapter show how to retrieve every row from a table. Optionally, a query can limit the result set to those rows in the target table that satisfy a *WHERE clause condition*. If the Boolean condition of the WHERE clause evaluates to TRUE for a particular row, Oracle includes the row in the query's result set. For example, the following query includes a WHERE clause condition (in bold) that limits the result set to only those records in the ORDERS table that have a STATUS code equal to B:

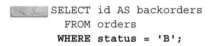

```
SELECT id AS backorders
    FROM orders
  WHERE status = 'B';
```

The result set is as follows:

```
BACKORDERS
----------
         2
         7
         9
        13
```

NOTE
If you submit a query and omit a WHERE clause, Oracle selects all rows from the targets specified in the query's FROM clause.

The next three exercises explain how to build WHERE clause conditions with relational operators, subqueries, and logical operators.

EXERCISE 3.10: Building WHERE Clause Conditions with Relational Operators

Oracle supports several relational operators that you can use to build WHERE clause conditions. A *relational* (or *comparison*) *operator* compares two operands to determine whether they are equal or one operand is greater than the other. A condition that uses a relational operator produces a Boolean value of TRUE or FALSE; however, if a null is involved in the condition, some relational operators produce an UNKNOWN result. Table 3-2 lists a subset of common relational operators that Oracle supports—see the *Oracle Database SQL Reference* for a complete list.

Condition	Returns TRUE when...	Returns FALSE when...	Returns UNKNOWN when...
x = y	x equals y and both x and y are not null.	x does not equal y and both x and y are not null.	either x or y is null.
x != y x ^= y x <> y	x does not equal y and both x and y are not null.	x equals y and both x and y are not null.	either x or y is null.
x > y	x is greater than y and both x and y are not null.	x is less than or equal to y and both x and y are not null.	either x or y is null.
x < y	x is less than y and both x and y are not null.	x is greater than or equal to y and both x and y are not null.	either x or y is null.
x >= y	x is greater than or equal to y and both x and y are not null.	x is less than y and both x and y are not null.	either x or y is null.
x <= y	x is less than or equal to y and both x and y are not null.	x is greater than y and both x and y are not null.	either x or y is null.
x IN (list|subquery)	x is present in y, where y is an explicitly specified list of values or list of values returned by a subquery.	x is not present in y.	either x is null or y contains a null.
x NOT IN (list|subquery)	x is not present in y, where y is an explicitly specified list of values or list of values returned by a subquery.	x is present in y.	either x is null or y contains a null.

TABLE 3-2. *Relational Operators Supported by Oracle Database 10g*

Condition	Returns TRUE when...	Returns FALSE when...	Returns UNKNOWN when...
x BETWEEN y AND z	x falls within the inclusive range of y and z.	x does not fall within the inclusive range of y and z.	either x, y, or z is null.
x NOT BETWEEN y AND z	x does not fall within the inclusive range of y and z.	x falls within the inclusive range of y and z.	either x, y, or z is null.
EXISTS (subquery)	the subquery returns one or more rows.	the subquery does not return any rows.	n/a
x LIKE y [ESCAPE z]	x matches the pattern y. y can include the wildcard characters % and _. % matches any string of zero or more characters, except null. _ matches any single character. Use the optional ESCAPE parameter only when you want Oracle to interpret literally a wildcard character within y—specify the wildcard character as the escape character.	x does not match the pattern y.	x is null.
x NOT LIKE y [ESCAPE z]	x does not match the pattern y. y can include the wildcard characters % and _, and you can include the optional ESCAPE parameter (explained in preceding row).	x matches the pattern y.	x is null.

TABLE 3-2. *Relational Operators Supported by Oracle Database 10g (continued)*

Condition	Returns TRUE when...	Returns FALSE when...	Returns UNKNOWN when...
REGEXP_LIKE(x, y[, z])	x contains matches for the POSIX standard Extended Regular Expression (ERE) y. The optional match parameter z is one or more character literals that let you control the pattern matching behavior: **i** specifies case-insensitive matching; **c** specifies case-sensitive matching; **n** allows the period metacharacter (.) to match a new line character (as well as all other characters); and **m** specifies that the source string may contain multiple lines and that you want the ^ and $ metacharacters to match the beginning and end, respectively, of any line in the source string. If you do not specify any match parameters, Oracle determines the case sensitivity for regular expression matches using the session's NLS_SORT parameter, the period metacharacter does not match a new line character, and the ^ and $ metacharacters match only the start and end, respectively, of an entire source string (even if it contains multiple lines). Regular expressions are a powerful tool that you can use for complex pattern matching and are beyond the scope of this book.	x does not contain matches for y.	x is null.
x IS NULL	x is null.	x is not null.	n/a
x IS NOT NULL	x is not null.	x is null.	n/a

TABLE 3-2. *Relational Operators Supported by Oracle Database 10g (continued)*

NOTE
In many of the conditions of Table 3-2, x or y can be a subquery, as long as the subquery returns a scalar value from zero or one row.

Let's try a couple of queries that use relational operators to build WHERE clause conditions. First, enter the following query with a WHERE clause (in bold) to display the ID and ORDERDATE of all records in the ORDERS tables that have an ORDERDATE greater than June 21, 2006:

```
SELECT id, orderdate
  FROM orders
 WHERE orderdate > TO_DATE('21-JUN-2006', 'DD-MON-YYYY');
```

The result set is as follows:

```
        ID ORDERDATE
---------- ---------
        11 22-JUN-06
        12 22-JUN-06
        13 22-JUN-06
        14 23-JUN-06
```

NOTE
In the previous example, the WHERE clause condition uses the SQL function TO_DATE to explicitly convert a character string to a DATE value. Oracle can also implicitly convert a value of one datatype to another. For example, when Oracle expects a DATE value as part of a WHERE clause condition, when you supply a string literal such as '21-JUN-06' and the string conforms to your session's current DATE format model, Oracle implicitly converts the string to a DATE and performs the comparison. While implicit datatype conversions such as these are convenient, they introduce the possibility of misinterpretation. For deterministic behavior, you should always specify dates with four-digit years using the TO_DATE function.

Next, enter the following query to list the ID and LASTNAME of all customer records that do not have a FAX number. Notice that the WHERE clause condition (in bold) uses the special IS NULL relational operator to test for the presence of a null in each record.

```
SELECT id, lastname
  FROM customers
 WHERE fax IS NULL;
```

The result set is as follows:

```
     ID LASTNAME
--------- --------------
      1 Joy
      8 Ayers
     10 Haagensen
```

The previous example introduces a very important rule regarding conditions that test for nulls: *Always* use the IS NULL or IS NOT NULL operators to test for the existence of nulls. *Never* try to identify nulls in a WHERE clause with a condition that uses a traditional equality operator such as WHERE fax = NULL; this type of condition will not deliver the desired results. Try it by revising the previous query and see for yourself.

EXERCISE 3.11: Building WHERE Clause Conditions with Subqueries

Some queries need to retrieve the answers based on multiple-part questions. For example, how would you build a query that reports the IDs of all orders placed by customers of a particular sales representative? This is really a two-part question, because the ORDERS table does not contain a field to record the sales representative that made the sale. However, the ORDERS table does include a field for the customer that made the purchase, and the CUSTOMERS table uses the S_ID column to indicate the sales representative for each customer record. Therefore, one way to answer the original question is by first building a list of customers that corresponds to the sales representative, and then using the list to retrieve the IDs of the orders that correspond to just those customers.

To answer a multiple-part question in SQL with just one query, the query can use a WHERE clause condition with a subquery as an operand. When a WHERE clause condition uses a subquery, Oracle conceptually evaluates the subquery (or *inner, nested query*) first to return a value or list of values to the relational operator in the condition before evaluating the *main* (or *outer*) *query*.

Let's try a query that uses a subquery to answer the question asked at the beginning of this exercise. Enter the following query, which uses a WHERE clause condition with the relational operator IN and a subquery (in bold) to report the ID and ORDERDATE of all orders placed by customers of sales representative number 2:

```
SELECT id, orderdate
   FROM orders
  WHERE c_id IN (
        SELECT id FROM customers
         WHERE s_id = 2 );
```

The result set is as follows:

```
    ID ORDERDATE
--------- ---------
     4 19-JUN-06
    11 22-JUN-06
    13 22-JUN-06
```

Now consider what you would do if you needed to answer the previous question, but you did not know the ID of the sales representative with the last name "Jonah." In this case, you would need to answer a three-part question with a single query. First, you would need to get the ID of the sales representative named Jonah, then get a list of Jonah's customers, and then list the ID and ORDERDATE that correspond to those customers only. To accomplish this feat with a single query, the subquery (in bold) of the main query must use a subquery itself. Enter the following query to try this out for yourself:

```
SELECT id, orderdate
   FROM orders
  WHERE c_id IN (
        SELECT id FROM customers
         WHERE s_id = (
               SELECT id FROM salesreps
                WHERE lastname = 'Jonah') );
```

The result set is as follows:

```
    ID ORDERDATE
--------- ---------
     4 19-JUN-06
    11 22-JUN-06
    13 22-JUN-06
```

Notice that the innermost subquery uses the equals relational operator (=) and a subquery to determine the ID of the sales representative with the last name "Jonah." Oracle supports the use of a subquery with many relational operators—see Table 3-2 for a short list of many relational operators that support subqueries and their corresponding descriptions.

EXERCISE 3.12: Building Composite WHERE Clause Conditions with Logical Operators

Oracle also supports the use of the logical operators AND and OR to build a composite WHERE clause condition—a condition that includes two or more conditions.

■ **AND**   Combines the results of two Boolean conditions. The entire condition evaluates to TRUE only when both conditions on either side of the AND operator are TRUE. It evaluates to FALSE when either or both conditions are FALSE, and it evaluates to UNKNOWN when both conditions are null, or when either condition is TRUE and the other is null.

■ **OR**   Combines the results of two conditions. The entire condition evaluates to FALSE only when both conditions on either side of the OR operator are FALSE. It evaluates to TRUE when either or both conditions are TRUE, and it evaluates to UNKNOWN when both conditions are null, or when either condition is FALSE and the other is null.

NOTE
For logic tables that encapsulate the preceding information and more information about logical operators, see the Oracle Database SQL Reference.

Enter the following query, which uses the AND logical operator (in bold) to build a composite WHERE clause condition that reports the ID and ORDERDATE of records in the ORDERS table that were ordered on or after June 21, 2006, and have a STATUS equal to B (on back order):

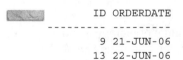
```
SELECT id, orderdate
  FROM orders
 WHERE orderdate >= TO_DATE('21-JUN-2006','DD-MON-YYYY')
   AND status = 'B';
```

The result set is as follows:

```
       ID ORDERDATE
--------- ---------
        9 21-JUN-06
       13 22-JUN-06
```

NOTE
Oracle also supports the logical operator NOT so that you can build a query with a WHERE clause condition that tests for records that contradict a condition.

Grouping and Sorting Data Within a Query's Result Set

The previous exercises in this chapter teach you how to include specific columns and rows in a query's result set. The next three sections explain how to format the output of a query's result set by grouping and sorting the records.

EXERCISE 3.13: Grouping Records in a Query's Result Set

Many queries need to answer questions based on *aggregates* or *summaries* of information rather than the details of individual records in a table. For example, you might want to query the ORDERS table to report how many orders each customer has placed or a count of orders on a particular date.

To group data in a query's result set, the query must include a *GROUP BY clause*. The list of columns in the GROUP BY clause specify how to aggregate the rows in the result set. A GROUP BY clause can list any column name in the table that appears in the query's FROM clause; however, a GROUP BY clause cannot reference column aliases defined in the SELECT clause.

When you build the SELECT clause of a query that includes a GROUP BY clause, you can include an expression that uses a group function, including the functions AVG, COUNT, MAX, MIN, STDDEV, SUM, and VARIANCE. You can also include an unaggregated column or expression in the SELECT clause, but the same column or expression must be one of the columns or expressions in the GROUP BY clause.

Let's try grouping some data in a query's result set by entering the following query, which uses the group SQL function COUNT and a GROUP BY clause (in bold) to display the total number of orders placed by each customer:

```
SELECT c_id AS customer,
       COUNT(id) AS orders_placed
  FROM orders
 GROUP BY c_id;
```

The result set is as follows:

```
CUSTOMER ORDERS_PLACED
--------- -------------
        1             2
        2             2
        3             1
        4             3
        5             1
        6             1
        7             2
        8             1
        9             1

9 rows selected.
```

To eliminate particular groups from a query's result set, you can add a *HAVING clause* to the query's GROUP BY clause. Much like a WHERE clause condition, Oracle includes only those groups in a query's result set that evaluate to TRUE for the HAVING clause condition. For example, enter the following query, which displays the ID and number of orders placed by customers that have placed more than one order:

```
SELECT c_id AS customer,
       COUNT(id) AS orders_placed
  FROM orders
 GROUP BY c_id
       HAVING COUNT(id) > 1;
```

The result set is as follows:

```
CUSTOMER ORDERS_PLACED
-------- -------------
       1             2
       2             2
       4             3
       7             2
```

NOTE
A query can use both a WHERE clause and the HAVING clause of a GROUP BY clause to eliminate data from the query's result set. Before forming groups, Oracle first removes all rows from the query's result set that do not satisfy the condition of the WHERE clause. Next, Oracle uses the expressions in the GROUP BY clause to form summary groups. Finally, Oracle removes the groups in the result set that do not satisfy the condition of the HAVING clause.

EXERCISE 3.14: Rolling Up Groups into Supergroups

Now that you understand basic grouping concepts, let's try something more advanced. A query that uses a basic GROUP BY clause divides the rows in the result set into groups, and then provides summary information for each group based on the aggregations declared in the SELECT list. For example, enter the following query, which counts how many orders each customer placed on individual days:

```
SELECT c_id, orderdate, COUNT(id) AS orders
  FROM orders
 GROUP BY (c_id, orderdate);
```

The results of the query are as follows:

```
     C_ID ORDERDATE      ORDERS
---------- ---------- ----------
        2 21-JUN-06          1
        4 22-JUN-06          2
        2 18-JUN-06          1
        3 18-JUN-06          1
        1 18-JUN-06          1
        7 22-JUN-06          1
        1 23-JUN-06          1
        4 19-JUN-06          1
        8 20-JUN-06          1
        9 21-JUN-06          1
        7 19-JUN-06          1
        5 19-JUN-06          1
        6 19-JUN-06          1
```

```
13 rows selected.
```

Now enter the next query, which counts how many orders each customer placed, without regard to what days the orders were placed:

```
SELECT c_id, COUNT(id) AS orders
   FROM orders
 GROUP BY (c_id);
```

The results of the query are as follows:

```
     C_ID     ORDERS
---------- ----------
        1          2
        6          1
        2          2
        4          3
        5          1
        8          1
        3          1
        7          2
        9          1
```

```
9 rows selected.
```

Now enter the next query, which counts how many orders were placed, without regard to what customer placed them or on which day they were placed:

```
SELECT COUNT(id) AS orders
   FROM orders
 GROUP BY ();
```

The results of the query are as follows:

```
ORDERS
----------
       14
```

Notice in the last three queries that you are gradually "rolling up" summary information from a more detailed level to a higher level. Wouldn't it be nice if you could accomplish the results with one query? You can! To "roll up" the information in the groups of a query's result set, or to create supergroups, you can use the ROLLUP operator of the GROUP BY clause. When you specify the ROLLUP operator before the list of columns in a GROUP BY clause, Oracle creates subtotals that summarize data from the most detailed level to the broadest level, moving from right to left through the list of grouping columns. ROLLUP will create subtotals (shown in bold in the following example) at $n+1$ levels, where n is the number of grouping columns. Let's try it. Enter the following query, which uses the ROLLUP operator:

```
SELECT c_id, orderdate, COUNT(id) AS orders
  FROM orders
 GROUP BY ROLLUP (c_id, orderdate);
```

The results of the query are as follows:

```
      C_ID ORDERDATE     ORDERS
---------- --------- ----------
         1 18-JUN-06          1
         1 23-JUN-06          1
         1                    2
         2 18-JUN-06          1
         2 21-JUN-06          1
         2                    2
         3 18-JUN-06          1
         3                    1
         4 19-JUN-06          1
         4 22-JUN-06          2
         4                    3
         5 19-JUN-06          1
         5                    1
         6 19-JUN-06          1
         6                    1
         7 19-JUN-06          1
         7 22-JUN-06          1
         7                    2
         8 20-JUN-06          1
         8                    1
         9 21-JUN-06          1
         9                    1
                            14
```

23 rows selected.

By using the ROLLUP operator of the GROUP BY clause, the result set of the final query combines all of the information that the preceding three queries provide. The highlighted rows point out that Oracle also calculates a count of each customer's orders, as well as a cumulative count of all orders. Because the query specifies the ROLLUP operator along with two grouping columns ($n=2$), the result set includes rows that aggregate data at three (2+1) levels. This type of query is common when an application needs to calculate subtotals (for example, to support an invoicing report in an order-entry application).

EXERCISE 3.15: Ordering Records in a Query's Result Set

As explained earlier in this chapter, relational databases do not explicitly maintain or guarantee the order of rows in a table. A query can sort the rows in its result set in ascending or descending order by including an *ORDER BY clause.* You can sort rows by any number of columns and expressions that are in the query's SELECT clause, or by any column in the target table even if it is not included in the SELECT clause. In the ORDER BY clause, specify a comma-separated list of the columns and expressions to sort on, either by name, by their position in the SELECT clause, or by their column alias in the SELECT list, and indicate whether you want ascending (ASC) or descending (DESC) order for each item. The default sort order for all columns and expressions in an ORDER BY clause is ascending order.

Enter the following query, which displays each customer record's ID, LASTNAME, and ZIPCODE, sorted in ascending order by the record's ZIPCODE:

```
SELECT id, lastname, zipcode
   FROM customers
 ORDER BY zipcode ASC;
```

The result set is as follows:

```
      ID LASTNAME                          ZIPCODE
--------- ----------------------------- -------
       3 Sams                              06103
       7 Wiersbicki                        11220
       5 Foss                              19144
       1 Joy                               21209
      10 Haagensen                         44124
       8 Ayers                             66604
       4 Elias                             75252
       6 Schaub                            85023
       2 Musial                            89501
       9 Clay                              95821

10 rows selected.
```

NOTE
By default, when you order a query's result set by an expression that returns nulls, Oracle places the rows with nulls last in the result set when you order in ascending order; by default, when you order in descending order, Oracle places the rows with nulls first in the result set. You can use the NULLS FIRST or NULLS LAST options of the ORDER BY clause to alter this behavior to your liking.

Joining Data in Related Tables

The previous examples in this chapter are all queries that target data from only one table. A query can also *join* information from multiple related tables. A query that targets an Oracle database can join information from related tables by using two different types of command syntax: older and in some cases Oracle-proprietary syntax, or newer syntax based on the latest versions of the ANSI/ISO SQL standard. This book introduces you to both types of join syntax because you will likely see both types of joins as you read about and use Oracle XE in various contexts.

The following simplified syntax listing demonstrates the older join syntax:

```
SELECT ...
   FROM table, table [, ...]
  WHERE join_condition
   [AND join_condition]
   [ ... other conditions ...]
[ORDER BY ...]
[GROUP BY ...];
```

When you want to join information from *n* number of tables using older join syntax, include a comma-separated list of the tables to join in the query's FROM clause. The query's WHERE clause should have *n*–1 *join conditions* that explain how to relate the data in the tables (see the examples of join conditions that follow). The join query's SELECT clause can contain columns and expressions that refer to some or all of the columns in the target tables; however, when two columns in different tables have identical names, you must qualify references to these columns throughout the query with a table name to avoid ambiguity.

The following simplified syntax listing demonstrates the newer join syntax:

```
SELECT ...
   FROM table JOIN table [JOIN table] ...
[WHERE condition]
[ORDER BY ...]
[GROUP BY ...];
```

Unlike with the older join syntax, the newer join syntax does not place join conditions in the WHERE clause; instead, a query that joins tables includes join specifications in the FROM clause that explicitly declare how to join related tables. The WHERE clause is optional, and necessary only when you want to restrict which rows appear in the query's result set.

The following two exercises contain examples of these syntax rules and explain two specific types of join queries using both syntax forms: inner joins and outer joins.

EXERCISE 3.16: Building an Inner Join of Two Tables

An *inner join* combines the rows of two related tables based on a common column (or combination of common columns). The result set of an inner join does not include rows in either table that do not have a match in the other table.

To specify an inner-join operation using older syntax, use a WHERE clause condition that relates the common columns in each table as operands on either side of the equality operator. For example, enter the following query, which performs an inner join of the CUSTOMERS and ORDERS tables:

```
SELECT c.id AS customer_id,
       c.lastname AS lastname,
       o.id AS order_id
  FROM customers c, orders o
 WHERE c.id = o.c_id
 ORDER BY c.id;
```

The result set is as follows:

```
CUSTOMER_ID LASTNAME                            ORDER_ID
----------- ----------------------------------- ----------
          1 Joy                                          1
          1 Joy                                         14
          2 Musial                                       2
          2 Musial                                      10
          3 Sams                                         3
          4 Elias                                        4
          4 Elias                                       11
          4 Elias                                       13
          5 Foss                                         5
          6 Schaub                                       6
          7 Wiersbicki                                   7
          7 Wiersbicki                                  12
          8 Ayers                                        8
          9 Clay                                         9

14 rows selected.
```

This example of an inner join retrieves a cross-product of all rows in the CUSTOMERS table that have placed orders. Notice that the result set of this query does not include any row for the customer with an ID of 10 because that customer has not placed any orders.

The previous example also shows the following:

■ You can prefix a column name in the SELECT list and other parts of a query by using a *qualifier*. In the context of a column, a qualifier explicitly identifies the table (and optionally, the "table owner") that contains the column. The qualification of a column is optional when there is no ambiguity as to the source of the column; however, the qualification of a column name with its table is mandatory when two tables in a join have columns with the same name.

■ You can declare a *table alias* for a table in the FROM clause. Once you declare an alias for a table name, all corresponding qualified column specifications that you use in other parts of the command must use the table alias rather than the table name.

■ A join that uses the equality operator in its join condition is known as an *equijoin*.

Now try the same inner join with the newer join syntax:

```
SELECT c.id AS customer_id,
       c.lastname AS lastname,
       o.id AS order_id
  FROM customers c
 INNER JOIN orders o
    ON c.id = o.c_id
 ORDER BY c.id;
```

Notice that unlike the older SQL join syntax, the newer join syntax does not place a join condition in the WHERE clause; instead, the query specifies one of the tables in the FROM clause followed by a join specification that explicitly states what table to join to the preceding table. To specify an inner join, a join specification can begin with the INNER keyword; however, an inner join is the default type of join, so the INNER keyword is not required. In this example, the join specification also indicates a join condition in an ON clause with the equality operator to join the rows of two related tables based on a common key column; when the join column has the same name in both tables, you can simplify the statement and omit the ON clause altogether.

EXERCISE 3.17: Building an Outer Join of Two Tables

Similar to an inner join, an *outer join* also combines the rows of two related tables based on a common column (or combination of common columns). However, the result set of an outer join includes rows from one of the tables even when there are not any matching rows in the other table.

When using older join syntax, the WHERE clause condition of an outer join is similar to that of an inner join, with one exception—you must place the outer-join operator, a plus sign delimited by parentheses, (+), after one or more of the columns in the join condition. Specifically, the outer-join operator follows the column in the join condition that corresponds to the table for which you expect no matching rows. For example, enter the following query, which performs an outer join of the CUSTOMERS and ORDERS tables, and includes all customers even when a customer does not have any matching orders:

```
SELECT c.id AS customer_id,
       c.lastname AS lastname,
       o.id AS order_id
  FROM customers c, orders o
 WHERE c.id = o.c_id(+)
 ORDER BY c.id;
```

The result set is as follows:

```
CUSTOMER_ID LASTNAME                        ORDER_ID
----------- ------------------------------ ----------
          1 Joy                                     1
          1 Joy                                    14
          2 Musial                                  2
          2 Musial                                 10
          3 Sams                                    3
          4 Elias                                   4
          4 Elias                                  11
          4 Elias                                  13
          5 Foss                                    5
          6 Schaub                                  6
          7 Wiersbicki                             12
          7 Wiersbicki                              7
          8 Ayers                                   8
          9 Clay                                    9
         10 Haagensen
```

15 rows selected.

Notice that the result set includes a row for the record in the CUSTOMERS table with an ID of 10 (in bold), even though the customer has not placed any orders. Oracle returns nulls for all columns that have no match in an outer join's result set.

Now let's try an equivalent outer join using the newer join syntax:

```
SELECT c.id AS customer_id,
       c.lastname AS lastname,
       o.id AS order_id
  FROM customers c
```

```
LEFT OUTER JOIN orders o
   ON c.id = o.c_id
ORDER BY c.id;
```

Notice that the newer syntax uses keywords that explicitly indicate that the outer join is a left, right, or full outer join. A left outer join returns all rows from the row source on the left of the join specification, a right outer join returns all rows from the row source on the right of the join specification, and a full outer join returns all rows from both row sources. In the preceding example, we use a left outer join because we want to list all customers whether or not they have placed any orders.

Inserting, Updating, and Deleting Rows in Tables

All of the previous examples in this chapter show you how to retrieve data from tables in an Oracle database using various queries (SELECT commands). Now let's take a look at how to input, modify, and delete table data using the SQL commands INSERT, UPDATE, and DELETE.

EXERCISE 3.18: Inserting New Rows into a Table

To insert a new row into a table, you use the SQL command *INSERT*. For example, enter the following statement, which inserts a new part into the PARTS table:

```
INSERT INTO parts
   (id, description, unitprice, onhand, reorder)
   VALUES (6, 'Mouse', 49, 1200, 500);
```

This example statement demonstrates how to use the most common clauses and parameters of the INSERT command:

- Use the INTO parameter to specify the target table.

- To insert a single row into the target table, use a VALUES clause that contains a comma-separated list of values for various columns in the table.

- Optionally (but recommended), use a comma-separated list of column names to specify the columns that correspond to the values in the VALUES clause. The number of columns in the list of column names must match the number of values in the VALUES clause. When you omit a column list altogether, the VALUES clause must specify values for every column in the target table in the order in which the columns appear in the table. For readability and limited validation of your VALUES clause, always include a list of columns.

EXERCISE 3.19: Updating Rows in a Table

To update column values in one or more rows of a table, use the SQL command *UPDATE*. For example, enter the following UPDATE statement, which updates the UNITPRICE value for a part in the PARTS table:

```
UPDATE parts
   SET unitprice = 55, onhand = 1100
 WHERE id = 6;
```

Notice that the SET clause of the example UPDATE statement updates the UNITPRICE and ONHAND values of a specific record in the PARTS table—the record identified by the condition of the WHERE clause. Be careful, because when an UPDATE statement omits selection criteria (in other words, a WHERE clause), the UPDATE statement updates all rows in the target table.

EXERCISE 3.20: Deleting Rows from a Table

To delete one or more rows from a table, you use the SQL command *DELETE*. For example, enter the following DELETE statement, which deletes a specific record from the PARTS table:

```
DELETE FROM parts
  WHERE id = 6 AND description = 'Mouse';
```

As this example demonstrates, a DELETE statement should always include a WHERE clause with a condition that targets specific rows in a table, unless you want to delete *all* rows in the table.

Committing and Rolling Back Transactions

As you learned earlier in this chapter, a database *transaction* is a unit of work performed by one or more closely related SQL statements. The following hands-on exercise teaches you how to commit or roll back a transaction.

EXERCISE 3.21: Committing and Rolling Back Transactions

Enter the following series of related SQL statements, which together form a transaction that inserts a new order into the ORDERS table and two associated line items into the ITEMS table:

```
INSERT INTO orders
   (id, c_id, orderdate, shipdate, paiddate, status)
   VALUES (15, 3, TO_DATE('23-JUN-2006','DD-MON-YYYY'),
           TO_DATE('23-JUN-2006','DD-MON-YYYY'), NULL, 'F');
```

```
INSERT INTO items
 (o_id, id, p_id, quantity)
  VALUES (15, 1, 4, 1);
INSERT INTO items
 (o_id, id, p_id, quantity)
  VALUES (15, 2, 5, 1);
```

To permanently *commit* the work of the transaction to the database, use the SQL command *COMMIT* (with or without the optional keyword *WORK*). Enter the following statement now:

```
COMMIT WORK;
```

After you commit the transaction, Oracle automatically starts the next transaction. At this point, the work of the previous transaction is permanent and cannot be undone.

Now consider the situation where you are in the middle of a new transaction, but make a mistake or cannot complete the transaction for some reason. In this case, you can undo, or *roll back*, the work of a transaction's SQL statements; just use the SQL command *ROLLBACK* (with or without the optional keyword WORK):

```
ROLLBACK WORK;
```

A fundamental principle that you must clearly understand is that a transaction is a unit of work. That is, although a transaction might be made up of several SQL statements, they all commit or roll back as a single operation. For example, when an application commits a transaction, Oracle permanently records the changes made by *all* SQL statements in the transaction. If for some reason Oracle cannot commit the work of any statement in a transaction, Oracle automatically rolls back the effects of *all* statements in the transaction.

When you start a database application and establish a connection to a database, Oracle implicitly starts a new transaction for your session. After you commit or roll back a transaction, Oracle again implicitly starts a new transaction for your session.

Transaction Design

The design of application transactions is very important, because a transaction's design can directly affect database integrity and the performance of applications. The following sections discuss several issues to consider when designing a database application's transactions.

Units of Work

Remember that a transaction is meant to encompass many closely related SQL statements that, together, perform a single unit of work as defined by the application's business rules. More specifically, a transaction should not encompass multiple units of work, nor should it encompass a partial unit of work.

For example, consider an application that should independently allow the input of customers, parts, and orders with their corresponding line items. In this context, the following example demonstrates bad transaction design:

```
INSERT INTO customers ... ;
INSERT INTO parts ... ;
INSERT INTO orders ... ;
INSERT INTO items ... ;
INSERT INTO items ... ;
COMMIT WORK ;
```

In this example, the bad transaction design encompasses three separate units of work:

1. The transaction inserts a new customer record.

2. The transaction inserts a new part record.

3. The transaction inserts the records for a new sales order.

In the context of your application, each unit of work in the transaction has nothing to do with the others. When a transaction encompasses more than a single unit of work, Oracle must maintain internal system information on behalf of the transaction for a longer period of time. Quite possibly, this can detract from system performance, especially when many transactions burden Oracle with the same type of bad transaction design.

To contrast the previous type of bad transaction design, consider another example:

```
INSERT INTO orders ... ;
COMMIT WORK ;
INSERT INTO items ... ;
COMMIT WORK ;
INSERT INTO items ... ;
COMMIT WORK ;
```

This example does the opposite of the previous example—there are three transactions to input the records for a single sales order. The overhead of many unnecessary small transaction commits can also detract from server performance. More importantly, partial transactions can risk the integrity of a database's data. For example, consider what happens if you use the preceding transaction design to insert a new sales order, but before you can commit the insert of all line items for the new sales order, your session abnormally disconnects from the database server. At this point, the database contains a partial sales order, at least until you reconnect to finish the sales order. In the interim, a shipping transaction might look at the partial sales order and not realize that it is working with incomplete information.

As a result, the shipping department might unknowingly send a partial product shipment to a customer and mark it as complete. The irate customer calls days later demanding to know why she didn't receive the other ordered products. When the shipping clerk looks at the order in the database, he sees the missing line items, but he cannot explain why the order did not contain the products and was marked as complete.

Read-Write Transactions

By default, when Oracle starts a new transaction for your session, the transaction is read-write. A *read-write transaction* can include any type of SQL statement, including DML statements that query, insert, update, and delete table rows. To explicitly declare a transaction as a read-write transaction, you can begin the transaction with the SQL command SET TRANSACTION and the READ WRITE option:

```
SET TRANSACTION READ WRITE;
```

Read-Only Transactions

A *read-only transaction* includes queries only. In other words, a read-only transaction does not modify the database in any way. Certain reporting applications might want to explicitly declare a transaction as read-only with the READ ONLY option of the SET TRANSACTION command:

```
SET TRANSACTION READ ONLY;
```

When you declare an explicit read-only transaction, Oracle guarantees *transaction-level read consistency* for the transaction. This means that the result sets of all queries in the transaction reflect the database's data as it existed at the beginning of the transaction, even though other transactions modify and commit work to the database. Reporting applications commonly use an explicit read-only transaction to encompass several queries and produce a report with consistent data.

Building SQL with Oracle Application Express

So far, this book has taught you that you can use the SQL*Plus command-line interface to execute any type of SQL statement, as well as special SQL*Plus commands like DESCRIBE. Oracle XE also provides several alternative, albeit less-functional, interfaces that you can use to code SQL. For example, Oracle Application Express provides a SQL command editor that is somewhat easier to use than SQL*Plus; the next chapter demonstrates how to use this tool. The following sections teach you how to get started with another of Oracle Application Express's SQL tools, a graphical query interface called the Query Builder.

Introducing Oracle Application Express's Query Builder

Oracle Application Express's Query Builder, available from the Database Home Page, is a user-friendly alternative to command-line tools like SQL*Plus. Using an intuitive GUI presented via a standard web browser, Query Builder makes it relatively easy for novice users to build simple SQL queries without any knowledge of SQL's SELECT command. The Query Builder is a great way to begin learning SQL if you have no experience with relational databases.

Exercise 3.22: Using Query Builder

This exercise teaches you the basics of Query Builder by duplicating many of the results produced by queries in earlier exercises of this chapter. First, launch the Database Home Page as explained in Exercise 2.13. Establish a connection using this chapter's practice account, HANDSONXE03, with the password PASSWORD.

Once you connect, click SQL, and then click Query Builder to start Query Builder. Figure 3-1 identifies the key parts of the Query Builder interface.

Notice the following GUI features of Query Builder:

- **Object Selection pane**   Located on the left, this pane displays the objects that you can use to build queries.

- **Design pane**   Located to the right of the Object Selection pane, this pane displays objects that you select from the Object Selection pane.

- **Output pane**   Located below the Design pane, this pane has several tabs that let you create conditions, view the SQL statement that corresponds to the Design pane, view query results, and manage saved SQL statements as you work with Query Builder.

- **Home, Logout, and Help links**   Located in the top-right corner of the page, these links let you quickly navigate to the Home, Logout, and Help pages of Oracle Application Express.

- **Breadcrumbs menu links**   Located just above the Object Selection pane, these links let you quickly navigate to other pages of Oracle Application Express.

- **Save and Run buttons**   Located in the upper-right corner of the Design pane, these buttons let you save and execute queries that you build with Query Builder.

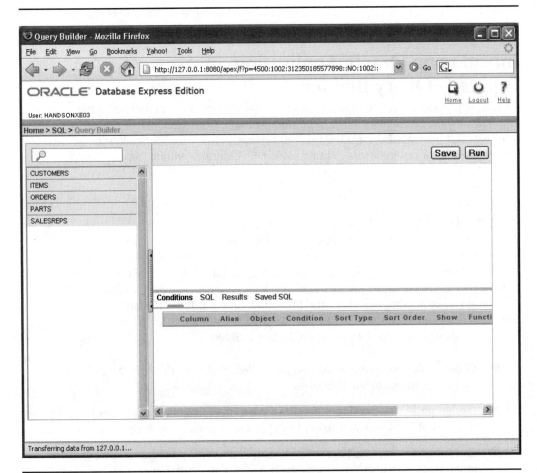

FIGURE 3-1. *Query Builder's graphical user interface*

Now that you know your way around, the remainder of this exercise explains how to use Query Builder to duplicate the queries that you coded with the SELECT command using SQL*Plus in Exercises 3.1, 3.2, 3.4, 3.7, 3.10–3.13, and 3.15–3.17.

To duplicate the query in Exercise 3.1 that retrieves all columns and rows from the ORDERS table, complete the following steps:

1. Click ORDERS in the Object Selection pane. The ORDERS table then appears in the Design pane.

2. To display all columns of the ORDERS table in the result set of the query, select each column's check box in the Design pane. You can check each column's check box one by one, or click Table Actions in the upper-left

corner of the ORDERS table, click Check All, and then click Close. Notice that as you select table columns in the Design pane, more detailed information about each column appears below in the Conditions tab of the Output pane.

3. Click Run to run the query.

The results of the query shown in the Results tab of the Output pane should match the results of Exercise 3.1, with the addition of a 15th row added by the transaction in Exercise 3.21. Figure 3-2 illustrates the completed steps and part of the query's output.

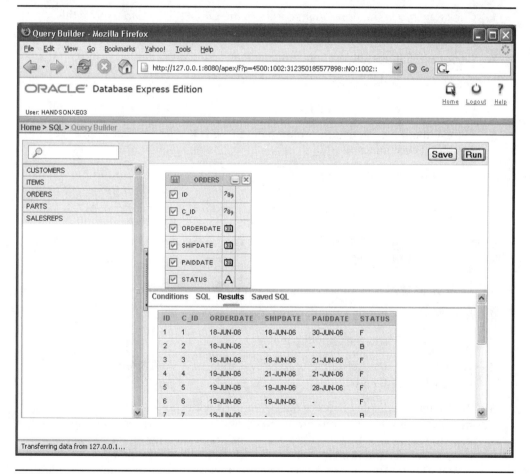

FIGURE 3-2. *Query Builder makes it easy to query a table's rows and columns.*

To duplicate the query in Exercise 3.2 that retrieves specific columns from all rows in the ORDERS table, complete the following steps:

1. Select only the check boxes next to the ID and ORDERDATE columns of the ORDERS table in the Design pane.

2. Click Run.

To duplicate the query in Exercise 3.4 that retrieves the ID and ONHAND columns of all rows in the PARTS table, using a column alias for the ONHAND column, complete the following steps:

1. Click Remove in the upper-right corner of the ORDERS table to remove this table from the Design pane.

2. Click PARTS in the Object Selection pane to add it to the Design pane.

3. Select the ID and ONHAND columns of the PARTS table.

4. Click the Conditions tab in the Output pane.

5. In the Output pane, enter the column alias **IN STOCK** as the alias for the ONHAND column.

6. Click Run to execute the query.

Figure 3-3 illustrates the completed query as described by the preceding steps.
To duplicate the first query in Exercise 3.7 that retrieves all COMPANYNAMEs in uppercase letters and all LASTNAMEs in lowercase letters from the CUSTOMERS table, complete the following steps:

1. Remove the PARTS table from the Design pane.

2. Add the CUSTOMERS table to the Design pane.

3. Click Conditions in the Output pane.

4. In the Design pane, select the LASTNAME and COMPANYNAME columns in the CUSTOMERS table.

5. By default, the display order of query columns corresponds to the order in which you select columns from the Design pane. If necessary, use the promote or demote buttons to the left of the column names in the Output pane to arrange the display order of the selected columns so that the COMPANYNAME column displays before the LASTNAME column.

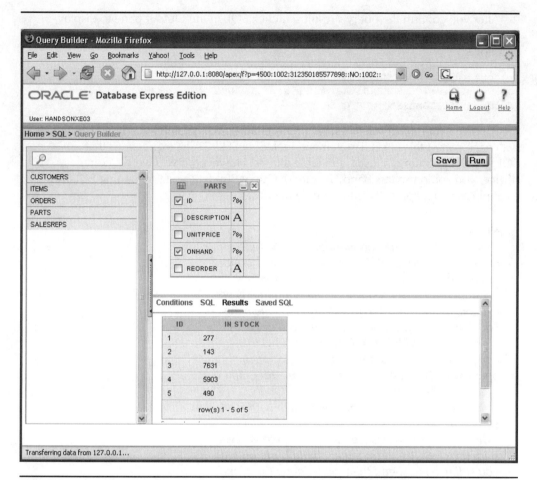

FIGURE 3-3. *The Conditions tab of the Output pane lets you reposition columns, declare column aliases, specify query conditions, and more.*

6. In the Output pane, select the UPPER function for the COMPANYNAME column and the LOWER function for the LASTNAME column. To see the Function lists for each column, you may have to use the vertical scroll bar at the bottom of the Output pane.

7. Click Run to execute the query.

After you confirm the query's result set, click SQL in the Output pane to display the SELECT statement that corresponds to the current query design. It should appear as follows:

```
select    upper(CUSTOMERS.COMPANYNAME) as "COMPANYNAME",
          lower(CUSTOMERS.LASTNAME) as "LASTNAME"
  from    "CUSTOMERS" "CUSTOMERS"
```

Based on your experiences earlier in this chapter, you should already be familiar with each part of this SELECT statement, including SELECT list expressions that use SQL functions, column aliases, and table aliases. However, if you were a complete novice, you could use this handy feature of Query Builder to begin learning SQL by example as you graphically build simple queries.

NOTE

At this point, you may be wondering why this exercise does not explain how to use Query Builder to build queries equivalent to those in Exercises 3.5 and 3.6. The reason is that Query Builder is not capable of building all types of SELECT statements. For example, you cannot use Query Builder to create queries with SELECT list expressions that concatenate two columns or perform arithmetic operations. The SQL functions available for column specifications are limited as well. And Query Builder is not capable of modifying data with DML statements such as INSERT, UPDATE, and DELETE. While Query Builder is a great tool to help you get started with SQL and to quickly build basic queries, you still need to spend the time learning the syntax of SQL commands. That's why I decided to teach you SQL using SQL*Plus rather than Query Builder.

Now skip ahead and duplicate the second query in Exercise 3.10 that lists the ID and LASTNAME of all customer records that do not have a FAX number:

1. The CUSTOMERS table should already be in the Design pane.

2. Click Conditions in the Output pane.

3. In the Design pane, select the ID and FAX columns and uncheck (remove) the COMPANYNAME column.

4. In the Conditions tab of the Design pane, modify the display order so that the ID column is before the LASTNAME column. For the LASTNAME column, remove the Function LOWER (select nothing). For the FAX column, disable the Show option and enter the following condition in the Condition field: **IS NULL**.

5. Click Run to execute the query.

The results of the query should be identical to the corresponding results in Exercise 3.10. If you have not already surmised, the preceding steps show you how to add a WHERE clause condition to a query—click the SQL tab of the Output pane to view the query. You should also be able to use Query Builder to build queries equivalent to the first, third, and fourth queries in Exercise 3.10. The Conditions field for a column in the Output pane accepts all syntactically correct WHERE clause conditions (starting with a relational operator), including conditions that use subqueries. Feel free to try these queries on your own.

Query Builder also lets you build queries with composite WHERE clause conditions that use the AND operator, but not the OR operator. For example, to duplicate the query in Exercise 3.12, complete the following steps:

1. Remove the CUSTOMERS table from the Design pane.

2. Add the ORDERS table to the Design pane.

3. Click Conditions in the Output pane.

4. In the Design pane, select the ID, ORDERDATE, and STATUS columns in the ORDERS table.

   ■ For the ORDERDATE column, enter the following condition: **>=TO_DATE('21-JUN-2006','DD-MON-YYYY')**

   ■ For the STATUS column, disable the Show option and enter the following condition: = **'B'**

5. Click Run to execute the query.

Query Builder also supports queries that use simple groupings. For example, to duplicate the first query in Exercise 3.13, complete the following steps:

1. The ORDERS table should already be in the Design pane. Select the C_ID and ID columns and then remove all others.

2. Click Conditions in the Output pane. Arrange the column display order so that the C_ID column is before the ID column. For the C_ID column, set Alias to **CUSTOMER** and select the Group By option. For the ID column, set Alias to **ORDERS_PLACED** and set Function to COUNT.

3. Click Run to execute the query.

You will not be able to duplicate the second query in Exercise 3.13 or the queries in Exercise 3.14 because Query Builder does not support extended GROUP BY clause features such as a HAVING clause condition and the ROLLUP operator.

To duplicate the query in Exercise 3.15 that sorts records in a query's result set, complete the following steps:

1. Remove the ORDERS table from the Design pane.

2. Add the CUSTOMERS table to the Design pane.

3. Click Conditions in the Output pane.

4. In the Design pane, select the ID, LASTNAME, and ZIPCODE columns.

5. Switch your focus to the Conditions tab of the Output pane. For the ZIPCODE column, specify Sort Order as 1 and set Sort Type to Asc.

6. Click Run to execute the query.

Query Builder also supports both inner and outer joins. To duplicate the inner join of the CUSTOMERS and ORDERS tables in Exercise 3.16, complete the following steps:

1. Add the ORDERS table to the Design pane. The CUSTOMERS table should already be present.

2. Click Conditions in the Output pane.

3. In the Design pane, select only the ID and LASTNAME columns of the CUSTOMERS table and the ID column of the ORDERS table, arranging their display order in this sequence. Do not select any other columns. To specify the join condition for the tables, drag the ID column of the CUSTOMERS table and drop it on the C_ID column of the ORDERS table; afterwards, a join condition bar should appear between the two tables. For the ID column of the CUSTOMERS table, specify **CUSTOMER_ID** for Alias and specify 1 for Sort Order. For the ID column of the ORDERS table, specify **ORDER_ID** for Alias.

4. Click Run to execute the query.

NOTE
The SQL tab of the Output pane reveals that Query Builder uses the older-style syntax when creating join queries.

To duplicate the outer join of the CUSTOMERS and ORDERS tables in Exercise 3.17, all that you have to do is modify the type of join condition for the current query design:

1. In the Design pane, click the Join condition bar. From the menu that appears, select Set Right Outer Join; afterwards, you should notice a + to the right of the C_ID column in the ORDERS table.

2. Click Run to execute the query.

3. Browse the results in the Results tab of the Output pane. Notice that the result set contains a row for customer 10 who has not placed any orders. If necessary, click the Next button at the bottom of the query results to advance to the final record in the result set. Figure 3-4 demonstrates this query in Query Builder.

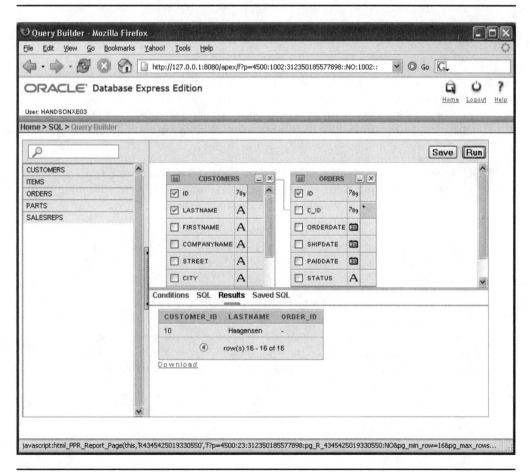

FIGURE 3-4. *Query Builder can build both inner and outer joins using a graphical approach.*

Chapter Summary

This chapter has provided you with a broad overview of SQL and a tutorial for using the most common SQL commands. In this chapter, you learned the following:

■ To accomplish work with Oracle, applications must use SQL commands.

■ Use the SQL command SELECT to build queries that retrieve data from database tables. A query's FROM clause specifies the table(s) to target. A query's SELECT clause determines what columns to include in the query's result set—the SELECT clause can contain simple column names as well as expressions that use operators, literals, or SQL functions to derive data. A query's optional WHERE clause condition determines which rows to include in the query's result set. You can use the optional ORDER BY clause to sort the records in a query's result set. Use the optional GROUP BY clause to summarize or aggregate data in a query's result set.

■ Use the SQL command INSERT to insert a row into a table. An INSERT statement's INTO parameter specifies the target table, and the VALUES clause contains a list of values for the various columns in the table. You can also include an optional list of column names before the VALUES clause to specify target columns in the table for the values in the VALUES clause.

■ Use the SQL command UPDATE to update rows in a table. Use the SET clause to identify the column values to change, and a WHERE clause to target specific rows in the table that you want to update.

■ Use the SQL command DELETE to delete rows from a table. A DELETE statement should always include a WHERE clause with a condition that targets specific rows in a table, unless you want to delete all rows in the table.

■ Use the SQL commands COMMIT and ROLLBACK to control the outcome of your session's current transaction. A COMMIT statement permanently commits the changes made by all SQL statements in the transaction. A ROLLBACK statement undoes the effects of all SQL statements in the transaction. Effectively, Oracle automatically starts a new transaction after you commit or roll back your current transaction.

■ Query Builder, part of Oracle Application Express, is an intuitive GUI presented via a standard web browser that makes it relatively easy for novice users to build simple SQL queries without any knowledge of SQL's SELECT command.

CHAPTER
4

Code Database Access Programs with PL/SQL

QL is nothing more than a data access language that allows applications to put data into and get data out of an Oracle database. In other words, SQL by itself is not a full-featured programming language that you can use to develop powerful database applications. To build a database application, you must use a procedural language that encompasses SQL to interact with an Oracle database. This chapter explains Oracle's very own procedural language, PL/SQL, which you can use to program an Oracle database server and associated applications. The following topics will be covered:

- PL/SQL coding basics

- Anonymous PL/SQL blocks

- Stored procedures, functions, and packages

- Database triggers

NOTE
By no means is this chapter a complete guide to PL/SQL. However, this chapter does provide an intermediate-level tutorial of PL/SQL's capabilities so that you can get started programming with Oracle XE.

Chapter Prerequisites

To practice the hands-on exercises in this chapter, you need to start SQL*Plus as instructed in Exercise 2.11 and then run the following command script:

```
location\handsonxe\sql\chap04.sql
```

where *location* is the file directory where you expanded the support archive that accompanies this book. For example, after starting SQL*Plus, you can run this chapter's SQL command script using the SQL*Plus command @, as in the following example (assuming that your chap04.sql file is in C:\temp\handsonxe\sql):

```
SQL> @C:\temp\handsonxe\sql\chap04.sql;
```

Once you reply to all of the prompts and the script completes successfully, you can exit SQL*Plus by using an EXIT command.

What Is PL/SQL?

PL/SQL is a procedural programming language that's built into Oracle XE. With PL/SQL, you can build programs to process information by combining PL/SQL procedural statements that control program flow with SQL statements that access an

Oracle database. For example, the following is a very simple PL/SQL program that updates a part's UNITPRICE, given the part's ID number. (This listing is not an exercise—it is just an example to study.)

```
CREATE OR REPLACE PROCEDURE updatePartPrice (
  partId IN INTEGER,
  newPrice IN NUMBER )
IS
  invalidPart EXCEPTION;
BEGIN
-- HERE'S AN UPDATE STATEMENT TO UPDATE A DATABASE RECORD
  UPDATE parts
    SET unitprice = newPrice
    WHERE id = partId;
-- HERE'S AN ERROR-CHECKING STATEMENT
  IF SQL%NOTFOUND THEN
    RAISE invalidPart;
  END IF;
EXCEPTION
-- HERE'S AN ERROR-HANDLING ROUTINE
  WHEN invalidPart THEN
    DBMS_OUTPUT.PUT_LINE('Invalid Part ID');
END updatePartPrice;
```

This example program is a procedure that is stored as a *program unit* in a database. Using PL/SQL, you can build many types of database access program units. All of the sections in this chapter include examples of PL/SQL programs. But before learning about full-blown PL/SQL programs, you need to understand the basic programmatic constructs and commands that the PL/SQL language offers.

NOTE
PL/SQL is similar to the programming language Ada, with many of its procedural constructs, but is optimized to fully interact with Oracle. PL/SQL has statements that allow you to declare variables and constants, control program flow, assign and manipulate data, and more.

PL/SQL Blocks

A PL/SQL program is structured using distinct *blocks* that group related declarations and statements. Each block in a PL/SQL program has a specific task and solves a particular problem. Consequently, you can organize a PL/SQL program so that it is easy to understand.

A PL/SQL block can include three sections, as the following pseudo-code illustrates—program declarations, the main program body, and exception handlers:

```
DECLARE
-- program declarations are optional
BEGIN
-- program body is required
EXCEPTION
-- exception handlers are optional
END;
```

Most of the examples in this chapter ask you to use the SQL Command editor that is part of Oracle Application Express to interactively type and execute anonymous PL/SQL blocks while learning the fundamentals of PL/SQL. An *anonymous PL/SQL block* has no name and is not stored permanently in an Oracle database. An application, such as SQL*Plus, simply sends the PL/SQL block to the database server for processing at run time.

Program Declarations

The *declaration section* of a PL/SQL block is where the block declares all variables, constants, exceptions, and so on, which are then accessible to all other parts of the same block. The declaration section of a PL/SQL block starts with the DECLARE keyword and implicitly ends with the BEGIN keyword of the program body. If the program does not need to make any declarations, the declaration section is not necessary.

The Program Body

The main program *body* of a PL/SQL block contains the executable statements for the block. In other words, the body is where the PL/SQL block defines its functionality. The body of a PL/SQL block begins with the BEGIN keyword and ends with the EXCEPTION keyword that starts the exception-handling section of the block; if the block does not include any exception handlers, the program body ends with the END keyword that ends the block altogether.

Exception Handlers

The optional *exception-handling section* of a PL/SQL block contains the *exception handlers* (error-handling routines) for the block. When a statement in the block's body *raises an exception* (detects an error), it transfers program control to a corresponding exception handler in the exception section for further processing. The exception-handling section of a PL/SQL block begins with the EXCEPTION keyword and ends with the END keyword. If a program does not need to define any exception handlers, the exception-handling section of the block is not necessary.

Program Comments

Although optional, all blocks of a PL/SQL program should include *comments* that document program declarations and functionality. Comments clarify the purpose of specific programs and code segments.

PL/SQL supports two different styles for comments, as the following code segment shows:

```
-- PRECEDE A SINGLE-LINE COMMENT WITH A DOUBLE-HYPHEN.
/* DELIMIT A MULTI-LINE COMMENT WITH A SLASH-ASTERISK
AS A PREFIX AND AN ASTERISK-SLASH AS A SUFFIX. A MULTI-LINE
COMMENT CAN CONTAIN ANY NUMBER OF LINES. */
```

The examples in the remainder of this chapter often use comments to help explain the functionality of code listings.

The Fundamentals of PL/SQL Coding

All procedural languages, such as PL/SQL, have fundamental language elements and functionality that you need to learn about before you can build programs using the language. The following sections introduce the basic elements of PL/SQL, including the following:

- How to declare program variables and assign values to them

- How to control program flow with loops and conditional logic

- How to embed SQL statements and interact with Oracle databases

- How to declare and use subprograms (procedures and functions) within PL/SQL blocks

- How to declare user-defined types, such as records and nested tables

- How to declare and use cursors to process queries that return multiple rows

- How to use exception handlers to handle error conditions

Working with Program Variables

All procedural programs typically declare one or more program variables and use them to hold temporary information for program processing. The next two exercises teach you how to declare program variables (and constants), initialize them, and assign values to them in the body of a PL/SQL program.

EXERCISE 4.1: Declaring Variables and Constants with Basic Datatypes

The declaration section of a PL/SQL program can include *variable* and *constant* declarations. The general syntax that you use to declare a scalar variable or constant is as follows:

 `variable [CONSTANT] datatype [[NOT NULL] {DEFAULT|:=} expression];`

NOTE
To declare a constant rather than a variable, include the CONSTANT keyword in the declaration. You must initialize a constant, after which the constant's value cannot change.

When you declare a variable, you can choose to initialize it immediately or wait until later in the body of the program; however, if you include the not null constraint, you must initialize the variable as part of its declaration. By default, PL/SQL initializes a variable as null unless the program explicitly initializes the variable.

A program can declare a variable or constant using any Oracle or ANSI/ISO datatype, user-defined type, or subtype listed in Table 4-1.

NOTE
A subtype is a constrained version of its base type.

For the first hands-on exercise in this chapter, start Oracle Application Express as explained in Chapter 2. Establish a connection using this chapter's practice account, HANDSONXE04, with the password PASSWORD. Click SQL, and then SQL Commands to start Oracle Application Express's graphical version of an ad hoc SQL command-line tool called the *SQL Commands* page, as shown in Figure 4-1.

The Input pane at the top of the SQL Commands page is where you enter SQL and anonymous PL/SQL blocks. Among other things, the Output pane below the Input pane shows the results of your work.

Notice above the Input pane that you can enable or disable transactional support for your work with the *Autocommit* option; if enabled (checked, the default), every SQL or PL/SQL block that you execute runs in its own transaction that is automatically committed; if disabled, you will be able to use the SQL commands COMMIT and ROLLBACK to control the outcome of transactions. For the purposes of the exercises in this chapter, *please disable Autocommit.*

Once you establish a connection to Oracle Application Express and open the SQL Commands page, enter into the Input pane the following anonymous PL/SQL block that declares and initializes several variables of different datatypes and then

Datatype	Subtype	Description
BINARY_INTEGER	NATURAL, NATURALN, POSITIVE, POSITIVEN, SIGNTYPE	Stores signed integers in the range −2,147,483,647 to 2,147,483,647. Uses library arithmetic. NATURAL and NATURALN store only nonnegative integers; the latter disallows nulls. POSITIVE and POSITIVEN store only positive integers; the latter disallows nulls. SIGNTYPE stores only −1, 0, and 1.
BINARY_FLOAT and BINARY_DOUBLE		Store single- and double-precision IEEE 754–format single-precision floating-point numbers. Useful for high-speed scientific computations.
NUMBER (*precision,scale*)	DEC, DECIMAL, DOUBLE PRECISION, FLOAT (*precision*), INTEGER, INT, NUMERIC, REAL, SMALLINT	Stores fixed or floating-point numbers in the range 1^{-130} to 10^{125}. Uses library arithmetic.
PLS_INTEGER		Stores signed integers in the range −2,147,483,647 to 2,147,483,647. Uses machine arithmetic for fast calculations.
CHAR (*size*)	CHARACTER (*size*)	Stores fixed-length character strings. Maximum size is 32,767 bytes; however, database maximum CHAR is 2000 bytes.
VARCHAR2 (*size*)	VARCHAR (*size*), STRING	Stores variable-length character strings. Maximum size is 32,767 bytes; however, database maximum CHAR is 4000 bytes.
DATE		Stores time-related information, including dates, hours, minutes, and seconds.

TABLE 4-1. *PL/SQL Scalar Datatypes and Related Subtypes*

Datatype	Subtype	Description
TIMESTAMP [(precision)] [WITH [LOCAL] TIME ZONE]		Stores dates, including a year, month, day, hour, minute, second, and fractional part of a second. Optionally, you can specify fractional precision for seconds; the default is six places to the right of the decimal place. You can also specify a WITH TIME ZONE option to store a time zone displacement with a timestamp. A time zone displacement is the difference in hours and minutes between local time and the Coordinated Universal Time (UTC) (formerly Greenwich Mean Time).
INTERVAL DAY (precision) TO SECOND (precision)		Stores a period of time as days, hours, minutes, and seconds, and the fractional part of a second. Optionally, you can specify a precision for both components of an interval; the defaults are two digits for the DAY component, and six digits for the fractional part of a second.
INTERVAL YEAR (precision) TO MONTH		Stores a period of time as years and months. Optionally, you can specify a precision for the YEAR component of an interval; the default is two digits.
BOOLEAN		Stores logical values (TRUE, FALSE, and NULL).
ROWID		Stores the physical row address of a row in a database table.
UROWID		Stores the physical, logical, or foreign (non-Oracle) address of a row in a database table.
CLOB		Stores large, single-byte character objects.
BLOB		Stores large binary objects.
BFILE		Stores file pointers to large objects (LOBs) managed by file systems external to the database.

TABLE 4-1. *PL/SQL Scalar Datatypes and Related Subtypes (continued)*

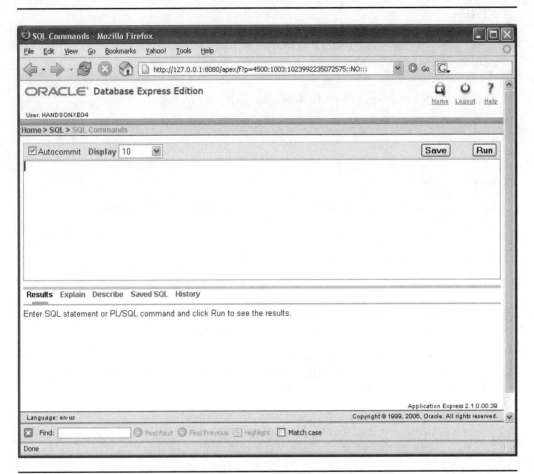

FIGURE 4-1. *Oracle Application Express's SQL Commands page is an editor that you can use to interactively build and execute SQL and PL/SQL, much like SQL*Plus.*

prints their current values to the Output pane. Click Run to execute the block once you have entered it correctly.

```
DECLARE
  l_outputString VARCHAR2(20) := 'Hello World';
  l_todaysDate DATE := SYSDATE;
  l_pi CONSTANT NUMBER := 3.14159265359;
BEGIN
  DBMS_OUTPUT.PUT_LINE(l_outputString);
  DBMS_OUTPUT.PUT_LINE(l_todaysDate);
  DBMS_OUTPUT.PUT_LINE(l_pi);
END;
/
```

NOTE
To end a PL/SQL program in the SQL Commands page, terminate the code with a line that includes only the backslash (/) character.

The output of the program should be similar to the following:

```
Hello World
20-MAR-06
3.14159265359

Statement processed.
```

There are a couple of subtle points to understand about this first example PL/SQL program:

- When a program declares a variable using a datatype that requires a constraint specification such as VARCHAR2, the declaration must specify the constraint; for example, VARCHAR2(20).

- To make your code more understandable, prefix all local variables (and other local constructs) with the letter *l* and an underscore, l_.

- The second variable declaration initializes l_todaysDate using the *SQL function SYSDATE,* which returns the current date and time set by the host operating system on which the database resides.

- The body of the example program uses the *DBMS_OUTPUT.PUT_LINE procedure* to direct output to the standard output. The DBMS_OUTPUT .PUT_LINE procedure is analogous in functionality to the println procedure in C and the System.out.println method of Java.

NOTE
If you try to execute this exercise's PL/SQL block with SQL*Plus, you will not see the output of a call to DBMS_OUTPUT.PUT_LINE unless you enable the SQL*Plus environment setting SERVEROUTPUT with a command such as SET SERVEROUTPUT ON.

EXERCISE 4.2: Assigning Values to Variables
Value assignment is one of the most common operations within any type of procedural program. The general syntax that you use to assign a value to a variable is as follows:

```
variable := expression
```

An *assignment statement* in a PL/SQL program assigns the value that results from an expression to a PL/SQL construct, such as a variable, using the *assignment operator* (:=). For example, execute the following PL/SQL block, which declares some variables, assigns values to them in the program body, and then uses the DBMS_OUTPUT .PUT_LINE procedure to output their current values to standard output:

```
DECLARE
  l_outputString VARCHAR2(20);
  l_todaysDate DATE;
  l_tomorrowsDate DATE;
  l_lastDayOfTheMonth DATE;
BEGIN
  l_outputString := 'Hello ' || 'World';
  l_todaysDate := SYSDATE;
  l_tomorrowsDate := SYSDATE + 1;
  l_lastDayOfTheMonth := LAST_DAY(SYSDATE);
  DBMS_OUTPUT.PUT_LINE(l_outputString);
  DBMS_OUTPUT.PUT_LINE(l_todaysDate);
  DBMS_OUTPUT.PUT_LINE(l_tomorrowsDate);
  DBMS_OUTPUT.PUT_LINE(l_lastDayOfTheMonth);
END;
/
```

The program output should be similar to the following:

```
Hello World
20-MAR-06
21-MAR-06
31-MAR-06
```

```
Statement processed.
```

Notice that the assignment statements in the body of the program use different types of expressions that build values to assign to variables. Several sections in the previous chapter teach you how to build expressions for a query's SELECT clause by using literals, operators, and SQL functions. Similarly, you can build expressions for the right side of an assignment statement in a PL/SQL program. For example, the expressions in the example program use literals, the concatenation and addition operators (|| and +), and the LAST_DAY and SYSDATE functions. Most SQL functions are also built in and supported in PL/SQL statements.

NOTE
The expression SYSDATE + 1 introduces the concept of date arithmetic. As you can see from the results, SYSDATE + 1 evaluates to the current date plus one. A complete discussion of date arithmetic is beyond the scope of this book; for more information, please see the Oracle Database SQL Reference.

Controlling Program Flow

Typical procedural programs have *flow*. That is, a program uses some sort of logic to control whether and when the program executes particular statements. PL/SQL programs can control program flow using iterative logic (loops), conditional logic (if-then-else), and sequential logic (goto). The following exercises teach you how to use the different program flow-control statements that PL/SQL offers.

EXERCISE 4.3: Using PL/SQL Loops

A PL/SQL program can use a *loop* to iterate the execution of a series of statements a certain number of times. Enter the following anonymous PL/SQL block, which teaches you how to use a *basic loop*. The beginning of a basic loop starts with a LOOP statement and ends with an END LOOP statement, as highlighted in bold.

```
DECLARE
  l_loopCounter INTEGER := 0;
BEGIN
 LOOP
  DBMS_OUTPUT.PUT(l_loopCounter || ' ');
  l_loopCounter := l_loopCounter + 1;
  EXIT WHEN l_loopCounter = 10;
 END LOOP;
 DBMS_OUTPUT.PUT_LINE('Loop Exited.');
END;
/
```

The program output should look like the following:

```
0 1 2 3 4 5 6 7 8 9 Loop Exited.

Statement processed.
```

It is important to understand that every basic loop definition should use either an *EXIT WHEN* or *EXIT* statement to terminate the loop—otherwise, the loop executes infinitely!

NOTE
The preceding example uses the DBMS_OUTPUT .PUT procedure to produce output without a trailing newline character.

Next, enter the following anonymous PL/SQL block, which teaches you how to use a different type of loop, a *WHILE loop*. The LOOP statement of a WHILE loop begins with a WHILE condition and ends with an END LOOP statement, as shown in bold.

```
DECLARE
  l_loopCounter INTEGER := 0;
BEGIN
 WHILE l_loopCounter < 10 LOOP
  DBMS_OUTPUT.PUT(l_loopCounter || ' ');
  l_loopCounter := l_loopCounter + 1;
 END LOOP;
 DBMS_OUTPUT.PUT_LINE('Loop Exited.');
END;
/
```

The program output should look like the following:

```
0 1 2 3 4 5 6 7 8 9 Loop Exited.

Statement processed.
```

Notice that the definition of a WHILE loop requires that you specify a condition to describe how the loop terminates.

Finally, enter the following anonymous PL/SQL block, which teaches you how to use a third type of loop, a *FOR loop*. The LOOP statement of a FOR loop begins with a FOR clause and ends with an END LOOP statement.

```
BEGIN
  FOR l_loopCounter IN 0 .. 10 LOOP
   DBMS_OUTPUT.PUT(l_loopCounter || ' ');
  END LOOP;
  DBMS_OUTPUT.PUT_LINE('Loop Exited.');
END;
/
```

The program output should be identical to the previous outputs in this exercise. Notice in the preceding example that a FOR loop can declare its integer counter variable as part of the FOR ... LOOP statement, and that a FOR loop automatically increments or decrements its counter variable so that you do not have to explicitly do so in the body of the loop.

EXERCISE 4.4: Using the PL/SQL Command IF ... ELSIF ... ELSE

An *IF* statement in a PL/SQL program provides for conditional logic. The basic syntax of an IF statement is as follows:

```
IF condition THEN
  statement1;
  statement2;
  ...
ELSIF condition THEN
  statement3;
```

```
statement4;
...
ELSE
 statement5;
 statement6;
...
END;
```

An IF statement functions as follows:

■ An IF statement evaluates a Boolean condition and, if the condition is TRUE, executes one or more statements that follow the THEN clause. When the condition of an IF clause evaluates to FALSE or UNKNOWN (for example, when the condition compares a value to an uninitialized null variable), the statements of the subsequent THEN clause do not execute.

■ An optional ELSIF clause indicates an alternative condition. When the condition of an ELSIF clause evaluates to TRUE, the statements of the subsequent THEN clause execute. When the condition of an ELSIF clause evaluates to FALSE or UNKNOWN, the statements of the subsequent THEN clause do not execute. An IF statement can include more than one ELSIF clause.

■ The optional ELSE clause specifies a series of statements to execute when all of the conditions in the preceding IF and ELSIF clauses do not evaluate to TRUE.

Enter the following anonymous PL/SQL block to get some experience with IF ... ELSIF ... ELSE logic:

```
BEGIN
  FOR l_i IN 1 .. 20 LOOP
   IF ((l_i MOD 3 = 0) AND (l_i MOD 5 = 0)) THEN
    DBMS_OUTPUT.PUT('multipleOfBoth');
   ELSIF l_i MOD 3 = 0 THEN
    DBMS_OUTPUT.PUT('multipleOf3');
   ELSIF l_i MOD 5 = 0 THEN
    DBMS_OUTPUT.PUT('multipleOf5');
   ELSE
    DBMS_OUTPUT.PUT(l_i);
   END IF;
   DBMS_OUTPUT.PUT(' ');
  END LOOP;
  DBMS_OUTPUT.PUT_LINE(' ');
END;
/
```

The program uses the SQL function MOD and the conditions in an IF statement to determine when the FOR loop counter is a multiple of 3, 5, or both 3 and 5. The output should look similar to the following:

```
1 2 multipleOf3 4 multipleOf5 multipleOf3 7 8 multipleOf3
multipleOf5 11 multipleOf3 13 14 multipleOfBoth 16 17
multipleOf3 19 multipleOf5

Statement processed.
```

Interacting with Databases

The previous example exercises are PL/SQL programs that generate simple output to demonstrate some basics of PL/SQL. However, the primary reason for using PL/SQL is to create database access programs. A PL/SQL program can interact with an Oracle database only through the use of SQL. The following exercises show you how a PL/SQL program can manipulate database information by using standard SQL DML statements and cursors.

EXERCISE 4.5: Manipulating Table Data with DML Statements

PL/SQL programs can include any valid INSERT, UPDATE, or DELETE statement to modify the rows in a database table. For example, enter the following anonymous PL/SQL block, which inserts a new record into the PARTS table:

```
DECLARE
  l_newId INTEGER := 6;
  l_newDesc VARCHAR2(250) := 'Mouse';
BEGIN
  INSERT INTO parts
    (id, description, unitprice, onhand, reorder)
    VALUES (l_newId, l_newDesc, 49, 1200, 500);
END;
/
```

The output produced by this program is simply the following line:

```
1 row(s) inserted.
```

A variable or constant in a PL/SQL block can satisfy the requirement for an expression in a DML statement. For example, the previous example program uses program variables to supply the first two values in the VALUES clause of the INSERT statement.

Now query the PARTS table to see the new record:

```
SELECT * FROM parts
  WHERE id = 6;
```

The textual representation of the result set you will see in the SQL Commands page of Application Express is as follows:

```
        ID DESCRIPTION      UNITPRICE    ONHAND REORDER
---------- ---------------- --------- --------- -------
         6 Mouse                   49      1200 500
```

All data modifications made by INSERT, UPDATE, and DELETE statements inside of a PL/SQL block are part of your session's current transaction. Although you can include COMMIT and ROLLBACK statements inside many types of PL/SQL blocks, transaction control is typically controlled outside of PL/SQL blocks so that transaction boundaries are clearly visible to those using your PL/SQL programs.

EXERCISE 4.6: Assigning a Value to a Variable with a Query

PL/SQL programs often use the *INTO clause* of the SQL command SELECT to assign a specific database value to a program variable. Oracle supports the use of a *SELECT ... INTO* statement only inside PL/SQL programs. Try out this type of assignment statement by entering the following anonymous PL/SQL block, which uses a SELECT ... INTO statement to assign a value to a program variable:

```
DECLARE
  l_partDesc VARCHAR2(250);
BEGIN
 SELECT description INTO l_partDesc
   FROM parts
  WHERE id = 3;
 DBMS_OUTPUT.PUT_LINE('Part 3 is a ' || l_partDesc);
END;
/
```

The program output is as follows:

```
Part 3 is a Laptop PC

Statement processed.
```

A SELECT ... INTO command must have a result set with only one row—if the result set of a SELECT ... INTO statement contains zero rows or more than one row, or returns a value that is not of an acceptable datatype, Oracle raises a corresponding exception. To process a query that returns more than one row, a PL/SQL program must use a cursor. You'll learn more about handling exceptions and cursors later in this chapter.

Declaring and Using Subprograms: Procedures and Functions

The declaration section of a PL/SQL block can declare a common subtask as a named *subprogram* (or *subroutine*). Subsequent statements in the main program body can then *call* (execute) the subprogram to perform work whenever necessary.

PL/SQL supports two types of subprograms: procedures and functions. A *procedure* is a subprogram that performs an operation. A *function* is a subprogram that computes a value and returns it to the program that called the function; in other words, a function is a procedure that returns a value.

EXERCISE 4.7: Declaring and Using a Procedure

The simplified syntax for declaring a procedure is as follows:

```
PROCEDURE procedure
  [(parameter [IN|OUT|IN OUT] datatype [{DEFAULT|:=} expression]
  [,...] )]
  declarations ...
{IS|AS}
 BEGIN
 statements ...
 END [procedure];
```

When you declare a subprogram such as a procedure, you can pass values into and out of the subprogram by using *parameters*. Typically, a calling program passes one or more variables as parameters to a subprogram. To clearly distinguish parameters from variables, constants, etc., declare parameters with the prefix p_.

For each parameter, you must specify a datatype in an unconstrained form; for example, VARCHAR2, not VARCHAR2(100). Furthermore, you should indicate the mode of each parameter as IN, OUT, or IN OUT:

- **IN parameter**   Passes a value into a subprogram, but a subprogram cannot change the value of the external variable that corresponds to an IN parameter.

- **OUT parameter**   Is initialized to null, after which a subprogram can manipulate an OUT parameter to change the value of the corresponding variable in the outside calling environment. A subprogram can set but cannot read the value of an OUT parameter.

- **IN OUT parameter**   Combines the capabilities of IN and OUT parameters.

Enter the following anonymous PL/SQL block, which declares a procedure to print horizontal lines of a specified width:

```
DECLARE
  PROCEDURE printLine(p_width IN INTEGER, p_chr IN CHAR DEFAULT '-') IS
  BEGIN
   FOR l_i IN 1 .. p_width LOOP
    DBMS_OUTPUT.PUT(p_chr);
   END LOOP;
   DBMS_OUTPUT.PUT_LINE('');
  END printLine;
BEGIN
 printLine(40, '*');                        -- print a line of 40 *s
 printLine(p_chr => '=', p_width => 20);    -- print a line of 20 =s
 printLine(10);                             -- print a line of 10 -s
END;
/
```

The program output is as follows:

```
****************************************
====================
----------

Statement processed.
```

The body of the example in this exercise calls the printLine procedure three times:

- The first procedure call provides values for both parameters of the procedure by using *positional notation*—each parameter value that you specify in a procedure call implicitly corresponds to the procedure parameter declared in the same position.

- The second procedure call provides values for both parameters of the procedure by using *named notation*—the name of a parameter and the *association operator* (=>) precede a parameter value. When using named notation, notice that you can specify parameters in any order.

- The third procedure call demonstrates that you must provide values for all procedure parameters without default values, but can optionally omit values for parameters with a default value.

EXERCISE 4.8: Declaring and Using a Function

The simplified syntax for declaring a function is as follows:

```
FUNCTION function
  [(parameter [IN|OUT|IN OUT] datatype [{DEFAULT|:=} expression]
  [,...] )]
  RETURN datatype
  declarations ...
{IS|AS}
  BEGIN
  statements ...
  END [function];
```

Notice that a function differs from a procedure only in that it returns a value to its calling environment. The specification of a function declares the type of the *return value*. Furthermore, the body of a function must include one or more *RETURN statements* to return a value to the calling environment.

Enter the following anonymous PL/SQL block, which declares and uses a function:

```
DECLARE
  l_tempTotal NUMBER;
  FUNCTION orderTotal(p_orderId IN INTEGER)
   RETURN NUMBER
  IS
   l_orderTotal NUMBER;
   l_tempTotal NUMBER;
  BEGIN
   SELECT SUM(i.quantity * p.unitprice) INTO l_orderTotal
    FROM items i, parts p
    WHERE i.o_id = p_orderId
    AND i.p_id = p.id
    GROUP BY i.o_id;
   RETURN l_orderTotal;
  END orderTotal;
BEGIN
  DBMS_OUTPUT.PUT_LINE('Order 1 Total: ' || orderTotal(1));
  l_tempTotal := orderTotal(2);
  DBMS_OUTPUT.PUT_LINE('Order 2 Total: ' || l_tempTotal);
END;
/
```

The program output is as follows:

```
Order 1 Total: 7094
Order 2 Total: 3196

Statement processed.
```

The main program body of the PL/SQL block calls the orderTotal function twice. A program can call a function anywhere an expression is valid—for example, as a parameter for a procedure call or on the right side of an assignment statement. A SQL statement can also reference a user-defined function in the condition of a WHERE clause.

Working with Record Types

So far in this chapter, you've seen how to declare simple, scalar variables and constants based on Oracle datatypes (for example, NUMBER) and subtypes of the base datatypes (for example, INTEGER). A block in a PL/SQL program can also declare *user-defined types* and then use the user-defined types to declare corresponding program variables. This section teaches you how to declare and use an elementary user-defined type, a record type. A *record type* consists of a group of one or more related fields, each of which has its own name and datatype. Typically, PL/SQL programs use a record type to create variables that match the structure of a record in a table. For example, you might declare a record type called partRecord and then use the type to create a record variable that holds a part's ID, DESCRIPTION, UNITPRICE, ONHAND, and REORDER fields. After you declare a record variable, you can manipulate the individual fields of the record or pass the entire record to subprograms as a unit.

The general syntax for declaring a record type is as follows:

```
TYPE recordType IS RECORD
(   field datatype [NOT NULL] {DEFAULT|:=} expression ]
 [, field ...]
)
```

The specification of an individual field in a record type is similar to declaring a scalar variable—you must specify the field's datatype, and you can specify an optional not null constraint, as well as initialize the field.

EXERCISE 4.9: Declaring and Using Record Types

Enter the following anonymous PL/SQL block, which demonstrates how to declare and use a record type. The declaration section of the block declares a user-defined record type to match the attributes of the PARTS table, and then declares two record variables using the new type. The body of the program demonstrates how to do the following:

■ Reference individual fields of record variables using dot notation

■ Assign values to the fields of a record variable

■ Pass a record variable as a parameter to a procedure call

■ Copy the field values of one record variable to the fields of another variable of the same record type

■ Use the fields of a record variable as expressions in an INSERT statement

```
DECLARE
 TYPE partRecord IS RECORD (
  id INTEGER,
  description VARCHAR2(250),
  unitprice NUMBER(10,2),
  onhand INTEGER,
  reorder INTEGER
 );
 l_selectedPart partRecord;
 l_copiedPart partRecord;
 PROCEDURE printPart (p_title IN VARCHAR2, p_thisPart IN partRecord) IS
 BEGIN
  FOR l_i IN 1 .. 50 LOOP
   DBMS_OUTPUT.PUT('-');
  END LOOP;
  DBMS_OUTPUT.PUT_LINE('');
  DBMS_OUTPUT.PUT_LINE(p_title || ': ID: ' || p_thisPart.id ||
   ' DESCRIPTION: ' || p_thisPart.description);
 END printPart;
BEGIN
/* Assign values to the fields of a record variable
|| using a SELECT .. INTO statement.
*/
 SELECT id, description, unitprice , onhand, reorder INTO l_selectedPart
  FROM parts WHERE id = 3;
 printPart('selectedPart Info', l_selectedPart);

/* Assign the field values of one record variable to
|| the corresponding fields in another record
|| variable of the same type. Then assign new
|| values to the fields of original record variable
|| to demonstrate that record copies are not by reference.
*/
 l_copiedPart := l_selectedPart;

 l_selectedPart.id := 7;
 l_selectedPart.description := 'Laser Printer';
 l_selectedPart.unitprice := 399;
 l_selectedPart.onhand := 780;
 l_selectedPart.reorder := 500;

 printPart('newPart Info', l_selectedPart);
 printPart('copiedPart Info', l_copiedPart);
```

```
/* Use the fields of a record variable as expressions
|| in the VALUES clause of an INSERT statement.
*/
 INSERT INTO parts
  VALUES (l_selectedPart.id, l_selectedPart.description,
   l_selectedPart.unitprice, l_selectedPart.onhand, l_selectedPart.reorder);
END;
/
```

The program output is as follows:

```
-----------------------------------------------
selectedPart Info: ID: 3 DESCRIPTION: Laptop PC
-----------------------------------------------
newPart Info: ID: 7 DESCRIPTION: Laser Printer
-----------------------------------------------
copiedPart Info: ID: 3 DESCRIPTION: Laptop PC

1 row(s) inserted.
```

NOTE
As an additional exercise, build a query of the PARTS table to view the new part inserted by the example program.

Using the %TYPE and %ROWTYPE Attributes

A PL/SQL program can use the *%TYPE and %ROWTYPE attributes* to declare variables, constants, individual fields in records, and record variables that match the properties of database columns and tables or other program constructs. The use of attributes not only simplifies the declaration of program constructs, but also makes programs flexible to database modifications. For example, after an administrator modifies the PARTS table to add a new column, a record variable declared using the %ROWTYPE attribute automatically adjusts to account for the new column at run time, without any modification of the program.

EXERCISE 4.10: Using the %TYPE Attribute

The declaration of a PL/SQL variable, constant, or field in a record variable can use the *%TYPE attribute* to capture the datatype of another program construct or column in a database table at run time. For example, enter the following anonymous PL/SQL block, which uses the %TYPE attribute to reference the columns in the PARTS table when declaring the partRecord type:

```
DECLARE
  TYPE partRecord IS RECORD (
    id parts.id%TYPE,
```

```
  description parts.description%TYPE,
  unitprice parts.unitprice%TYPE,
  onhand parts.onhand%TYPE,
  reorder parts.reorder%TYPE
);
l_selectedPart partRecord;
BEGIN
 SELECT id, description, unitprice , onhand, reorder INTO l_selectedPart
  FROM parts WHERE id = 3;
 DBMS_OUTPUT.PUT_LINE('ID: ' || l_selectedPart.id);
 DBMS_OUTPUT.PUT_LINE('DESCRIPTION: ' || l_selectedPart.description);
 DBMS_OUTPUT.PUT_LINE('UNIT PRICE: ' || l_selectedPart.unitprice);
 DBMS_OUTPUT.PUT_LINE('CURRENTLY ONHAND: ' || l_selectedPart.onhand);
 DBMS_OUTPUT.PUT_LINE('REORDER AT: ' || l_selectedPart.reorder);
END;
/
```

The program output is as follows:

```
ID: 3
DESCRIPTION: Laptop PC
UNIT PRICE: 2100
CURRENTLY ONHAND: 7631
REORDER AT: 1000

Statement processed.
```

EXERCISE 4.11: Using the %ROWTYPE Attribute

A PL/SQL program can use the *%ROWTYPE attribute* to easily declare record variables and other constructs at run time. For example, enter the following anonymous PL/SQL block, which shows how to use the %ROWTYPE attribute to simplify the declaration of a record variable that corresponds to the fields in the PARTS table:

```
DECLARE
  l_selectedPart parts%ROWTYPE;
BEGIN
 SELECT id, description, unitprice , onhand, reorder INTO l_selectedPart
  FROM parts WHERE id = 3;
 DBMS_OUTPUT.PUT_LINE('ID: ' || l_selectedPart.id);
 DBMS_OUTPUT.PUT_LINE('DESCRIPTION: ' || l_selectedPart.description);
 DBMS_OUTPUT.PUT_LINE('UNIT PRICE: ' || l_selectedPart.unitprice);
 DBMS_OUTPUT.PUT_LINE('CURRENTLY ONHAND: ' || l_selectedPart.onhand);
 DBMS_OUTPUT.PUT_LINE('REORDER AT: ' || l_selectedPart.reorder);
END;
/
```

The program output is as follows:

```
ID: 3
DESCRIPTION: Laptop PC
UNIT PRICE: 2100
CURRENTLY ONHAND: 7631
REORDER AT: 1000

Statement processed.
```

Notice that a record variable that you declare using the %ROWTYPE attribute automatically has field names that correspond to the fields in the referenced table.

> **NOTE**
> *One of the great things about using the %TYPE and %ROWTYPE attributes is that they make your program declarations flexible to inevitable changes in data structures. For example, the preceding two examples function properly with the DESCRIPTION column of the PARTS table declared as VARCHAR2(1), VARCHAR2(50), VARCHAR2(250), and so on.*

Working with Cursors

Whenever an application submits a SQL statement to Oracle, the server opens at least one cursor to process the statement. A *cursor* is essentially a work area for a SQL statement. When a PL/SQL program (or any other application) submits an INSERT, UPDATE, or DELETE statement, Oracle automatically opens a cursor to process the statement. Oracle also can automatically process SELECT statements that return just one row. However, database access programs frequently must process a query that returns a set of database records, rather than just one row.

To process the rows of a query that correspond to a multiple-row result set, a PL/SQL program must explicitly declare a cursor, open it, fetch rows from the cursor one at a time, and then close the cursor. Oracle supports several approaches for cursor processing:

- **Named cursor declaration, OPEN, FETCH, CLOSE statements** You can explicitly declare a cursor with a name in the declaration section of a block by using the PL/SQL command *CURSOR*. In the block's body or exception-handling section, you can then open the cursor with the PL/SQL command *OPEN*, fetch rows from the cursor with the PL/SQL command *FETCH* (normally within a loop), and finally close the cursor with the PL/SQL command *CLOSE*. This approach is the most tedious, error-prone, and poorest performing choice.

- **Explicit cursor FOR loop** You can declare a cursor with the CURSOR command and then use a *cursor FOR loop* to automatically declare a variable or record capable of receiving the rows in the cursor, open the cursor, fetch rows from the cursor, and close the cursor after the last row is fetched from the cursor. This approach is simpler, less error-prone, and much better performing than the previous approach, but still requires the explicit declaration of a cursor.

- **Implicit cursor FOR loop** Along with a matching variable or record, you can declare the cursor *in* a FOR loop itself and process corresponding rows one by one. This approach is by far the simplest and performs equally as well as an explicit cursor FOR loop.

The next exercise demonstrates and compares each of the preceding approaches.

NOTE
When using a cursor to process a large number of rows, explicit and implicit cursor FOR loops deliver much better performance than the OPEN/ FETCH/CLOSE approach because cursor FOR loops implicitly fetch arrays of 100 rows at a time from the corresponding cursor; by contrast, when you use OPEN/FETCH/CLOSE to process a cursor, Oracle fetches one row at a time.

EXERCISE 4.12: Declaring and Using a Cursor

To familiarize yourself with the steps necessary to declare and use a cursor, enter the following anonymous PL/SQL block, which declares and uses a very simple cursor to print out selected columns in all the rows of the PARTS table:

```
BEGIN
  FOR l_currentPart IN (SELECT id, description FROM parts ORDER BY id)
  LOOP
    DBMS_OUTPUT.PUT_LINE(l_currentPart.id||' '||l_currentPart.description);
  END LOOP;
END;
/
```

The program output is as follows:

```
1 Fax Machine
2 Copy Machine
3 Laptop PC
4 Desktop PC
5 Scanner
```

```
6 Mouse
7 Laser Printer

Statement processed.
```

The preceding approach for cursor processing is straightforward and performs well. But realize that as you work more with Oracle, you are undoubtedly going to see cursor processing that uses the other, more complex aforementioned approaches. For example, you could implement the previous block equivalently as the following:

```
DECLARE
  -- Step 1: Declare the cursor.
  CURSOR l_nextPartsRow IS
    SELECT id, description FROM parts
      ORDER BY id;
  -- record variable that matches the cursor
  l_currentPart l_nextPartsRow%ROWTYPE;
BEGIN
  -- Step 2. Open the cursor.
  OPEN l_nextPartsRow;

  FETCH l_nextPartsRow INTO l_currentPart;
  -- Step 3. Using a WHILE loop, fetch individual rows from the cursor.
  WHILE l_nextPartsRow%FOUND LOOP
    DBMS_OUTPUT.PUT_LINE(l_currentPart.id||' '||l_currentPart.description);
    FETCH l_nextPartsRow INTO l_currentPart;
  END LOOP;

  -- Step 4. Close the cursor.
  CLOSE l_nextPartsRow;
END;
/
```

Notice that after fetching the first row from the cursor, this version of the block uses a WHILE loop to fetch subsequent rows from the open cursor, one by one. A PL/SQL program can use a *cursor attribute* to make decisions when processing cursors. The condition of the WHILE loop in the example program uses the %FOUND cursor attribute to detect when the last row of the cursor has been fetched. Table 4-2 lists the cursor attributes available with PL/SQL for basic cursors.

You might see yet another version of the previous block that uses an explicit cursor FOR loop:

```
DECLARE
  CURSOR l_partsRows IS
    SELECT id, description FROM parts
      ORDER BY id;
BEGIN
```

Explicit Cursor Attribute	Description
cursor %FOUND	The %FOUND attribute evaluates to TRUE when the preceding FETCH statement corresponds to at least one row in a database; otherwise, %FOUND evaluates to FALSE.
cursor %NOTFOUND	The %NOTFOUND attribute evaluates to TRUE when the preceding FETCH statement does not correspond to at least one row in a database; otherwise, %NOTFOUND evaluates to FALSE.
cursor %ISOPEN	The %ISOPEN attribute evaluates to TRUE when the target cursor is open; otherwise, %ISOPEN evaluates to FALSE.
cursor %ROWCOUNT	The %ROWCOUNT attribute reveals the number of rows fetched so far for an explicitly declared cursor.

TABLE 4-2. *Attributes of Explicitly Declared Cursors*

```
FOR l_currentPart IN l_partsRows LOOP
  DBMS_OUTPUT.PUT_LINE(l_currentPart.id||' '||l_currentPart.description);
END LOOP;
END;
/
```

This version of the block is simpler than the previous version, but still not as simple as the first version at the beginning of this exercise.

EXERCISE 4.13: Manipulating a Cursor's Current Row

As a program fetches individual rows from a cursor's result set, it is accessing the cursor's *current row*. When a cursor needs to update or delete the current row of a cursor, the method you use for targeting the row varies depending on the approach that you take to process the cursor. When you use an implicit cursor FOR loop to process a cursor, the cursor should select each row's *ROWID* and use a WHERE clause condition that uses the target row's ROWID. For example, enter the following to try this technique with an implicit cursor FOR loop:

```
BEGIN
  FOR l_currentPart
    IN (SELECT rowid, id, description FROM parts WHERE id >= 6 FOR UPDATE)
```

```
LOOP
  DELETE FROM parts
    WHERE rowid = l_currentPart.rowid;
  DBMS_OUTPUT.PUT_LINE('Deleted part ' || l_currentPart.id || ', ' ||
    l_currentPart.description);
  END LOOP;
END;
/
```

NOTE
A ROWID is a physical address that tells Oracle where to physically find the corresponding row in the database. As the previous block demonstrates, you can reference a row's ROWID by using the ROWID *pseudocolumn.*

The preceding block deletes the two new records inserted into the PARTS table by previous example programs in this chapter. Notice that when you declare a cursor with the intention of updating or deleting rows fetched by the cursor, you must declare the cursor's defining query with the *FOR UPDATE* keywords; this requirement forces Oracle to lock the rows in the cursor's result set, which prevents other transactions from updating or deleting the same rows until your transaction commits or rolls back.

Assuming that your PARTS table has rows for parts 6 and 7 (a Mouse and a Laser Printer, respectively), which were inserted by earlier exercises in this chapter, the program output should be as follows:

```
Deleted part 6, Mouse
Deleted part 7, Laser Printer

1 row(s) deleted.
```

A PL/SQL program that explicitly declares a cursor can take advantage of the special *CURRENT OF clause* in the WHERE condition of an UPDATE or DELETE statement to process the current row of a cursor. The following anonymous PL/SQL block is equivalent to the previous block:

```
DECLARE
  CURSOR l_partsRows (p_partId INTEGER) IS
    SELECT * FROM parts
    WHERE id >= l_partId
    FOR UPDATE;
BEGIN
  FOR l_currentPart IN l_partsRows (6) LOOP -- selects parts 6 and 7
    DELETE FROM parts
```

```
  WHERE CURRENT OF l_partsRows;
  DBMS_OUTPUT.PUT_LINE('Deleted part ' || l_currentPart.id || ', ' ||
  l_currentPart.description);
 END LOOP;
END;
/
```

Besides the CURRENT OF clause, this program also shows that when you declare a cursor, you can declare one or more *cursor parameters* that the PL/SQL program uses to define the cursor's record selection criteria at run time (shown in bold). When a program opens a cursor that has a cursor parameter, the program can indicate a value for each cursor parameter (shown in bold).

Working with Collections

PL/SQL blocks can also declare and use collections. A *collection* in a PL/SQL program is a variable that is made up of an ordered set of like elements. To create a collection, you must first declare either a nested table type or a varray (varying array) type, and then declare a variable of the collection type. The next few sections explain more about nested tables and varrays.

NOTE
This chapter does not explain a third collection type, PL/SQL tables (index-by tables). See the Oracle PL/SQL User's Guide and Reference *for more information.*

Nested Tables

A PL/SQL program can use a *nested table type* to create variables that have one or more columns and an *unlimited* number of rows, just like tables in a database. The general syntax for declaring a nested table type is as follows:

```
TYPE tableType IS TABLE OF
  { datatype | {variable|table.column}%TYPE | table%ROWTYPE }
  [NOT NULL] ;
```

The following exercises teach you how to declare, use, and manipulate nested tables.

EXERCISE 4.14: Declaring and Initializing a Nested Table

Enter the following anonymous PL/SQL block, which demonstrates how to declare a nested table type, and then use the type to declare a new collection variable. The following example also demonstrates how to initialize a collection with its constructor method and then reference specific elements in the nested table collection by subscript.

```
DECLARE
-- declare a nested table type of INTEGERs
 TYPE integerTable IS TABLE OF INTEGER;
-- declare and initialize a collection with its constructor
 l_tempIntegers integerTable := integerTable(1, 202, 451);
BEGIN
 FOR l_i IN 1 .. 3 LOOP
  DBMS_OUTPUT.PUT_LINE('Element #' || l_i || ' is ' || l_tempIntegers(l_i));
 END LOOP;
END;
/
```

The program output is as follows:

```
Element #1 is 1
Element #2 is 202
Element #3 is 451

Statement processed.
```

This very simple example demonstrates a few fundamental points you need to understand about nested tables:

■ Before you can use a collection, such as a nested table, you must initialize it using the type's corresponding *constructor*. PL/SQL automatically provides a constructor with the same name as the collection type. When you call a constructor to initialize a collection variable, you can specify a comma-separated list of initial elements for the collection, or a set of empty parentheses to initialize the collection as null.

■ A nested table collection can have any number of rows. The size of a table can increase or decrease dynamically, as necessary. The next practice exercise shows how to add and delete elements in a nested table.

EXERCISE 4.15: Using Collection Methods with a Nested Table

PL/SQL supports several different *collection methods* that you can use to manipulate collections. To use a collection method, an expression in a PL/SQL program names the collection with the collection method as a suffix, using dot notation. Table 4-3 lists the collection methods that are available in PL/SQL.

Enter the following anonymous PL/SQL block, which demonstrates how to use several collection methods with a nested table of records. The highlighted text points out calls to a collection's constructor and collection methods.

Collection Method	Description
COUNT	Returns the number of elements currently in the collection.
DELETE[(x[,y] ...)]	Deletes some or all of the collection's elements without deallocating the space used by the elements.
EXISTS(x)	Returns TRUE if the xth element in the collection exists. Otherwise, the method returns FALSE.
EXTEND[(x[,y])]	Appends x copies of the yth element to the tail end of the collection. If y is omitted, appends x null elements to the collection. If both x and y are omitted, appends a single null element to the collection.
FIRST	Returns the index number of the first element in the collection.
LAST	Returns the index number of the last element in the collection.
LIMIT	Returns the maximum number of elements that a varray's collection can contain.
NEXT(x)	Returns the index number of the element after the xth element of the collection.
PRIOR(x)	Returns the index number of the element before the xth element of the collection.
TRIM(x)	Trims x elements from the end of the collection.

TABLE 4-3. *Collection Methods*

```
DECLARE
    -- declare a nested table type of PARTS
    TYPE partsTable IS TABLE OF parts%ROWTYPE;
    -- declare and initialize a collection with its constructor
    tempParts partsTable := partsTable();
    -- counter variable to hold subscript information
    currentElement INTEGER;
    -- procedure to output elements of a collection
    PROCEDURE printParts(p_collection IN partsTable, p_title IN VARCHAR2)
    IS
    BEGIN
      DBMS_OUTPUT.PUT_LINE('');
      DBMS_OUTPUT.PUT_LINE(p_title || ' elements: ' || p_collection.COUNT);
      currentElement := p_collection.FIRST;
```

```
  FOR i IN 1 .. p_collection.COUNT
  LOOP
   DBMS_OUTPUT.PUT('Element #' || currentElement || ' is ');
   IF tempParts(currentElement).id IS NULL THEN
    DBMS_OUTPUT.PUT_LINE('an empty element.');
   ELSE
    DBMS_OUTPUT.PUT_LINE('ID: '|| tempParts(currentElement).id ||
     ', ' || 'DESCRIPTION: ' || tempParts(currentElement).description);
   END IF;
   currentElement := p_collection.NEXT(currentElement);
  END LOOP;
 END;
BEGIN
 -- ADD ELEMENTS TO AND POPULATE THE COLLECTION
 FOR currentPart IN (SELECT * FROM parts ORDER BY id)
 LOOP
  tempParts.EXTEND(2);
  tempParts(tempParts.LAST) := currentPart;
 END LOOP;
 -- PRINT ELEMENTS OF COLLECTION
 printParts(tempParts, 'Densely populated');
 -- DELETE EMPTY COLLECTION ELEMENTS
 FOR i IN 1 .. tempParts.COUNT LOOP
  IF tempParts(i).id IS NULL THEN
   tempParts.DELETE(i);
  END IF;
 END LOOP;
 -- OUTPUT SPARSE VERSION OF THE COLLECTION
 printParts(tempParts, 'Sparsely populated');
END;
/
```

The program output is as follows:

```
Densely populated elements: 10
Element #1 is an empty element.
Element #2 is ID: 1, DESCRIPTION: Fax Machine
Element #3 is an empty element.
Element #4 is ID: 2, DESCRIPTION: Copy Machine
Element #5 is an empty element.
Element #6 is ID: 3, DESCRIPTION: Laptop PC
Element #7 is an empty element.
Element #8 is ID: 4, DESCRIPTION: Desktop PC
Element #9 is an empty element.
Element #10 is ID: 5, DESCRIPTION: Scanner
```

```
Sparsely populated elements: 5
Element #2 is ID: 1, DESCRIPTION: Fax Machine
Element #4 is ID: 2, DESCRIPTION: Copy Machine
Element #6 is ID: 3, DESCRIPTION: Laptop PC
Element #8 is ID: 4, DESCRIPTION: Desktop PC
Element #10 is ID: 5, DESCRIPTION: Scanner
```

Besides demonstrating how to use the EXTEND, COUNT, FIRST, NEXT, and DELETE collection methods, this example shows that while nested tables are initially *dense* (elements have consecutive subscripts), they can later become *sparse* (elements can have nonconsecutive subscripts) if the program deletes elements from the collection. With this possibility in mind, the loops that output elements in the example program do not rely on the loop's counter variable to reference collection elements.

Varying Arrays

A program can also declare a *varying array* (*varray*) *type* to create table-like variables that have one or more columns and a *limited* number of rows. The general syntax for declaring a varray type is as follows:

```
TYPE varrayType IS {VARRAY | VARYING ARRAY} (size) OF
{ datatype | {variable|table.column}%TYPE | table%ROWTYPE }
   [NOT NULL] ;
```

For the most part, varray collections are similar to nested table collections, with the following important differences:

- When you declare a varray type, you must declare the number of elements in the varray, which remains constant.

- Varrays must remain *dense*. A program cannot delete elements from a varray.

Handling Program Exceptions

A good program is not complete unless it contains routines to process the errors that can occur during program execution. Rather than embed error-handling routines into the body of a program, a PL/SQL program addresses error-handling requirements using exceptions and associated exception handlers. An *exception* is a named error condition. A PL/SQL program *raises* a named exception when it detects an error, and then it passes control to an associated *exception handler* routine that is separate from the main program body. The next two exercises teach you more about exceptions and exception handling, including predefined and user-defined exceptions.

EXERCISE 4.16: Handling Predefined Exceptions

PL/SQL includes many *predefined exceptions* that correspond to several common Oracle errors. When a program encounters a predefined exception, it automatically transfers program control to the associated exception handler—a program does not have to explicitly perform checks for predefined exceptions.

PL/SQL identifies many predefined exceptions such as NO_DATA_FOUND and TOO_MANY_ROWS:

- A PL/SQL program automatically raises the NO_DATA_FOUND exception when a SELECT INTO statement has a result set with no rows.

- A PL/SQL program automatically raises the TOO_MANY_ROWS exception when a SELECT INTO statement has a result set with more than one row.

NOTE
For a complete list of predefined exceptions, see the Oracle PL/SQL User's Guide and Reference.

For example, enter the following anonymous PL/SQL block, which includes exception handlers to handle the NO_DATA_FOUND and TOO_MANY_ROWS predefined PL/SQL exceptions:

```
DECLARE
  PROCEDURE printOrder (p_thisOrderDate IN DATE) IS
    l_thisId INTEGER;
  BEGIN
    SELECT id INTO l_thisId FROM orders
      WHERE orderdate = p_thisOrderDate;
    DBMS_OUTPUT.PUT_LINE('Order ID ' || l_thisId
      || ' on ' || p_thisOrderDate);
  EXCEPTION
    WHEN no_data_found THEN
      DBMS_OUTPUT.PUT_LINE('No data found for SELECT .. INTO');
  END printOrder;
BEGIN
  printOrder(TO_DATE('23-JUN-2006', 'DD-MON-YYYY'));
  printOrder(TO_DATE('24-JUN-2006', 'DD-MON-YYYY'));
  printOrder(TO_DATE('18-JUN-2006', 'DD-MON-YYYY'));
  printOrder(TO_DATE('19-JUN-2006', 'DD-MON-YYYY'));
EXCEPTION
  WHEN too_many_rows THEN
    DBMS_OUTPUT.PUT_LINE('Too many rows found for SELECT .. INTO');
END;
/
```

The program output is as follows:

```
Order ID 14 on 23-JUN-06
No data found for SELECT .. INTO
Too many rows found for SELECT .. INTO

Statement processed.
```

There are several important points that this example demonstrates about exception handling in general:

- You can include an exception-handling section in any PL/SQL block—both the anonymous PL/SQL block and its subprogram (the printOrder procedure) have their own exception-handling sections.

- The first call to the printOrder procedure does not raise any exceptions and prints the ID of the only order placed on 23-Jun-2006.

- The second call to the printOrder procedure raises the predefined exception NO_DATA_FOUND, because the SELECT ... INTO statement in the procedure does not retrieve any rows. The NO_DATA_FOUND exception handler that is local to the procedure handles the exception by printing a message, and then returns control to the calling program, the anonymous PL/SQL block, which then calls the printOrder procedure a third time.

- The third call to the printOrder procedure raises the predefined exception TOO_MANY_ROWS, because the SELECT ... INTO statement in the procedure returns more than one row. The procedure's exception-handling section does not handle the TOO_MANY_ROWS exception locally, so the exception propagates to the calling program (the anonymous PL/SQL block itself), which does have an exception handler for TOO_MANY_ROWS. The exception handler prints a message, and then passes control to the calling program, which in this case is the SQL Commands page of Oracle Application Express. Execution of the anonymous PL/SQL block stops, and the fourth call to the printOrder procedure never executes.

NOTE
When an unhandled exception is raised in or propagates to the outermost PL/SQL block, the block stops execution and returns the error number and message that correspond to the exception to the calling program.

EXERCISE 4.17: Declaring and Handling User-Defined Exceptions

A program can also declare *user-defined exceptions* in the declaration section of a block. However, a program must perform explicit checks for a user-defined exception to raise the exception. Enter the following anonymous PL/SQL block, which demonstrates the use of user-defined exceptions (in bold) and corresponding exception handlers:

```
DECLARE
  l_partNum INTEGER := 10;
  l_errNum INTEGER;
  l_errMsg VARCHAR2(2000);
  l_invalidPart EXCEPTION;
BEGIN
 UPDATE parts
    SET description = 'Test'
  WHERE id = l_partNum;
-- Explicitly check for the user-defined exception
 IF SQL%NOTFOUND THEN
  RAISE l_invalidPart;
 END IF;
 DBMS_OUTPUT.PUT_LINE('Part updated.');
EXCEPTION
 WHEN l_invalidPart THEN
  DBMS_OUTPUT.PUT_LINE('Invalid Part ID #' || l_partNum);
 WHEN OTHERS THEN
  l_errNum := SQLCODE;
  l_errMsg := SUBSTR(SQLERRM, 1, 100);
  DBMS_OUTPUT.PUT_LINE(l_errNum ||' '||l_errMsg);
END;
/
```

The program output is as follows:

```
Invalid Part ID #10
1 row(s) updated.
```

The example in this section introduces several interesting points about exception handling:

- You declare a user-defined exception in the declaration section of a PL/SQL block with the *EXCEPTION keyword*.

- You raise a user-defined exception with the PL/SQL command *RAISE*.

- A PL/SQL program can use the *WHEN OTHERS exception handler* to handle all exceptions that do not have a specific handler.

- A PL/SQL program can use the special *SQLCODE* and *SQLERRM functions* to return the most recent Oracle error number and message, respectively.

Types of PL/SQL Programs

Now that you understand the basics of the PL/SQL language, it's time to learn more about the different types of programs you can create with PL/SQL, including anonymous PL/SQL blocks, procedures, functions, packages, and database triggers.

Anonymous PL/SQL Blocks

The previous examples in this chapter are all anonymous PL/SQL blocks. An *anonymous block* is a PL/SQL block that appears within your application. An anonymous PL/SQL block has no name and is not stored in the database. The application simply sends the block of code to the database server for processing at run time.

Stored Procedures and Functions

Several exercises in this chapter taught you how to declare and use PL/SQL subprograms (procedures and functions) within PL/SQL blocks to encapsulate frequently used tasks. You can also store procedures and functions as compiled bits of application logic inside an Oracle database as named schema objects.

Database-stored subprograms offer many benefits for application development, such as the following:

- **Code reusability and developer productivity**   By centralizing common procedures and functions in the database, any application can make use of these common routines to perform work. Judicious use of stored procedures and functions can thus increase developer productivity and simplify application development.

- **Data integrity**   Once you validate stored subprograms, they can be trusted by applications as data access methods that will not undermine the integrity of database information.

- **Security**   Stored subprograms are compiled data access programs that hide the underlying database structures they access. Furthermore, only the owner of a subprogram requires privileges to access underlying data structures, not every user that calls the subprogram.

The next two practice exercises demonstrate how to create stored procedures and functions in an Oracle database.

EXERCISE 4.18: Creating and Using Stored Procedures

To create a stored procedure in an Oracle database, use the SQL command *CREATE PROCEDURE*. Specification of a stored PL/SQL subprogram is basically the same as when you declare a subprogram in the declaration section of a PL/SQL block.

However, when you declare a stored procedure, you can use the following options to indicate the privilege domain that Oracle uses when executing the procedure:

- **AUTHID CURRENT_USER** If you create the procedure with the AUTHID CURRENT_USER option, Oracle executes the procedure (when called) by using the privilege domain of the user calling the procedure, including roles. To execute the procedure successfully, the *caller* must have the privileges necessary to access all database objects referenced in the body of the stored procedure using SQL.

- **AUTHID DEFINER** If you create the procedure with the default AUTHID DEFINER option, Oracle executes the procedure by using the privilege domain of the owner of the procedure, excluding roles. To execute the procedure successfully, the procedure *owner* must have the privileges necessary to access all database objects referenced in the body of the stored procedure using SQL. To simplify privilege management for application users, the default AUTHID DEFINER option should be your typical choice when creating a stored procedure—this way, you do not have to grant privileges to all the users that need to call the procedure.

NOTE
For more information about database access privileges and roles, see Chapter 7.

Enter the following example, which demonstrates how to create and store the familiar printLine procedure in an Oracle database:

```
CREATE OR REPLACE PROCEDURE printLine(
    p_width IN INTEGER,
    p_chr IN CHAR DEFAULT '-')
AUTHID DEFINER
IS
BEGIN
  FOR l_i IN 1 .. p_width LOOP
   DBMS_OUTPUT.PUT(p_chr);
  END LOOP;
  DBMS_OUTPUT.PUT_LINE('');
END printLine;
/
```

Now, you can use the printLine procedure in any other PL/SQL program just by calling the stored procedure in the database. For example, try entering the following anonymous PL/SQL blocks, which use the printLine stored procedure:

```
BEGIN
   printLine(40, '*');              -- print a line of 40 *s
   printLine(p_width => 20, p_chr => '=');   -- print a line of 20 =s
   printLine(10);                   -- print a line of 10 -s
END;
/
```

The program output is as follows:

```
****************************************
====================
----------

Statement processed.
```

EXERCISE 4.19: Creating and Using Stored Functions

To create a stored function in an Oracle database, use the SQL command *CREATE FUNCTION*. Specify a function just as you would in the declaration section of a PL/SQL block—do not forget to declare the function's return type, and to use one or more RETURN statements in the body of the function to return the function's return value. Enter the following example, which demonstrates how to create and store the orderTotal function in an Oracle database:

```
CREATE OR REPLACE FUNCTION orderTotal(p_orderId IN INTEGER)
   RETURN NUMBER
IS
  l_orderTotal NUMBER;
BEGIN
  SELECT SUM(i.quantity * p.unitprice) INTO l_orderTotal
    FROM items i, parts p
   WHERE i.o_id = p_orderId
     AND i.p_id = p.id
   GROUP BY i.o_id;
  RETURN l_orderTotal;
END orderTotal;
/
```

Now, enter the following block to print the value of order 5:

```
BEGIN
   DBMS_OUTPUT.PUT_LINE('Order 5 totals $' || orderTotal(5));
END;
/
```

The results are as follows:

```
Order 5 totals $6995
Statement processed.
```

Packages

A *package* is a group of procedures, functions, and other PL/SQL constructs, all stored together in a database as a unit. Packages are especially useful for organizing a number of PL/SQL procedures and functions that relate to a particular database application.

A package has two parts:

- **Package specification**   Defines the interface to the package. In a package specification, you declare all package variables, constants, cursors, procedures, functions, and other constructs that you want to make available to programs outside the package. In other words, everything that you declare in a package's specification is *public*. You declare a package specification with the SQL command CREATE PACKAGE.

- **Package body**   Defines all public procedures and functions declared in the package specification. Additionally, a package body can include other construct definitions not in the specification; such package constructs are *private* (available only to programs within the package). You declare a package body with the SQL command CREATE PACKAGE BODY.

NOTE
The separation of a package's specification (application programming interface, or API) from its body lets you modify the logic that implements the package without breaking dependencies that rely on the package's API.

All variables, constants, and cursors declared in either a package specification or body outside of a subprogram are considered *global*. Unlike local variables, constants, and cursors declared within specific procedures and functions, global constructs are available to all package procedures and functions and have a state that persists independent of any particular package subprogram on a per-session basis. So that others can readily understand your code, use the convention of declaring global package variables (and other global package constructs) with the prefix g_.

EXERCISE 4.20: Declaring and Using a Package

Enter the statements in this exercise to create a very simple package called partMgmt, which demonstrates some of the functionality available with PL/SQL packages. First, create the package specification:

```
CREATE OR REPLACE PACKAGE partMgmt IS
-- Public subprograms
 PROCEDURE insertPart (p_partRecord IN parts%ROWTYPE);
 PROCEDURE updatePart (p_partRecord IN parts%ROWTYPE);
 PROCEDURE deletePart (p_partId IN INTEGER);
 PROCEDURE printPartsProcessed;
END partMgmt;
/
```

Next, create the package body by using the following statement. Make sure to individually enter and execute the CREATE PACKAGE and CREATE PACKAGE BODY statements using the SQL Commands Input pane, as it does not permit you to run more than one statement at a time.

```
CREATE OR REPLACE PACKAGE BODY partMgmt AS
-- Private global variable
 g_rowsProcessed INTEGER := 0;

-- Public subprograms
 PROCEDURE insertPart (p_partRecord IN parts%ROWTYPE) IS
 BEGIN
  INSERT INTO parts
   (id, description, unitprice, onhand, reorder)
   VALUES (p_partRecord.id, p_partRecord.description,
    p_partRecord.unitprice, p_partRecord.onhand,
    p_partRecord.reorder);
  g_rowsProcessed := g_rowsProcessed + 1;
 END insertPart;

 PROCEDURE updatePart (p_partRecord IN parts%ROWTYPE) IS
 BEGIN
  UPDATE parts
    SET description = p_partRecord.description,
        unitprice = p_partRecord.unitprice,
        onhand = p_partRecord.onhand,
        reorder = p_partRecord.reorder
   WHERE id = p_partRecord.id;
  g_rowsProcessed := g_rowsProcessed + 1;
 END updatePart;

 PROCEDURE deletePart (p_partId IN INTEGER) IS
 BEGIN
  DELETE FROM parts
   WHERE id = p_partId;
  g_rowsProcessed := g_rowsProcessed + 1;
 END deletePart;
```

```
PROCEDURE printPartsProcessed IS
BEGIN
 DBMS_OUTPUT.PUT_LINE(
  'Parts processed this session: ' || g_rowsProcessed);
END printPartsProcessed;

END partMgmt;
/
```

Now, enter the following anonymous PL/SQL block, which uses the insertPart procedure of the partMgmt package to insert a new part in the PARTS table:

```
DECLARE
 l_newPart parts%ROWTYPE;
BEGIN
 l_newPart.id := 6;
 l_newPart.description := 'Mouse';
 l_newPart.unitprice := 49;
 l_newPart.onhand := 1200;
 l_newPart.reorder := 500;

 partMgmt.insertPart(l_newPart);
END;
/
```

Notice that when you reference a package object (for example, a global variable or subprogram), you must use dot notation to qualify the package object with its package name. Now, enter the following anonymous PL/SQL block to update the new part's ONHAND quantity using the updatePart procedure in the partMgmt package:

```
DECLARE
 l_aPart parts%ROWTYPE;
BEGIN
 SELECT * INTO l_aPart FROM parts
  WHERE id = 6;
 l_aPart.onhand := 1123;

 partMgmt.updatePart(l_aPart);
END;
/
```

Now, enter the following anonymous PL/SQL block to execute the deletePart procedure of the partMgmt package to delete the newest part:

```
BEGIN
 partMgmt.deletePart(6);
END;
/
```

TIP
The SQL*Plus command EXECUTE, which is not supported by the SQL Commands interface, is another way of executing PL/SQL subprograms. The EXECUTE command is equivalent to surrounding a procedure call with the BEGIN and END keywords that delimit the start and end of an anonymous PL/SQL block. When calling a function, you have to provide a variable to accept the return value from the function. See the SQL*Plus User's Guide and Reference *for more information and examples of using the SQL*Plus commands, but do not try to use them in the SQL Commands page, because most are not supported.*

Finally, enter the following anonymous PL/SQL block to output the number of rows in the PARTS table processed by the current session using the partMgmt package:

```
BEGIN
  partMgmt.printPartsProcessed;
END;
/
```

The program output is as follows:

```
Parts processed this session: 3

PL/SQL procedure successfully completed.
```

The printPartsProcessed procedure demonstrates that the rowsProcessed global variable retains its state, independent of calls to individual package subprograms.

NOTE
If the previous results show that the number of parts processed in your session is 0, then you forgot to disable the Autocommit option of the SQL Commands page, as instructed in Exercise 4.1. When Autocommit is enabled, the SQL Commands page does not maintain session state among transactions.

Prebuilt Utility Packages
Oracle includes several prebuilt utility packages that provide useful tools for application building. Table 4-4 lists a subset of the prebuilt packages available with Oracle.

Package Name	Description
DBMS_ALERT	Procedures and functions that allow applications to name and signal alert conditions without polling
DBMS_AQ DBMS_AQADM	Procedures and functions to queue the execution of transactions and administer queuing mechanisms
DBMS_CRYPTO	Procedures and functions to encrypt and decrypt data on disk when security is a concern
DBMS_DESCRIBE	Procedures that describe the API for stored procedures and functions
DBMS_LOB	Procedures and functions to manipulate BLOBs, CLOBs, NCLOBs, and BFILEs
DBMS_LOCK	Procedures and functions that allow applications to coordinate access to shared resources
DBMS_METADATA	Procedures and functions to retrieve metadata about schema objects from a database's data dictionary as XML or SQL DDL
DBMS_OUTPUT	Procedures and functions that allow a PL/SQL program to generate terminal output
DBMS_PIPE	Procedures and functions that allow database sessions to communicate using pipes (communication channels)
DBMS_RANDOM	Procedures and functions to generate random numbers and strings for applications
DBMS_ROWID	Procedures and functions that allow applications to easily interpret a base-64 character external ROWID
DBMS_SCHEDULER	Procedures and functions to schedule jobs
DBMS_SESSION	Procedures and functions to control an application user's session
DBMS_SPACE	Procedures and functions for analyzing storage space usage and estimating space requirements
DBMS_STATS	Procedures and functions for maintaining statistics that help optimize SQL statement execution

TABLE 4-4. *Some of the Many Prebuilt Packages Available with Oracle*

Package Name	Description
DBMS_TRANSACTION	Procedures to perform a limited amount of transaction control
UTL_FILE	Procedures and functions to read and write text files to the server's file system
UTL_HTTP	Procedures and functions to access data via the Hypertext Transfer Protocol (HTTP)
UTL_SMTP	Procedures and functions to send e-mail via the Simple Mail Transfer Protocol (SMTP)

TABLE 4-4. *Some of the Many Prebuilt Packages Available with Oracle* (continued)

NOTE
See the Oracle PL/SQL Packages and Types Reference *for complete information about the APIs for all prebuilt packages and examples of their use.*

Database Triggers

A *database trigger* is a stored procedure that *fires* (executes) when an event happens. The most basic type of trigger that you can use is a *DML trigger* that is associated with a specific table; when applications target the table with a SQL DML statement that meets the trigger's execution conditions, Oracle automatically fires the trigger to perform work. You use triggers to customize Oracle's reaction to application events.

NOTE
Oracle also supports triggers that fire based on database- and schema-level events. See the Oracle Database SQL Reference *for more information about these types of triggers.*

To create a DML trigger, you use the SQL command *CREATE TRIGGER*. The simplified syntax (not complete) for the CREATE TRIGGER command is as follows:

```
CREATE [OR REPLACE] TRIGGER trigger
  {BEFORE|AFTER}
  {DELETE|INSERT|UPDATE [OF column [,column] ... ]}
  [OR {DELETE|INSERT|UPDATE [OF column [,column] ... ]} ] ...
```

```
   ON table }
FOR EACH ROW [WHEN condition] ]
... PL/SQL block ...
END [trigger]
```

A DML trigger definition includes the following unique parts:

■ A trigger's definition includes a list of *trigger statements*, including INSERT, UPDATE, and/or DELETE, that fire the trigger. A trigger is associated with one, and only one, table.

■ A trigger can be set to fire before or after the trigger statement to provide specific application logic.

■ A trigger's definition indicates whether the trigger is a statement trigger or a row trigger. A *statement trigger* fires only once, no matter how many rows the trigger statement affects.

EXERCISE 4.21: Creating and Using Database Triggers

Enter the following CREATE TRIGGER statement to create a DML trigger that automatically logs some basic information about the DML changes made to the PARTS table. The logPartChanges trigger is an after-statement trigger that fires once after the triggering statement, no matter how many rows the trigger statement affects.

```
CREATE OR REPLACE TRIGGER logPartChanges
AFTER INSERT OR UPDATE OR DELETE ON parts
DECLARE
 l_statementType CHAR(1);
BEGIN
 IF INSERTING THEN
  l_statementType := 'I';
 ELSIF UPDATING THEN
  l_statementType := 'U';
 ELSE
  l_statementType := 'D';
 END IF;
 INSERT INTO partsLog
  VALUES (SYSDATE, l_statementType, USER);
END logPartChanges;
/
```

Notice in the logPartChanges trigger that when a trigger allows different types of statements to fire the trigger, the *INSERTING, UPDATING,* and *DELETING predicates* allow conditional statements to identify the type of statement that actually fired the trigger.

Now create the logDetailedPartChanges trigger, which is an after-row trigger that logs more detailed information about DML modifications that target the PARTS table. A row trigger fires once for every row affected by the triggering statement.

```
CREATE OR REPLACE TRIGGER logDetailedPartChanges
AFTER INSERT OR UPDATE OR DELETE ON parts
FOR EACH ROW
BEGIN
  INSERT INTO detailedpartslog
   (changedate, userid,
    newid, newdescription, newunitprice, newonhand, newreorder,
    oldid, olddescription, oldunitprice, oldonhand, oldreorder)
   VALUES (SYSDATE, USER,
    :new.id, :new.description, :new.unitprice,
    :new.onhand, :new.reorder,
    :old.id, :old.description, :old.unitprice,
    :old.onhand, :old.reorder
    );
END logDetailedPartChanges;
/
```

NOTE
Optionally, a row trigger can include a trigger restriction—a Boolean condition that determines when to fire the trigger.

Notice in the logDetailedPartChanges trigger that *:new* and *:old correlation values* allow a row trigger to access new and old field values of the current row. When a trigger statement is an INSERT statement, all old field values are null. Similarly, when a trigger statement is a DELETE statement, all new field values are null.

Finally, test out your new triggers and see what they actually do. Enter the following SQL statements, which insert, update, and delete rows in the PARTS table, and then query the PARTSLOG and DETAILEDPARTSLOG tables:

```
INSERT INTO parts
  (id, description, unitprice, onhand, reorder)
  VALUES (6, 'Mouse', 49, 1200, 500);

UPDATE parts
 SET onhand = onhand - 10;

DELETE FROM parts
  WHERE id = 6;

SELECT * FROM partsLog;

SELECT newid, newonhand, oldid, oldonhand FROM detailedpartslog;
```

The textual representation of the result sets for the queries should be similar to the following:

```
CHANGEDATE C USERID
---------- - ----------
03-DEC-05  I ANONYMOUS
03-DEC-05  U ANONYMOUS
03-DEC-05  D ANONYMOUS


    NEWID NEWONHAND     OLDID OLDONHAND
--------- --------- --------- ---------
        6      1200
        1       267         1       277
        2       133         2       143
        3      7621         3      7631
        4      5893         4      5903
        5       480         5       490
        6      1190         6      1200
                            6      1190
```

An important point to understand about database triggers is that DML triggers execute within the context of the current transaction. Therefore, if you were to roll back the current transaction, you would get the "no rows selected" message when you subsequently queried the PARTSLOG and DETAILEDPARTSLOG tables. Try it for yourself.

Chapter Summary

This chapter has provided you with a broad overview of the extended capabilities that PL/SQL offers for creating powerful database access programs. You've learned about the basics of the language itself, as well as how to create PL/SQL programs using stored procedures, functions, packages, and database triggers. And you've also gained some valuable experience using the SQL Commands page of Oracle Application Express and seen how it differs slightly from SQL*Plus.

CHAPTER
5

Build a Basic
Relational Schema

very database application is built upon a set of related database objects that store the application's data and allow the application to function. This chapter introduces Oracle database objects, such as tables, and discusses the logical concepts of database objects. Discussions of data storage (storage parameters, partitioning, and so on) will come in subsequent chapters of this book. This chapter's topics include the following:

■ Schemas

■ Tables

■ Integrity constraints

■ Views

■ Sequences

■ Synonyms

■ Indexes

Chapter Prerequisites

To practice the hands-on exercises in this chapter, you need to start SQL*Plus as instructed in Exercise 2.11 and run the following command script:

```
location\handsonxe\sql\chap05.sql
```

where *location* is the file directory where you expanded the support archive that accompanies this book. For example, after starting SQL*Plus, you can run this chapter's SQL command script using the SQL*Plus command @, as in the following example (assuming that your chap05.sql file is in C:\temp\handsonxe\sql):

```
SQL> @C:\temp\handsonxe\sql\chap05.sql;
```

Once you reply to all of the prompts and the script completes successfully, *leave the current SQL*Plus session open*—you'll need it later on in several of this chapter's exercises.

Schemas

It is easier to solve most problems when you are organized and have a well-designed plan to achieve your goal. If you are unorganized, you will most certainly realize your goals less efficiently, if at all. Designing an information management system that uses Oracle XE is certainly no different.

Databases organize related objects within a database *schema*. For example, it's typical to organize within a single database schema all of the tables and other database objects necessary to support an application. This way, it's clear that the purpose of a certain table or other database object is to support the corresponding application system. Figure 5-1 illustrates the idea of an application schema.

Schemas, an Entirely Logical Concept

It's important to understand that schemas do not *physically* organize the storage of objects. Rather, schemas *logically* organize related database objects. In other words, the logical organization of database objects within schemas is purely for the benefit of organization and has absolutely nothing to do with the physical storage of database objects.

The logical organization that schemas offer can have practical benefits. For example, consider a database with two schemas, S1 and S2. Each schema can have a table called T1. Even though the two tables share the same name, they are uniquely identifiable because they are within different database schemas. Using standard dot notation, the complete names for the different tables would be S1.T1 and S2.T1.

If the idea of logical versus physical organization is confusing to you, consider how operating systems organize files on disk. The layout of folders and files in a graphical file management utility, such as Microsoft Windows Explorer, does not necessarily correspond to the physical location of the folders and files on a particular disk drive.

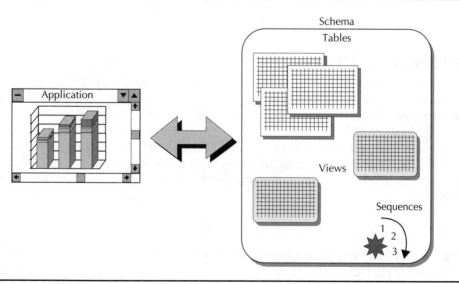

FIGURE 5-1.   *A schema is a logical organization of related database objects.*

File folders represent the logical organization of operating system files. The underlying operating system decides where to physically store the blocks for each operating system file, independent of the logical organization of encompassing folders.

Subsequent chapters of this book explain more about how Oracle can physically organize the storage of database objects using physical storage structures.

The Correlation of Schemas and Database User Accounts

With Oracle, the concept of a database schema is directly tied to the concept of a database user. That is, a schema in an Oracle database has a one-to-one correspondence with a user account such that a user and the associated schema have the same name. As a result, people who work with Oracle often blur the distinction between users and schemas, commonly saying things like "the user SCOTT owns the EMP and DEPT tables" rather than "the schema SCOTT contains the EMP and DEPT tables." These two statements are more or less equivalent in the context of an Oracle database.

NOTE
The scripts that you executed to support the practice exercises of this chapter and previous chapters create new database users/schemas (HANDSONXE03, HANDSONXE04, and so on) that contain similar sets of tables and other database objects (PARTS, CUSTOMERS, and so on).

Database Tables

Tables are the basic data structure in any relational database. A *table* is nothing more than an organized collection of *records*, or *rows*, that all have the same *attributes*, or *columns*. Figure 5-2 illustrates a typical CUSTOMERS table in a relational database.

Each customer record in the example CUSTOMERS table has the same attributes, including an ID, a company name, a last name, a first name, and so on.

When you create tables, the two primary things that you must consider are the following:

- The table's columns, which describe the table's structure

- The table's integrity constraints, which describe the data that is acceptable within the table

The following sections explain more about columns and integrity constraints.

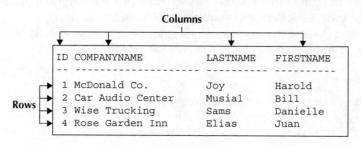

FIGURE 5-2.   *A table is a set of records with the same attributes.*

Columns and Datatypes

When you create a table for an Oracle database, you establish the structure of the table by identifying the columns that correspond to the table's attributes. Furthermore, every column in a table has a *datatype*, which describes the basic type of data that is acceptable in the column, much like when you declare the datatype of a variable in a PL/SQL program. For example, the ID column in the CUSTOMERS table uses the basic Oracle datatype NUMBER because the column stores ID numbers.

Oracle supports many fundamental datatypes that you can use when creating a relational database table and its columns, including CHAR, VARCHAR2, NUMBER, BINARY_FLOAT, BINARY_DOUBLE, DATE, TIMESTAMP, CLOB, BLOB, BFILE, and many more. The following sections explain some of the more commonly used Oracle datatypes.

CHAR and VARCHAR2: Oracle's Character Datatypes

The Oracle datatypes CHAR and VARCHAR2 are the datatypes most commonly used for columns that store character strings. The Oracle datatype *CHAR* is appropriate for columns that store fixed-length character strings, such as two-letter U.S. state codes. Alternatively, the Oracle datatype *VARCHAR2* is useful for columns that store variable-length character strings, such as names and addresses. The primary difference between these character datatypes relates to how Oracle stores strings shorter than the maximum length of a column:

- When a string in a CHAR column is less than the column's size, Oracle pads (appends) the end of the string with blank spaces to create a string that matches the column's size.

- When a string in a VARCHAR2 column is less than the column's maximum size, Oracle stores only the string and does not pad the string with blanks.

Thus, when the strings in a column vary in length, Oracle can store them more efficiently in a VARCHAR2 column than in a CHAR column. In general, use VARCHAR2 for a column that contains small strings that vary in size; do not use CHAR unless all strings in the column have the same length.

NOTE
CHAR stores fixed-length character strings up to 2000 bytes; if you do not specify a size, the default is 1. VARCHAR2 stores variable-length character strings up to 4000 bytes; you must specify a size.

NUMBER, BINARY_FLOAT, and BINARY_DOUBLE: Oracle's Numeric Datatypes

Oracle's NUMBER datatype is useful for columns that store numbers. You can optionally specify a precision and scale to constrain the acceptable type of numbers in a NUMBER column. *Precision* refers to the total number of digits in a number, and *scale* refers to the number of digits to the right of the decimal place. If you do not specify a precision for a NUMBER column, the default is the maximum of 38. If you specify NUMBER with a precision but without a scale, the default scale is 0.

Do not specify a precision or scale (just NUMBER) for columns in which you want to store floating-point numbers (numbers without a fixed number of digits before and after the decimal point, such as 1.2, 11.23, and 1.234) with decimal precision. Optionally, you can use either the BINARY_FLOAT or BINARY_DOUBLE datatype rather than NUMBER to take advantage of more efficient binary precision for floating-point numbers and calculations involving floating-point numbers.

NOTE
The IEEE-compliant BINARY_FLOAT and BINARY_ DOUBLE datatypes provide more efficient binary precision than the native Oracle NUMBER datatype, but at the expense of accuracy; NUMBER can maintain up to 38 digits of precision, whereas BINARY_FLOAT and BINARY_DOUBLE provide 6 and 13 digits of precision, respectively.

DATE and TIMESTAMP: Oracle's Time-Related Datatypes

You can use Oracle's DATE datatype for columns that store time-related information such as dates, including century, year, month, day, hour, minute, and second. If you need to store dates with fractional seconds or dates with information about a time zone, you can use the TIMESTAMP, TIMESTAMP WITH TIME ZONE, or TIMESTAMP WITH LOCAL TIME ZONE datatype.

CLOBs, BLOBs, and More: Oracle's Multimedia Datatypes

Because databases are secure, fast, and safe storage areas for data, they are often employed as data repositories for multimedia applications. To support such content-rich applications, Oracle supports several different *large object (LOB)* datatypes, described in the following list, that can store unstructured information, such as text documents, static images, video, audio, and more.

- **CLOB column** Stores single-byte *character large objects (CLOBs)* such as documents up to 4GB times the database block size (a possible range of 8 terabytes [TB] to 128TB).

- **BLOB column** Stores *binary large objects (BLOBs)* such as graphics, video clips, or sound files up to 4GB times the database block size (a possible range of 8TB to 128TB).

- **BFILE column** Stores file pointers to LOBs managed by file systems external to the database. For example, a BFILE column might be a list of filename references for photos stored on a CD-ROM.

A table can have multiple CLOB, BLOB, and BFILE columns. For efficiency, a table stores only small *locators* (pointers) for the LOBs in a column, rather than the actual large objects themselves. A LOB column typically has storage characteristics independent from those of the encompassing table, making it easier to address the large disk requirements typically associated with LOBs. For example, it's possible to separate the storage of primary table data and related LOBs in different physical locations (for example, disk drives).

SQL automatically supports VARCHAR2 semantics for CLOB data so that it is relatively simple to code applications with simple LOB manipulation tasks. For example, when you execute an INSERT statement that provides a VARCHAR2 literal for a CLOB column, Oracle implicitly converts the VARCHAR2 value into a CLOB value. Likewise, a query can include a CLOB column in its SELECT list, use SQL operators such as =, IN, ALL, etc., and SQL functions such as CONCAT, INITCAP, SUBSTR, REPLACE, etc., that accept VARCHAR2 expressions when working with data from a CLOB column, and indicate WHERE clause conditions that include a CLOB column. APIs such as the supplied PL/SQL package DBMS_LOB also exist that offer more diverse functionality for manipulating LOBs.

NOTE
For backward compatibility, Oracle continues to support older Oracle datatypes designed for large objects, such as LONG and LONG RAW. However, Oracle's newer LOB datatypes have many advantages over the older Oracle large datatypes.

Oracle's National Language Support Character Datatypes

Oracle's *National Language Support (NLS)* features allow databases to store and manipulate character data in many languages. Some languages have character sets that require several bytes for each character. The special Oracle datatypes *NCHAR*, *NVARCHAR2*, and *NCLOB* are datatypes that are counterparts to the CHAR, VARCHAR2, and CLOB datatypes, respectively.

ANSI Datatypes and Others

Oracle also supports the specification of Oracle datatypes using other standard datatypes. For example, Table 5-1 lists the ANSI/ISO standard datatypes that Oracle supports.

Default Column Values

When you declare a column for a table, you can also declare a corresponding *default column value*. Oracle uses the default value of a column when an

ANSI/ISO Datatypes	Corresponding Oracle Datatype
CHARACTER CHAR	CHAR
CHARACTER VARYING CHAR VARYING	VARCHAR2
NATIONAL CHARACTER NATIONAL CHAR NCHAR	NCHAR
NATIONAL CHARACTER VARYING NATIONAL CHAR VARYING NCHAR VARYING	NVARCHAR2
NUMERIC DECIMAL INTEGER INT SMALLINT FLOAT DOUBLE PRECISION REAL	NUMBER

TABLE 5-1. *Oracle Supports the Specification of Oracle Datatypes Using ANSI/ISO Standard Datatypes*

application inserts a new row into the table but omits a value for the column. For example, you might indicate that the default value for the ORDERDATE column of the ORDERS table be the current system time when an application creates a new order.

NOTE
Unless you indicate otherwise, the initial default value for a column is null (an absence of value).

Data Integrity and Integrity Constraints

Data integrity is a fundamental principle of the relational database model. Saying that a database has integrity is another way of saying that the database contains only accurate and acceptable information. For obvious reasons, data integrity is a desirable attribute for a database.

To a small degree, a column's datatype establishes a more limited domain of acceptable values for the column—it limits the type of data that the column can store. For example, a DATE column can contain valid dates and times, but not numbers or character strings. But while simple column datatypes are useful for enforcing a basic level of data integrity, there are typically more complex integrity rules that must be enforced in a relational database. In fact, the relational database model itself outlines several inherent data integrity rules that a *relational database management system (RDBMS)* must uphold. The next few sections describe these common integrity rules and related issues.

Domain Integrity, Nulls, and Complex Domains

Domain integrity defines the domain of acceptable values for a column. For example, you might have a rule that a customer record is not valid unless the customer's state abbreviation code is one of the 50 or so U.S. state codes.

Besides using column datatypes, Oracle supports two types of integrity constraints that allow you to further limit the domain of a column:

- **Not null constraint**   Applied to a column to eliminate the possibility of nulls (absent or unknown values) in the column.

- **Check constraint**   Used to declare a complex domain integrity rule as part of a table. A check constraint commonly contains an explicit list of the acceptable values for a column. For example, M and F in a column that contains gender information; AL, AK, … WY in a column that contains U.S. state codes; and so on.

Entity Integrity, Primary Keys, and Alternate Keys

Entity integrity ensures that every row in a table is uniquely identified by a non-null unique key. As a result, entity integrity eliminates the possibility of duplicate records in the table and makes every row in the table uniquely identifiable.

The primary key of a table ensures its entity integrity. A *primary key* is a column that uniquely identifies each row in a table and is not null. To simplify application coding, well-designed relational databases build a table with a primary key that is nothing more than an arbitrary numeric identifier for rows in the table. For example, a CUSTOMERS table might include an ID column to uniquely identify the customer records within it. This way, even if two customers, say John Smith and his son John Smith (Jr.), have the same name, address, phone number, and so on, they have distinct ID numbers that make them different.

A table's primary key is sometimes a *composite key*; that is, it is composed of more than one column. For example, the primary key in a typical line-item table of an order-entry system might have a composite primary key that consists of the ORDER_ID and ITEM_ID columns. In this example of a composite primary key, many line-item records can have the same line-item ID (1, 2, 3, ...), but no two line-item records can have the same order ID and line-item ID combination (order ID 1, line-item IDs 1, 2, 3, ...; order ID 2, line item-IDs 1, 2, 3, ...; and so on).

Optionally, a table might require secondary levels of entity integrity. *Alternate keys*, also called *unique keys*, are columns or sets of columns that do not contain duplicate values within them. For example, the EMAIL column in the EMPLOYEES table might be made an alternate key to guarantee that all employees have unique e-mail addresses.

Referential Integrity, Foreign Keys, and Referential Actions

Referential integrity, sometimes called *relation integrity*, establishes the relationships among different columns and tables in a database. Referential integrity ensures that each column value in a *foreign key* of a *child* (or *detail*) *table* matches a value in the primary or an alternate key of a related *parent* (or *master*) *table*. For example, a row in the CUSTOMERS (child) table is not valid unless the customer's S_ID field refers to a valid sales representative ID in the SALESREPS (parent) table. When the parent and child tables are the same, this is called *self-referential integrity*. Figure 5-3 illustrates the terminology and concepts related to referential integrity.

Referential Actions   Referential integrity ensures that each value in a foreign key always has a matching parent key value. To guarantee referential integrity, an RDBMS must also be able to address database operations that manipulate parent keys. For example, when a user deletes a sales order, what happens to the dependent line items for that order? *Referential actions* describe what will be done in cases where an application updates or deletes a parent key that has dependent child records (children).

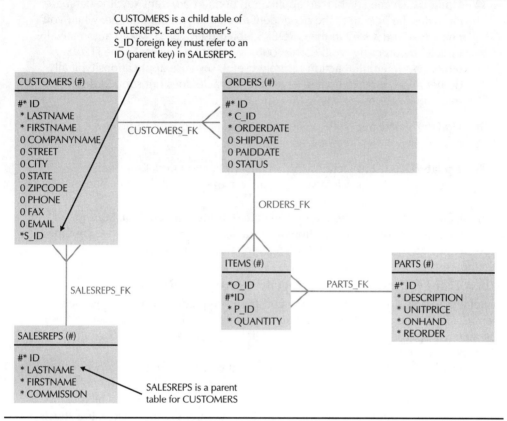

FIGURE 5-3. *Referential integrity describes the relationships among columns and tables in a relational database.*

The relational database model describes several referential actions:

■ **Update/Delete Restrict**   The database does not allow an application to update a parent key or delete a parent row that has one or more dependent child records. For example, you cannot delete a sales order from the ORDERS table if it has associated line items in the ITEMS table.

■ **Delete Cascade**   When an application deletes a row from the parent table, the RDBMS cascades the delete by deleting all dependent records in a child table. For example, when you delete an order from the ORDERS table, the database automatically removes all corresponding line items from the ITEMS table.

■ **Update Cascade**   When an application updates a parent key, the database cascades the update to the dependent foreign keys. For example, when you change an order's ID in the ORDERS table, the RDBMS would automatically update the order ID of all corresponding line-item records in the ITEMS table. This referential action is rarely useful, because applications typically do not allow users to update key values. Oracle does not support this referential action.

■ **Update/Delete Set Null**   When an application updates or deletes a parent key, all dependent keys are set to null.

■ **Update/Delete Set Default**   When an application updates or deletes a parent key, all dependent keys are set to a meaningful default value.

By default, Oracle enforces the update/delete restrict referential actions for all referential integrity constraints. Optionally, Oracle can perform the delete cascade or delete set null referential action for a referential integrity constraint.

When Does Oracle Enforce Integrity Constraint Rules?
By default, Oracle enforces all integrity constraints immediately after an application submits a SQL statement to insert, update, or delete rows in a table. When a statement causes a data integrity violation, Oracle automatically rolls back the effects of the statement.

Optionally, Oracle can delay the enforcement of a *deferrable integrity constraint* until just before the commit of a transaction. When you commit a transaction and the transaction has modified table data such that it does not conform to all integrity constraints, Oracle automatically rolls back the entire transaction (that is, the effects of all statements in the transaction).

Typical database applications should choose to immediately check data integrity as each SQL statement is executed. Deferrable constraints are typically useful for specialized situations such as large data loads that might need to update many tables with lots of data and temporarily violate integrity rules until just before the end of the transaction. See the *Oracle SQL Reference* if you would like more information about configuring and using deferrable constraints.

Now that you have a basic understanding of schemas, tables, columns, datatypes, and integrity constraints, the exercises in the following section explain how to put your newfound knowledge into practice.

Creating Tables and Integrity Constraints
When working with Oracle XE, you can build and manage tables, integrity constraints, and most other types of schema objects by using either of two different approaches:

■ You can use a command-line tool such as SQL*Plus to enter SQL DDL commands such as CREATE TABLE, ALTER TABLE, CREATE VIEW, and so on.

■ You can use the Oracle Application Express Object Browser page point-and-click graphical user interface to simplify the creation of SQL DDL commands that build schema objects.

The exercises in this section expose you to both approaches.

EXERCISE 5.1: Start the Object Browser

To complete this exercise, launch the Database Home Page of Oracle Application Express as explained in Exercise 2.13. Establish a connection using this chapter's practice account, HANDSONXE05, with the password PASSWORD. Once you launch the Database Home Page, click Object Browser to start the Object Browser page, as shown in Figure 5-4.

Notice that the Object Browser page has two panes. The *Object Selection pane* on the left side of the page lists objects of various types contained in the current schema; at this point, your schema has no objects, so the Object Selection pane

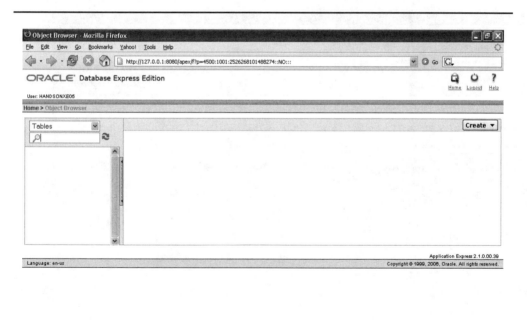

FIGURE 5-4. *Oracle Application Express Object Browser page*

is empty. The *Detail pane* on the right side of the page shows information about the object currently selected in the Object Selection pane. You will learn more about using the Detail pane later on once we have some objects to work with.

NOTE
The top-left corner of the page indicates your current schema (for example, User: HANDSONXE05*).*

EXERCISE 5.2: Create the PARTS Table

To create the familiar PARTS table used in previous chapters with the Object Browser page of Oracle Application Express, click the down arrow of the Create menu in the upper-right corner of the Detail pane, then click Table to display the Create Table wizard. The Columns page of the Create Table wizard lets you indicate the names, datatypes, and not null constraints for the columns in the table. Fill out this page as shown in Figure 5-5.

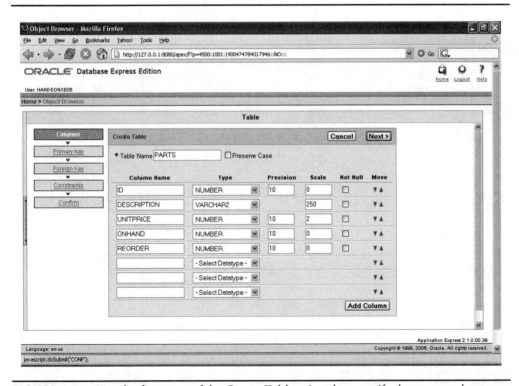

FIGURE 5-5. *Use the first page of the Create Table wizard to specify the names, datatypes, and not null constraints for the columns of a new table.*

Note the following points in Figure 5-5:

■   The ID, ONHAND, and REORDER columns use the NUMBER datatype
    constrained to a precision of 10 and a scale of 0; these columns will be
    able to store integers up to ten significant digits of precision. Because scale
    defaults to 0 for the NUMBER datatype when you specify a precision,
    entering 0 for the scale is not required, but makes your intentions clear.

■   The UNITPRICE column uses the NUMBER datatype constrained to a
    precision of 10 and a scale of 2; this column will be able to hold numbers
    up to ten digits of precision and will round numbers after two digits to the
    right of the decimal place.

■   The DESCRIPTION column uses the VARCHAR2 datatype to accept
    variable-length strings up to 250 bytes in length.

When you are finished, click Next to continue. The Primary Key page of the
Create Table wizard asks you to indicate information about the table's primary key.
Fill out this page as shown in Figure 5-6.
Note the following points in Figure 5-6:

■   You must first indicate whether the table has a primary key and, if so,
    whether you want to automatically generate a primary key value for each
    row that you insert into the table. Subsequent sections of this chapter
    explain some techniques for primary key generation; for the purposes of this
    exercise, select Not Populated.

■   You can specify a name for the primary key constraint; a good convention
    to follow is the name of the table followed by the suffix _PK; for example,
    specify **PARTS_PK** in the Primary Key Constraint Name field.

■   You must select a column (or columns) as the basis for the primary key
    constraint; select ID(NUMBER) (the ID column and its datatype, NUMBER)
    from the Primary Key drop-down list. Once you create the PARTS table,
    every record in the table must have an ID (nulls are implicitly disallowed)
    that is unique from all others.

The next two pages of the Create Table wizard provide interfaces for creating
foreign keys (referential integrity constraints), check constraints, and unique key
(alternate key) constraints. The PARTS table does not require these types of integrity
constraints, so click Confirm (on the left) to skip ahead; subsequent exercises
demonstrate how to use the skipped pages of the Create Table wizard.

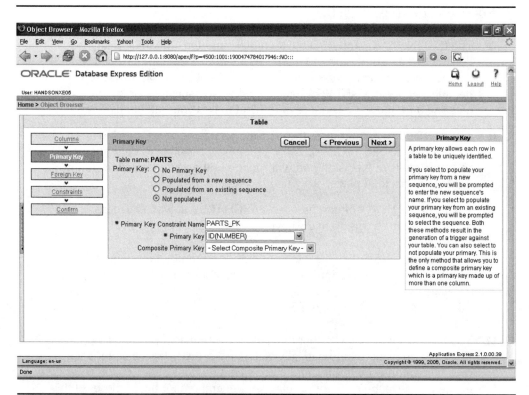

FIGURE 5-6. *Use the second page of the Create Table wizard to specify the table's primary key.*

The Confirm page of the Create Table wizard requests confirmation to create the new table. Before creating the PARTS table, click SQL to display the underlying SQL statement that the wizard will execute to complete your request. The SQL should match the following:

```
CREATE table "PARTS" (
    "ID"          NUMBER(10,0),
    "DESCRIPTION" VARCHAR2(250),
    "UNITPRICE"   NUMBER(10,2),
    "ONHAND"      NUMBER(10,0),
    "REORDER"     NUMBER(10,0),
    constraint    "PARTS_PK" primary key ("ID")
)
/
```

Notice that, in the context of this lesson, the Create Table wizard of the Object Browser page is nothing more than a tool that simplifies the creation of a CREATE TABLE statement. This first example of a CREATE TABLE statement illustrates that after specifying a unique name for the new table, you can indicate a comma-separated list of column specifications that describes the structure of the table. Each column specification includes a column name and datatype specification. Also notice that the CREATE TABLE command supports the declaration of integrity constraints such as a primary key. For complete information about the SQL command CREATE TABLE, refer to the *Oracle SQL Reference*.

To create the HANDSONXE05.PARTS table, click Create on the final page of the Create Table wizard. Your current schema, HANDSONXE05, now has a new table, PARTS, that you can query, insert records into, and so on. The new table's name should appear in the list of objects in the Object Selection pane and details about the new table should appear in the Detail pane, as shown in Figure 5-7.

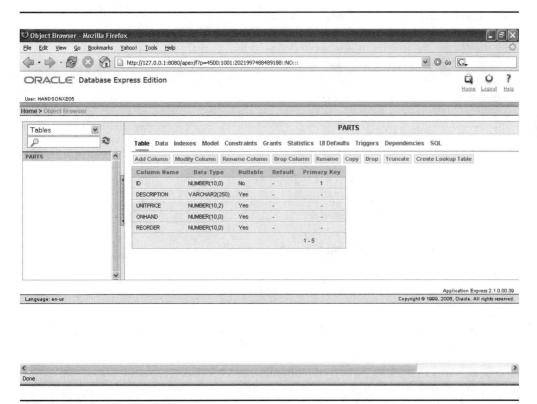

FIGURE 5-7.   *Use the Object Selection and Detail panes of the Object Browser to create, browse, and modify database objects.*

Now that an object is available, note the following about each pane of the Object Browser page:

- The Object Selection pane on the left side of the page lists objects of various types contained in the current schema. You can control what objects to focus on by using the Object drop-down list and the object search field at the top of the pane.

- The Detail pane on the right side of the page shows information about the object currently selected in the Object Selection pane. Once you select an object, you can click the tabs along the top edge of the Detail pane (for example, Table, Data, Indexes) to view various types of information about the current object. Click the buttons just underneath the sequence of tabs to edit the selected object in a particular way (for example, Add Column, Modify Column, Rename Column).

EXERCISE 5.3: Create the CUSTOMERS Table

Now let's create a somewhat incomplete version of the familiar CUSTOMERS table with the Create Table wizard. Please understand that you are going to purposely make some omissions and mistakes while creating the CUSTOMERS table in this exercise so that you can learn how to modify the table later on. Complete the following steps with the Object Browser:

1. Click Create | Table.

NOTE
Sometimes, the Create button may be out of view and require that you use the horizontal scroll bar of your browser to make it accessible.

2. Specify **CUSTOMERS** in the Table Name field.

3. While still on the Columns page, enter the following column specifications (Column Name, Type, etc.); click Add Column to add more columns to the display, when necessary:

   - Specify the **ID** column using the NUMBER datatype constrained to a precision of **10** and a scale of **0**.

   - Specify the **LASTNAME** column using the VARCHAR2 datatype with a size of **100**.

   - Specify the **FIRSTNAME** column using the VARCHAR2 datatype with a size of **50**.

- Specify the **COMPANYNAME** column using the VARCHAR2 datatype with a size of **100**.

- Specify the **STREET** column using the VARCHAR2 datatype with a size of **100**.

- Specify the **CITY** column using the VARCHAR2 datatype with a size of **100**.

- Specify the **STATE** column using the VARCHAR2 datatype with a size of **50**.

- Specify the **ZIPCODE** column using the NUMBER datatype constrained to a precision of **10** and a scale of **0**.

- Specify the **PHONE** and **FAX** columns using the VARCHAR2 datatype with a size of **30**.

- Specify the **EMAIL** column using the VARCHAR2 datatype with a size of **100**.

- The following columns should be marked Not Null: LASTNAME, FIRSTNAME, and PHONE.

4. Click Confirm (on the left) to continue.

5. Click SQL and review the CREATE TABLE statement that the wizard builds (shown next). In particular, notice that when you specify a column in a CREATE TABLE statement, you can declare it as NOT NULL to declare a not null integrity constraint for the column.

```
CREATE table "CUSTOMERS" (
    "ID"            NUMBER(10,0),
    "LASTNAME"      VARCHAR2(100) NOT NULL,
    "FIRSTNAME"     VARCHAR2(50) NOT NULL,
    "COMPANYNAME"   VARCHAR2(100),
    "STREET"        VARCHAR2(100),
    "CITY"          VARCHAR2(100),
    "STATE"         VARCHAR2(50),
    "ZIPCODE"       NUMBER(10,0),
    "PHONE"         VARCHAR2(30) NOT NULL,
    "FAX"           VARCHAR2(30),
    "EMAIL"         VARCHAR2(100)
)
/
```

6. Click Create to create the HANDSONXE05.CUSTOMERS table.

Choosing Dataytpes Wisely

When you are designing the tables in a database schema, sometimes it can be tricky to choose the correct datatype for a column. For example, let's take a look at what happens after you declare the ZIPCODE column in the CUSTOMERS table with the

NUMBER datatype as in Exercise 5.2. Consider what will happen when you insert a customer record with the ZIPCODE 01003—Oracle is going to store this number as 1003, certainly not what you intended. You also would not be able to insert a Canadian postal code such as J7N1H3. And consider what would happen if you were to insert a customer record with a ZIP code and an extension such as 91222-0299—Oracle would evaluate this numeric expression and store the resulting number 90923. These simple examples illustrate that the selection of a column's datatype is certainly an important consideration, and is not to be taken lightly. Exercise 5.4 teaches you how to change the datatype of the ZIPCODE column to store postal codes correctly.

EXERCISE 5.4: Modify a Column's Datatype

After you create a table, you can modify it in many different ways by using the Object Browser page of Oracle Application Express. Complete the following steps of this exercise to learn how to change the datatype of the ZIPCODE column from NUMBER to VARCHAR2:

1. Select CUSTOMERS in the Object Selection pane.

2. Click Table in the Detail pane.

3. Click Modify Column in the Detail pane.

4. Complete the following steps to modify the ZIPCODE column's datatype from NUMBER(10,0) to VARCHAR2(50):

   ■ Select ZIPCODE(NUMBER) in the Column list.

   ■ Select VARCHAR2 in the Datatype list.

   ■ Specify **50** in the Length field.

   ■ Select Null (do not require a value) in the Nullable list.

5. Click Next.

6. Click SQL and review the SQL statement that the Object Browser page builds. Notice that to modify a column's datatype, you can use the MODIFY clause of the SQL command ALTER TABLE, as shown next. For complete information about the ALTER TABLE command, refer to the *Oracle SQL Reference*.

```
alter table "CUSTOMERS" modify
("ZIPCODE" VARCHAR2(50) )
/
```

7. Click Finish.

NOTE
*Keep in mind that you can modify a column's
datatype specification as long as all of the current
data in the column conforms to the change you want
to make. For example, you can always increase the
size of a CHAR or VARCHAR2 column, but you
cannot reduce the column's size if a string in the
column is longer than the new size of the column.*

EXERCISE 5.5: Add a Primary Key to a Table

The Object Browser page makes it easy to add integrity constraints to a table. For example, complete the following steps to add a primary key to the CUSTOMERS table:

1. Select CUSTOMERS in the Object Selection pane.

2. Click Constraints in the Detail pane. Notice the list of not null constraints already in place for the CUSTOMERS table. The next exercise explains more about the names of constraints.

3. Click Create.

4. Complete the following steps to add a primary key constraint:

   ■ Specify **CUSTOMERS_PK** in the Constraint Name field.

   ■ Select Primary Key in the Constraint Type field.

   ■ Select ID(NUMBER) in the Primary Key Column 1 list.

5. Click Next.

6. Click SQL and review the SQL statement that the Object Browser page builds (shown next). Notice that to add a constraint to a table, you can use the ADD CONSTRAINT clause of the SQL command ALTER TABLE.

```
alter table "CUSTOMERS" add constraint
"CUSTOMERS_PK" primary key ("ID")
/
```

7. Click Finish. Observe the new constraint you just added in the Detail pane.

8. Click Table in the Detail pane. Observe in the Detail pane of the Object Browser page that all columns that comprise a primary key are not "Nullable"; this is a reminder of the fact that the primary key for every row in a table must be unique and not null.

EXERCISE 5.6: Add a Composite Unique Key to a Table

Complete the following steps to add a composite unique key to the CUSTOMERS table:

1. Select CUSTOMERS in the Object Selection pane.

2. Click Constraints in the Detail pane.

3. Click Create.

4. Complete the following steps to add a unique constraint:

   ■ Specify **CUSTOMERS_UK1** in the Constraint Name field.

   ■ Select Unique in the Constraint Type field.

   ■ Select LASTNAME(VARCHAR2) in the Unique column 1 list.

   ■ Select FIRSTNAME(VARCHAR2) in the Unique column 2 list.

5. Click Next.

6. Click SQL and review the SQL statement that the Object Browser page builds (shown next). Notice that you can add a unique constraint to a table by using the ADD CONSTRAINT clause of the SQL command ALTER TABLE.

```
alter table "CUSTOMERS" add constraint
"CUSTOMERS_UK1" unique ("LASTNAME","FIRSTNAME")
/
```

7. Click Finish.

Once you modify the CUSTOMERS table and return to the Object Browser page, take a close look at the names of the constraints for the CUSTOMERS table: all of the constraints that you explicitly named are readily identifiable (CUSTOMERS_PK, CUSTOMERS_UK1), but there are also a number of constraints that begin with the prefix SYS_C. These constraints correspond to the not null constraints associated with the table's LASTNAME, FIRSTNAME, and PHONE columns. Although the SQL commands CREATE TABLE and ALTER TABLE provide a way for you to explicitly name not null constraints, the Object Browser interfaces of Oracle Application Express do not expose this functionality. When you do not indicate a name for a constraint, Oracle generates a unique name for a constraint starting with the aforementioned prefix.

EXERCISE 5.7: Add a Not Null Constraint to a Table

Complete the following steps to prevent nulls in the DESCRIPTION column of the PARTS table:

1. Select PARTS in the Object Selection pane.

2. Click Table in the Detail pane.

3. Click Modify Column.

4. Complete the following steps to add a not null constraint:

   ■ Select DESCRIPTION(VARCHAR2) in the Column List field.

   ■ Select NOT NULL (require a value) in the Nullable list.

   ■ Notice that there is no way to name the not null constraint.

   ■ Do not modify any other items on the page.

5. Click Next.

6. Click SQL and review the ALTER TABLE statement that the Object Browser page builds:

```
alter table "PARTS" modify
("DESCRIPTION" NUMBER(10,0) NOT NULL)
/
```

7. Click Finish.

For your information, if you were using SQL*Plus and an ALTER TABLE statement to add a not null constraint to a table, you could name the not null constraint by adding the CONSTRAINT parameter to the previously displayed command:

```
alter table "PARTS" modify
("DESCRIPTION" NUMBER(10,0) CONSTRAINT description_nn NOT NULL)
/
```

This is an example of selected shortcomings of the Object Browser interface that you'll need to work around with SQL commands.

EXERCISE 5.8: Create the SALESREPS Table

To continue, create the SALESREPS table for the HANDSONXE05 schema as follows:

1. Click Create | Table.

2. Specify **SALESREPS** in the Table Name field.

3. While still on the Columns page, enter the following column specifications (Column Name, Type, etc.):

   ■ Specify the **ID** column using the NUMBER datatype constrained to a precision of **10** and a scale of **0**.

   ■ Specify the **LASTNAME** column using the VARCHAR2 datatype with a size of **100**.

   ■ Specify the **FIRSTNAME** column using the VARCHAR2 datatype with a size of **50**.

   ■ Specify the **COMMISSION** column using the NUMBER datatype constrained to a precision of **10** and no scale (leave scale blank).

   ■ Mark the LASTNAME column as Not Null.

4. Click Next or Primary Key (on the left) to continue.

5. On the Primary Key page, complete the following steps:

   ■ Select Not populated.

   ■ Specify **SALESREPS_PK** in the Primary Key Constraint Name field.

   ■ Select ID(NUMBER) in the Primary Key list.

6. Click Confirm to continue.

7. Click SQL and review the CREATE TABLE statement that the wizard builds:

```
CREATE table "SALESREPS" (
    "ID"         NUMBER(10,0),
    "LASTNAME"   VARCHAR2(100) NOT NULL,
    "FIRSTNAME"  VARCHAR2(50),
    "COMMISSION" NUMBER(10),
    constraint  "SALESREPS_PK" primary key ("ID")
)
/
```

8. Click Create to create the HANDSONXE05.SALESREPS table.

EXERCISE 5.9: Create the ORDERS Table

In this exercise, you are going to create the ORDERS table for the HANDSONXE05 schema. This table has a referential integrity constraint (foreign key) that refers to the primary key of the CUSTOMERS table and a check constraint.

1. Click Create | Table.

2. Specify **ORDERS** in the Table Name field.

3. While still on the Columns page, enter the following column specifications (Column Name, Type, etc.):

- Specify the **ID** and **C_ID** columns using the NUMBER datatype constrained to a precision of **10** and a scale of **0**.

- Specify the **ORDERDATE**, **SHIPDATE**, and **PAIDDATE** columns using the DATE datatype.

- Specify the **STATUS** column using the CHAR datatype with a size of **1**.

- Mark the C_ID and ORDERDATE columns as Not Null.

4. Click Next or Primary Key to continue.

5. On the Primary Key page, complete the following steps:

- Select Not populated.

- Specify **ORDERS_PK** in the Primary Key Constraint Name field.

- Select ID(NUMBER) in the Primary Key list.

6. Click Next or Foreign Key to continue.

7. On the Foreign Keys page, complete the following steps to add a foreign key for the C_ID column of the ORDERS table that refers to the ID column of the CUSTOMERS table. The goals are to ensure that the C_ID field of each record in the ORDERS table refers to an ID in the CUSTOMERS table, and to prevent the deletion of parent records in the CUSTOMERS table that have dependent rows (children) in the ORDERS table.

- Specify **ORDERS_FK1** in the Name field.

- To enforce the default delete restrict referential action for the new referential integrity constraint, select Disallow Delete.

- To indicate the column that makes up the foreign key in the new ORDERS table, select the C_ID column in the Select Key Column(s) field and then click the adjacent right-arrow button to move the selected column to the Key Column(s) field.

- To indicate the referenced column in the parent CUSTOMERS table, click the button to the right of the References Table field, click CUSTOMERS from the ensuing table pop-up list, select the ID column in the Select Reference Column(s) field and then click the adjacent right-arrow button to move the selected column to the Reference Column(s) field. If a list of columns does not automatically appear for the table that you specify in the References Table field, click the down arrow next to the field.

- Click Add.

- Confirm the declaration of the new foreign key in the list of foreign keys at the top of the page. If you mistakenly declare a constraint, use the corresponding Delete button (a red X) to delete the constraint declaration. Then try creating the constraint again using the items in the lower portion of the page.

8. Click Next or Constraints to continue.

9. On the Constraints page, complete the following steps to add a check constraint that limits the domain of the STATUS column to the status code characters B and F:

   - Specify **ORDERS_CK1** in the Name field.

   - Select Check.

   - Enter the following condition in the entry field: **status IN ('F','B')**.

   - Click Add.

   - Confirm the declaration of the new check constraint at the top of the page.

10. Click Finish or Confirm to continue.

11. Click SQL and review the SQL statements that the wizard builds (shown next). Notice that you can add a foreign key or check constraint to a table by using the ADD CONSTRAINT clause of the SQL command ALTER TABLE.

```
CREATE table "ORDERS" (
    "ID"          NUMBER(10,0),
    "C_ID"        NUMBER(10,0) NOT NULL,
    "ORDERDATE"   DATE NOT NULL,
    "SHIPDATE"    DATE,
    "PAIDDATE"    DATE,
    "STATUS"      CHAR(1),
    constraint   "ORDERS_PK" primary key ("ID")
)
/

ALTER TABLE "ORDERS" ADD CONSTRAINT "ORDERS_FK1"
FOREIGN KEY ("C_ID")
REFERENCES "CUSTOMERS" ("ID")

/
alter table "ORDERS" add
constraint ORDERS_CK1
check (status IN ('F','B'))
/
```

12. Click Create to create the HANDSONXE05.ORDERS table.

Once you create the ORDERS table, notice in the Table tab of the Design pane that the STATUS column can contain nulls (Nullable is Yes). Why? This is a good place to point out some important facts that newcomers must clearly understand when designing tables with integrity constraints:

■ Constraints other than primary key and not null constraints do not prohibit nulls. To prohibit nulls from unique keys, foreign keys, and the underlying columns of a check constraint, you must explicitly declare not null constraints for the underlying columns.

■ When you allow nulls in unique keys, foreign keys, or the underlying columns of a check constraint, and the condition of the constraint evaluates to TRUE or UNKNOWN for a given row, the row complies with the constraint.

■ When you prohibit nulls in unique keys, foreign keys, or the underlying columns of a check constraint, a given row complies with the constraint only when the condition of the constraint evaluates to TRUE for the row.

Always keep these subtle points about nulls and integrity constraints in mind when designing tables to ensure that you properly enforce the business rules for your system.

EXERCISE 5.10: Create the ITEMS Table

In this exercise, you are going to create the ITEMS table for the HANDSONXE05 schema. This table has referential integrity constraints that refer to the primary keys of the ORDERS and PARTS tables; one foreign key uses the default referential action delete restrict, while the other foreign key uses the delete cascade referential action.

1. Click Create | Table.

2. Specify **ITEMS** in the Table Name field.

3. While still on the Columns page, enter the following column specifications (Column Name, Type, etc.):

   ■ Specify the **O_ID**, **ID**, **P_ID**, and **QUANTITY** columns using the NUMBER datatype constrained to a precision of **10** and a scale of **0**.

   ■ Mark all columns as Not Null.

4. Click Next or Primary Key to continue.

5. On the Primary Key page, complete the following steps:

   ■ Select Not populated.

   ■ Specify **ITEMS_PK** in the Primary Key Constraint Name field.

■ Select O_ID(NUMBER) in the Primary Key list.

■ Select ID(NUMBER) in the Composite Primary Key list. This means that each row in the ITEMS table must have a unique O_ID/ID (order ID/item ID) combination.

6. Click Next or Foreign Key to continue.

7. On the Foreign Key page, complete the following steps to add a foreign key for the O_ID column of the ORDERS table that refers to the ID column of the ORDERS table. The goals are to ensure that the O_ID field of each record in the ITEMS table refers to an ID in the ORDERS table, and that whenever a transaction deletes a record in the ORDERS table, Oracle automatically cascades the delete by deleting the associated records in the ITEMS table.

■ Specify **ITEMS_FK1** in the Name field.

■ To enforce the delete cascade referential action for the new referential integrity constraint, select Cascade Delete.

■ To indicate the column that makes up the foreign key in the new ITEMS table, select the O_ID column in the Select Key Column(s) field and then click the right-arrow button to move the selected column to the Key Column(s) field.

■ To indicate the referenced column in the parent ORDERS table, click the button to the right of the References Table field, click ORDERS from the ensuing table pop-up list, select the ID column in the Select Reference Column(s) field, and then click the right-arrow button to move the selected column to the Reference Column(s) field. If a list of columns does not automatically appear for the table that you specify in the References Table field, click the down arrow next to the field.

■ Click Add.

■ Confirm the declaration of the new foreign key in the list of foreign keys at the top of the page.

8. While still on the Foreign Keys page, complete the following steps to add another foreign key. This foreign key is for the P_ID column of the ORDERS table that refers to the ID column of the PARTS table. The goals are to ensure that the P_ID field of each record in the ITEMS table refers to an ID in the PARTS table, and to prevent the deletion of parent records in the PARTS table that have children in the ITEMS table.

■ Specify **ITEMS_FK2** in the Name field.

■ To enforce the delete restrict referential action for the new referential integrity constraint, select Disallow Delete.

■ To indicate the column that makes up the foreign key in the new ITEMS table, select the P_ID column in the Select Key Column(s) field and then click the right-arrow button to move the selected column to the Key Column(s) field.

■ To indicate the referenced column in the parent PARTS table, click the button to the right of the References Table field, click PARTS from the ensuing table pop-up list, select the ID column in the Select Reference Column(s) field, and then click the right-arrow button to move the selected column to the Reference Column(s) field.

■ Click Add.

■ Confirm the declaration of the new foreign key in the list of foreign keys at the top of the page. The Foreign Keys page should look like Figure 5-8 before continuing.

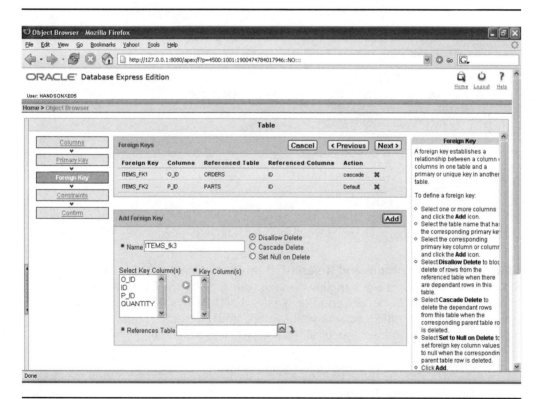

FIGURE 5-8. *Use the Foreign Keys page of the Create Table wizard to declare one or more referential integrity constraints for a new table.*

9. The ITEMS table does not require any check constraints. Therefore, click Confirm to continue.

10. Click SQL and review the SQL statements that the wizard builds (shown next). A couple of interesting things to observe include the specification of the composite primary key for the ITEMS table and the specification of the DELETE CASCADE option in the ADD CONSTRAINT clause of the ALTER TABLE statement for the ITEMS_FK1 constraint. As always, refer to the *Oracle SQL Reference* for complete information about the SQL commands CREATE TABLE .and ALTER TABLE.

```
CREATE table "ITEMS" (
    "O_ID"      NUMBER(10,0)  NOT NULL,
    "ID"        NUMBER(10,0)  NOT NULL,
    "P_ID"      NUMBER(10,0)  NOT NULL,
    "QUANTITY"  NUMBER(10,0)  NOT NULL
)
/

alter table "ITEMS" add constraint  "ITEMS_PK"
primary key ("O_ID","ID")
/

ALTER TABLE "ITEMS" ADD CONSTRAINT "ITEMS_FK1"
FOREIGN KEY ("O_ID")
REFERENCES "ORDERS" ("ID")
ON DELETE CASCADE
/
ALTER TABLE "ITEMS" ADD CONSTRAINT "ITEMS_FK2"
FOREIGN KEY ("P_ID")
REFERENCES "PARTS" ("ID")
/
```

11. Click Create to create the HANDSONXE05.ORDERS table.

EXERCISE 5.11: Add a Column and Referential Integrity Constraint to a Table

Suppose that you realize a design flaw exists in your schema: the CUSTOMERS table must be able to track each customer's sales representative. This requires a new column in the CUSTOMERS table as well as a referential integrity constraint. To get started, complete the following steps to learn how to add a column to a table:

1. Select CUSTOMERS in the Object Selection pane.

2. Click Table in the Detail pane.

3. Click Add Column.

4. Complete the following steps to add the S_ID column to the table:

   ■ Specify **S_ID** in the Add Column field.

   ■ Select NOT NULL (require a value) in the Nullable field.

   ■ Select NUMBER in the Type field.

   ■ Specify **10** in the Precision field.

   ■ Specify **0** in the Scale field.

5. Click Next to continue.

6. Click SQL and review the SQL statement that the wizard builds:

```
alter table "CUSTOMERS" add
("S_ID" NUMBER(10,0) NOT NULL)
/
```

7. Click Finish.

Now complete the following steps to add a referential integrity constraint to the CUSTOMERS table. The goals are to ensure that each customer record's S_ID refers to an ID in the SALESREPS table, and to prevent the deletion of parent records in the SALESREPS table that have children in the CUSTOMERS table.

1. Select CUSTOMERS in the Object Selection pane.

2. Click Constraints in the Detail pane.

3. Click Create.

4. Complete the following steps to add the foreign key to the table:

   ■ Specify **CUSTOMERS_FK1** in the Constraint Name field.

   ■ Select Foreign Key in the Constraint Type field.

   ■ Do not select the On Delete Cascade check box.

   ■ Select S_ID in the Foreign Key Column(s) field.

   ■ Select SALESREPS in the Reference Table Name field.

   ■ Select ID in the Reference Table Column List field.

5. Click Next to continue.

6. Click SQL and review the SQL statement that the wizard builds:

```
alter table "CUSTOMERS" add constraint
"CUSTOMERS_FK1" foreign key ("S_ID") references "SALESREPS" ("ID")
/
```

7. Click Finish.

The steps of this exercise so far have not introduced anything that should appear new to you. The reason that I built the exercise this way is to demonstrate that as you get more comfortable with SQL, a much more efficient way of doing things (in my opinion) is to learn and use SQL from the command line. For example, if you were using SQL*Plus, the following ALTER TABLE statement would both add the S_ID column to the CUSTOMERS table *and* declare a foreign key constraint that refers to the SALESREPS table, all in one command:

```
ALTER TABLE customers
 ADD s_id NUMBER(10,0)
  CONSTRAINT s_id_nn NOT NULL
 ADD CONSTRAINT customers_fk1
   FOREIGN KEY (s_id)
   REFERENCES salesreps (id);
```

Feel free to use the Object Browser interface as you get started with Oracle XE; but by all means, study the SQL that the tool is building for you, and then start trying it out for yourself with SQL*Plus or the SQL Commands page of Oracle Application Express.

Rules for Building Foreign Keys
When declaring foreign key constraints for a table, here are a few important points to remember:

- A foreign key must refer to a primary or unique key of a table; if you try to declare a foreign key that does not refer to a primary or unique key that is enabled, Oracle returns an error.

- The datatypes of the column or columns in a foreign key must match the datatypes of the column or columns in the referenced parent key.

- A column in a foreign key cannot use any of the following datatypes: LOB, LONG, LONG RAW, VARRAY, NESTED TABLE, OBJECT, BFILE, REF, or TIMESTAMP WITH TIME ZONE.

EXERCISE 5.12: Test Integrity Constraints

At this point, we've got all of our tables built. This exercise has you insert some rows into various tables to confirm that the integrity constraints we created in the previous exercises actually enforce our business rules:

1. Click PARTS in the Object Selection pane.

2. Click Data in the Detail pane. Notice that the table has no rows.

3. Click Insert Row.

4. Complete the following steps to insert a new row:

   ■ Specify **1** for the Id field.

   ■ Specify **Fax Machine** for the Description field.

   ■ Specify **299** for the Unitprice field.

   ■ Specify **277** for the Onhand field.

   ■ Specify **50** for the Reorder field.

5. Click Create and Create Another. The row complies with all integrity constraints, so you should see the message "Row created" at the top of the page.

6. Complete the following steps to insert another new row:

   ■ Specify **2** for the Id field.

   ■ Leave the Description field blank (null).

   ■ Specify **4895** for the Unitprice field.

   ■ Specify **143** for the Onhand field.

   ■ Specify **25** for the Reorder field.

7. Click Create. This time, Oracle returns the following error number and message:

   ```
   error ORA-01400: cannot insert NULL into
   ("HANDSONXE05"."PARTS"."DESCRIPTION")
   ```

8. The not null constraint for the DESCRIPTION column of the PARTS table prohibits nulls in the column. Re-enter the row information but specify **Copy Machine** for the Description field, click Create, and the row will insert without error.

The Object Browser's Detail pane now displays the new rows in the PARTS table, as shown in Figure 5-9.

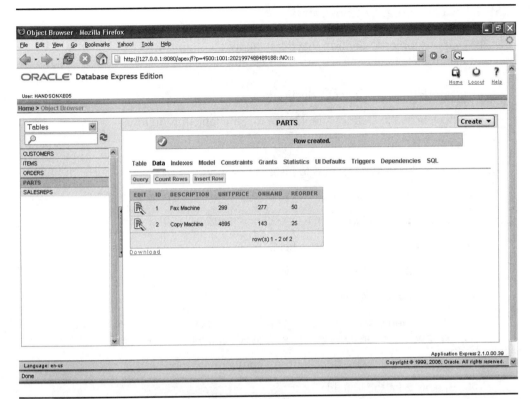

FIGURE 5-9. *The PARTS table with two rows*

Let's continue our testing:

1. Click SALESREPS in the Object Selection pane.

2. Click Data in the Detail pane. Notice that the table has no rows.

3. Click Insert Row.

4. Complete the following steps to insert a new row:

   ■ Specify **1** for the Id field.

   ■ Specify **Pratt** for the Lastname field.

   ■ Specify **Nick** for the Firstname field.

   ■ Specify **5** for the Commission field.

5. Click Create and Create Another. The row complies with all integrity constraints, so you should see the message "Row created" at the top of the page.

6. Complete the following steps to insert another new row:

- Specify **2** for the Id field.

- Specify **Jonah** for the Lastname field.

- Specify **Suzanne** for the Firstname field.

- Specify **5** for the Commission field.

7. Click Create and Create Another. Again, the new row complies with all integrity constraints, so you should see the message "Row created" at the top of the page.

8. Complete the following steps to insert a new row:

- Specify **2** for the Id field.

- Specify **Greenberg** for the Lastname field.

- Specify **Bara** for the Firstname field.

- Specify **5** for the Commission field.

9. Click Create. This time, Oracle returns the following error number and message:

```
error ORA-00001: unique constraint
(HANDSONXE05.SALESREPS_PK) violated
```

10. The primary key constraint of the SALESREPS table prohibits two records from having the same ID. In this example, the third row attempts to use an ID number of 2, which is already in use by another record. Simply re-enter the row information but specify 3 for the Id field, click Create, and the row will insert without error.

Once you finish, the Detail pane of the Object Browser should look similar to Figure 5-10.

NOTE
By default, the Object Browser interface implicitly commits after each row insert.

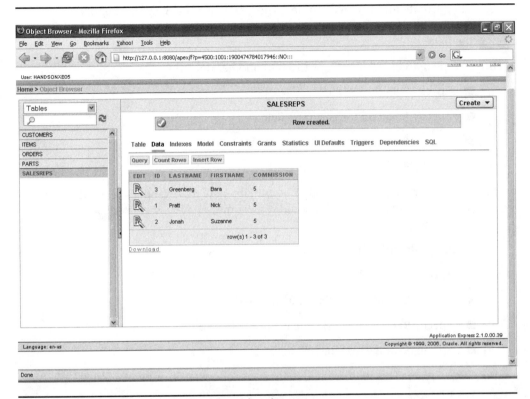

FIGURE 5-10. *The SALESREPS table with a few rows*

Now, let's test a referential integrity constraint and see what happens:

1. Click CUSTOMERS in the Object Selection pane.

2. Click Data in the Detail pane. Notice that the table has no rows.

3. Click Insert Row.

4. Complete the following steps to insert a new row:

   ■ Specify **1** for the Id field.

   ■ Specify **Joy** for the Lastname field.

   ■ Specify **Harold** for the Firstname field.

   ■ Specify **McDonald Co.** for the Companyname field.

   ■ Specify **4458 Stafford St.** for the Street field.

   ■ Specify **Baltimore** for the City field.

- Specify **MD** for the State field.

- Specify **21209** for the Zipcode field.

- Specify **410-983-5789** for the Phone field.

- Leave the Fax field empty.

- Specify **harold_joy@mcdonald.com** for the Email field.

- Specify **3** for the S_ID field.

5. Click Create and Create Another. The row complies with all integrity constraints, so you should see the message "Row created" at the top of the page.

6. Complete the following steps to insert another new row:

- Specify **2** for the Id field.

- Specify **Musial** for the Lastname field.

- Specify **Bill** for the Firstname field.

- Specify **Car Audio Center** for the Companyname field.

- Specify **12 Donna Lane** for the Street field.

- Specify **Reno** for the City field.

- Specify **NV** for the State field.

- Specify **89501** for the Zipcode field.

- Specify **775-859-2121** for the Phone field.

- Specify **775-859-2121** for the Fax field.

- Specify **musial@car-audio.net** for the Email field.

- Specify **5** for the S_ID field.

7. Click Create. This time, Oracle returns the following error number and message:

```
error ORA-02291: integrity constraint
(HANDSONXE05.CUSTOMERS_FK1) violated - parent key not found
```

8. The CUSTOMERS_FK1 referential integrity constraint in the CUSTOMERS table does not permit a customer record with an S_ID that fails to match an ID in the SALESREPS table. In this case, an INSERT statement attempts to insert a record that refers to a sales representative with an ID of 5, which does not exist. Re-enter the row information but specify 1 for the S_Id field, click Create, and the row will insert without error.

Views

Once you define the tables in a database, you can start to focus on other things that enhance the usability of the application schema. You can start by defining views of the tables in your schema. A *view* is a database object that presents table data. Why and how would you use views to present table data?

- You can use a simple view to expose all rows and columns in a table but hide the name of the underlying table. For example, you might create a view called CUST that presents all customer records in the CUSTOMERS table.

- You can use a view to protect the security of specific table data by exposing only a subset of the rows and/or columns in a table. For example, you might create a view called CUST_CA that presents only the LASTNAME, FIRSTNAME, and PHONE columns in the CUSTOMERS table for customers that reside in the state of California.

- You can use a view to simplify application coding. A complex view might join the data of related parent and child tables to make it appear as though a different table exists in the database. For example, you might create a view called ORDER_ITEMS that joins related records in the ORDERS and ITEMS tables.

- You can use a view to present derived data that is not actually stored in a table. For example, you might create a view of the ITEMS table with a column called TOTAL that calculates the line total for each record.

As you can see from this list, views provide a flexible means of presenting the table data in a database. In fact, you can create a view of any data that you can represent with a SQL query. That's because a view is really just a query that Oracle stores as a schema object. When an application uses a view to do something, Oracle derives the data of the view based on the view's *defining query*.

Creating Views

The exercises in this section teach you how to create some different types of views by using the Object Browser page of Oracle Application Express and the SQL command CREATE VIEW.

Read-Only Views

One type of view that Oracle supports is a *read-only view*. As you might expect, database applications can use a read-only view to retrieve corresponding table data, but cannot insert, update, or delete table data through a read-only view.

EXERCISE 5.13: Create and Use a Read-Only View

Complete the following steps using the Object Browser page of Oracle Application Express to create a read-only view of the ORDERS table that corresponds to the orders that are currently on backlog:

1. Click Create | View.

2. Specify **BACKLOGGED_ORDERS** in the View Name field.

3. Specify the following query in the Query field. To create a read-only view, you must specify a defining query with the WITH READ ONLY option to explicitly declare that the view is read-only; otherwise, Oracle creates the view as an updateable view. The interface does not provide an option or radio button list to choose what type of view to create (at least not at the time I wrote this book).

   ```
   SELECT * FROM orders WHERE status = 'B' WITH READ ONLY
   ```

4. Click Next to continue.

5. Click SQL to review the SQL statement built by the Object Browser (shown next). Notice that you can create a view with the SQL command CREATE VIEW.

   ```
   create or replace view "BACKLOGGED_ORDERS" as
   SELECT * FROM orders WHERE status = 'B' WITH READ ONLY
   /
   ```

6. Click Create.

7. Notice that the Detail pane lists information about the view, including the base table columns, their datatypes, etc.

To get an idea of what you can do with the new view, switch to your SQL*Plus session (left over from running the support script at the beginning of the chapter) and enter the following commands that target the new BACKLOGGED_ORDERS read-only view:

```
SELECT * FROM backlogged_orders;

INSERT INTO backlogged_orders
(id, c_id, orderdate, shipdate, paiddate, status)
VALUES (1, 1, SYSDATE, SYSDATE, SYSDATE, 'B');
```

Notice that you can query the view (although there are no rows) but cannot insert a row into the underlying ORDERS table through the read-only view.

NOTE
I suggest using SQL*Plus in several exercises of this chapter only in the interest of brevity. Please realize that you can always enter and update data by using the Object Browser page of Oracle Application Express, similar to the steps in Exercise 5.12. Feel free to use the interface if you prefer doing this rather than entering SQL statements.

Updateable Views

Oracle also allows you to define *updateable views* that an application can use to insert, update, and delete table data or query data. However, all columns of an updateable view are not *inherently updateable* unless Oracle can correctly map an insert, update, or delete operation through the view to the underlying base table data of the view. For example, when the SELECT list in the defining query of a view contains *virtual columns* (expressions, or references to pseudocolumns such as ROWID), you can update base table rows using the view only when an UPDATE statement does not refer to any of the view's virtual columns.

When you create an updateable view, you can create the view as a *constrained view* to prohibit specific insert and update operations with the view. A view with a WITH CHECK OPTION constraint disallows INSERT and UPDATE statements that would otherwise create rows that the view's defining query could not in turn materialize from its base tables.

EXERCISE 5.14: Create an Updateable View

Complete the following steps using the Object Browser page of Oracle Application Express to replace the current version of the BACKLOGGED_ORDERS view with a constrained updateable view:

1. Select BACKLOGGED_ORDERS in the Object Selection pane.

2. Click Code.

3. Click Edit.

4. Edit the definition of the view by replacing WITH READ ONLY with **WITH CHECK OPTION**.

5. Click Compile.

6. The following message confirms that your edit was successful:

```
PL/SQL code successfully compiled
```

You can use this new version of the view to insert rows into the ORDERS base table that have a STATUS equal to B, update current orders as long as you do not change an order's STATUS code from B, or delete orders that have STATUS equal to B. For example, use your current SQL*Plus session to enter the following SQL statements, which should all succeed:

```
INSERT INTO backlogged_orders
   (ID, ORDERDATE, STATUS, C_ID)
VALUES (1, SYSDATE, 'B',1);

UPDATE backlogged_orders
   SET paiddate = SYSDATE
 WHERE id = 1;

DELETE FROM backlogged_orders
 WHERE status = 'B';
```

Now try the following INSERT statement:

```
INSERT INTO backlogged_orders
   (ID, ORDERDATE, STATUS, C_ID)
VALUES (1, SYSDATE, 'F',1);
```

The result should be the following error, because the INSERT statement attempts to create a row that the view cannot materialize:

```
ORA-01402: view WITH CHECK OPTION where-clause violation
```

Now enter the following statements:

```
INSERT INTO backlogged_orders
   (ID, ORDERDATE, STATUS, C_ID)
VALUES (1, SYSDATE, 'B',1);

UPDATE backlogged_orders
   SET status = 'F'
 WHERE id = 1;
```

The INSERT statement succeeds, but the UPDATE statement returns the same error as before. Why? Because the UPDATE statement tries to update the row so that the view would not be able to materialize the row any longer.

End this exercise by rolling back your changes:

```
ROLLBACK;
```

Updateable Join Views

A *join view* (a view with a defining query that joins information from two or more tables) can be updateable, subject to the following restrictions:

- You can insert rows into an *unconstrained join view* (a join view created without the WITH CHECK OPTION) if an INSERT statement targets only columns in a single key-preserved base table of the view. (See the text following this list for the definition of a key-preserved table.)

- You can update rows in a join view if an UPDATE statement targets only columns from a single key-preserved base table of the view; additionally, if the join view is a constrained view, an UPDATE statement cannot update columns used in a join condition, or columns referenced more than once in the view.

- You can delete rows from a join view if the view is based on only one key-preserved base table.

A base table of a view is considered a *key-preserved table* if every primary key or unique key value in the base table is also unique in the result set of the join view—in other words, if the entity integrity of the base table is preserved through the join view. The next exercise demonstrates this concept of a key-preserved table.

EXERCISE 5.15: Create an Updateable Join View

Complete the following steps using the Object Browser page of Oracle Application Express to create an updateable join view of the ORDERS and CUSTOMERS tables:

1. Click Create | View.

2. Specify **ORDER_INFO** in the View Name field.

3. Specify the following query in the Query field:

```
SELECT o.id, o.orderdate, o.shipdate,
       o.paiddate, o.status,
       c.firstname || ' ' || c.lastname AS customer
  FROM customers c
  JOIN orders o
    ON c.id = o.c_id
```

4. Click Next to continue.

5. Click SQL to review the SQL statement built by the Object Browser:

```
create or replace view "ORDER_INFO" as
SELECT o.id, o.orderdate, o.shipdate,
       o.paiddate, o.status,
       c.firstname || ' ' || c.lastname AS customer
```

```
   FROM customers c
   JOIN orders o
      ON c.id = o.c_id
 /
```

6. Click Create.

Now switch back to SQL*Plus and insert a couple of orders in the ORDERS base table, and then query the new ORDER_INFO view so that you can further investigate the view's properties:

```
INSERT INTO orders
(id, orderdate, status, c_id)
VALUES (1, TO_DATE('18-JUN-2006','DD-MON-YYYY'), 'B', 1);

COMMIT;

INSERT INTO orders
(id, orderdate, status, c_id)
VALUES (2, TO_DATE('18-JUN-2006','DD-MON-YYYY'), 'B', 1);

COMMIT;

SELECT * FROM order_info
 ORDER BY id;
```

The results of the query are as follows:

```
 ID ORDERDATE SHIPDATE  PAIDDATE  STATUS CUSTOMER
---- --------- --------- --------- ------ -------------
   1 18-JUN-06                     B      Harold Joy
   2 18-JUN-06                     B      Harold Joy
```

Notice that the join view preserves the entity integrity of the ORDERS table (the table's primary key corresponds to the ORDER_ID column of the view); therefore, the columns of the ORDERS table selected by the view are updateable because the ORDERS table is key-preserved. In contrast, the view does not preserve the entity integrity for the CUSTOMERS table—notice the duplicate customers listed in the CUSTOMER column, which the view derives from the join on the primary key of the CUSTOMERS table; therefore, you cannot inherently update an order's customer through the ORDER_INFO view because the CUSTOMERS base table is not key-preserved. You can prove these conclusions by trying some DML statements with the new ORDER_INFO view:

```
UPDATE order_info
   SET shipdate = TO_DATE('18-JUN-2006','DD-MON-YYYY'),
       status   = 'F'
 WHERE id = 1;
```

```
INSERT INTO order_info
(id, orderdate, status, customer)
VALUES (3, TO_DATE('18-JUN-2006','DD-MON-YYYY'), 'B', 'Harold Joy');
```

The UPDATE statement should succeed, because it targets only inherently updateable columns in the view. However, the INSERT statement returns an error, because it targets a virtual column derived from the CUSTOMERS table:

```
SQL> INSERT INTO order_info
  2  (id, orderdate, status, customer)
  3  VALUES (3, TO_DATE('18-JUN-2006','DD-MON-YYYY'), 'B', 'Harold Joy');
(id, orderdate, status, customer)
                         *
ERROR at line 2:
ORA-01733: virtual column not allowed here
```

INSTEAD OF Triggers and Updateable Views

You can make any view updateable when you define one or more *INSTEAD OF triggers* for the view. An INSTEAD OF trigger provides the logic that describes what should happen when INSERT, UPDATE, or DELETE statements target the view.

To create an INSTEAD OF trigger, you cannot use the Object Browser interface of Oracle Application Express: you must use the following abbreviated syntax of the SQL command CREATE TRIGGER:

```
CREATE [OR REPLACE] TRIGGER trigger
  INSTEAD OF
  {DELETE|INSERT|UPDATE [OF column [,column] ... ]}
   [OR {DELETE|INSERT|UPDATE [OF column [,column] ... ]} ] ...
   ON table|view }
   ... PL/SQL block ...
   END [trigger]
```

EXERCISE 5.16: Create an INSTEAD OF Trigger for a View

Using SQL*Plus, enter the following statements to create an INSTEAD OF trigger that defines the logic for handling an INSERT statement that targets the ORDER_INFO view:

```
-- commit the current transaction before executing DDL
COMMIT;

CREATE OR REPLACE TRIGGER io_order_info_insert
INSTEAD OF INSERT ON order_info
DECLARE
  l_customer_id INTEGER;
BEGIN
    SELECT id INTO l_customer_id
      FROM customers
     WHERE UPPER(firstname) || ' ' || UPPER(lastname) =
           UPPER(:new.customer);
```

```
      INSERT INTO orders
      (id, orderdate, shipdate, paiddate, status, c_id)
      VALUES (:new.id, :new.orderdate, :new.shipdate,
              :new.paiddate, :new.status, l_customer_id);
EXCEPTION
  WHEN no_data_found THEN
      RAISE_APPLICATION_ERROR(-20000, 'Invalid or no customer specification');
END;
/
```

NOTE
The SQL command CREATE TRIGGER is a DDL command, as are most of the other commands that this chapter discusses. When you execute a DDL command, Oracle automatically commits the work of the encompassing transaction; you cannot roll back the effects of a transaction that ends with a DDL command. For safety, commit or roll back your current transaction if it includes DML actions before executing a DDL statement. The COMMIT statement in the beginning of this exercise commits the transaction started in the previous exercise.

What's RAISE_APPLICATION_ERROR?

The exception in the trigger of this exercise calls the standard utility procedure *RAISE_APPLICATION_ERROR*. A PL/SQL program can call RAISE_APPLICATION_ERROR to raise an exception and return a custom error number (SQLCODE) and message (SQLERRM) to the calling program. A call to the RAISE_APPLICATION_ERROR procedure must include at least two actual parameters: a user-defined error number in the range –20000 to –20999, and a string of 2048 bytes or less that serves as the user-defined error message.

Before building PL/SQL programs that use RAISE_APPLICATION_ERROR, you should understand how and when to use it properly. RAISE_APPLICATION_ERROR is useful when you want to work around the limitation of propagating user-defined exceptions outside the scope of the program that declared the exception. Along with the EXCEPTION_INIT compiler directive, RAISE_APPLICATION_ERROR is particularly useful when client-side PL/SQL programs want to trap and handle user-defined exceptions raised during calls to server-side PL/SQL programs. Unfortunately, many texts about PL/SQL document RAISE_APPLICATION_ERROR simply as a way to display application-defined error messages, which could just as easily be done with DBMS_OUTPUT routines.

Now, when an INSERT statement targets the ORDER_INFO view, Oracle will translate the statement using the logic of the INSTEAD OF trigger to insert rows into the underlying ORDERS table. Using SQL*Plus, try the previous INSERT statement again and query the view's ORDERS base table to see the results:

```
INSERT INTO order_info
(id, orderdate, status, customer)
VALUES (3, TO_DATE('18-JUN-2006','DD-MON-YYYY'), 'B', 'Harold Joy');

COMMIT;

SELECT * FROM order_info ORDER BY id;
```

Witness that the INSTEAD OF trigger translates the customer name "Harold Joy" that the INSERT statement provides into the correct customer ID from the CUSTOMERS table and uses it as the foreign key in the ORDERS table:

```
        ID ORDERDATE SHIPDATE  PAIDDATE  STATUS CUSTOMER
---------- --------- --------- --------- ------ -------------
         1 18-JUN-06 18-JUN-06           F      Harold Joy
         2 18-JUN-06                     B      Harold Joy
         3 18-JUN-06                     B      Harold Joy
```

Sequences

An OLTP application, such as an airline reservation system, typically supports a large number of concurrent users. As each user's transaction inserts one or more new rows into various database tables, coordinating the generation of unique primary keys among multiple, concurrent transactions can be a significant challenge for the application.

Fortunately, Oracle has a feature that makes the generation of unique values a trivial matter. A *sequence* is a schema object that generates a series of unique integers, and is appropriate only for tables that use simple, numerical columns as keys, such as the ID columns used in all tables of our practice schema. When an application inserts a new row into a table, the application simply requests a database sequence to provide the next available value in the sequence for the new row's primary key value. What's more, the application can subsequently reuse a generated sequence number to coordinate the foreign key values in related child rows. Oracle manages sequence generation with an insignificant amount of overhead, allowing even the most demanding of online transaction processing (OLTP) applications to perform well.

You can create sequences to suit an application's particular needs:

- You can start a sequence with any number you choose: 0, 93, −345, etc.

- You can create a sequence that generates a series of ever increasing or decreasing numbers that increment by a constant interval, such as 1, 2, 3, 4, etc.; 0, 10, 20, 30, etc.; 0, −1, −2, −3, etc.; 1000, 990, 980, 970, etc.

■ You can create a sequence that generates and regenerates a cyclical set of numbers, such as 1 to 1000 by 1, 999 to –999 by –1, etc.

Creating and Using Sequences

The exercises in this section teach you how to create and use sequences by using the Object Browser page of Oracle Application Express and the SQL commands.

EXERCISE 5.17: Create a Sequence

There are several ways to create a sequence by using the Object Browser page. For example, complete the following steps to create a sequence for sales order IDs:

1. Click Create | Sequence.

2. Specify **ORDER_IDS** in the Sequence Name field.

3. Remember, we already have some records in the ORDERS table with the IDs 1, 2, and 3); therefore, specify **4** in the Start With field.

4. For order IDs, we want an ever increasing series of values that increase by one. With this in mind, leave the Minimum Value and Maximum Value fields blank, and then specify **1** in the Increment field. Do not select CYCLE.

5. To improve the performance of a sequence that must generate numbers at a very fast rate, Oracle can pre-generate, cache, and optionally guarantee ordered assignment for sets of a sequence's numbers. These options are not appropriate for our sequence, so leave the Number to Cache field empty and do not select ORDER.

6. Click Next or Confirm to continue.

7. Click SQL to review the SQL statement built by the Object Browser (shown next). Notice that to create a sequence, you can use the SQL command CREATE SEQUENCE; see the *Oracle SQL Reference* for more information about this command.

```
create sequence "ORDER_IDS"
start with 4
increment by 1
nocache
nocycle
noorder
/
```

8. Click Create.

EXERCISE 5.18: Use and Reuse a Sequence Number

To generate a new sequence number for your user session, a SQL statement must reference the sequence and its NEXTVAL pseudocolumn. Using SQL*Plus, enter the following INSERT statement to insert a new sales order and use the ORDER_IDS sequence to generate a unique order ID.

NOTE

A pseudocolumn is similar to a column in a table. SQL statements can reference pseudocolumns to retrieve data, but cannot insert, update, or delete data by referencing a pseudocolumn.

```
INSERT INTO orders
    (id, c_id, orderdate, status)
    VALUES (order_ids.NEXTVAL,2,TO_DATE('18-JUN-06','DD-MON-YYYY'),'B');
```

NOTE

Once a session generates a new sequence number, only that session can reuse the sequence number— other sessions generating sequence numbers with the same sequence receive subsequent sequence numbers of their own.

To reuse the *current sequence number assigned to your session*, a SQL statement must reference the sequence and its CURRVAL pseudocolumn. Using the CURRVAL pseudocolumn, your session can reuse your current sequence number any number of times, even after a transaction commits or rolls back. For example, enter the following INSERT statements to insert several new line items into the ITEMS table for the current order, and then commit the transaction:

```
INSERT INTO items
    (o_id, id, p_id, quantity)
    VALUES (order_ids.CURRVAL,1,1,1);

INSERT INTO items
    (o_id, id, p_id, quantity)
    VALUES (order_ids.CURRVAL,2,2,4);

INSERT INTO items
    (o_id, id, p_id, quantity)
    VALUES (order_ids.CURRVAL,3,1,5);

COMMIT;
```

To see your handiwork, enter the following queries:

```
SELECT * FROM orders;

SELECT * FROM items;
```

The results should be similar to the following. The highlighted numbers were generated by the ORDER_IDS sequence.

```
SQL> SELECT * FROM orders;

        ID      C_ID ORDERDATE SHIPDATE  PAIDDATE  STATUS
---------- ---------- --------- --------- --------- ------
         1         1 18-JUN-06 18-JUN-06                 F
         2         1 18-JUN-06                           B
         3         1 18-JUN-06                           B
         4         2 18-JUN-06                           B

SQL> SELECT * FROM items;

      O_ID        ID      P_ID   QUANTITY
---------- ---------- ---------- ----------
         4         1         1          1
         4         2         2          4
         4         3         1          5
```

Synonyms

A *synonym* is nothing more than an alias or alternate name for a table, view, sequence, or other schema object. Because a synonym is just an alternate name for an object, it requires no storage other than its definition. When an application uses a synonym, Oracle forwards the request to the synonym's underlying base object.

Among other things, you can use a synonym to hide the true schema and name of an object and make it harder for a malicious program or user to target the underlying object. You might also use a synonym to simplify a long or cryptic object name.

Private and Public Synonyms

Oracle allows you to create both private and public synonyms. A *private synonym* is a synonym within a database schema that a developer typically uses to mask the true name of a table, view, stored procedure, or other database object in an application schema.

On the other hand, a *public synonym* is an object alias that is available to every user in a database. Public synonyms are most often used to mask the names of system-oriented database structures such as data dictionary views, Oracle predefined

PL/SQL packages, etc. When a database supports multiple applications, application developers rarely have the privileges to create public synonyms, so as to avoid possible naming conflicts.

Creating Synonyms

The exercises in this section teach you how to create and use synonyms by using the Object Browser page of Oracle Application Express and the SQL commands.

EXERCISE 5.19: Create a Private Synonym

Complete the following steps to create the private synonym CUST in the HANDSONXE05 schema:

1. Click Create | Synonym.

2. Specify **CUST** in the Synonym Name field.

3. To create the new synonym as a private synonym, select Private in the Public or Private list.

4. To create the new synonym as an alias for the HANDSONXE05. CUSTOMERS table, enter **HANDSONXE05** in the Schema field and **CUSTOMERS** in the Object field.

5. Ignore the Database Link field. This field allows you to create synonyms for objects in remote Oracle databases, a topic that is beyond the scope of this book.

6. Click Next or Confirm to continue.

7. Click SQL to review the SQL statement built by the Object Browser (shown next). Notice that to create a synonym, you can use the SQL command CREATE SYNONYM; see the *Oracle SQL Reference* for more information about this command.

```
create  synonym "CUST"
for "HANDSONXE05"."CUSTOMERS"
/
```

8. Click Create.

EXERCISE 5.20: Using a Synonym

The use of a synonym is transparent—just reference the synonym anywhere you would reference its underlying object. For example, switch back to your SQL*Plus session and enter the following query that uses the new CUST synonym:

```
SELECT id, lastname FROM cust;
```

The result set is as follows:

```
        ID LASTNAME
--------- ---------------
         1 Joy
         2 Musial
```

NOTE
Synonyms do not enable someone to bypass the rules of object security—a user can access an object by using a synonym only if the user has the privileges for the synonym's underlying base object. This rule applies to both private and public synonyms. See Chapter 7 for more information about privileges and database security.

Indexes

The performance of an application is always critical. That's because the productivity of an application user directly relates to the amount of time that the user must sit idle while the application tries to complete work. With database applications, performance depends greatly on how quickly an application can access table data. Typically, disk I/O is the primary performance-determining factor for table access—the less disk I/O that's necessary to access table data, the better the dependent applications will perform. In general, it's best to try to minimize the amount of disk access that applications must perform when working with database tables.

NOTE
This section introduces indexes to support subsequent sections of this book. For complete information about the various types of indexes that Oracle supports and other performance-related topics, see Chapter 10.

The judicious use of table indexes is the principal method of reducing disk I/O and improving the performance of table access. Just like an index in a book, an *index* of a table column (or set of columns) allows Oracle to quickly find specific table records without having to scan the entire table. When an application queries a table and uses an indexed column in its selection criteria, Oracle automatically uses the index to quickly find the target rows with minimal disk I/O. Without an index, Oracle has to perform a *full table scan* of the entire table from disk to locate rows that match a selection criteria.

The presence of an index for a table is entirely optional and transparent to users and developers of database applications. For example:

- Applications can access table data with or without associated indexes.

- When an index is present and it will help the performance of an application request, Oracle automatically uses the index; otherwise, Oracle ignores the index.

- Oracle automatically updates an index to keep it in synch with its table.

Although indexes can dramatically improve the performance of application requests, it's unwise to index every column in a table. Indexes are meaningful only for the key columns that application requests specifically use to find rows of interest. Furthermore, index maintenance generates overhead—unnecessary indexes can actually slow down OLTP systems and large data loads into tables.

Oracle supports several different types of indexes to satisfy many types of application requirements. The most frequently used type of index in an Oracle database is a B* index, more commonly referred to as a normal index. The following sections explain more about normal indexes, which you can create for a table's columns.

Normal (B*) Indexes

The default and most common type of index for a table column is a normal index. A *normal index* is an ordered B* of index nodes, each of which contains one or more index entries. Each *index entry* corresponds to a row in the table and contains two elements:

- The indexed column value (or set of values) for the row

- The ROWID (or physical disk location) of the row

A normal index contains an entry for every row in the table, unless the index entry for a row is null. Figure 5-11 illustrates a typical normal index.

When using a normal index, Oracle descends the tree of index nodes looking for index values that match the selection criteria of the query. When it finds a match, Oracle uses the corresponding ROWID to locate and read the associated table row data from disk.

Using Normal Indexes Appropriately

Normal indexes are useful for all types of applications and most types of columns in a table. With OLTP applications, where data is constantly being inserted, updated, and deleted, normal indexes are the preferred type of index. Normal indexes work

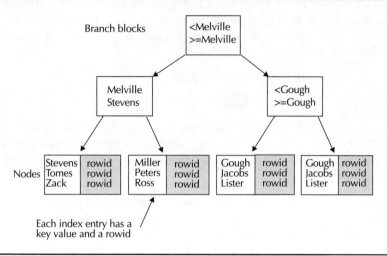

Branch blocks

Nodes

Each index entry has a
key value and a rowid

FIGURE 5-11. *A normal (B*) index*

best for key columns that contain many distinct values relative to the total number
of key values in the column. The primary and alternate keys in a table are perfect
examples of columns that should have normal indexes. Conveniently, Oracle
automatically creates normal indexes for all primary key and unique integrity
constraints of a table (or automatically uses unique indexes already in place for such
constraints).

Creating Normal Indexes

The next exercise demonstrates how to easily create indexes for the tables in an
application schema by using the Object Browser page of Oracle Application Express
and the SQL command CREATE INDEX.

EXERCISE 5.21: Create a Normal Index

To facilitate faster joins between the ITEMS and PARTS tables, complete the
following steps to create a normal index for the columns in the PARTS_FK foreign
key column of the ITEMS table:

1. Click Create | Index.

2. Specify **ITEMS** in the Table Name field, or click the button to the right of the
   Table Name field and click ITEMS from the ensuing table pop-up list.

3. You can create a normal index or a text index. A *text index* is a special kind of index that you can use to index the contents within text columns (for example, documents). In our situation, we want a normal index, so select Normal from the Type of Index list.

4. Click Next or Index Definition to continue.

5. Specify **ITEMS_IDX1** in the Index Name field.

6. You can create indexes that allow or prevent duplicate values in the index. The P_ID column in the ITEMS table makes up a foreign key that does not contain a unique value for each row. Therefore, select Non Unique from the Uniqueness list.

7. You must specify one or more columns for an index. To create the index for this exercise, select P_ID from the Index Column 1 list. (By default, Oracle XE sorts the values of each column in an index in ascending order. Although not exposed by Oracle Application Express's Object Browser interface, you can indicate ascending or descending order for each column of an index.)

8. Click Next or Confirm to continue.

9. Click SQL to review the SQL statement built by the Object Browser (shown next). Notice that to create a normal index, you can use the SQL command CREATE INDEX; see the *Oracle SQL Reference* for more information about this command.

```
create index "ITEMS_IDX1"
 on "ITEMS" ("P_ID")
 /
```

10. Click Finish.

The Detail pane of the Object Brower page displays information about the new index, as shown in Figure 5-12. Also notice the other indexes listed in the Object Selection pane that Oracle XE automatically created for the primary and unique key constraints declared for the various tables in the HANDSONXE05 schema (CUSTOMERS_PK, CUSTOMERS_UK1, etc.).

NOTE
Rather than create a unique index, it's better to declare an equivalent unique constraint for a table so that the entity integrity rule that you are enforcing is readily visible along with other integrity constraints in the database.

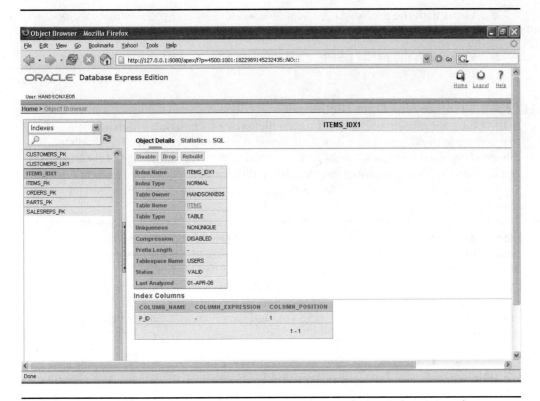

FIGURE 5-12.   *Use the Object Browser page to create and view information about indexes.*

The Data Dictionary: A Unique Schema

Every Oracle database uses a number of system tables and views to keep track of *metadata*—data about the data in a database. This collection of system objects is called the Oracle database's *data dictionary* or *system catalog*. Oracle organizes a database's data dictionary within the SYS schema.

Categories of Data Dictionary Views

Oracle's data dictionary contains several different categories of data dictionary views:

- **Views with the prefix DBA_**   Present all information in the corresponding data dictionary base tables. Because the DBA views are comprehensive, they are accessible only to users that have been granted the SELECT_CATALOG_ROLE role or the SELECT ANY TABLE system privilege. (See Chapter 7 for more information about privileges, roles, and database security.)

- **Views with the prefix ALL_** Available to all users and show things specific to the privilege domain of the current user.

- **Views with the prefix USER_** Available to all users and show things in the current user's schema.

EXERCISE 5.22: Query the Data Dictionary

In this practice exercise, you query the data dictionary several times to make sure that you understand how it can be useful as you work with Oracle XE. To complete this exercise, you must use either SQL*Plus or the SQL Commands page of Oracle Application Express; you cannot use the Query Builder page of Oracle Application Express because it does not provide a way to select from data dictionary views (at least that was the case at the time I wrote this book).

First, let's build a query to reveal information about the integrity constraints created in the previous exercises in this chapter. Where do you start? At this point, I would not expect a beginner to know which data dictionary view to target—there are literally hundreds to choose from. Fortunately, the data dictionary contains a "table of contents" view named *DICTIONARY* that you can use to help find views of interest. Because we want to query information about constraints, use SQL*Plus to enter the following commands that help you find data dictionary views that correspond to constraints:

```
DESCRIBE DICTIONARY;

SELECT table_name, comments
  FROM dictionary
 WHERE REGEXP_LIKE(comments, 'constraint', 'i');
```

The results of the query should appear similar to the following:

```
TABLE_NAME              COMMENTS
-------------------     ----------------------------------------------------
USER_CONSTRAINTS        Constraint definitions on user's own tables
ALL_CONSTRAINTS         Constraint definitions on accessible tables
USER_CONS_COLUMNS       Information about accessible columns in constraint
                          definitions

ALL_CONS_COLUMNS        Information about accessible columns in constraint
                          definitions
```

Excellent. Now we know about some views that might contain the information we want. Remember that our goal is to report information about *the constraints in our current schema*, not information about all constraints in the database or all constraints that the current session has access to. We need to query the USER_CONSTRAINTS data dictionary view.

First, enter the following DESCRIBE command to reveal the columns available in the USER_CONSTRAINTS view:

```
DESCRIBE user_constraints;
```

Name	Null?	Type
OWNER	NOT NULL	VARCHAR2(30)
CONSTRAINT_NAME	NOT NULL	VARCHAR2(30)
CONSTRAINT_TYPE		VARCHAR2(1)
TABLE_NAME	NOT NULL	VARCHAR2(30)
SEARCH_CONDITION		LONG
R_OWNER		VARCHAR2(30)
R_CONSTRAINT_NAME		VARCHAR2(30)
DELETE_RULE		VARCHAR2(9)
STATUS		VARCHAR2(8)
DEFERRABLE		VARCHAR2(14)
DEFERRED		VARCHAR2(9)
VALIDATED		VARCHAR2(13)
GENERATED		VARCHAR2(14)
BAD		VARCHAR2(3)
RELY		VARCHAR2(4)
LAST_CHANGE		DATE
INDEX_OWNER		VARCHAR2(30)
INDEX_NAME		VARCHAR2(30)
INVALID		VARCHAR2(7)
VIEW_RELATED		VARCHAR2(14)

As you can see, the USER_CONSTRAINTS view contains many columns for recording the properties of integrity constraints. For this exercise, enter the following query to display the name of each constraint, the table that it is associated with, the type of constraint, and whether the constraint is deferrable:

```
SELECT constraint_name, table_name,
  DECODE(constraint_type,
    'C','CHECK',
    'P','PRIMARY KEY',
    'U','UNIQUE',
    'R','REFERENTIAL',
    'O','VIEW WITH READ ONLY',
    'OTHER') constraint_type,
  deferrable
 FROM user_constraints
ORDER BY 2, 3, 1;
```

If you completed the previous exercises in this chapter, the result set of the query should be similar to the following results:

```
CONSTRAINT_NAME   TABLE_NAME            CONSTRAINT_TYPE       DEFERRABLE
---------------   --------------------  --------------------  --------------
SYS_C004566       BACKLOGGED_ORDERS     OTHER                 NOT DEFERRABLE
SYS_C004543       CUSTOMERS             CHECK                 NOT DEFERRABLE
SYS_C004544       CUSTOMERS             CHECK                 NOT DEFERRABLE
SYS_C004545       CUSTOMERS             CHECK                 NOT DEFERRABLE
SYS_C004563       CUSTOMERS             CHECK                 NOT DEFERRABLE
CUSTOMERS_PK      CUSTOMERS             PRIMARY KEY           NOT DEFERRABLE
CUSTOMERS_FK1     CUSTOMERS             REFERENTIAL           NOT DEFERRABLE
CUSTOMERS_UK1     CUSTOMERS             UNIQUE                NOT DEFERRABLE
SYS_C004556       ITEMS                 CHECK                 NOT DEFERRABLE
SYS_C004557       ITEMS                 CHECK                 NOT DEFERRABLE
SYS_C004558       ITEMS                 CHECK                 NOT DEFERRABLE
SYS_C004559       ITEMS                 CHECK                 NOT DEFERRABLE
ITEMS_PK          ITEMS                 PRIMARY KEY           NOT DEFERRABLE
ITEMS_FK1         ITEMS                 REFERENTIAL           NOT DEFERRABLE
ITEMS_FK2         ITEMS                 REFERENTIAL           NOT DEFERRABLE
ORDERS_CK1        ORDERS                CHECK                 NOT DEFERRABLE
SYS_C004551       ORDERS                CHECK                 NOT DEFERRABLE
SYS_C004552       ORDERS                CHECK                 NOT DEFERRABLE
ORDERS_PK         ORDERS                PRIMARY KEY           NOT DEFERRABLE
ORDERS_FK1        ORDERS                REFERENTIAL           NOT DEFERRABLE
SYS_C004548       PARTS                 CHECK                 NOT DEFERRABLE
PARTS_PK          PARTS                 PRIMARY KEY           NOT DEFERRABLE
SYS_C004549       SALESREPS             CHECK                 NOT DEFERRABLE
SALESREPS_PK      SALESREPS             PRIMARY KEY           NOT DEFERRABLE

24 rows selected.
```

Notice that Oracle generated unique names starting with the prefix SYS_ for all of the constraints that you did not explicitly name. The decoded expression in the query's SELECT clause translates codes in the CONSTRAINT_TYPE column to readable information.

Now suppose that you want to report information about sequences. Again, let's find out what dictionary views might be available to provide the information for this new report:

```
SELECT table_name, comments
  FROM dictionary
 WHERE REGEXP_LIKE(comments, 'sequence', 'i');
```

The output should be similar to the following:

```
TABLE_NAME                 COMMENTS
-------------------        --------------------------------------------------
USER_CATALOG               Tables, Views, Synonyms and Sequences owned by the
                             user

ALL_CATALOG                All tables, views, synonyms, sequences accessible
                           to the user

USER_SEQUENCES             Description of the user's own SEQUENCEs
ALL_SEQUENCES              Description of SEQUENCEs accessible to the user
USER_AUDIT_OBJECT          Audit trail records for statements concerning obje
                           cts, specifically: table, cluster, view, index, se
                           quence, [public] database link, [public] synonym,
                           procedure, trigger, rollback segment, tablespace,
                           role, user

SEQ                        Synonym for USER_SEQUENCES

6 rows selected.
```

Suppose that you first want to see the sequences "owned" by your current schema; considering the output of the previous query, USER_SEQUENCES looks like the view to target:

```
DESCRIBE USER_SEQUENCES;

SELECT sequence_name
  FROM user_sequences;
```

The result should show only the name of the sequence that you created earlier in this chapter:

```
SEQUENCE_NAME
-------------------------------
ORDER_IDS
```

Now suppose that you are interested in all of the sequences accessible to you. Considering the previous query of the DICTIONARY view, ALL_SEQUENCES looks like the view to target:

```
DESCRIBE ALL_SEQUENCES;

SELECT sequence_owner, sequence_name
  FROM all_sequences;
```

Aha! Notice in the output (shown next) that the HANDSONXE05 session not only has access to the ORDER_IDS sequence created earlier in this chapter, but also has the privileges to use several other sequences. The purpose of these sequences is not relevant to the context of this chapter.

```
        SEQUENCE_OWNER                      SEQUENCE_NAME
        ----------------------------        ----------------------------
        SYS                                 SCHEDULER$_JOBSUFFIX_S
        XDB                                 XDB$NAMESUFF_SEQ
        MDSYS                               TMP_COORD_OPS
        MDSYS                               SDO_IDX_TAB_SEQUENCE
        MDSYS                               SAMPLE_SEQ
        FLOWS_020100                        WWV_SEQ
        FLOWS_020100                        WWV_FLOW_SESSION_SEQ
        HANDSONXE05                         ORDER_IDS

        8 rows selected.
```

Exploring Other Object Browser Features

The previous exercises in this chapter expose you to many key facets of Oracle Application Express's Object Brower interface. Before this chapter ends, the next few exercises preview a few more interesting features of this useful tool. For complete information, refer to the *Application Express User's Guide* online at OTN.

EXERCISE 5.23: Reveal Object Dependencies

The nature of certain types of database objects establishes dependencies among objects in an Oracle database. For example, the data that a view represents corresponds directly to the data in its base table. Therefore, the view *depends on* its base table. Likewise, a PL/SQL package, procedure, or function that references database objects such as tables, views, and other PL/SQL routines is dependent on those objects.

To ensure that dependent objects remain valid, Oracle automatically records and manages the object dependencies in the data dictionary. Oracle automatically manages dependencies by marking a dependent object for revalidation when someone alters one of its base objects. At run time, Oracle attempts to validate an object marked as "invalid" before actually using the object during SQL statement execution. For complete information about Oracle's dependency-management features, please refer to the *Oracle Database Concepts* guide, which is part of the online Oracle documentation at OTN.

To demonstrate and reveal dependencies for an object, use the Object Browser page to complete the following steps:

1. Click Views in the Object Selection pane.

2. Click ORDER_INFO in the list of views in the Object Selection pane.

3. Click Dependencies in the Detail pane.

Minimizing the Side Effects of Dependencies

When developing applications, it is good practice to utilize the many features of Oracle that can help reduce an application's direct dependence on database objects in an effort to minimize unnecessary application modifications when inevitable changes to schema objects happen.

For example, when declaring PL/SQL program variables, constants, records, etc., that correspond to database fields or records, use the %TYPE and %ROWTYPE attributes whenever possible. Using them not only simplifies the declaration of program constructs, but also makes programs flexible to database modifications. For example, after a change to the CUSTOMERS table that adds a new column, a record variable declared in a stored procedure using the %ROWTYPE attribute automatically adjusts to account for the new column at run time, without any modification of the procedure. The procedure just might continue to function properly without any modification (or it may not, but at least you might get lucky).

Packages offer more than just a way to encapsulate related PL/SQL constructs—you can use the specification/body format of a package to eliminate direct object dependencies and insulate PL/SQL programs from unnecessary recompilations. For example, consider a stored procedure P1 that calls another stored procedure P2 that depends on table T1. Now suppose that you add a column to T1 that in no way affects the functionality of P1 or P2; nonetheless, Oracle invalidates both P1 and P2. Alternatively, consider what happens if you create P2 as part of package PK1. The modification to T1 does not cause Oracle to invalidate P1. Why? P1 depends on the specification for PK1, which does not change. In this scenario, Oracle invalidates only the PK1 package body that contains the logic for P2.

Synonyms and views are incredibly useful for eliminating an application's direct dependence on database objects. For example, consider two applications that access a table. The first application's SQL directly refers to the table, while the second application's SQL always refers to a synonym or view of the table. Suppose that, for whatever reason, you rename the table or move the table to a different schema. The first application is now broken until after you modify every SQL statement in the application that refers to the table. After redefining the synonym or view that refers to the table, the second application requires absolutely no modification.

These are just a few ways that sound knowledge and use of Oracle's many unique features can minimize the side effects caused by an application's dependence on database objects.

Notice in the Detail pane that the selected view is involved in several dependency chains, as shown in Figure 5-13:

■ The view depends on the CUSTOMERS and ORDERS table of the HANDSONXE05 schema due to the fact that the view's defining query targets these tables.

■ The IO_ORDER_INFO_INSERT trigger depends on the view—that is, the view that the trigger is defined for.

As you build more and more complex schemas, keep in mind the dependencies that exist among objects. Before modifying or dropping objects, check for dependencies that might be broken and cause errors in application functionality.

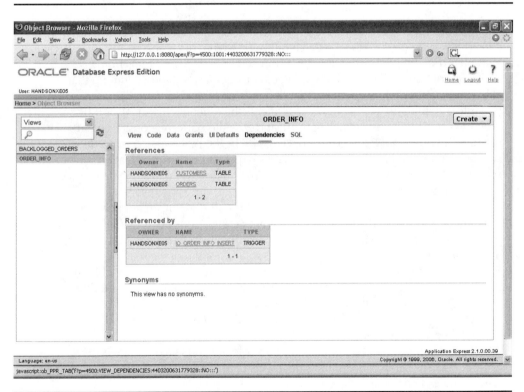

FIGURE 5-13. *Use the Object Browser page to display object dependencies.*

EXERCISE 5.24: Gather Object Statistics

To make sure SQL statements execute as quickly as possible, all database applications rely on Oracle's SQL statement optimizer. When you submit a SQL statement, the optimizer's job is to determine a good *execution plan* for the statement—an optimal way to execute the statement.

To determine the relative *cost* for a SQL statement execution plan, Oracle's optimizer uses statistics about the database system, host operating system, and data structures that the statement targets. As transactions insert, update, and delete table rows, the optimizer will not be able to make good choices for SQL statement execution plans unless the optimizer statistics that correspond to the table and indexes accurately reflect information about the table's current data.

Conveniently, all Oracle XE databases create and schedule a nightly job that automatically and efficiently collects optimizer statistics for system and user-defined objects so that Oracle's optimizer can do its job well. If you create a new table and indexes, load some data into the table, and do not want to wait for the nightly job to update the statistics for the new data structures, you can manually *analyze* tables and indexes whenever you want to.

To complete this exercise, use the Object Browser page to manually analyze the HANDSONXE05.ORDERS table:

1. Click Tables in the Object Selection pane.

2. Click ORDERS in the list of views in the Object Selection pane.

3. Click Statistics in the Detail pane.

4. Notice that there are currently no statistics for the ORDERS table.

5. Click Analyze.

6. Notice that the Analyze Table page provides for three different operations:

   ■ You can compute optimizer statistics for the target table by scanning all available data in the table. Computing statistics can generate significant overhead when collecting statistics for a large table.

   ■ A more efficient way of gathering statistics for a large table is to estimate statistics using a representative sample of the rows in a table. A setting in the range 0.000001 to 100 indicates the sample size that you want Oracle to use for estimating optimizer statistics.

   ■ You can also validate a table. A discussion of this feature is not relevant to the context of this exercise; please refer to the *Oracle Database Concepts* guide, which is part of the online Oracle documentation at OTN, for more information about validating a table.

7. The ORDERS table contains very few rows; therefore, select Compute Statistics.

8. Click Next to continue.

9. Click Finish.

Notice in the Detail pane that the ORDERS table has four rows, requires five blocks of database storage, has an average row length of 23 bytes, etc., as shown in Figure 5-14.

EXERCISE 5.25: Generate Object DML

Once you build and validate an application schema, it's important to document your work so that others can easily understand or rebuild the schema. The Object Browser has a feature that makes this job easy.

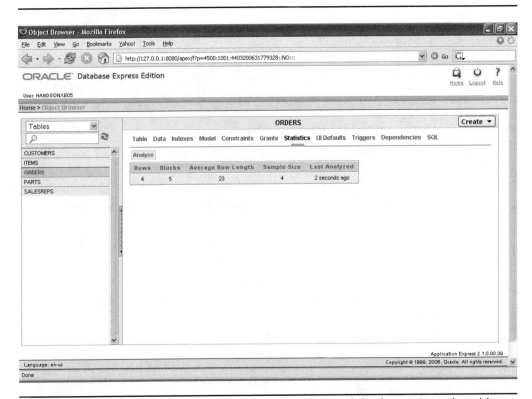

FIGURE 5-14. *Use the Object Browser page to update and display statistics for tables and indexes.*

To demonstrate, let's report all of the SQL DDL statements that are necessary to create the HANDSONXE05.ITEMS table, related constraints, indexes, etc. Complete the following steps:

1. Click Tables in the Object Selection pane if Tables is not already selected.

2. Click ITEMS in the list of tables in the Object Selection pane.

3. Click SQL in the Detail pane.

The Detail pane then reveals the SQL that you can use to create the current version of the ITEMS table and all related database objects. The output should be similar to the following:

```
CREATE TABLE   "ITEMS"
    (  "O_ID" NUMBER(10,0) NOT NULL ENABLE,
       "ID" NUMBER(10,0) NOT NULL ENABLE,
       "P_ID" NUMBER(10,0) NOT NULL ENABLE,
       "QUANTITY" NUMBER(10,0) NOT NULL ENABLE,
       CONSTRAINT "ITEMS_PK" PRIMARY KEY ("O_ID", "ID") ENABLE,
       CONSTRAINT "ITEMS_FK1" FOREIGN KEY ("O_ID")
         REFERENCES   "ORDERS" ("ID") ON DELETE CASCADE ENABLE,
       CONSTRAINT "ITEMS_FK2" FOREIGN KEY ("P_ID")
         REFERENCES   "PARTS" ("ID") ENABLE
    )
/


CREATE INDEX   "ITEMS_IDX1" ON   "ITEMS" ("P_ID")
/
```

The output demonstrates how a single CREATE TABLE statement can declare the structure of a table along with all of the table's constraints, as opposed to using a CREATE TABLE statement followed by one or more ALTER TABLE statements. Separate CREATE INDEX statements are always necessary; you cannot create a nonunique index as part of a CREATE TABLE statement.

Chapter Summary

This chapter has introduced many different types of objects that you can create in a basic relational database schema:

■ **Tables**   Tables are the basic data structure in any relational database. A table is nothing more than an organized collection of rows that all have the same columns. A column's datatype describes the basic type of data that is acceptable in the column. To create and alter a table's structure, you can use the Object Browser page of Oracle Application Express or the SQL commands CREATE TABLE and ALTER TABLE.

■ **Integrity constraints** To enforce business rules that describe the acceptable data for columns in a table, you can declare integrity constraints for a table. You can use domain integrity constraints, such as not null constraints and check constraints, to explicitly define the domain of acceptable values for a column. You can use entity integrity constraints, such as primary key and unique constraints, to prevent duplicate rows in a table. And finally, you can use referential integrity constraints to establish and enforce the relationships among different columns and tables in a database. You can declare all types of integrity constraints when you create a table or after table creation by using the Object Browser page of Oracle Application Express or by using the SQL commands CREATE TABLE and ALTER TABLE.

■ **Views** A view is a schema object that presents data from one or more tables. A view is nothing more than a query that Oracle stores in a database's data dictionary as a schema object. When you use a view to do something, Oracle derives the data of the view from the view's defining query. To create a view, use the Object Browser page of Oracle Application Express or the SQL command CREATE VIEW.

■ **Sequences** A sequence is a schema object that generates a series of unique integers. Sequences are most often used to generate unique primary keys for ID-type columns. When an application inserts a new row into a table, the application can request a database sequence to generate the next available value in the sequence for the new row's primary key value. The application can subsequently reuse a generated sequence number to coordinate the foreign key values in related child rows. To create a sequence, use the Object Browser page of Oracle Application Express or the SQL command CREATE SEQUENCE. To generate and then reuse a sequence number, reference the sequence's NEXTVAL and CURRVAL pseudocolumns, respectively.

■ **Synonyms** To mask the true name of a schema object, you can create a synonym. A synonym is an alias for a table, view, sequence, or other schema object that you store in the database. You create synonyms with the Object Browser page of Oracle Application Express or the SQL command CREATE SYNONYM.

■ **Indexes** To improve the performance of table access, you can create an index for one or more columns in the table. Use the Object Browser page of Oracle Application Express or the SQL command CREATE INDEX to create an index.

CHAPTER
6

Build an Application with
Oracle Application Express

his chapter teaches you how to quickly design, build, test, and deploy a simple database application from start to finish using the Oracle Application Express application development environment that is an integral part of Oracle XE. In many ways, this chapter is the most important chapter in the book, because it sheds light on how you are expected to use many of the skills that you have learned in the previous chapters. This chapter's topics include the following:

- The stages of the application development lifecycle

- Software modeling and the Unified Modeling Language (UML)

- The steps for uploading and executing SQL scripts that build an application schema

- The steps for loading data into a schema from structured data files

- The steps for creating, modifying, and deploying Oracle Application Express applications

Chapter Prerequisites

To practice the hands-on exercises in this chapter, you need to start SQL*Plus as instructed in Exercise 2.11 and run the following command script:

```
location\handsonxe\sql\chap06.sql
```

where *location* is the file directory where you expanded the support archive that accompanies this book. For example, after starting SQL*Plus, you can run this chapter's SQL command script using the SQL*Plus command @, as in the following example (assuming that your chap06.sql file is in C:\temp\handsonxe\sql):

```
SQL> @C:\temp\handsonxe\sql\chap06.sql;
```

Once you reply to all of the prompts and the script completes successfully, you can exit SQL*Plus by using an EXIT command.

NOTE
Relative to the previous chapters in this book, this chapter contains more involved exercises that might take longer to complete. Consequently, you are not expected to complete the entire chapter in one sitting. Feel free to start, stop, and pick up where you left off as you go through the material in this chapter. As with other chapters, I encourage you to repeat the chapter's exercises as many times as you like; just remember to re-execute the chap06.sql support script between iterations.

Introducing the Application Development Lifecycle

Before you start building an application, it is very worthwhile to learn more about the process of developing computer applications, and specifically database applications. The procedure for developing a database application seems like it might be a straightforward concept, right? Designing everything on the fly as you go, you build a set of tables and related schema objects along with an application interface that, altogether, does something that you have a relatively good understanding of. *This approach could not be more wrong,* but surprisingly many applications are built this way. Such haphazard development styles typically result in an application that does not meet its objectives, is not easy to use, and does not perform well. Significant amounts of time are then necessary to rework the application.

People with experience developing computer applications know that, just like any other type of problem-solving task, application development requires a systematic approach to yield good results. A general, recognized model known as the *application development lifecycle (ADLC)* outlines a sequence of well-defined stages for building first-rate computer applications from the ground up, as Figure 6-1 outlines and the following sections discuss.

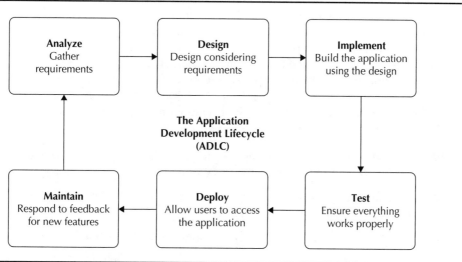

FIGURE 6-1.   *The application development lifecycle (ADLC)*

Analyzing Processes and Defining Requirements

The first phase in an ADLC is commonly referred to as the *analysis stage*. The purpose of this stage is to carefully analyze and define the processes that you are trying to computerize with the proposed application. Using your newfound understanding, it's important to meticulously document a list of requirements that the application must meet to successfully computerize the associated processes.

The analysis stage typically includes interviews of people who play a role in the current processes that you aim to computerize—after all, these are the people who can best explain the current processes of interest and suggest possible improvements to implement when building the application.

For example, assume that you are hired to help organize the day-to-day operations of a technical services support group that manages more than a hundred database applications and Oracle databases executing on dozens of host computers. Your first day on the job, you ask a coworker: "Where can I find the latest documentation on your environment and all of the system's components? Hostnames, database names, application names, that kind of thing." The answer: "Well, let's see, your new account e-mail messages for each host should help you get started on the names of the host computers. To see what databases are on a host, just log in to the host and look in its configuration files. Oh, and there's a company web page and a spreadsheet or two on the shared network drive that have some information about the applications out there." Immediately, you realize that the worst first problem that you must solve is simple to understand: a lack of organization. Your initial application requirements are to pull together all of the scattered information about the environment into a central database, and then build an application that the group can use going forward to keep track of the system. Subsequent meetings with system administrators (SAs), database administrators (DBAs), and application administrators (AAs) provide you with insight into the daily operations carried out by staff members. The initial list of requirements that you assemble for the planned application ends up looking something like this:

■ Maintain information about each host computer, including its name, operating system, operating system version, and number of CPUs.

■ Maintain information about each database, including its name, Oracle version number, and supporting host computer.

■ Maintain information about each application, including its name, purpose, version, and supporting database.

■ Provide a web-based interface for the application that is intuitive and easy to use.

■ Do not spend any money for software.

■ Use minimal hardware resources on an existing server.

Continue reading to learn how to use the list of requirements going forward to build an application that allows SAs, DBAs, and AAs to update information about the system environment on an ongoing basis.

 NOTE
The example application/system introduced in this section is carried forward throughout the remaining sections of the chapter. The example application is henceforth referred to as SysMgmt.

Designing the Application to Meet the Requirements

The next stage in the ADLC is the *design stage*. The purpose of this stage is to design an application that meets the requirements previously documented during the analysis stage. The quality of an application's design ultimately determines how well the initial version of the application meets its objectives.

The design stage is the time to experiment. Try this, try that—determine the application design that best meets the agreed-upon objectives. Make your designs available for review by the eventual users of the proposed application and encourage them to point out omissions and weaknesses of your designs. The initial design that you lay out might work just fine, but be prepared to go through umpteen different iterations of the design to get something that everyone is finally happy with.

Implementing the Application Using the Design

The *implementation stage* of the ADLC is the creative part of the process. The purpose of the implementation stage is to build the first version of an application based on a design that meets all requirements.

Before implementing, be careful that you pick a development tool or development environment that can build an application that meets all requirements. For example, based on the list of requirements and budget available for the SysMgmt application, the choice is easy: use Oracle XE to build a database that pulls together all available information about the system components, and build an Oracle Application Express web-based application that everyone can use to maintain system information.

The implementation of a database application usually has at least two distinct phases: build the database schema (tables, sequences, triggers, etc.), and then build the application interface. The specific procedures for completing each task depend on the tools that you choose for building the application. For example, if you use a UML diagramming tool during the design phase that can generate SQL DDL commands from class diagrams, creating the database schema for the application is trivial: you simply run a SQL command script using a utility like SQL*Plus. Many UML tools can also generate class definitions for programming languages such as Java and C++. On the other hand, if you did not use UML diagrams to design the application or are using a minimal diagramming tool, the implementation process will no doubt require a much more manual approach.

NOTE
The bulk of the exercises in this chapter explain how to accomplish the implementation phase in detail while using Oracle Application Express.

Testing That the Application Meets the Requirements

During the *test stage* of the application development lifecycle, provide access to a "beta" version of the application in a test environment so that people can test the application, test it some more, and then test it again until everyone is satisfied that the application adequately meets all requirements. You should also put together a rigorous test plan that strictly validates the functionality of each and every application component; this type of *regression testing* helps ensure that the application itself does not introduce unforeseen data integrity violations that are not necessarily prevented by database integrity constraints. If necessary, modify the components of the system to adjust for any problems uncovered during the test stage.

You might want to limit access to the application so that only developers or a particular group of users can test it. At other times, it might make sense to provide unrestricted access to the application for testing. The decision is up to you based on your plan for ensuring that the application meets all requirements.

To test the response time and load generated by a new application, make sure to test it in an environment that is representative of the environment in which you plan to deploy it. For example:

- If you plan to deploy an application on a server that is shared among multiple applications, test it on a server that carries a similar load.

- If you expect an application's table to accumulate a large number of rows, build scripts to load sets of fictitious data into the application's tables so that users can see how well the application performs with a representative amount of data.

Deploying the Application

The next stage of the ADLC is the *deployment stage*. Once you are satisfied that the application has been thoroughly tested and validated, you can move the application to a "production" environment where users can begin using the new application and realizing the benefits of computerizing the associated operations.

Maintaining the Application

After the production version of the application has been in use for a while, users inevitably find bugs or make enhancement requests. The *maintenance stage* of the ADLC is the stage in which you respond to such issues. For enhancements, make sure to complete the analysis, design, implementation, testing, and deployment stages with respect to the new features.

Software Modeling and the Unified Modeling Language

Software modeling is a tool that every application developer should use during the design stage of application development. Software models are blueprints of an application's processes, database elements, component interactions, etc. Software models of an application design are an effective means for communicating your plan, ensuring that the design meets all necessary requirements, and identifying the design's weaknesses *before* coding actually begins.

There are many different software-modeling approaches that are popular. Among these is the *Unified Modeling Language (UML)*. With UML, you construct models of your software. If you have experience with object-oriented problem solving, many UML concepts should already be familiar to you, such as the following:

- A *model* is an abstraction or visual representation of a problem.

- A *domain* is the environment from which a problem originates.

- A model is made up of *objects* that interact by sending each other *messages*.

- An object is defined from a class; a *class* is essentially a blueprint for an object.

- A class definition includes *attributes* that describe the data that objects of the class can maintain.

- A class definition also includes *operations* (*methods*) that describe the things that objects of the class can perform.

- An object's attribute values determine its *state*.

NOTE
Search the Web or refer to a good book if you need some background information about object-oriented concepts.

The latest UML specification defines many types of diagrams that are generally categorized as structure or behavior diagrams. *Structure diagrams* illustrate the *static* structure of the system that you are modeling. *Behavior diagrams* show the *dynamic* interaction of system components. The intention of this section is merely to introduce UML and provide examples of some basic UML diagrams that demonstrate their value during the design stage of the ADLC; for a complete presentation of UML, modeling diagrams, and techniques, please use the many useful links to documentation and tutorials available at www.uml.org.

Use Case Diagrams

During the software development design stage, behavior diagrams known as *use case* diagrams help you to flesh out and communicate the requirements of particular systems that the application intends to computerize. A use case diagram illustrates what a particular system does by way of actors, use cases, and communications. An *actor*, represented by a stick figure, is the person or thing that initiates the events that occur. A *use case*, represented by an oval, is a single task or goal. A *communication*, represented by a line, is the connection between an actor and a use case.

Figure 6-2 is a simple use case diagram for the SysMgmt application that illustrates the tasks that an SA performs in our case-study application. The diagram clearly identifies the SA as an actor in the domain whose tasks include creating, altering, and dropping host computers. Figures 6-3 and 6-4 are use case diagrams that illustrate similar tasks for DBAs with databases and AAs with applications. Modeling even very simple use case diagrams such as these forces you to think methodically about what things are happening in the system and, as a result, what tasks the proposed application must support. When others review your use case diagrams, expect feedback such as "You forgot about this" and "Those people don't do that, they do this." Then, it's back to the drawing board until you have a crystal clear picture of everything that is going on before you start trying to build the application.

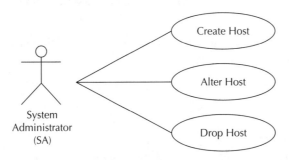

FIGURE 6-2. *A use case diagram that shows the host computer system management tasks performed by system administrators in the SysMgmt application*

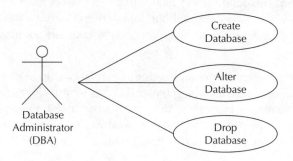

FIGURE 6-3. *A use case diagram that shows the database management tasks performed by database administrators in the SysMgmt application*

Class Diagrams

The design stage should also include diagrams known as *class diagrams* to illustrate the structure of the system, including the system's classes and class associations. A *class*, the design for a new type of object, appears in a class diagram as a rectangle divided into three stacked layers: the class name, its attributes, and its operations. Each attribute has a name, a type, and an optional default value. Each operation has a name, parameter list, and return value type.

A line connecting two classes represents a *relationship* or *association* between the two classes. You can indicate several different types of associations in a class diagram. For example:

- **Bidirectional association**   Signifies that both classes in the relationship know about each other; show this type of relationship with a solid line between two classes.

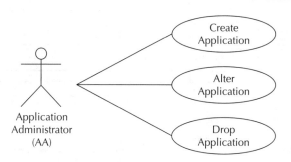

FIGURE 6-4. *A use case diagram that shows the application management tasks performed by application administrators in the SysMgmt application*

- ■ **Unidirectional association** Indicates that two classes have a relationship, but that only one class knows about the relationship; draw this type of relationship using a solid line with an open arrowhead pointing to the known class.

- ■ **Inheritance (also called generalization)** A relationship between a child class and a super class in which the *child class* inherits all attributes and operations from its *super class*. A child class can optionally add new functionality or override inherited functionality. Show inheritance with a solid line that has a closed arrowhead pointing at the super class.

The *multiplicity value* at the end of an association specifies the possible instances of the class associated with a single instance of the class on the other end. Multiplicities are single numbers or ranges of numbers.

Figure 6-5 is the class diagram for the proposed SysMgmt application. Notice how easy it is to understand the type of data and operations necessary to manage

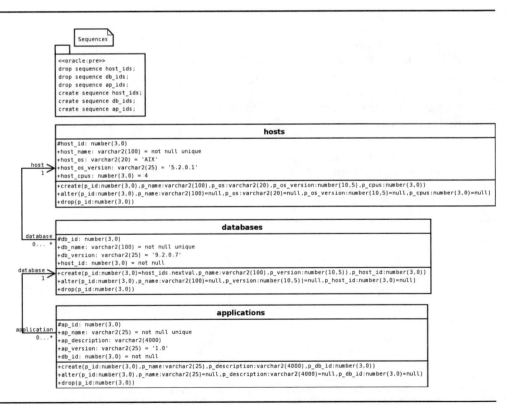

FIGURE 6-5. *A class diagram that shows the static structure of the SysMgmt application*

hosts, databases, and applications. When others review a class diagram, expect feedback such as "For databases, we also need to keep track of…" and "The version number for a host's operating system needs to allow for longer string values." Again, make necessary changes until everyone agrees on the plan going forward.

Building the Application Schema

With our application's design in hand, it is now a relatively trivial task to actually build the schema necessary to support the application. You have a few choices for creating the schema:

- You can start a SQL*Plus session or use the SQL Commands page of Application Express to manually code SQL DDL statements that create objects in the schema.

- You can use the Object Browser page of Application Express to manually build the objects in the schema.

- If you use a UML tool that can generate SQL scripts from your class diagrams, you can simply load and run the SQL scripts using Application Express.

The third alternative is by far the easiest, most reliable, and fastest approach you can take, if available, and the method that the next exercise demonstrates.

EXERCISE 6.1: Upload and Run a SQL Script

In the interest of brevity, this book's support archive includes a SQL script generated by a UML tool called *Dia* (http://dia-installer.sourceforge.net). The tool generates the SQL script, a series of SQL DDL commands, from a class diagram that corresponds to our case-study application. This exercise teaches you how to upload the sysmgmt1 .sql script and run it to create the SysMgmt application's schema.

Launch the Database Home Page of Oracle Application Express as explained in Exercise 2.13. Establish a connection using this chapter's practice account, **HANDSONXE06**, with the password **PASSWORD**.

Once you launch the Database Home Page, complete the following steps to upload the sysmgmt1.sql script:

1. From the Database Home Page, click SQL I SQL Scripts to display the SQL Scripts page.

2. Click Upload to display the Upload Script page.

3. Click Browse and navigate your file system to select the sysmgmt1.sql script extracted from this book's support archive.

4. Specify **SYSMGMT1** or any other suitable name in the Script Name field of the Upload Script page.

5. Click Upload.

6. Notice the new script icon in the SQL Scripts page, as shown in Figure 6-6.

To run the newly uploaded script and create the schema objects for the SysMgmt application in the current HANDSONXE06 schema, complete the following steps:

1. Click the script's icon on the SQL Scripts page.

2. Browse the contents of the script to become familiar with the SQL DDL commands that make up the script.

3. Click Run.

4. Click Run to confirm your request to run the script.

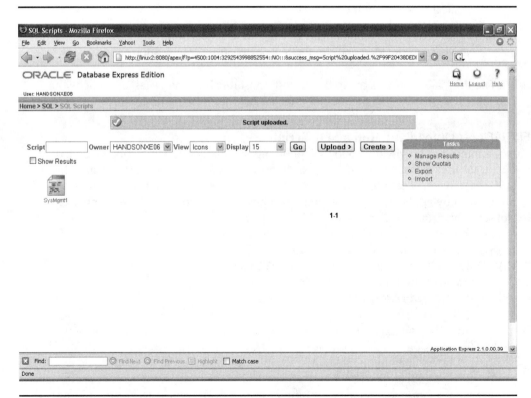

FIGURE 6-6. *The SQL Scripts page shows SQL scripts that have been uploaded and can be run to carry out work.*

5. The Manage Script Results page is a summary report of all script runs. Notice that the initial status of the script run is Submitted.

6. Wait a few seconds and then click Go. The status of the script run should change to Complete.

7. Click View Results for the script run.

8. Browse the success or failure of various SQL statements in the script. It is expected that certain statements will fail depending on whether this is the first time you are running the script; for example, there are several DROP statements that will fail if this is the first time you are executing the script.

To check the work that the script performed, complete the following steps:

1. Click Home.

2. Click Object Browser.

3. Select Tables and then confirm the existence and browse the structure of the following tables: APPLICATIONS, DATABASES, and HOSTS. For example, the HOSTS table should appear as in Figure 6-7.

4. Select Sequences and then confirm the existence and browse the structure of the following sequences: AP_IDS, DB_IDS, and HOST_IDS.

EXERCISE 6.2: Set User Interface Defaults

To promote consistent interfaces and functionality among the pages in an Oracle Application Express application, you should set *user interface defaults* for all tables and views in the application schema *before* you start to build the application. This exercise teaches you how to set user interface defaults for the tables in the application schema.

TIP
When the Detail pane contains a wide set of information that is not completely viewable, click the button along the left edge of the Detail pane to temporarily maximize the Detail pane to the full window. Click the same button again to make the Object Selection pane viewable once again.

1. On the Object Browser page, select Tables.

2. Select APPLICATIONS (that is, the APPLICATIONS table from the list of tables).

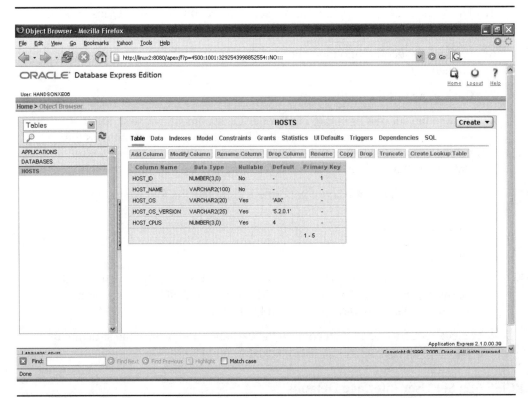

FIGURE 6-7. *The HOSTS table in the Object Browser, as created by the SQL script*

3. Click UI Defaults.

4. If this is the first time that you are setting user interface defaults for a particular table, click Create Defaults; otherwise, skip to the next step.

5. Browse the report of default user interface settings for the APPLICATIONS table. Notice that you can set user interface defaults for a table's columns on both reports and forms. When looking at this report, use the following information to help make your decisions:

   ■ Both forms and reports use a column's *Label* to identify it on the page. In general, you should translate the default labels generated for cryptic column names into user-friendly labels.

   ■ A column's *Report Sequence* and *Form Sequence* indicate the order of presentation for the column with respect to other columns on a report or form, respectively. Modify these settings if the default column order is not appropriate.

- A report can include a Search field that makes it convenient for users to find specific records in the report. A column's default *Searchable* setting indicates whether Oracle Application Express generates a report with Search field criteria that considers the column's data for filtering the results in a report. Make a column searchable only if users often search for records in the table using the data in the column as search criteria. Primary key and foreign key columns that contain nonmeaningful numeric keys typically should not be searchable, to avoid false positives for searches of numerical data. A subsequent exercise explains more about searchable report columns.

- A column's *Required* attribute indicates whether the column can contain nulls. Oracle Application Express determines the default setting for each column based on whether the column is part of a primary key or is declared as not null. As long as you correctly declare constraints for your tables, no changes should be necessary for each column's Required attribute.

6. Click Grid Edit to display a form for editing the APPLICATION table's user interface defaults.

7. Replace the text in the Form Region Title field with **Create/Edit Application**.

8. Replace the text in the Report Region Title field with **Application**.

9. Specify the following in the Label field of the table's columns:

   - **Application** for the AP_ID column

   - **Name** for the AP_NAME column

   - **Description** for the AP_DESCRIPTION column

   - **Version** for the AP_VERSION column

   - **Database** for the DB_ID column

10. Select Yes for every column's Include in Reports and Include in Forms lists.

11. Select Yes for the Searchable list of the AP_NAME, AP_DESCRIPTION, and AP_VERSION columns; set all other columns to No.

12. Click Apply Changes to save your work.

Repeat the preceding steps to create, display, and edit the user interface defaults for the remaining two tables, DATABASES and HOSTS. To save yourself a few mouse clicks, click User Interface Defaults on the breadcrumbs menu after you update a table's settings. Next, click the icon for the new table that you want to work with, click Create User Interface Defaults to create defaults for the table, and then click Grid Edit.

NOTE
User interface defaults remain in the Oracle Application Express repository, even after you drop a table from a database. If you are repeating this chapter's exercises, you will notice that you do not have to create user interface defaults for each of the example tables.

For the DATABASES table:

1. Specify **Create/Edit Database** in the Form Region Title field.

2. Specify **Database** in the Report Region Title field.

3. Specify the following in the Label field of the table's columns:

   ■ **Database** for the DB_ID column

   ■ **Name** for the DB_NAME column

   ■ **Version** for the DB_VERSION column

   ■ **Host** for the HOST_ID column

4. Select Yes for every column's Include in Reports and Include in Forms lists.

5. Select Yes for the Searchable list of the DB_NAME and DB_VERSION columns; set all other columns to No.

6. Click Apply Changes to save your work.

For the HOSTS table:

1. Specify **Create/Edit Host** in the Form Region Title field.

2. Specify **Host** in the Report Region Title field.

3. Specify the following in the Label field of the table's columns:

   ■ **Host** for the HOST_ID column

   ■ **Name** for the HOST_NAME column

   ■ **Operating System (OS)** for the HOST_OS column

   ■ **OS Version** for the HOST_OS_VERSION column

   ■ **CPUs** for the HOST_CPUS column

4. Select Yes for every column's Include in Reports and Include in Forms lists.

5. Select Yes for the Searchable list of every column except HOST_ID.

6. Click Apply Changes to save your work.

At this point, you are done modifying the user interface defaults for all tables in your schema.

Loading Schema Data

Before starting to build the application, it is a good idea to quickly add some data to your tables. Otherwise, the first cut of your application will be hard to grade because reports and forms based on an empty table display nothing more than a message indicating that there are no records to display.

To load data into a table with Oracle Application Express, you have a few options:

■ You can manually create records with the Object Browser page.

■ You can load data from comma-separated or tab-delimited text files.

■ You can load data from XML files.

The following sections cover all three methods.

Loading Data Manually

The previous chapter explains how to insert rows into a table using the Object Browser page. To review your skills and reveal a weakness in your application schema, complete the following exercises.

EXERCISE 6.3: Manually Enter Data

Complete the following steps to insert a new record into the HOSTS table:

1. Click Home.

2. Click Object Browser.

3. Select Tables | HOSTS in the Object Selection pane.

4. Click Data.

5. Click Insert Row.

6. Specify the following information for the fields of the HOSTS table:

- The HOST_ID field should be populated by the HOST_IDS sequence. Therefore, generate a new sequence number by referencing the NEXTVAL pseudocolumn of the sequence. For example, specify **handsonxe06.host_ids.nextval**.

- Specify **server1.mycompany.com** in the HOST_NAME field.

- Specify **AIX** in the HOST_OS field.

- Specify **5.2.0.0** in the HOST_OS_VERSION field.

- Specify **4** in the HOST_CPUS field.

7. Click Create.

EXERCISE 6.4: Create Triggers to Generate Primary Keys

The previous exercise reveals an opportunity for improvement in the current version of your schema—explicit references to a sequence are necessary to generate the primary key when inserting a new row into a table. In this exercise, you create a simple trigger for each table that automatically generates primary keys for new rows:

1. From the Object Browser page, click Create | Trigger.

2. Specify **HOSTS** in the Table Name field (or select the table name from the pop-up select list).

3. Click Next.

4. Specify **HOSTS_TPK** in the Trigger Name field.

5. Select BEFORE from the Firing Point list.

6. Select insert from the Options list.

7. Select For Each Row.

8. Specify the following statement in the Trigger Body field. The simple trigger generates a new sequence number and assigns the value to the HOST_ID field for the new row being inserted.

```
SELECT handsonxe06.host_ids.nextval
  INTO :new.host_id
  FROM dual;
```

9. Notice a subtle point about how the trigger body references the sequence: the reference to the synonym is *fully qualified*; that is, the reference to the sequence is prefixed by the encompassing schema name. When reviewing application code, fully qualified references to schema objects in an application make it much easier for other developers and system tuners to readily understand what objects the application uses. It is always good practice to follow this example of fully qualified object references when designing new applications.

10. Click Next.

11. Optionally, click SQL to review the CREATE TRIGGER statement that the Object Browser page generates:

```
create or replace trigger "HOSTS_TPK"
BEFORE
insert on "HOSTS"
for each row
begin
SELECT handsonxe06.host_ids.nextval
  INTO :new.host_id
  FROM dual;
end;
/
```

12. Click Finish.

The new trigger should appear in the Object Browser page similar to what's shown in Figure 6-8.

To complete this exercise, repeat the preceding steps to create similar before-insert-row triggers for the DATABASES and APPLICATIONS tables:

■ The DATABASES_TPK trigger should use the DB_IDS sequence, as follows:

```
create or replace trigger "DATABASES_TPK"
BEFORE
insert on "DATABASES"
for each row
begin
SELECT handsonxe06.db_ids.nextval
  INTO :new.db_id
  FROM dual;

end;
/
```

■ The APPLICATIONS_TPK trigger should use the AP_IDS sequence, as follows:

```
create or replace trigger "APPLICATIONS_TPK"
BEFORE
insert on "APPLICATIONS"
for each row
begin
SELECT handsonxe06.ap_ids.nextval
  INTO :new.ap_id
  FROM dual;
end;
/
```

Make sure that all three triggers exist and are valid before continuing; otherwise, subsequent exercises will fail.

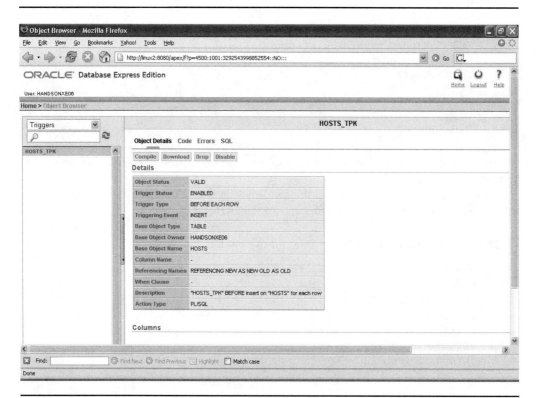

FIGURE 6-8. *When inserting a new row into the HOSTS table, the HOSTS_TPK trigger generates a new sequence number from the HOST_IDS sequence for the HOST_ID column of the new row.*

Loading Spreadsheet and Text File Data

Organizations typically have useful data stored all over the place and in various formats: spreadsheets, PC databases, text files, and so on. Fortunately, Oracle XE and Oracle Application Express have utilities that make it easy to load structured data from various file formats into a database. The next two exercises teach you how to load such data.

EXERCISE 6.5: Load Data from a Text File

Most spreadsheet and PC database programs can export data to simple text files in one of two structured formats: with fields separated by commas (*comma-separated values*, or *CSVs*) or fields delimited by tabs (*tab delimited*). This exercise teaches you how to load records from text files into the DATABASES table of our application.

Each UNIX server (in our fictitious application) that manages Oracle databases in our system has a configuration file named /etc/oratab that contains each database's name, version, and other information. For example, here's what the server1 .mycompany.com server's /etc/oratab file might look like:

```
db1:/usr/opt/oracle/product/10.2.0.1:Y
db2:/usr/opt/oracle/product/9.2.0.7:Y
db3:/usr/opt/oracle/product/10.2.0.1:Y
db4:/usr/opt/oracle/product/10.2.0.1:Y
db5:/usr/opt/oracle/product/9.2.0.7:Y
db6:/usr/opt/oracle/product/9.2.0.7:Y
db7:/usr/opt/oracle/product/9.2.0.7:Y
db8:/usr/opt/oracle/product/9.2.0.7:Y
```

Notice that the file uses colons to delimit fields and carriage returns to start new records. For each record, the first field indicates the database's name (for example, db1); the second field indicates the database's ORACLE_HOME (for example, /usr/opt/oracle/product/10.2.0.1); and the third field indicates whether the database should automatically start after a system reboot (for example, Y).

Using a text editor and some basic search-and-replace commands, you can easily transform this type of file into the db1.csv file in this book's support archive, as shown in the following code. The CSV file contains only the data relevant to the DATABASES table: the database name, its Oracle version, and the HOST_ID of server1.mycompany .com. To make the load easier to complete, you can add field names that correspond to the DATABASES table in the first row of the file.

```
db_name,db_version,host_id
db1,10.2.0.1,1
db2,9.2.0.7,1
db3,10.2.0.1,1
db4,10.2.0.1,1
db5,9.2.0.7,1
```

```
db6,9.2.0.7,1
db7,9.2.0.7,1
db8,9.2.0.7,1
```

Notice that the file omits the DB_ID for each record: the data load will rely on the newly created DATABASES_TPK trigger (and DB_IDS sequence) to automatically generate primary keys for each new record.

To load the records from the CSV file into the DATABASES table, complete the following steps:

1. Click Home.

2. Click Utilities.

3. Click Data Load/Unload.

4. Click Load.

5. Click Load Text Data to display the Load Data page.

6. Select Existing Table for the Load To field.

7. Select Upload from for the Load From field.

8. Click Next.

9. Confirm that you are loading data into the HANDSONXE06 schema. Then click Next.

10. Select DATABASES from the Table Name list.

11. Click Next.

12. Click Browse and navigate the file systems that are accessible from your local computer to select the db1.csv file extracted from this book's support archive. Do not modify any other page settings.

13. Click Next.

14. The page displays a formatted version of the records and fields pending for the load. If necessary, you can eliminate fields in the data file from loading, rearrange fields, and so forth: in our example, no work is necessary. After reviewing the information, click Load Data to commence the data load.

15. Review the Text Data Load Repository page to confirm that the load completed without errors, as shown in Figure 6-9.

16. Optionally, return to the Object Browser page (using steps that should be familiar to you by now) to view the new records inserted in the DATABASES table.

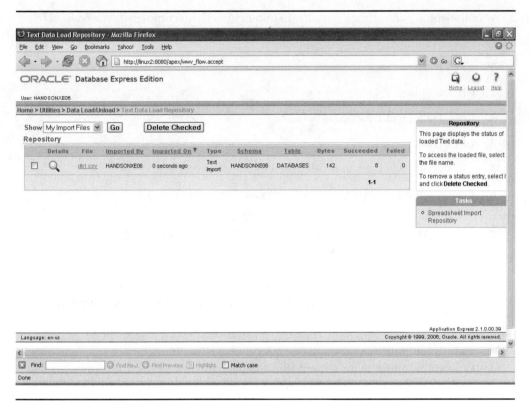

FIGURE 6-9. *The Text Data Load Repository page displays historical records of data uploaded from text files.*

Loading XML Data

Extensible Markup Language (XML) data files are another common format that many software programs support for storing data in a structured format. XML allows applications and application designers to create customized tags that enable the definition, transmission, validation, and interpretation of data between applications and organizations.

EXERCISE 6.6: Load Data from an XML File

This exercise teaches you how to use Oracle XE to upload data into an Oracle database from an XML file. This book's support archive contains a file named ap1 .xml. This XML file was generated by a spreadsheet and contains information about a few of the applications running on the fictitious server1.mycompany.com. To load data from this XML file into the APPLICATIONS table, complete the following steps:

1. Click Home.

2. Click Utilities.

3. Click Data Load/Unload.

4. Click Load.

5. Click Load XML Data to display the Load XML Data page.

6. Confirm that you are loading data into the HANDSONXE06 schema. Then click Next.

7. Specify **APPLICATIONS** in the Table field (or use the pop-up list).

8. Click Next.

9. Click Browse and navigate the file systems that are accessible from your local computer to select the ap1.xml file extracted from this book's support archive.

10. Click Load Data.

11. Optionally, return to the Object Browser page to view the new records inserted in the APPLICATIONS table.

NOTE
The XML file that you attempt to load must be well formed; *if it is not, the load fails and Oracle XE returns an error. Detailed information about XML is beyond the scope of this book; please refer to* Oracle Database 10g XML & SQL: Design, Build & Manage XML Applications in Java, C, C++ & PL/SQL *(McGraw-Hill/Osborne, 2004) for more information.*

Creating the SysMgmt Application

Now that each table has a few records, the following exercise teaches you just how easy it is to create a simple application with Oracle Application Express based on existing database tables. The component of Oracle Application Express that you use to build applications is called the Application Builder. The *Application Builder* has a tremendous number of features, most of which are beyond the context of this chapter.

The purpose of the subsequent exercises in this chapter is to expose you to many common Application Builder features and make you comfortable with the Application Builder development approach for rapid application development (RAD).

EXERCISE 6.7: Create the SysMgmt Application with the Create Application Wizard

To quickly create an application with Oracle Application Express that meets our business requirements, complete the following steps:

1. Click Home.

2. Click Application Builder.

3. The primary Application Builder page displays a list of applications in the Oracle Application Express repository; you are about to develop your first application, so this page should initially be empty and display the message "No applications found."

4. Click Create to launch the Create Application wizard, which presents a few simple pages and creates a new application quickly.

5. Notice that the Create Application wizard provides two different approaches for building a new application: build an application from scratch or build a simple application from spreadsheet data. You can also install demonstration applications to learn by example. For the purposes of this exercise, click Create Application.

6. Use the Name page of the wizard to indicate basic information about your application by completing the following steps:

   ■ The Name field indicates a name for the new application. Specify **SysMgmt** for the Name field.

   ■ The Application field indicates a unique identifier for the application (in other words, a primary key). Make a note of the system-generated key value, but do not modify it.

   ■ The Create Application option list indicates how you want to create the new application. Select From scratch for the Create Application option list.

   ■ Select HANDSONXE06 from the Schema list.

7. Click Next.

8. Use the Pages page of the wizard to quickly add pages to the new application based on existing database tables. Oracle Application Express can create

many different types of pages for an application. For example, *reports* are read-only pages that display information in database tables; *forms* are read/write pages that facilitate data entry and modification; *charts* and *graphs* represent database data in visual formats. Complete the following steps to create a report and form for all three tables in the schema:

a. Both a report and a form based on the HOSTS table are necessary. Therefore, in the Add Page region of the page, click Report and Form.

b. Specify **HOSTS** in the Table Name field (or use the pop-up list).

c. When selected, the Include Analysis Pages check box starts another wizard to guide you through the process of creating reports that summarize information. For the purposes of this exercise, do not select Include Analysis Pages.

d. Click Add Page.

e. Notice the two new pages for the HOSTS table that are now part of the application and their hierarchical arrangement: the parent page is a report and the child page is a form. The hierarchical arrangement of the pages represents the navigation between the two pages.

f. Complete the same series of steps to add a report and form based on the DATABASES table. In the Add Page region of the page, click Report and Form.

g. The Subordinate to Page drop-down list box indicates the hierarchical relationship of the page(s) that you are adding relative to other pages in the application; for the purpose of this exercise, select Top Level Page.

h. Specify **DATABASES** in the Table Name field (or use the pop-up list).

i. Click Add Page.

j. Notice the two new pages for the DATABASES table that are now part of the application.

k. Complete the same series of steps to add a report and form based on the APPLICATIONS table. In the Add Page region of the page, click Report and Form.

l. Select Top Level Page in the Subordinate to Page list.

m. Specify **APPLICATIONS** in the Table Name field (or use the pop-up list).

n. Click Add Page.

o. Notice the two new pages for the APPLICATIONS table that are now part of the application.

p. Before continuing, confirm that there is a total of six pages, as shown in Figure 6-10. If you made a mistake, delete the erroneous pages and then add new versions of the correct pages by using the preceding steps.

9. Click Next.

10. Use the Tabs page of the wizard to indicate the primary means of navigation for the application. Tabs are a commonly used navigation style for web-based applications and should be effective for our example application; therefore, select One Level of Tabs.

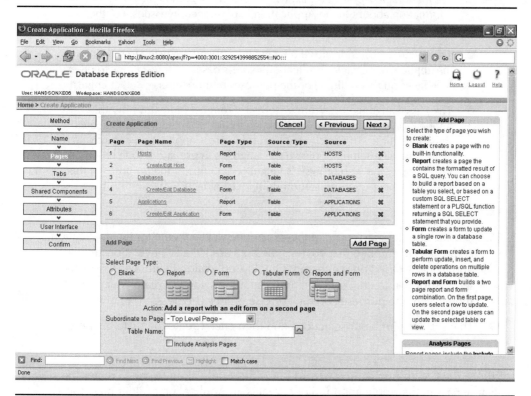

FIGURE 6-10.   *The six pages of the SysMgmt application as created by the Create Application wizard of Oracle Application Express*

11. Click Next.

12. Use the Shared Components page of the wizard to indicate whether you want to copy shared components from other Oracle Application Express applications to the new application. Because this is the first application you are developing, No is the only sensible selection.

13. Click Next.

14. Use the Attributes page to indicate several application attributes:

- The Authentication Scheme list indicates how you want to enforce security for the new application. Oracle Application Express supports a variety of authentication schemes for applications; however, a complete discussion of Oracle Application Express security is beyond the scope of this book. See the *Oracle Application Express User's Guide,* online at OTN, for more information about Oracle Application Express security issues. For the purposes of this exercise, select Application Express Authentication.

- The Language list indicates the language that you are using to develop the application; Oracle Application Express bases all translations to other languages on this setting. For the purposes of this exercise, select English.

- The User Language Preference Derived From list indicates how the application determines what language to use when someone executes the application. An Oracle Application Express application can have a static language setting or derive the language to use at run time based on, for example, the web browser's language setting. For the purposes of this exercise, select Use Application Primary Language.

15. Click Next.

16. Use the User Interface page of the wizard to select a theme for the application. A *theme* is a template that governs the appearance and navigation style for applications based on the theme. Oracle Application Express has several themes for you to choose from, and also allows you to create your own themes. For the purposes of this exercise, select Theme 2.

17. That's it! Confirm your selections and then click Create to create the new application.

Once the Create Application wizard of Oracle Application Express creates the new application, the Application Builder creates an Application Builder page for the application (not a page *of* the application) that displays information about the application, including the name of the application and several links for working with the application. When you are using an iconic view (select Icons from the View list, and then click Go), the page shows nothing more than a list of icons that represent the current pages in the application, as shown in Figure 6-11.

To see more details about each page in the application, select Details from the View list and then click Go; the main Application Builder page then shows a more in-depth list of the current pages in the application, as shown in Figure 6-12.

Subsequent exercises teach you more about using this interface. For now, confirm that your new application's attributes appear similar to those in Figures 6-11 and 6-12. In particular, notice that Oracle Application Express names the reports and forms by adopting the user interface defaults that you previously set for corresponding tables.

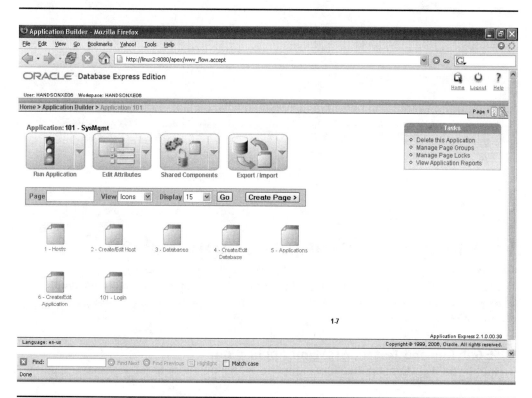

FIGURE 6-11. *The Icons view of the SysMgmt application's pages*

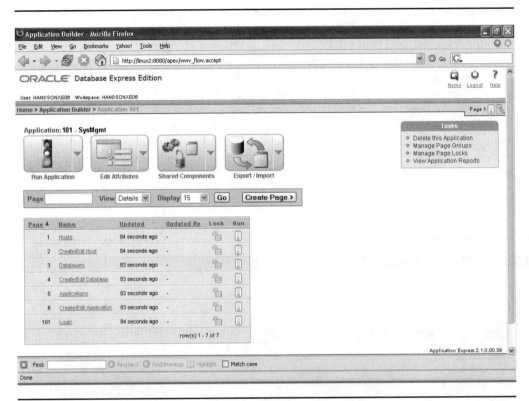

FIGURE 6-12. *The Details view of the SysMgmt application's pages*

Running and Testing the Application

After you develop an application, the next step is to run the application and see how it works. Throughout this testing stage of the application development lifecycle, make sure to take specific notes about application functionality that requires modification.

EXERCISE 6.8: Run and Test the SysMgmt Application

To launch the SysMgmt application, complete the following steps:

1. From the primary Application Builder page, click the icon of the application that you want to run to display the application's page. This step should be necessary only if you explored a bit since finishing the previous exercise.

2. From the application's page, click Run Application.

3. The SysMgmt application is set to use database authentication; therefore, enter a username and password of a user who has the privileges to use the application. For the purposes of this application, specify **HANDSONXE06** in the User Name field and **PASSWORD** in the Password field; then click Login.

Once the SysMgmt application launches, you should see the Hosts report page, similar to Figure 6-13.

EXERCISE 6.9: Navigate Application Report Pages

The top of each SysMgmt application page has a series of three tabs with the titles Hosts, Databases, and Applications. These tabs make it easy to switch among the pages related to the HOSTS, DATABASES, and APPLICATIONS tables.

1. Click the Databases tab to display a report of databases.

2. Click the Applications tab to display a report of applications.

3. Click the Hosts tab to return to the Hosts report.

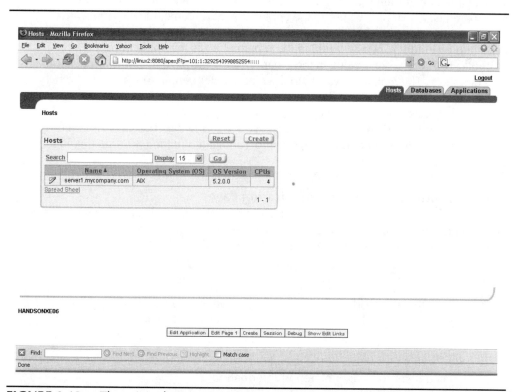

FIGURE 6-13. *The original Hosts report page of the SysMgmt application*

NOTE
The bottom of each page displays the Developer's
toolbar *with convenient links that make it easy to
stop running the application and edit the application
or a specific page. Subsequent exercises demonstrate
how to use several links in the Developer's toolbar
during application development and testing.*

EXERCISE 6.10: Understand Oracle Application Express URLs

As you move among the pages of the application, carefully notice how the URL
changes in your web browser. Oracle Application Express URLs should be similar to
the following:

http://127.0.0.1:8080/apex/f?p=**100:1**: ...

The first part of the URL, http://127.0.0.1:8080/apex/f, remains static as you move
among pages. This portion of the URL indicates the address of the application and
web server. The dynamic part of the URL that changes as you switch pages is a query
string, which begins after the ? character. A query string in a URL contains one or
more parameters that pass values to the application at run time. Oracle Application
Express query strings contain the p parameter, which is assigned several values
delimited by colons. The first value in the p parameter is the application's ID; for
example, 100. The second value in the p parameter is the page ID in the application;
for example, 1. The remaining values in the p parameter pertain to session and other
information not relevant to this discussion.

Notice that as you switch among pages in the application, the page number
changes to indicate the number of the page you are viewing. The page number in
the URL should correspond to the page number indicated in the Edit Page link in the
Developer's toolbar on the page.

EXERCISE 6.11: Browse and Review Application Pages

Now that you have a general understanding of the SysMgmt application's navigation,
layout, and user interface, complete this exercise's steps to review each page and
make notes for refining their appearance and functionality:

1. Click the Applications tab.

2. Notice that the header of the report region on the Applications report page
   contains a Create button: this button is a link to the Create/Edit Application
   form page.

3. Notice that the header of the report region also includes a Search field and
   related items for searching report information.

4. Specify **finch** in the Search field.

5. Click Go.

6. Notice that the report now displays only one record, a record with a Description that contains the string "finch." All other records have been filtered out of the report display.

7. Click Reset to remove the search filter and again display the first 15 records in the APPLICATIONS table.

8. Notice that the labels of the columns in the Applications report correspond to the user interface defaults that you previously set for the columns of the APPLICATIONS table.

9. Notice that the Database column of the Applications report contains each application's foreign key that refers to the DB_ID of a parent record in the DATABASES table. Make a note to modify the appearance of the Database column's data so that it lists the name of the database rather than the database's DB_ID.

10. Notice that the leftmost column in the report contains icons that are links for editing the corresponding record. Click the Edit icon to edit the first record in the Applications report.

11. This is your first look at the Create/Edit Application form page of the new application. Notice that the breadcrumbs navigation menu above the form indicates that the form page is hierarchically a child page of the parent Applications report page. You can easily click the Applications link in the breadcrumbs menu to return to the Applications report page, but don't do it yet.

12. Notice that the labels for the entry fields in the form correspond to the user interface defaults that you previously set for the columns of the APPLICATIONS table.

13. Notice that required fields have a small icon to the left of the column label.

14. Similar to the Applications report, notice that the Database field of the Create/Edit Applications form expects and displays a foreign key value that refers to the DB_ID of a parent record in the DATABASES table. Make a note to modify the Database field of the Create/Edit Applications form so that it displays a list of available databases rather than a database's DB_ID.

Repeat the preceding steps for the reports and forms based on the HOSTS and DATABASES tables. Make notes to edit the appearance/functionality of the Host field of the report and form pages based on the DATABASES table, similar to Steps 9 and 14.

Refining the Application

Applications that you build quickly with the Oracle Application Express Create Application wizard typically require a certain degree of refinement to account for issues such as those found in the previous exercise. The exercises in this section teach you several ways that you can refine the SysMgmt application to make it appear and function better.

EXERCISE 6.12: Create Lists of Values (LOVs) for Forms

A *list of values (LOV)* is a common application component that provides a standardized list of acceptable values for a field in a form. Technically speaking, each option in an LOV has a pair of associated values: a value that the LOV displays (a *display value*) and a value that the LOV returns to the associated field (a *return value*). LOVs are therefore useful for displaying human-readable values that correspond to cryptic code values such as foreign key values or status codes. This exercise teaches you how to create LOVs for hosts and databases that you can then use to improve the pages of the SysMgmt application.

To create a LOV for hosts, complete the following steps:

1. Click Edit Application in the Developer's toolbar to cease running the application and return to the SysMgmt application's page.

2. Click Shared Components to display the application's Shared Components page. *Shared components* are application components that pages in one or more Oracle Application Express applications can reuse.

3. After browsing the page information, click Lists of Values in the User Interface section of the Shared Components page.

4. The Lists of Values page displays icons for all LOVs that exist. Notice that the Create Application wizard generates a standard LOV named Report Row Per Page that the report pages in the application use to control the number of rows displayed per page.

5. Click Create.

6. Select From Scratch from the Create List of Values options.

7. Click Next.

8. Specify **HOSTS** in the Name field.

9. Your goal is to create a list of available hosts, which is not necessarily a static list. Therefore, select Dynamic from the Type options.

10. Click Next.

11. To generate a dynamic LOV, you must enter a SQL query in the Query field. The query's SELECT list must include only two expressions in the following order, as the example query in the Query field illustrates: a display value with the column alias *d* and a return value with the column alias *r*. (You should already be familiar with building queries that contain column aliases from your experience in Chapter 3.) The query that you specify generally returns more than one row and can have a WHERE clause, an ORDER BY clause, join information from one or more tables, etc.—click Examples if you would like to see example queries that are acceptable. To return a list of hosts and corresponding primary key values, enter the following query in the Query field:

```
SELECT host_name d, host_id r
  FROM handsonxe06.hosts
 ORDER BY 1
```

12. Click Create List of Values. Oracle Application Express checks the syntax of the query you submit to make sure it will parse at run time; if it will not, Oracle Application Express returns an error and allows you to correct your problem before continuing.

13. Notice that an icon for the new LOV appears in the Lists of Values page.

Now repeat Steps 5 through 13 to create a dynamic LOV for databases. Name the LOV **DATABASES** and specify the following query for the LOV:

```
SELECT db.db_name || '.' || h.host_name d, db_id r
  FROM handsonxe06.databases db
  NATURAL JOIN handsonxe06.hosts h
 ORDER BY 1
```

Notice that the display values that the join query returns are a concatenation of each database's name with its corresponding server's name; this extra information makes it clear which database to select just in case there are duplicate database names among servers in the organization (for example, db1 on server1 would be db1.server1 and db1 on server2 would be db1.server2).

EXERCISE 6.13: Add LOVs to Forms

Complete this exercise to modify specific form pages of the SysMgmt application to make use of the new LOVs. For example, to add the HOSTS LOV to the Create/Edit Database page, complete the following steps:

1. In the breadcrumbs navigation menu, click the link to your application's page (for example, **Application 100**).

2. From the application's page, click the link or icon for the Create/Edit Database form page, which should be page 4.

3. Take a moment to observe how Oracle Application Express organizes the various components that make up a form page:

   ■ A *region* is an area on a page that displays content.

   ■ A *page template* controls the order in which regions appear on a page.

   ■ Each region can contain various *elements*, such as reports, HTML, menus, and lists.

   ■ Regions can also contain *items* such as text fields, buttons, radio button groups, select lists, etc. Oracle Application Express assigns each item on a page a unique name prefixed by the letter *P*, the page's number, and an underscore (for example, P4_).

   ■ A *region template* controls the appearance of a region's elements and items.

4. Your goal in this exercise is to modify the HOST_ID field of the Create/Edit Database form page so that it uses the HOSTS LOV. Therefore, click the P4_HOST_ID link in the Items section of the page.

5. Take a moment to scroll the page and learn about the many attributes that you can set for a form field.

6. Again, the goal is to modify the HOST_ID form field so that it uses the HOSTS LOV. Therefore, select Select List from the Display As list in the Name section of the page. A shortcut for carrying out this step is to click [Select List] directly underneath the Display As list.

7. Next, you must indicate the LOV to use as the field's select list. Scroll down the page until the List of Values section is visible; click LOV at the top of the page to quickly scroll down the page directly to this section. Then select HOSTS from the Named LOV list.

8. Scroll back to the top of the page and click Apply Changes to save your work.

9. To run the application and immediately load this new version of the Create/Edit Database form page, click the streetlight icon in the top-right corner of the page. The new version of the form with the LOV should appear similar to Figure 6-14.

10. Click the Host list and notice that only one host is available. As you add new hosts to your database, the select list on this form will adapt accordingly.

Next, complete a similar series of steps so that the Database field of the Create/Edit Application form page uses the DATABASES LOV. This is a good opportunity to learn another way to use the Developer's toolbar.

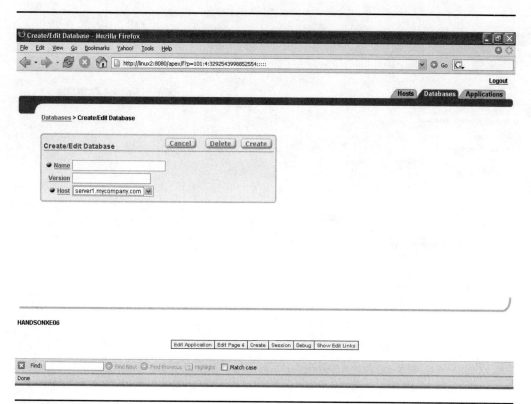

FIGURE 6-14. *The Create/Edit Database form page with the new list of values for the Host field*

11. Click the Applications tab.

12. Click Create to display the Create/Edit Application form page.

13. On the Developer's toolbar, click Edit Page 6.

14. Notice that you immediately navigate to the form page's definition page.

15. Repeat Steps 4 through 10 of this exercise to make use of the DATABASES LOV for the P6_DB_ID field of the Create/Edit Application form page. Notice that when you run the new version of the page and click the Database list in the form, all of the databases (db1 through db8) are available as options. When you finish, the new version of the Create/Edit Application form page should appear similar to Figure 6-15.

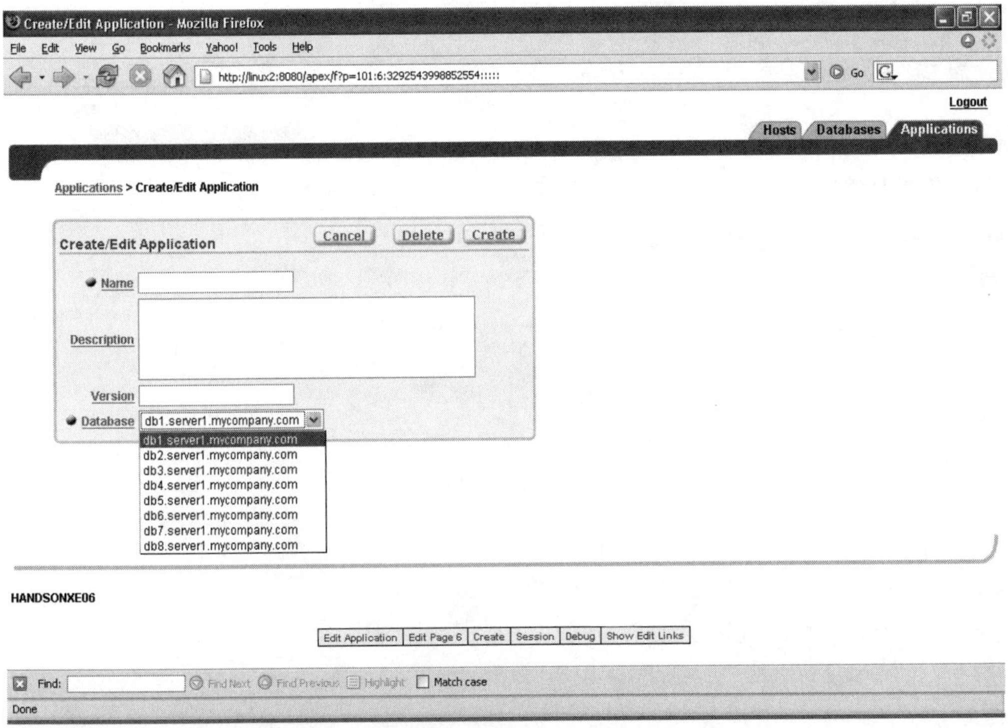

FIGURE 6-15. *The Create/Edit Application form page with the new list of values for the Database field*

EXERCISE 6.14: Modify a Report's Query and Make New Columns Searchable

The report pages in the current version of the application also display foreign key IDs: the Databases report shows the HOST_ID for its host and the Applications report shows the DB_ID for its database. This exercise teaches you one way to modify the report so that these fields contain more meaningful information that is also searchable.

To modify the Databases report page so that the Host Name column displays database names rather than database IDs, complete the following steps:

1. Click Databases (the Databases tab) to display the Databases report page.

2. On the Developer's toolbar, click Edit Page 3.

3. Take a moment to observe how Oracle Application Express organizes the various components that make up a report page, which is somewhat different from how it organizes form pages.

4. Although similar, reports have read-only *column attributes* that display information rather than fields that provide a means for data input on forms. To access a report's attributes, click the link for the report: for the purposes of this exercise, click Databases (not Region) in the Regions section of the page.

5. Notice that a region on a report page has two tabs with settings that you can use to control the region's appearance. The Region Definition tab provides access to settings that control the overall appearance of the region. The Report Attributes tab provides access to specific settings for report attributes.

6. Your goal is to modify the report so that it returns the name of a database's host rather than the HOST_ID foreign key. You could use the HOSTS LOV to do this, but the hostname information would not be searchable because the underlying data in each Databases report record would still be the HOST_ID value. To display the hostname for each database and make the new information searchable, you need to modify the data that the report's query actually retrieves; therefore, click the Report Definition tab, if necessary.

7. Click Source to jump to the Source section of the report definition.

8. The Region Source field contains the query that generates the information that the report displays. Notice the following points about the current query:

   ■ The query selects information for all columns in the HOSTS table.

   ■ When the P3_REPORT_SEARCH report field is not null, the query's WHERE clause condition limits the result set of the query to rows in which the uppercase string in the P3_REPORT_SEARCH field occur at least once in either the DB_NAME or DB_VERSION field. When the P3_REPORT_SEARCH field is null, the query returns all rows in the HOSTS table.

9. Modify the query so that it joins the DATABASES and HOSTS table to retrieve the hostname for each database record; replace the HOST_ID expression in the select list with the HOST_NAME expression. Also modify the query's WHERE clause so that the new HOST_NAME field is searchable, as follows (the edits that you should make are indicated in bold):

```
select
"DB_NAME",
"DB_ID",
"HOST_NAME",
"DB_VERSION"
 from    "DATABASES"
natural join "HOSTS"
```

```
where
(
 instr(upper("DB_NAME"),
  upper(nvl(:P3_REPORT_SEARCH,"DB_NAME"))) > 0 or
 instr(upper("DB_VERSION"),
  upper(nvl(:P3_REPORT_SEARCH,"DB_VERSION"))) > 0 or
 instr(upper("HOST_NAME"),
  upper(nvl(:P3_REPORT_SEARCH,"HOST_NAME"))) > 0
)
```

10. Scroll back to the top of the page and click Apply Changes to save your work.

11. To run the application and immediately load this new version of the Databases report page, click the streetlight icon in the top-right corner of the page. The new version of the report should appear similar to Figure 6-16.

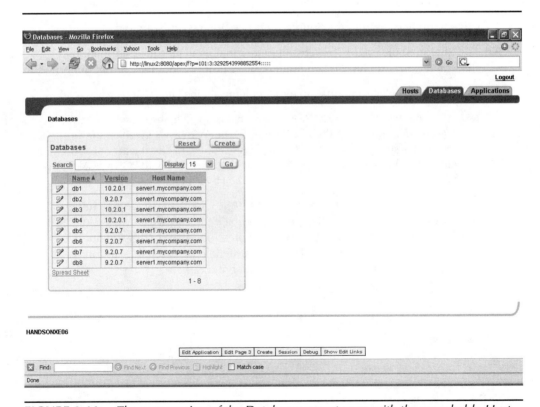

FIGURE 6-16. *The new version of the Databases report page with the searchable Host Name column*

12. Notice that the Host Name column in the report now displays the name of each database's host rather than each host's ID.

13. Test the new search function to make sure that it works properly. For example, a search for the string server1 should display all records in the table; a search for the string server2 should display no records in the table.

TIP
It is very important to note the columns of an application's tables that you make searchable—these are the columns that you want to create indexes for so that the application's queries can efficiently find specific rows in a table with index scans rather than full table scans.

Now repeat steps similar to the previous steps in this exercise to replace the DB_ID column of the Applications report page with the DATABASE_NAME column. Modify the report to use the following query (the edits that you should make are indicated in bold):

```
select
"AP_DESCRIPTION",
"AP_NAME",
"DB_NAME" || '.' || "HOST_NAME" AS "DATABASE",
"AP_VERSION",
"AP_ID"
 from    "APPLICATIONS"
 natural join "DATABASES"
 natural join "HOSTS"
where
(
 instr(upper("AP_DESCRIPTION"),
  upper(nvl(:P5_REPORT_SEARCH,"AP_DESCRIPTION"))) > 0  or
 instr(upper("AP_NAME"),
  upper(nvl(:P5_REPORT_SEARCH,"AP_NAME"))) > 0  or
 instr(upper("AP_VERSION"),
  upper(nvl(:P5_REPORT_SEARCH,"AP_VERSION"))) > 0  or
 instr(upper("DB_NAME" || '.' || "HOST_NAME"),
  upper(nvl(:P5_REPORT_SEARCH,"DB_NAME" || '.' || "HOST_NAME"))) > 0
)
```

Again, make sure to test the new search function. For example, a search for the string db3 should display only the applications that are served by db3.server1 .mycompany.com; a search for db6 should display no records. When you finish, the new version of the Applications report page should appear similar to Figure 6-17.

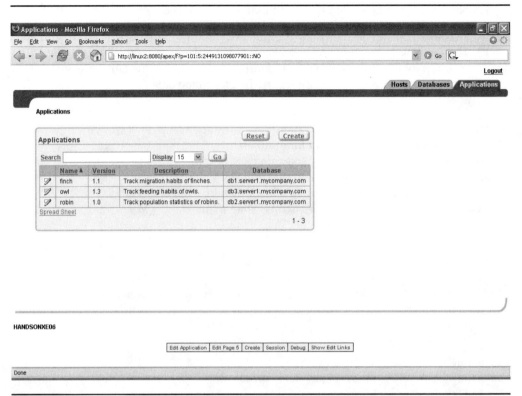

FIGURE 6-17. *The new version of the Applications report page with the searchable Database column*

Maintaining the Application

An application's requirements will inevitably change over the lifecycle of the application. For example, after you develop, refine, and finish testing the first version of the SysMgmt application, suppose that the DBAs request a new requirement: the need to track information about all daily database backups. To meet the latest requirement, make sure that you take the time to *analyze* and *design* for the new feature.

For example, during a meeting with the staff DBAs to review the functionality of the SysMgmt application, they indicate the need to track information about technical support service requests for databases. Consequently, you draw a new use case diagram (see Figure 6-18) that shows how DBAs must be able to create, modify, and drop service request information related to the various databases in the system.

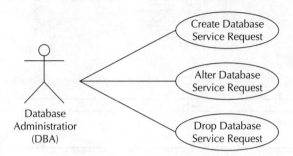

FIGURE 6-18. *A use case diagram that shows the database service request management tasks performed by database administrators in the SysMgmt application*

An updated class diagram (see Figure 6-19) clearly identifies the attributes that DBAs consider important when tracking database service requests, which includes the following:

- The database that the service request corresponds to

- The version of the database, host operating system, and host operating system version *at the time that the service request was filed*

- An optional reference identifier that corresponds to a technical service request filed with Oracle's technical support department, MetaLink

- A summary of the problem that the service request addresses

- Detailed information about the problem

- Detailed information about the problem resolution

- A database can have zero or many database service requests.

Next, you design new application components that are necessary to meet the new requirements. In this example, the database requires a new table to track the required information for database service requests. Each database service request should have a unique ID generated by a sequence. The new table must have a foreign key that refers to the existing DATABASES table. The application itself requires a new form for creating, modifying, and deleting database service requests, and a new report for displaying information about them. To populate the historical fields in the table, you decide to create a trigger.

Now that you have a plan, this section's exercises introduce you to some techniques that you can use to adapt an existing Oracle Application Express application as needs change.

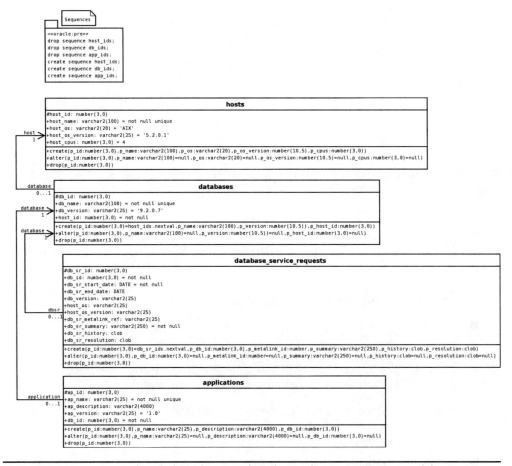

FIGURE 6-19. *An updated class diagram that shows the static structure of the SysMgmt application*

EXERCISE 6.15: Create a New Table

The first task to meet the new requirements is to create a new table named DATABASE_ SERVICE_REQUESTS. This exercise lists steps for using the familiar Object Browser page to accomplish related tasks.

1. If necessary, click Edit Application in the Developer's toolbar to cease running the application.

2. Click Home.

3. Click Object Browser.

4. Click Create | Table.

5. Specify **DATABASE_SERVICE_REQUESTS** in the Table Name field.

6. On the Columns page, enter the following column specifications (Column Name, Type, etc.):

   ■ Specify the **DB_SR_ID** and **DB_ID** columns using the NUMBER datatype constrained to a precision of **3** and a scale of **0**.

   ■ Specify the **DB_SR_START_DATE** and **DB_SR_END_DATE** columns using the DATE datatype.

   ■ Specify the **DB_VERSION**, **HOST_OS**, **HOST_OS_VERSION**, and **DB_SR_ METALINK_REF** columns using the VARCHAR2 datatype with a size of **25**.

   ■ Specify the **DB_SR_SUMMARY** column using the VARCHAR2 datatype with a size of **250**.

   ■ Specify the **DB_SR_HISTORY** and **DB_SR_RESOLUTION** columns using the CLOB datatype.

   ■ Mark the **DB_ID**, **DB_SR_START_DATE**, and **DB_SR_SUMMARY** columns as Not Null.

7. Click Next or Primary Key to continue.

8. On the Primary Key page, complete the following steps:

   ■ Unlike with previous application tables, you need to create a sequence for the new table's primary key. To do it conveniently while creating the table, select the Populated from a new sequence radio button.

   ■ Specify **DATABASE_SERVICE_REQUESTS_PK** in the Primary Key Constraint Name field.

   ■ Specify **DB_SR_IDS** in the Sequence Name field.

   ■ Select DB_SR_ID(NUMBER) in the Primary Key list.

9. Click Next or Foreign Key to continue.

10. On the Foreign Key page, complete the following steps to add a foreign key for the DB_ID column of the DATABASE_SERVICE_REQUESTS table that refers to the DB_ID column of the DATABASES table. The goals are to ensure that the DB_ID field of each record in the DATABASE_SERVICE_ REQUESTS table refers to a DB_ID in the DATABASES table and to prevent transactions from updating the primary keys in or deleting rows from the DATABASES table.

   ■ Specify **DATABASE_SERVICE_REQUESTS_FK1** in the Name field.

   ■ To enforce the delete cascade referential action for the new referential integrity constraint, select the Disallow Delete radio button.

- To indicate the column that makes up the foreign key in the new DATABASE_SERVICE_REQUESTS table, select the DB_ID column in the Select Key Column(s) field and then click the right-arrow button to move the selected column to the Key Column(s) field.

- To indicate the referenced column in the parent DATABASES table, specify **DATABASES** in the References Table field, show the specified table's columns, select the DB_ID column in the Select Reference Column(s) field, and then click the right-arrow button to move the selected column to the Reference Column(s) field.

- Click Add.

- Confirm the declaration of the new foreign key in the list of foreign keys at the top of the page.

11. The table does not require any check or unique constraints; therefore, click Confirm to continue.

12. Click SQL and confirm the SQL DDL statements that the wizard builds:

```
CREATE table "DATABASE_SERVICE_REQUESTS" (
     "DB_SR_ID"             NUMBER(3,0),
     "DB_ID"                NUMBER(3,0) NOT NULL,
     "DB_SR_START_DATE"     DATE NOT NULL,
     "DB_SR_END_DATE"       DATE,
     "DB_VERSION"           VARCHAR2(25),
     "HOST_OS"              VARCHAR2(25),
     "HOST_OS_VERSION"      VARCHAR2(25),
     "DB_SR_METALINK_REF"   VARCHAR2(25),
     "DB_SR_SUMMARY"        VARCHAR2(250) NOT NULL,
     "DB_SR_HISTORY"        CLOB,
     "DB_SR_RESOLUTION"     CLOB,
     constraint   "DATABASE_SERVICE_REQUESTS_PK"
       primary key ("DB_SR_ID")
)
/

CREATE sequence "DB_SR_IDS"
/

CREATE trigger "BI_DATABASE_SERVICE_REQUESTS"
  before insert on "DATABASE_SERVICE_REQUESTS"
  for each row
begin
    select "DB_SR_IDS".nextval into :NEW.DB_SR_ID from dual;
end;
/
```

```
ALTER TABLE "DATABASE_SERVICE_REQUESTS"
 ADD CONSTRAINT "DATABASE_SERVICE_REQUESTS_FK1"
FOREIGN KEY ("DB_ID")
REFERENCES "DATABASES" ("DB_ID")

/
```

13. Click Create to create the HANDSONXE05.DATABASE_SERVICE_REQUESTS table and related objects.

EXERCISE 6.16: Set UI Defaults for the New Table

After you create a new table for an application, remember to set associated user interface defaults before starting to design new application pages based on the table. Complete the following steps to set UI defaults for the new DATABASE_SERVICE_ REQUESTS table:

1. From the Object Browser page (click Home | Object Browser), select Tables | DATABASE_SERVICE_REQUESTS if the table is not already selected.

2. Click UI Defaults.

3. Click Create Defaults.

4. Click Grid Edit.

5. Specify **Create/Edit Database Service Request** in the Form Region Title field.

6. Specify **Database Service Requests** in the Report Region Title field.

7. Specify the following in the Label field of the table's columns:

   ■ **Service Request** for the DB_SR_ID column

   ■ **Database** for the DB_ID column

   ■ **Start Date** for the DB_SR_START_DATE column

   ■ **End Date** for the DB_SR_END_DATE column

   ■ **Oracle Version** for the DB_VERSION column

   ■ **Operating System (OS)** for the HOST_OS column

   ■ **OS Version** for the HOST_OS_VERSION column

   ■ **Metalink** for the DB_SR_METALINK_REF column

   ■ **Summary** for the DB_SR_SUMMARY column

   ■ **History** for the DB_SR_HISTORY column

   ■ **Resolution** for the DB_SR_RESOLUTION column

8. Select Yes for the Searchable field of the DB_VERSION, HOST_OS, HOST_OS_VERSION, DB_SR_METALINK_REF, and DB_SR_SUMMARY columns; all other columns should be set to No.

9. Do not adjust any other UI defaults.

10. Click Apply Changes to save your work.

EXERCISE 6.17: Create a New Trigger

To make data entry easier for a new database service request, you decide to create a trigger that populates the DB_SR_START_DATE, DB_VERSION, HOST_OS, and HOST_OS_VERSION columns with default values based on corresponding information at the time a new service request is created. To create the new trigger, complete the following steps:

1. Click Home | Object Browser.

2. Select the DATABASE_SERVICE_REQUESTS table.

3. Click Triggers.

4. Click Create.

5. Specify **DATABASE_SERVICE_REQUESTS_T1** for the Trigger Name field.

6. Select BEFORE in the Firing Point list.

7. Select insert in the Options list.

8. Select For Each Row.

9. Specify the following in the Trigger Body field:

```
SELECT SYSDATE INTO :NEW.db_sr_start_date FROM dual;

SELECT db_version, host_os, host_os_version
  INTO :NEW.db_version, :NEW.host_os, :NEW.host_os_version
  FROM handsonxe06.databases
  NATURAL JOIN handsonxe06.hosts
 WHERE db_id = :NEW.db_id;
```

10. Click Next.

11. Click SQL and confirm that the following SQL statement displays:

```
create or replace trigger "DATABASE_SERVICE_REQUESTS_T1"
BEFORE
insert on "DATABASE_SERVICE_REQUESTS"
for each row
```

```
begin
SELECT SYSDATE INTO :NEW.db_sr_start_date FROM dual;

SELECT db_version, host_os, host_os_version
  INTO :NEW.db_version, :NEW.host_os, :NEW.host_os_version
  FROM handsonxe06.databases
  NATURAL JOIN handsonxe06.hosts
 WHERE db_id = :NEW.db_id;
end;
/
```

12. Click Finish to create the new trigger.

EXERCISE 6.18: Add Rows to the DATABASE_SERVICE_REQUESTS Table

Complete the following steps to insert two rows into the DATABASE_SERVICE_
REQUESTS table and test the new triggers:

1. Select Home | Object Browser | Browse | Tables.

2. Select DATABASE_SERVICE_REQUESTS.

3. Click Data.

4. Click Insert Row.

5. Specify the following information for the fields of the DATABASE_SERVICE_
    REQUESTS table:

    ■ The DB_SR_ID field will be automatically populated by the DB_SR_IDS
       sequence and BI_DATABASE_SERVICE_REQUESTS trigger; therefore, do not
       specify anything for this field.

    ■ Specify **1** in the DB_ID field.

    ■ The DB_SR_START_DATE, DB_VERSION, HOST_OS, and HOST_OS_
       VERSION fields will automatically be populated by the DATABASE_SERVICE_
       REQUESTS_T1 trigger; therefore, do not specify anything for these fields.

    ■ Do not specify anything for the DB_SR_END_DATE field; this value is
       unknown as of this time.

    ■ Specify **5983257.1** in the DB_SR_METALINK_REF field.

    ■ Specify **The data file for the USERS tablespace was damaged by a disk
       failure and required recovery**. in the DB_SR_SUMMARY field.

    ■ You cannot specify anything for the DB_SR_HISTORY and DB_SR_
       RESOLUTION fields because they are CLOB columns, which the Create
       Row page of the Object Browser does not support.

6. Click Create and Create Another.

7. Similar to Step 5, specify the following values for another new row:

   ■ Skip the DB_SR_ID field to rely on the trigger.

   ■ Specify **2** in the DB_ID field.

   ■ Skip the DB_SR_START_DATE, DB_VERSION, HOST_OS, and HOST_OS_
     VERSION fields to rely on triggers.

   ■ Do not specify anything for the DB_SR_END_DATE field.

   ■ Specify **5823552.1** in the DB_SR_METALINK_REF field.

   ■ Specify **During a large data load, the archiving location ran out of space
     and made the instance hang.** in the DB_SR_SUMMARY field.

   ■ Skip the DB_SR_HISTORY and DB_SR_RESOLUTION fields.

8. Click Create.

9. Notice how the triggers automatically populate several fields for the new
   rows, as expected.

EXERCISE 6.19: Add New Application Pages

Now complete the following steps to create a new report and form page based on
the DATABASE_BACKUPS table:

1. Click Home | Application Builder.

2. Click SysMgmt (its icon).

3. Click Create Page.

4. Notice the many types of pages that you can add to an application. For
   complete information about the various types of pages supported by Oracle
   Application Express, use the help system or read the Oracle Application
   Express documentation that is online at OTN. For the purposes of this
   exercise, click Form.

5. You want to add both a form and a report; therefore, click Form on a Table
   with Report.

6. Confirm that you are working with the HANDSONXE06 schema, and then
   click Next.

7. Specify **DATABASE_SERVICE_REQUESTS** in the Table/View Name field
   (or use the select window feature).

8. Click Next.

9. Specify the following information for this page of the Create Report Page wizard:

   ■ Select Yes for the Use User Interface Defaults option list.

   ■ Specify the next available page number in the Page field; for example, **7**. You can use the adjacent button to show a pop-up list of current application pages and their page numbers.

   ■ Specify **Database Service Requests** in both the Page Name and Region Title fields.

   ■ Do not change any of the remaining settings.

10. Click Next.

11. Select Use an existing tab set and reuse an existing tab within that tab set from the Tab Options list.

12. Select TS1 (Hosts, Databases, Applications) from the Tab Set list.

13. Click Next.

14. The new report page should appear in the application under the Databases tab; therefore, select T_DATABASES from the Use Tab list.

15. Click Next.

16. The new report page should include all columns of the DATABASE_SERVICE_ REQUESTS table; therefore, select all columns in the Select Column(s) list.

17. Click Next.

18. Use the default Edit Link Image so that it matches the appearance of the other report pages in the application; click Next.

19. Specify the following information for this page of the Create Form Page wizard:

   ■ Specify the next available page number in the Page field; for example, **8**. You can use the adjacent button to show a list of current application pages and their page numbers.

   ■ Specify **Create/Edit Database Service Request** in both the Page Name and Region Title fields.

   ■ Do not change any of the remaining settings.

20. Click Next.

21. Select Use an existing tab set and reuse an existing tab within that tab set from the Tab Options list.

22. Select TS1 (Hosts, Databases, Applications) from the Tab Set list.

23. Click Next.

24. Select T_DATABASES from the Use Tab list.

25. Click Next.

26. Select DB_SR_ID from the Primary Key list.

27. Click Next.

28. The table already has a trigger to generate primary keys; therefore, click Existing Trigger.

29. Click Next.

30. The new form page should include all columns of the DATABASE_SERVICE_ REQUESTS table; therefore, select all columns in the Select Column(s) list.

31. Click Next.

32. The new form should allow all DML operations; therefore, select Yes for the Insert, Update, and Delete lists to enable all options for the form page.

33. Click Next.

34. Confirm your selections and click Finish.

35. Click Run Page to view the new report page. Notice that the DB_ID is listed for the Database column; you will want to change this so that the more meaningful database name appears.

36. Click the edit icon in the first row of the report or the Create button to view the new form page. Notice that the date fields for the form have date pickers to facilitate easy date entry in the new form.

37. Click the Hosts tab.

38. Click the Databases tab.

39. Notice that there is no way to show the new Database Service Requests report page. That's a hitch.

EXERCISE 6.20: Add a Navigation Menu

The most glaring problem that requires attention immediately after adding the new report and form pages is that there is no way to navigate to them. Oracle Application Express offers many different components that you can use to facilitate navigation within an application, including breadcrumbs, lists, navigation bar entries, tabs, and trees. Considering that the SysMgmt application is likely to evolve and require many new pages under each top-level page (Hosts, Databases, and Applications), an extensible strategy is to add a menu to each top-level page that makes it easy to navigate to each related subpage in the application. This exercise teaches you how to add a navigation menu to the Databases report page that users can use to navigate to the related Database Service Requests report page. Follow these steps:

1. Click Edit Application in the Developer's toolbar.

2. Click Databases.

3. Click the Create button (+) in the Lists section to create a new list.

4. Specify **LINKS_1** in the Name field.

5. Select Vertical Unordered List without Bullet in the List Template list.

6. Click Create.

That was easy; however, immediately after you create a new list, the list is empty, so it doesn't serve any purpose. To make the list useful, you need to make the new list a collection of the navigation links that you want to appear on the Databases report page. At this time, the navigation menu requires just a single entry (link) that targets the new Database Service Requests report page. To add the new entry to the list, complete the following steps:

1. Click Create List Entry.

2. In the Entry section of the page, specify **Database Service Requests** in the List Entry Label field; this is the text that Oracle Application Express displays for the new entry in the list. Notice that it's possible to specify an image as well.

3. In the Target section of the page, use the page selection list or specify the page number for the Database Service Requests report page in the Page field. The expected page is page **7**.

4. Click Create.

5. Notice that the List Entries page displays information about the list's entries, as shown in Figure 6-20.

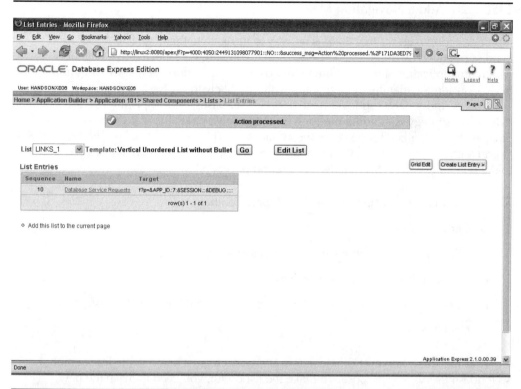

FIGURE 6-20. A new list that contains navigation links

Now complete the following steps to add the new list to the current page:

1. Click Add this list to the current page (look under the list's entries).

2. To add the list to the Databases report page, you must first create a new region to contain the list. Specify **Related Links** in the Title field to specify the title for the new region.

3. A page template controls the appearance of a page's layout. A region template controls the appearance of a particular region on a page. Select Reports Region for the Region Template list.

4. A region's display point controls the display sequence of a region relative to other regions on the same page. For a visual representation of the region's display point, click the flashlight icon adjacent to the Display Point list. To make the new navigation menu appear in the upper-right corner of the reports region of the page, click the Region Pos 03 link in the pop-up window. The pop-up window then closes and updates the Display Point list

with your selection (Page Template Region Position 3). In the future, you can make your selection directly from the Display Point list or use the shortcut links below the select list.

5. Click Next to continue.

6. Select LINKS_1 in the List select list.

7. Click Create List Region.

8. Notice that the Regions section of the page definition now shows the new region to display the list.

Now test the new list to see if it works:

1. Click Run (the streetlight icon) in the upper-right corner to run the current page.

2. Notice the new Related Links section on the Databases report page, as shown in Figure 6-21.

3. Click Database Service Requests to display the Display Service Requests report page. From here, you can navigate to the related form page with the edit icons and Create button.

The new menu now provides an avenue to navigate *to* the new Database Service Requests report and related form. But notice that it is unclear where you are in the application, and that there is no way to navigate *back to* the Databases page without multiple mouse clicks. The next exercise corrects this navigation problem.

EXERCISE 6.21: Copy Breadcrumbs to the New Report and Form Pages

A *breadcrumbs menu* is an application component that provides two useful benefits: navigation and a visual representation of your current location in the application. This exercise teaches you how to add new links for the new report and form pages to the application's breadcrumb menu, and then add the breadcrumb region and menu to the new pages:

1. While the SysMgmt application is executing, click the Hosts tab.

2. Click Edit Page 1 on the Developer's toolbar.

3. Notice that the Regions section of the page includes a region to display the breadcrumbs menu. The easiest way to add the same breadcrumbs region and menu to the new pages is to copy the region from one page to another. Click the Copy icon in the upper-right corner of the Regions section.

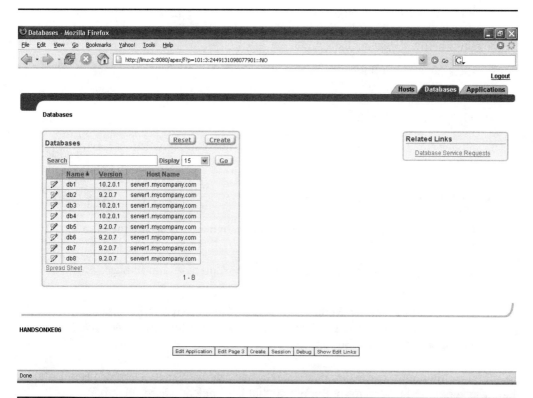

FIGURE 6-21. *The new version of the Databases report page with a Related Links navigation menu*

4. Click Breadcrumbs to copy the Breadcrumbs regions.

5. Specify **7** in the To Page field, or click the button adjacent to the To Page field and select the Database Service Requests page from the pop-up window.

6. Click Next.

7. Click Copy Region to accept the defaults for the new region.

8. Navigate to page 7 and notice that it now includes a new Breadcrumbs region to display the breadcrumbs menu.

9. Repeat the steps similar to Steps 3 through 7 to copy the Breadcrumbs region from the current page to the Create/Edit Database Service Requests page (page 8).

Now, both new pages have the ability to display the application's breadcrumb menu, but will not do so until we add links for each page to the menu. To add entries (links) to the breadcrumbs menu, complete the following steps.

1. To edit the breadcrumbs menu itself, click Breadcrumb (not Breadcrumbs) in the Regions section of whatever application page definition you are currently viewing.

2. The Breadcrumb Entries page displays the existing entries for the breadcrumbs menu. Notice the hierarchical arrangement, display sequence numbers, and referenced application pages of the existing entries. The highest display sequence should be 60.

3. Click Create Breadcrumb Entry to create a new entry.

4. The Breadcrumb section of the Create/Edit Breadcrumb Entry page indicates the page on which the breadcrumb entry is current; specify **7** in the Page field, or use the pop-up window to select the page number of the Database Service Requests page.

5. The Entry section of the Create/Edit Breadcrumb Entry page indicates the details for the breadcrumb entry.

   ■ Specify a higher sequence number than 60 such as 70 in the Sequence field.

   ■ The parent page for the Database Service Requests page is the Databases page; therefore, select **Databases** in the Parent Entry list.

   ■ Enter **Database Service Requests** in both the Short Name and Long Name fields.

6. The Target section of the Create/Edit Breadcrumb Entry page specifies the page to navigate to when a user clicks the link; specify **7** in the Page field, or use the pop-up window to select the page number of the Database Service Requests page.

7. Click Create to create the new entry.

8. Notice the new entry for the Database Service Requests page in the Breadcrumb Entries page and its hierarchical arrangement relative to entry for the Databases page.

9. Repeat steps similar to Steps 3 through 8 for the Create/Edit Database Service Requests page. Make sure that the parent of the new entry is set to the Database Service Requests page. When you are finished, the breadcrumbs menu entries should appear as in Figure 6-22.

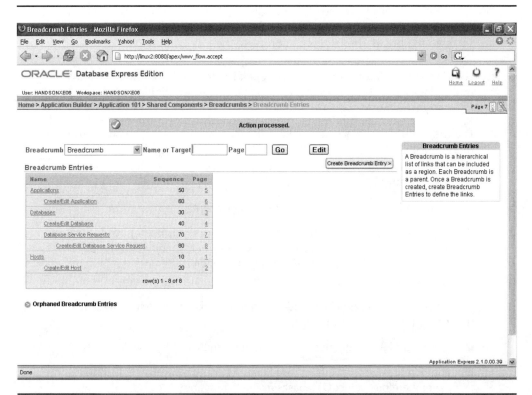

FIGURE 6-22. *The modified version of the SysMgmt's breadcrumb menu*

To test your new breadcrumbs menu, click Run to run the current page. The Create/Edit Database Service Request form page should appear as in Figure 6-23.

EXERCISE 6.22: Add Search and Display Controls to the New Report

The new Database Service Requests report page lacks the search functionality that the other report pages in the application currently support. This relatively long exercise teaches you how to add the same capability to the new report page, along with a control for repagination.

The first part of the job is to create page components that facilitate the search function and repagination on the new report page; the easiest way to accomplish this task and ensure that the new report page is consistent with other report pages is to copy the components from one page to another:

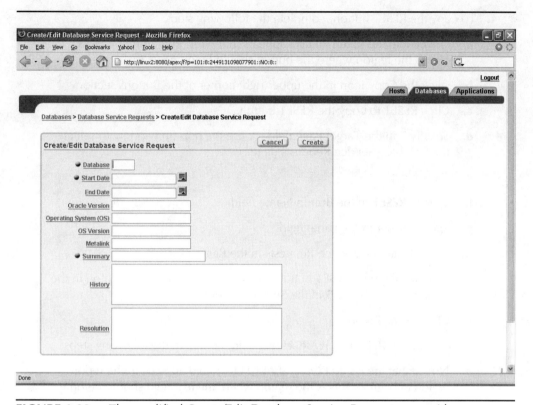

FIGURE 6-23. *The modified Create/Edit Database Service Request page with a breadcrumbs menu*

1. While the SysMgmt application is executing, navigate to the Databases report page any way you choose.

2. Notice that the Databases report contains four different items to support the search and display functionality: a Reset button to clear nondefault display settings; a Search text field where you can enter search string criteria; a Display list to control how many records the report displays; and a Go button to update the display of the report based on the settings of the previously mentioned two items. Your goal is to duplicate this functionality on the Database Service Requests report page.

3. Click Edit Page 3 in the Developer's toolbar to display the current page's definition.

4. To copy the RESET button, complete the following steps:

a. Notice that the RESET button appears in the report region of page 3. This is the region where the button should be on page 7.

b. Click the Copy icon in the upper-right corner of the Buttons section.

c. Click RESET to copy the RESET button.

d. Specify **7** in the Target Page field (or use the pop-up window to select the Database Service Requests page).

e. Click Next.

f. Specify **RESET** in the Button Name field.

g. Specify **Reset** in the Label field.

h. Select Database Service Requests in the Region list.

i. To make the new RESET button appear before the CREATE button in the same region, specify **5** in the Sequence field.

j. Click Copy Button.

5. To copy the P3_REPORT_SEARCH text field, complete the following steps:

a. Notice that the P3_REPORT_SEARCH text field appears in the report region of page 3. This is the region where the text field should be on page 7.

b. Click the Copy icon in the upper-right corner of the Items section.

c. Click P3_REPORT_SEARCH to copy the P3_REPORT_SEARCH text field.

d. Specify **7** in the Target Page field.

e. Click Next.

f. Specify **P7_REPORT_SEARCH** in the Item Name field. Notice that the prefix for the text field's name reflects the page on which it exists (P7_).

g. Specify **Search** in the Label field.

h. Select Database Service Requests in the Region list.

i. Specify **10** in the Sequence field.

j. The text field is used to enter search criteria. Therefore, select Static Assignment (value equals source attribute) in the Source Type list.

k. Click Copy Item.

6. To copy the P3_ROWS select list, complete the following steps:

   a. Notice that the P3_ROWS select list appears in the report region of page 3. This is the region where the select list should be on page 7.

   b. Click the Copy icon in the upper-right corner of the Items section.

   c. Click P3_ROWS to copy the P3_ROWS select list.

   d. Specify **7** in the Target Page field.

   e. Click Next.

   f. Specify **P7_ROWS** in the Item Name field. Notice that the prefix for the text field's name reflects the page on which it exists (P7_).

   g. Specify **Display** in the Label field.

   h. Select Database Service Requests in the Region list.

   i. Specify **20** in the Sequence field.

   j. Do not modify the copied settings for the Source Type list and Source fields, which should be Static Assignment and 15, respectively.

   k. Click Copy Item.

7. To copy the P3_GO button, complete the following steps:

   a. Notice that the P3_GO button appears in the report region of page 3. This is the region where the button should be on page 7.

   b. Click the Copy icon in the upper-right corner of the Items section.

   c. Click P3_GO to copy the P3_GO button.

   d. Specify **7** in the Target Page field.

   e. Click Next.

   f. Specify **P7_GO** in the Item Name field. Notice that the prefix for the text field's name reflects the page on which it exists (P7_).

   g. Specify Go in the Label field.

   h. Select Database Service Requests in the Region list.

   i. Specify **30** in the Sequence field.

   j. The Source Type list determines what the button does when it is clicked. Select Static Assignment so that the button assigns a value when it is clicked.

    k. The Source field determines the value to assign based on the setting of the Source Type list. Specify **Go** in the Source field.

    l. Click Copy Item.

8. Navigate from the definition of page 3 to the definition of page 7: specify **7** in the Page field in the upper-left corner of the page definition page and then click Go.

9. Notice the items recently copied to this page (page 7), as shown in Figure 6-24.

To support the search functionality, the next part of the job is to modify the report's query so that it takes into account the current value of the new P7_REPORT_SEARCH field. To do this, modify the report query by adding a WHERE clause using

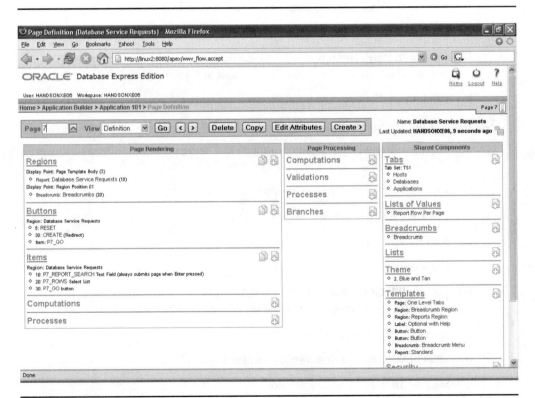

FIGURE 6-24. *The modified Database Service Requests report page with copied items*

the steps that follow. At the same time, modify the report's query so that it displays a more meaningful database name rather than a DB_ID.

1. Click Database Service Requests in the Regions section of the page.

2. Click Source to jump to the Source section of the page.

3. Modify the query as follows. The new query joins the DATABASE_SERVICE_
REQUESTS table with the DATABASES table, replaces the DB_ID select
list expression with the DB_NAME expression, and adds a WHERE clause
condition that takes into account the P7_REPORT_SEARCH text field value to
search the DB_NAME, DB_VERSION, HOST_OS, HOST_OS_VERSION, DB_
SR_METALINK_REF, and DB_SR_SUMMARY fields; you should be familiar
with these types of report query modifications from previous exercises in this
chapter. The edits that you should make are indicated in bold.

```
select "DB_SR_ID",
"DB_NAME" AS "DATABASE",
"DB_SR_START_DATE",
"DB_SR_END_DATE",
"DB_VERSION",
"HOST_OS",
"HOST_OS_VERSION",
"DB_SR_METALINK_REF",
"DB_SR_SUMMARY",
dbms_lob.substr("DB_SR_HISTORY",4000,1) "DB_SR_HISTORY",
dbms_lob.substr("DB_SR_RESOLUTION",4000,1) "DB_SR_RESOLUTION"
from "#OWNER#"."DATABASE_SERVICE_REQUESTS"
natural join "#OWNER#"."DATABASES"
where
(
 instr(upper("DB_NAME"),
  upper(nvl(:P7_REPORT_SEARCH,"DB_NAME"))) > 0 or
 instr(upper("DB_VERSION"),
  upper(nvl(:P7_REPORT_SEARCH,"DB_VERSION"))) > 0 or
 instr(upper("HOST_OS"),
  upper(nvl(:P7_REPORT_SEARCH,"HOST_OS"))) > 0 or
 instr(upper("HOST_OS_VERSION"),
  upper(nvl(:P7_REPORT_SEARCH,"HOST_OS_VERSION"))) > 0 or
 instr(upper("DB_SR_METALINK_REF"),
  upper(nvl(:P7_REPORT_SEARCH,"DB_SR_METALINK_REF"))) > 0 or
 instr(upper("DB_SR_SUMMARY"),
  upper(nvl(:P7_REPORT_SEARCH,"DB_SR_SUMMARY"))) > 0

)
```

Next, bind the Display list to control the number of rows that the report displays at any given time. To do this, complete the following steps:

1. Scroll to the top of the page and click the Report Attributes tab. Oracle Application Express implicitly saves your report definition modifications.

2. Click Layouts and Pagination to jump to the Layouts and Pagination section.

3. Specify **P7_ROWS** in the Number of Rows (Item) field to link the setting of the P7_ROWS select list to the number of rows to display on the report page.

4. Click Apply Changes to save your work.

At this point, all of the controls necessary to control the display of rows in the report are built and configured. However, items that control application behavior, such as buttons, do not know what actions to perform until you build associated processes and branches that explicitly explain what to do when a user utilizes each control. A *page process* does something when Oracle Application Express renders or submits a page. For example, when you reset a report page, a process can repaginate the report so that the report displays the original result set of the report. A *branch* forks application processing to display a page or URL, or execute a PL/SQL procedure. For example, to reset a report page's display after entering some search criteria or changing the number of rows to display, the page can create and use a branch back to itself.

To code the desired behavior for the new controls in the Database Service Requests report, the following processes and branch are necessary:

■ When the user clicks the Go button (P7_GO) to submit a page, a process must repaginate the report to display the first set of rows in the result set.

■ When a user clicks the Reset button (RESET) to submit a page, a process must reset the Search field (P7_REPORT_SEARCH) and Display list (P7_ROWS) to their default settings.

■ In the previous two scenarios, when the Database Service Requests report submits, the page branches back to itself.

Complete the following steps to create a process that resets the Database Service Requests report when someone clicks the P7_GO button:

1. On the page definition page for the Database Service Requests report, click Create in the Processes section to create a new process.

2. Click Reset Repagination.

3. The process should take place after submitting the page; therefore, select On Submit – After Computations and Validations from the Point select list.

4. Specify **Reset Pagination – Go Button** for the Name field.

5. Specify **10** for the Sequence field.

6. The new process should execute whenever someone clicks the Go button; therefore, select P7_GO for the When Button Pressed select list.

7. The new process should unconditionally fire whenever someone clicks the P7_GO button; therefore, select Process Not Conditional from the Condition Type list.

8. Click Create Process.

Complete the following steps to create a process that resets the settings of the P7_REPORT_SEARCH field and P7_ROWS list to their default values when someone clicks the RESET button:

1. On the page definition page for the Database Service Requests report, click Create in the Processes section to create a new process.

2. Click Session State.

3. The process is necessary to clear the settings of values currently cached by Oracle Application Express for the previously mentioned page items; therefore, select the Clear Cache for Items (ITEM,ITEM,ITEM) option and then click Next.

4. Specify **Reset Display** for the Name field.

5. Specify **20** for the Sequence field.

6. The process should take place after submitting the page; therefore, select On Submit – After Computations and Validations from the Point select list.

7. Click Next.

8. Notice the required syntax for specifying the page items that you want to clear (comma separated, no spaces). Specify **P7_REPORT_SEARCH,P7_ROWS**.

9. Click Next.

10. Oracle Application Express can display a different message when the process succeeds or fails. Specify **Page reset.** for the Success Message field; specify **Reset failed.** for the Failure Message field.

11. Click Next.

12. The new process should execute whenever someone clicks the Reset button; therefore, select RESET for the When Button Pressed select list.

13. The new process should unconditionally fire whenever someone clicks the RESET button; therefore, select Process Not Conditional from the Condition Type list.

14. Click Create Process.

Complete the following steps to create a branch that "reloads" the Database Service Requests page:

1. On the page definition page for the Database Service Requests report, click Create in the Branches section to create a new branch.

2. The branch should take place after submitting the page; therefore, select On Submit – After Computations and Validations from the Branch Point select list.

3. The branch target is a page in the application; therefore, select Branch to Page from the Branch Type select list.

4. Click Next.

5. The branch target is the Database Service Requests report page itself, which should be page 7; therefore, specify 7 in the Branch to Page field (or use the pop-up window to select the page).

6. Click Next.

7. Do not associate the branch with a particular button; select Select Button from the When Button Pressed select list.

8. Click Create Branch.

Finally, it's time to test the new display functionality on the Database Service Requests report page. Click Run and then test the Search field, Display list, and Go and Reset buttons to make sure that they work just as they do on the other report pages of the application. For example:

■ Specify **598** in the Search field and then click Go. The report should only display the database service request that has the MetaLink reference 5983257.1.

■ Specify **582** in the Search field and then click Go. The report should only display the database service request that has the MetaLink reference 5823552.1.

■ Click Reset. The report should display both records in the table.

More thorough testing is appropriate: for example, make sure that the new search functionality correctly filters data from the report for all fields that are searchable.

EXERCISE 6.23: Add an Analysis Page to the Application

Just when you think everything is perfect, another new enhancement request appears: the DBAs would like a page that summarizes information about the versions of Oracle that are deployed in the environment so that they can better track their migration project from Oracle9*i* to Oracle Database 10*g*. This exercise shows you how to add a chart to the application and demonstrates how to extend the Related Links navigation menu on the Databases page.

To add a new Chart page to the application that summarizes the versions of Oracle currently in use, complete the following steps:

1. Click Edit Application in the Developer's toolbar.

2. Click Create Page.

3. Click Chart.

4. The DBAs want exact numbers of each version of Oracle that is deployed. Considering this requirement, click "Bar, Vertical."

5. Specify the next available page number in the Page field, which should be page 9.

6. Specify **Database Versions in Use** in the Page Name field.

7. Select Chart Region in the Region Template list.

8. Specify **Chart** in the Region Name field.

9. Do not modify the default setting in the Chart Color Theme list.

10. Click Next.

11. Select "Use an existing tab set and reuse an existing tab within that tab set."

12. Select TS1 in the Tab Set list.

13. Click Next.

14. The information in this new chart is related to databases; therefore, select T_DATABASES in the Use Tab list.

15. Click Next.

16. Use the Identify Query page of the wizard to specify a query that returns the data for the new chart. Oracle Application Express expects the first SELECT list expression to be used as link text (to drill down for more information), the second expression to be used as the data label, and the third expression to be the data value; to see an example, click the Query Example link below the wizard form. For the purposes of this exercise, specify the following query in the SQL field. Notice that the first expression in the SELECT list returns NULL for every row (links are not required), and that the other two expressions in the SELECT list declare column aliases so that the labels in the chart are more comprehensible.

```
SELECT NULL, db_version as "DATABASE VERSION",
       count(db_version) AS "NUMBER"
  FROM handsonxe06.databases
 GROUP BY db_version
```

17. Click Next.

18. Confirm your settings, and then click Finish.

19. Click Run Page to see the initial version of the new Database Versions in Use page, which should appear as shown in Figure 6-25.

NOTE
Certain web browsers such as Mozilla Firefox may not be able to display charts generated by Oracle Application Express until after you install an SVG plug-in.

The application's new Database Versions in Use page looks great. However, the page has similar navigation problems as when you added the other new pages to the application. To modify the Related Links navigation menu on the Databases page, complete the following steps:

1. Click Edit Application in the Developer's toolbar.

2. Navigate to the Databases page.

3. Click LINKS_1 in the Lists section to modify the list.

4. Click Create List Entry.

5. Select No Parent Entry in the Parent List Entry list.

6. Specify **20** in the Sequence field.

7. Specify **Database Versions Summary** in the List Entry Label field.

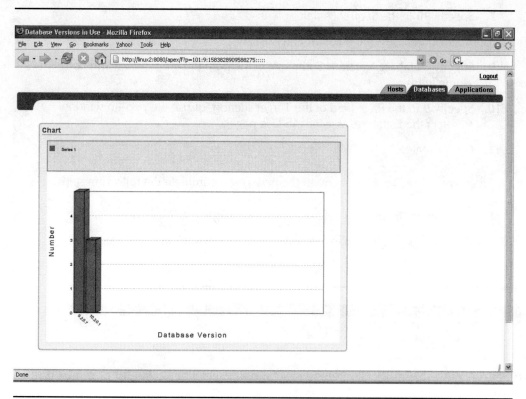

FIGURE 6-25. *The initial version of the Database Versions in Use page*

8. Specify **9** in the Page field of the Target section (or use the pop-up window to select the Database Versions in Use page).

9. Click Create.

To create a new entry in the breadcrumbs menu, complete the following steps:

1. Navigate to the main SysMgmt application page.

2. Click Shared Components.

3. Click Breadcrumbs.

4. Click Breadcrumb.

5. Click Create Breadcrumb Entry.

6. Specify **9** in the Page field of the Breadcrumb section (or use the pop-up window to select the Database Versions in Use page).

7. Specify **90** in the Sequence field.

8. Select Databases in the Parent Entry list.

9. Specify **Database Versions Summary** in the both the Short Name and Long Name fields.

10. Specify **9** in the Page field of the Target section (or use the pop-up window to select the Database Versions in Use page).

11. Click Create.

To copy the breadcrumbs menu to the new page, complete the following steps:

1. Navigate to the main SysMgmt application page.

2. Click any page other than the new Database Versions in Use page.

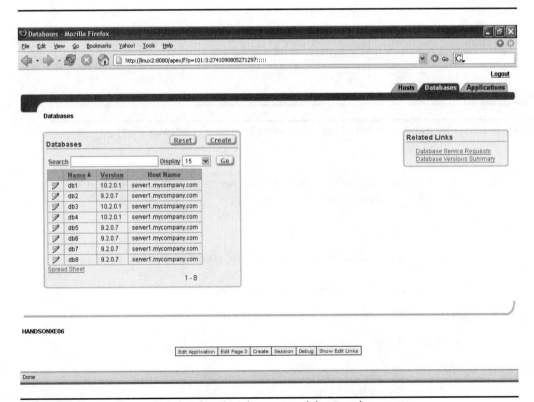

FIGURE 6-26. *The updated Related Links menu of the Databases page*

3. Click the Copy icon in the upper-right corner of the Regions section.

4. Click Breadcrumbs to copy the Breadcrumbs regions.

5. Specify **9** in the To Page field, or click its adjacent button and select the Database Versions in Use page from the pop-up window.

6. Click Next.

7. Click Copy Region to accept the defaults for the new region.

Now test the new navigation functionality to and from the Database Versions in Use page. The Databases page should appear as shown in Figure 6-26 (on the opposite page).

The Database Versions in Use page should now have a breadcrumb menu, as shown in Figure 6-27.

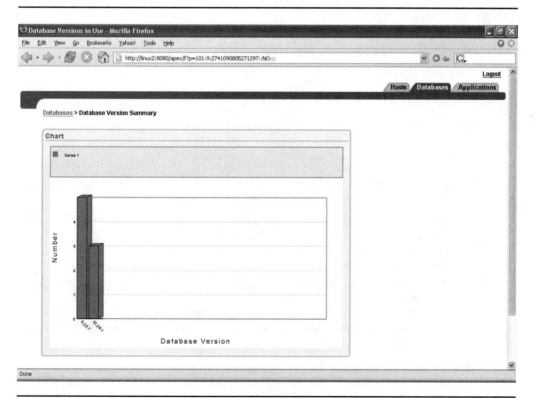

FIGURE 6-27. *The updated Database Versions in Use page with the breadcrumbs menu*

Deploying the Application

Once you finish building, testing, and tweaking an Oracle Application Express application, you can deploy it whenever necessary. The first choice you have to make is where you want to deploy the application. Oracle Application Express has facilities that make it easy to deploy an application wherever Oracle Application Express and Oracle are available. The exercises in this section teach you how to put an application into "production" mode on the same computer that you are using to develop the application, and how to move an application from a development environment to a production server.

EXERCISE 6.24: Modify Application Attributes for Deployment

It's a trivial task to deploy an Oracle Application Express application on the same computer that you use to develop the application: all that is necessary is the modification of a few simple application attributes. For example, complete the following steps to deploy the example SysMgmt application on the same computer that you have used to develop the application:

1. Navigate to the application's main page.

2. Click Edit Attributes.

3. Click Edit Standard Attributes.

4. Use the Standard Attributes page to modify basic application settings such as the application's name, version number, and availability. For the purposes of this brief exercise, focus on the following settings:

   - Specify **SysMgmt** in the Application Alias field. You can use this alias or the application ID in a URL when you want to run the application.

   - The setting of the Status list controls whether the application is available for use. For example, select Available to make the application available to all types of users but without the Developer's toolbar; select Available with Edit Links to make the application available to all types of users with the Developer's toolbar; and select Available to Developer's Only to make the application available only to users who have developer privileges. See the online help system or the *Oracle Application Express User's Guide* for more information about other options of the Status list. For the purposes of this exercise, select Available.

   - The setting of the Build Status list determines whether the application is still in development or not; specify Run and Build Application for the purposes of this exercise.

5. Click Apply Changes.

To test the execution of the application, complete the following steps:

1. Click Logout to end your current session.

2. Load the application's URL in your web browser using the application's ID or the alias that you previously set. For example, load the following URL:

    ```
    http://127.0.0.1:8080/apex/f?p=SysMgmt
    ```

3. Specify **HANDSONXE06** in the User Name field and **PASSWORD** in the Password field, and then click Login.

4. Feel free to navigate and use the application. As you use the application, notice that the Developer's toolbar is no longer available.

When you need to modify an application that is Available with a Build Status set to Run and Build Application, launch the Database Home Page, log in, and then use the Application Builder to load and modify the application.

EXERCISE 6.25: Deploy the Application on Another Computer

In the real world, it's unlikely that you will deploy a production Oracle Application Express application on the same computer that you use to develop it. Fortunately, it is very easy to copy an Oracle Application Express application from one computer to another for deployment. The steps in this exercise demonstrate this process.

When you create an application with Oracle Application Express, you are creating metadata in database tables that Oracle Application Express can use to dynamically generate the application's web pages and logic at run time. Moving an application from one computer to another requires nothing more than exporting the application's metadata and importing it into another Oracle database.

To copy an application, two primary steps are necessary: generate a SQL DDL script that you can use to create the application's schema, and export and import the application's metadata. If two computers are available to you with Oracle XE, or you would like to simulate the application copy process by creating a second version of the SysMgmt application on your development computer, use the steps in this exercise.

To quickly generate a SQL DDL script that can build the current version of the HANDSONXE06 schema, complete the following steps:

1. Start a web browser *on the computer targeted for application deployment.* This exercise assumes that Oracle XE is installed and started on the target computer, or that Oracle Application Express 2.x and a supporting version of Oracle are installed and started on the target computer.

2. Launch the Database Home Page on *the development computer* (not the target computer) and log in as **HANDSONXE06**.

3. Click Utilities.

4. Click Generate DDL.

5. Click Create Script.

6. Click Next.

7. Select all Object Type options.

8. Use either of the following techniques to create a SQL script on the target computer:

   ■ Select Display Inline from the Output options, click Generate DDL, copy the contents of the output from your clipboard into a text editor, and then save it as a simple text file that is available within the target computer's file system.

   ■ Select Save as Script File from the Output options, click Generate DDL, specify a name for the script (for example, **sysmgmt_ddl**), and click Create Script; this process generates a script in the Oracle Application Express repository (not in your file system). From the SQL Scripts page, click the new script, click Download, and then specify a filename that is valid for a file system available to the target computer.

Complete the following steps to export the SysMgmt application itself:

1. Click Home.

2. Click Application Builder.

3. Click SysMgmt.

4. Click Export/Import.

5. Click Export.

6. Do not modify the default settings for the application export; click Export Application.

7. Use your browser to save the generated SQL script to a file system available to the target computer.

At this point, you have two SQL scripts that you can use to deploy the application on any computer on which Oracle Application Express is available. Complete the following steps to use the scripts for application deployment:

1. Click Logout to end your Oracle Application Express session on the development computer.

2. Launch the Database Home Page on *the target computer.*

3. Create the HANDSONXE06 user/schema in the target database to support the SysMgmt application. You can use this chapter's support script, chap06. sql, to quickly carry out this step. If you are creating a second version of the SysMgmt application on the development computer, skip this step.

4. Using steps similar to those in Exercise 6.1, upload and run the SQL script that contains the DDL statement necessary to create the application schema in the target database's HANDSONXE06 schema.

Complete the following steps to import the SysMgmt application into the target computer's Oracle Application Express repository:

1. Click Home.

2. Click Application Builder.

3. Click Import.

4. Click Browse and navigate your file system to select the SQL script that contains the SysMgmt application's metadata.

5. Click Next.

6. Click Install.

7. After the application installs, click Run Application to test the application on the target computer.

Managing Application Access and Application Users

Application deployment is not complete until after you grant application access to users that plan to utilize the application. The authentication scheme that you choose for an application dictates what you need to do in order to provide user access to the application. A complete discussion of the authentication schemes that Oracle Application Express supports is beyond the scope of this chapter. However, this short section demonstrates the steps necessary to manage user access to the example SysMgmt application that uses the Application Express Authentication scheme.

EXERCISE 6.26: Create an Application Express User

When an application uses the *Application Express Authentication* scheme, you manage application access with Application Express end-user accounts. Application Express end users do not have the privileges for application development, and can only access applications that do not use an external authentication scheme.

To create an Application Express user account, complete the following steps:

1. Log out of the application if it is executing.

2. Launch the Database Home Page.

3. Log in as **HANDSONXE06**.

4. Click Application Builder.

5. Click Manage Application Express Users.

6. Click Create User.

7. Specify **STEVE** in the User Name field.

8. Specify **PASSWORD** in the Password field. Specify the same password in the Confirm Password field. Note that Application Express end-user account passwords are case sensitive.

9. Specify **steveb@dbdomain.com** in the Email Address field.

10. Click Create User.

11. Repeat steps similar to Steps 6 through 10 for as many users as you need to create.

To test the new user account with the SysMgmt application, complete the following steps:

1. Click Logout.

2. Start the application with the application's URL. For example:

    ```
    http://myserver:8080/f?p=SysMgmt
    ```

3. Log in using the new user account.

Chapter Summary

This chapter has been a brief introduction to the application development process, with special focus on Oracle Application Express. You learned the following concepts:

■   The application development lifecycle (ADLC) includes analysis, design, implementation, test, deployment, and maintenance stages.

■   Software modeling with Unified Modeling Language (UML) diagrammers can greatly improve the efficiency and effectiveness of the design stage. Structure diagrams such as class diagrams illustrate the static structure of the system that you are modeling. Behavior diagrams such as use case diagrams show the dynamic interaction of system components.

■   To build an application schema quickly, you can use Oracle XE to upload and run SQL scripts generated from UML class diagrams.

■   Oracle XE can easily load data from structured data file formats such as comma-separated values, tab-delimited fields, and XML files generated by spreadsheet and PC database programs.

■   The component of Oracle Application Express that you use to build web-based applications is called the Application Builder. The many wizards of the Application Builder make it easy to quickly build web pages for reports, forms, and charts based on an Oracle database.

■   An Oracle Application Express application is generated at run time from metadata in a database. Deploying an application from one computer to another requires nothing more than exporting the application's metadata and importing it into another Oracle database.

PART
III

Database Administration

CHAPTER
7

Secure Database Access

ow that you have a fundamental understanding of application development with Oracle XE, this part of the book focuses on the issues that you need to know about to manage the underlying Oracle database that you use to support database applications. Although Oracle XE itself automatically performs many routine database administration tasks, it is critical that you learn about the *database administrator (DBA)* tasks that the system routinely performs as well as others that you must perform yourself. This chapter begins by discussing several database security topics that are pertinent to Oracle XE.

With any multiuser computer system, security is a particularly important issue to address. Oracle database systems are certainly no exception. Without adequate security controls, malicious users might invade an Oracle database, view confidential information, and make unauthorized changes to database information. This chapter explains the various security features of Oracle XE that you can use to control user access to an Oracle database and Oracle Application Express applications:

- User management and authentication

- Privilege management and roles

- Database resource limits

- User password management

Chapter Prerequisites

To practice the hands-on exercises in this chapter, you need to start SQL*Plus as instructed in Exercise 2.11 and run the following command script:

```
location\handsonxe\sql\chap07.sql
```

where *location* is the file directory where you expanded the support archive that accompanies this book. For example, after starting SQL*Plus, you can run this chapter's SQL command script using the SQL*Plus command @, as in the following example (assuming that your chap07.sql file is in C:\temp\handsonxe\sql):

```
SQL> @C:\temp\handsonxe\sql\chap07.sql;
```

Once you reply to all of the prompts and the script completes successfully, *leave the current SQL*Plus session open*—you'll need it later on in several of this chapter's exercises.

User Management

The first line of defense against unwanted database access is controlling who can access the system in the first place. As you already know from previous chapters in this book, to use Oracle XE, a user must log in and provide a *username*. The following sections explain more about managing user access specifically in an Oracle XE database.

Oracle Database Users and Oracle Application Express Users

Before continuing, it is important to understand the distinction between two types of user accounts that previous chapters of this book introduce in the context of Oracle XE. In most of the previous chapters, you use Oracle XE database user accounts such as HANDSONXE03, HANDSONXE04, etc., to start utilities such as SQL*Plus and the Database Home Page to execute support scripts and otherwise complete work. A *database user account* is an account that Oracle XE manages in the database's data dictionary.

Exercise 6.26 briefly introduces the concept of Oracle Application Express users. An *Application Express user account* is an account that Oracle Application Express manages in its repository, separate from the underlying Oracle database's data dictionary. Oracle Application Express users can access an Oracle database only by using an Oracle Application Express application that relies on the Application Express Authentication scheme. You cannot use an Oracle Application Express user account to directly access an Oracle database (for example, using SQL*Plus or the Database Home Page of Oracle XE).

This is a book about Oracle XE; therefore, this chapter focuses on database user accounts. For complete information about Oracle Application Express authentication schemes and Oracle Application Express user accounts, please refer to the *Oracle Application Express User's Guide*.

Default Database User Accounts

Every Oracle database has at least two default database user accounts:

- **SYS**   Owns the database's data dictionary objects. Connect to Oracle using the SYS account only when it is absolutely necessary; for example, to shut down, start up, or recover the database. Later in this chapter, you'll learn about a special option of the CONNECT command that is required when using the SYS account (AS SYSDBA).

- **SYSTEM**   The default DBA account that you can use to get started with a new database. However, for accountability reasons, it's always best to create distinct user accounts capable of database administration rather than use the default SYSTEM account.

The passwords for the SYS and SYSTEM accounts are set during Oracle XE installation.

NOTE
Most Oracle databases include many other default or internal user accounts that support optional features of Oracle. For a complete list of default Oracle user accounts, see Chapter 2 of the Oracle Database 10*g* Administrator's Guide.

Database User Properties

Every Oracle database user has several associated attributes:

- A unique username, for obvious reasons

- An authentication method, such as a password

- A status, either locked or unlocked

- Database space usage settings that control and target database space resources

The following sections briefly introduce each type of database user account attribute.

Database Usernames

Each database username must be unique among all other usernames and roles, can be 1 to 30 characters long, must begin with an alphabetic character, and is not case sensitive. A username can include any alphanumeric character, as well as the underscore character (_), the dollar sign ($), and the pound sign (#), but cannot include single or double quotes, and cannot be an Oracle reserved word such as SELECT, CREATE, etc. See the *Oracle Database 10*g *SQL Reference* for a complete list of Oracle reserved words.

Database User Authentication

For each database user, you must indicate how you want to *authenticate* use of the database user account. *User authentication* ensures that when a user attempts to connect to an Oracle database, the user is truly who they claim to be and not someone else attempting to pose as the user.

In most cases, Oracle XE uses passwords to carry out database user authentication. When a user starts an application such as SQL*Plus or the Database Home Page, the application prompts for a database username and associated password. Oracle XE then authenticates the connection request with the user account information managed by the database itself. Because Oracle XE carries out all of the work, this process is commonly referred to as *Oracle database authentication,* but some people also refer to this as *password authentication.*

NOTE
Oracle, including Oracle XE, supports several other types of authentication mechanisms for database users, including operating system (external) authentication and network authentication, just to name a few. However, this chapter focuses only on database authentication, because it is the only type of database user authentication method that the Oracle XE administration interface of the Database Home Page supports. Please refer to the Oracle Database 10g Administrator's Guide *for more information about other types of authentication.*

When relying on password authentication, it's important to have a policy in place that ensures passwords have a certain degree of complexity. For example, *strong passwords* have the following characteristics:

■ Has both upper- and lowercase letters. However, Oracle passwords are not case sensitive, by default, unless you take some special steps, as explained later in this chapter.

■ Is at least eight characters long.

■ Has digits, punctuation marks, or other symbols (do not use a word where some letters are simply replaced by look-alike digits such as r**8** and r**&**om for "r**ate**" and "r**and**om").

■ Is not based on the username.

■ Is not a real word (e.g., something you'd find in a dictionary or a list of proper nouns).

A good security policy should also request or enforce that users change their passwords at least every six months. Oracle XE can enforce security policies for passwords; for more information about managing user passwords, see several exercises in the section "Managing Resource Limit Profiles" later in this chapter.

Locked and Unlocked User Accounts

Oracle lets you *lock* and *unlock* a user account at any time so that you can control database access through the account without having to drop and re-create it. A user cannot connect to Oracle after you lock the user's account. To subsequently allow a user access through an account, you must unlock the account. Why would you want to lock and unlock user accounts?

- You might want to lock a user's account when the user takes a temporary leave of absence from work, but plans on returning in the future.

- When a person leaves your company, you might want to lock the user's account rather than drop the account, especially if the user's schema contains tables and other objects that you want to preserve.

- You typically lock a user account that functions only as a schema for logically organizing all of an application's database objects. In other words, no one should typically access an application via the application's underlying user/schema.

A User's Default Tablespace

A tablespace is a logical storage division of a database that organizes the physical storage of database information; the next chapter in this book explains all about tablespaces. For now, understand that each database user has a *default tablespace* setting. When the user creates a new database object, such as a table or index, and does not explicitly indicate a tablespace for the object, Oracle stores the new database object in the user's default tablespace. Unless you specify otherwise, a user's default tablespace corresponds to the database's default tablespace setting. Chapter 8 explains more about setting the database's default tablespace.

A User's Temporary Tablespace

Often, SQL statements require temporary workspace to complete. For example, a query that joins and sorts a large amount of data might require temporary workspace to build the result set. When necessary, Oracle allocates temporary workspace for a user's SQL statements in the user's *temporary tablespace*. Unless you specify otherwise, a user's temporary tablespace is the database's default temporary tablespace. Chapter 8 explains more about setting the database's default temporary tablespace.

EXERCISE 7.1: Display Information About Database Users

To manage and display information about Oracle XE database user accounts, you can use the administration interface that is part of the Database Home Page. For example, to display information about current database users, complete the following steps:

1. Launch the Database Home Page.

2. To manage database users, you must establish a connection that has the necessary administrator privileges. Therefore, establish a connection using the default database administration account **SYSTEM** and then specify the password that you set for this account during Oracle XE installation.

3. Once you are connected as SYSTEM, click Administration.

4. Click Database Users.

5. Notice that the Manage Database Users page displays a list of database users in the Oracle XE database.

Feel free to modify the View, Show, and Display select lists, and then click Go to see how you can customize the display of database users in the display. In particular, notice that the Show select list determines what types of users to include in the current display:

- **Internal users**   In the context of Oracle XE, database user accounts that Oracle XE uses to support Oracle database features. For example, SYS and SYSTEM are the default database administration accounts present in every Oracle database; ANONYMOUS is a user account that Oracle Application Express uses to establish database connections on behalf of applications. You should not modify or drop internal user accounts unless you have a specific reason to do so and understand the implications of the change you are making.

- **Database users**   Normal database users, such as those created by the support scripts for previous chapters of this book, including HANDSONXE03, HANDSONXE04, and so on.

In Icons view, such as shown in Figure 7-1, the Manage Database Users page displays different-color icons for internal users and database users and displays nothing more than each user's name.

In Details view, such as shown in Figure 7-2, the Manage Database Users page displays more information about each user, including each user's account status, default tablespace, and temporary tablespace settings.

EXERCISE 7.2: Create a Database User
To create a database user, complete the following steps:

1. On the Manage Database Users page, click Create.

2. Use the Create Database User page to specify the following information for the new database user account:

   - Specify **HANDSONXE_USER1** in the Username field; case is not sensitive.

   - Specify **changepw123** in the Password and Confirm Password fields; case is not sensitive. Notice that the fields display *s rather than the characters you enter for the password so that someone looking over your shoulder cannot read what you specify.

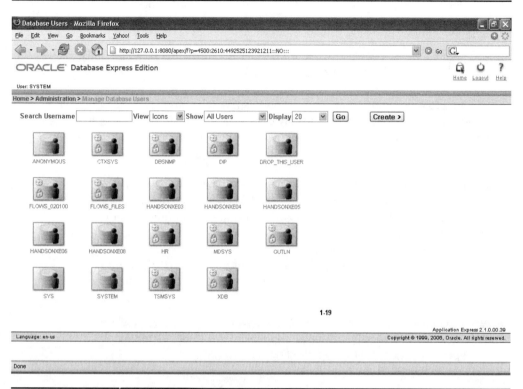

FIGURE 7-1. *The Manage Database Users page when using Icons view*

- Enable Expire Password so that Oracle XE forces the user to change their password the first time that they try to use the account.

- Select Unlocked from the Account Status list so that the user account is accessible.

- Notice that the nonmodifiable Default Tablespace and Temporary Tablespace settings are USERS and TEMP, respectively; Oracle XE derives these settings from database default settings.

- The settings in the User Privileges section of the page determine the privileges that you want to grant to the new user account; subsequent sections in this chapter explain more about privileges and roles. For the purposes of this exercise, select the CONNECT option and disable all other roles and privileges in this section.

   3. Confirm the settings of the page appear as in Figure 7-3 and then click Create to create the new user.

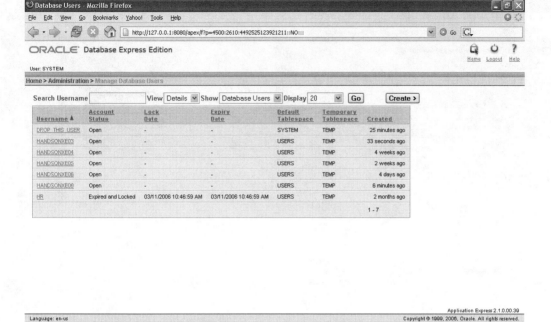

FIGURE 7-2. *The Manage Database Users page when using Details view*

NOTE
By default, Oracle usernames and passwords are not case sensitive. You can make a username case sensitive if you delimit it with double quotes. However, I do not recommend using this technique to force case-sensitive usernames; doing so would require that users explicitly delimit corresponding usernames when establishing a database connection, which is not intuitive.

After Oracle XE creates the new user, you return to the Manage Database Users page, which now displays information about the new user. Notice in Details view that the new user's account status is Expired, which indicates that the user must change their password the next time they try to use the account.

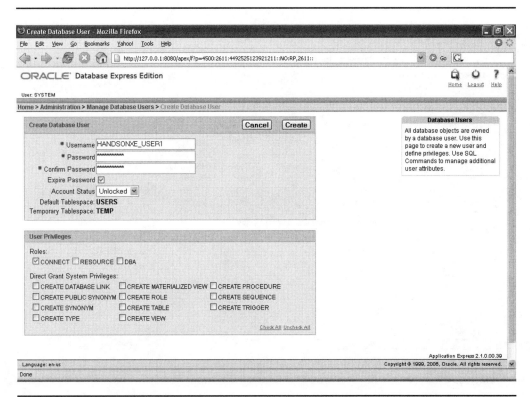

FIGURE 7-3. *Use the Create Database User page to create a new database user.*

NOTE
The Create Database User page uses the SQL commands CREATE USER and GRANT to create a new database user and grant the user privileges. Unfortunately, this page does not have a SQL link that you can use to reveal the SQL used to carry out work. Refer to the Oracle Database 10g SQL Reference *for more information about these commands.*

EXERCISE 7.3: Test the New Database User Account

To test the new user account and witness what happens when a user tries to use an expired account, complete the following steps:

1. Click Logout.

2. Click Login.

3. Specify **HANDSONXE_USER1** in the Username field.

4. Specify **changepw123** in the Password field.

5. Click Login.

6. Notice that you must change the account's password before continuing.

7. Specify the current password, **changepw123**, in the Old Password field.

8. Specify a new strong password, such as **j8tyrrs7**, in the New Password and Confirm Password fields; by default, the case that you use for characters does not matter.

9. Click Apply Changes.

10. Click Done.

11. Log in using HANDSONXE_USER1's new password.

EXERCISE 7.4: Modify Your Own Password

Any database user can change their password whenever necessary. For example, to change the password of the HANDSONXE_USER1 user account, complete the following steps:

1. Launch the Database Home Page and log in as **HANDSONXE_USER1**; this step should not be necessary unless you are not immediately continuing from the previous exercise.

2. Click Home | Administration.

3. Click Change My Password from the list of Tasks.

4. On the Change My Password page, specify the current password, **j8tyrrs7**, in the Old Password field.

5. Specify a new strong password, such as **tr7ghh13**, in the New Password and Confirm Password fields.

6. Click Apply Changes.

NOTE
The Change My Password page uses the SQL command ALTER USER to reset a user account's password. Refer to the Oracle Database 10g SQL Reference *for more information about the ALTER USER command.*

EXERCISE 7.5: Alter or Drop a Database User

A user with administrative privileges can alter the settings of a database user account or drop a database user account altogether, as follows:

1. Launch the Database Home Page and log in as **SYSTEM**. If you are continuing from the previous exercise, click Logout, click Login, and then log in as **SYSTEM**.

2. Click Administration.

3. Click Database Users.

4. Click the target database user to modify; for the purposes of this exercise, click DROP_THIS_USER.

5. Notice that the Manage Database User page is similar to the Create Database User page of Exercise 7.2. You can use the Manage Database User page to alter a user account in the following ways:

   ■ Change a user's password

   ■ Expire a user's password

   ■ Lock or unlock a user account

   ■ Drop a user

   When you make a change to a user account that you want to save, click Alter User to apply your changes; when you want to drop a user, click Drop; when you do not want to alter or drop a user, click Cancel.

6. For the purposes of this exercise, click Drop to drop the DROP_THIS_USER user account.

7. The ensuing Drop Database User page prompts you to confirm your request. When you want to drop a user that currently "owns" one or more schema objects, you must select the Cascade option; if you do not, Oracle returns an error so that you do not mistakenly drop objects that would otherwise be time-consuming to recover. For the purposes of this exercise, select Cascade and then click Drop User.

8. When you return to the Manage Database Users page, notice that DROP_ THIS_USER is no longer present in the display of database users.

After you complete each chapter in this book, feel free to use the steps in this exercise to lock or altogether drop the database user accounts created by this book's support scripts. In general, it is always good practice to remove obsolete database accounts that are otherwise potential security holes.

Dependencies and Dropping Users

Make sure that you carefully consider the possible side effects before dropping a user that "owns" database objects or Oracle Application Express applications. For example, when you drop a user that owns tables, Oracle automatically drops referential integrity constraints in other schemas that refer to the primary key and unique key constraints in the user's schema; Oracle also invalidates, but does not drop, dependent objects in other database schemas, including objects such as views, synonyms, stored procedures, functions, packages, and database triggers. Carelessly dropping a database user that owns tables can have crippling effects on the functionality of an application.

It's also important to think carefully before you drop a database user that owns Oracle Application Express applications—when you do so, Oracle XE automatically drops the user's applications from the Oracle Application Express repository. Before dropping a user that owns Oracle Application Express applications, utilize the techniques in Chapter 6 for exporting a user's schema and application data to create "backups" of the user's applications. As the saying goes, better safe than sorry.

Privilege Management

After you create the users for an Oracle database system, they cannot connect to the database server nor do anything of consequence unless they have the *privileges* to perform specific database operations. For example, consider the following limitations:

- A user cannot connect to an Oracle database unless the user has the CREATE SESSION system privilege.

- A user cannot create a table in his or her corresponding schema unless the user has the CREATE TABLE system privilege.

- A user cannot delete rows from a table in a different schema unless the user has the DELETE object privilege for the table.

Types of Database Privileges

If you read the preceding list closely, you'll notice that there are two different kinds of privileges that control access to an Oracle database: system privileges and object privileges.

System Privileges

A *system privilege* is a powerful privilege that enables a user to perform some type of system-wide operation. For example, the following examples are just a few of more than 150 system privileges in Oracle Database 10*g*:

■ **CREATE SESSION**   Enables a user to establish a database connection/session

■ **CREATE TABLE**   Enables a user to create a table in his or her corresponding schema

■ **CREATE ANY TABLE**   Enables a user to create a table in any schema of the database

■ **SELECT ANY TABLE**   Enables a user to query any table in the database

■ **EXECUTE ANY PROCEDURE**   Enables a user to execute any stored procedure, stored function, or packaged component in the database

Because system privileges are very powerful privileges that can affect the security of the entire database system, carefully consider what types of users require system privileges. For example:

■ A database administrator is the only type of user that should have the powerful ALTER DATABASE system privilege, a privilege that allows someone to alter the physical structure and availability of the database system.

■ Developers typically require several system privileges, including the CREATE TABLE, CREATE VIEW, and CREATE PROCEDURE system privileges to build database schemas that support front-end applications.

■ Every user in the system typically has the CREATE SESSION system privilege, the privilege that allows a user to connect to the database.

Object Privileges

An *object privilege* enables a user to perform a specific type of operation on a specific database object, such as a table, view, or stored procedure. The following are some examples of object privileges:

■ A user with the SELECT object privilege for the CUST view can query the view to retrieve information.

■ A user with the INSERT object privilege for the CUSTOMERS table can insert new rows into the table. The user can insert table rows by directly referencing the table or by referencing a view or synonym based on the table.

- A user with the REFERENCES object privilege for a table can reference the table when declaring a referential integrity constraint.

- A user with the EXECUTE privilege for the deleteHost procedure can execute the procedure.

 NOTE
For complete lists of all system and object privileges, refer to the Oracle Database 10g SQL Reference.

Granting and Revoking Privileges

You can give a user a system or object privilege by *granting* the privilege to the user. To withdraw a privilege from a user, you *revoke* the privilege from the user. Oracle does not let just anyone grant and revoke privileges to and from users. Consider the following requirements when managing individual system and object privileges for database users:

- You can grant a user a system privilege only if you are a grantee of the system privilege yourself with the administrative rights to grant the privilege to other users; because of related SQL syntax, this is commonly referred to as the WITH ADMIN OPTION. You can also grant any system privilege to any other user if you are a grantee of the GRANT ANY PRIVILEGE system privilege.

- You can grant a user a database object privilege only if you own the associated database object or if you are a grantee of the object privilege yourself with the administrative rights to grant the privilege to other users; because of related SQL syntax, this is commonly referred to as the WITH GRANT OPTION. You can also grant any object privilege to any database object if you are a grantee of the GRANT ANY OBJECT PRIVILEGE system privilege.

EXERCISE 7.6: Grant System Privileges to a User

You can easily grant a subset of some of the most useful system privileges to a database user with the Database Home Page, as follows:

1. Launch the Database Home Page, log in as **SYSTEM**, and click Administration | Database Users; this step should not be necessary if you are continuing from the previous exercise.

2. Click the user that you want to manage to display the familiar Manage Database User page; for the purposes of this exercise, click HANDSONXE_USER1.

3. Notice the following in the User Privileges section of the page:

   ■ You can individually select from a limited list of several different system privileges, such as CREATE DATABASE LINK, CREATE PUBLIC SYNONYM, and CREATE TRIGGER.

   ■ You can click Check All or Uncheck All to select or unselect all available system privileges, respectively.

4. Click All System Privileges Granted to HANDSONXE_USER1 at the bottom of the page to display a list of all system privileges to which HANDSONXE_USER1 currently has access. HANDSONXE_USER1 should currently have access only to the CREATE SESSION system privilege.

5. Suppose that HANDSONXE_USER1 is a new user account intended for application development. In this case, enable the CREATE PUBLIC SYNONYM, CREATE SYNONYM, CREATE TABLE, CREATE VIEW, CREATE

Granting System Privileges with the SQL Command GRANT

The Manage Database User page uses the SQL command GRANT to grant system privileges to a user. However, the Manage Database User page provides the capability to grant only a limited set of system privileges to a user, and does not provide the capability to grant a user a system privilege with administrative rights. To accomplish either of these tasks, you must use the following abbreviated form of the SQL command GRANT:

```
GRANT privilege [, privilege] ...
  TO user [, user] ...
  [WITH ADMIN OPTION]
```

The following example demonstrates how you might grant an application developer appropriate system privileges with administrative rights:

```
GRANT CREATE SESSION, CREATE TABLE, CREATE VIEW, CREATE ANY INDEX,
  CREATE SEQUENCE
TO handsonxe_user1
WITH ADMIN OPTION;
```

To quickly grant a system privilege to every database user, grant the privilege to the keyword PUBLIC rather than to a specific user. *PUBLIC* is a special group in an Oracle database that you can use to make a privilege available quickly to every user in the system. However, use this feature carefully so that you do not open up security holes in your database.

PROCEDURE, CREATE SEQUENCE, and CREATE TRIGGER options. Do not modify any other page settings. Before continuing, make sure that the page looks similar to Figure 7-4.

6. Click Alter User to grant HANDSONXE_USER1 the selected system privileges.

EXERCISE 7.7: Revoke System Privileges from a User

If you make a mistake while granting a user system privileges with the Manage Database User page, or later decide that a user should no longer have a particular system privilege as part of their *privilege domain* or *security domain* (set of available privileges), you can also revoke the system privilege by using the Manage Database User page. For example, the CREATE PUBLIC SYNONYM system privilege is typically not appropriate for application developers—with it, a developer who does not have a global perspective might unknowingly create public synonyms that potentially cause

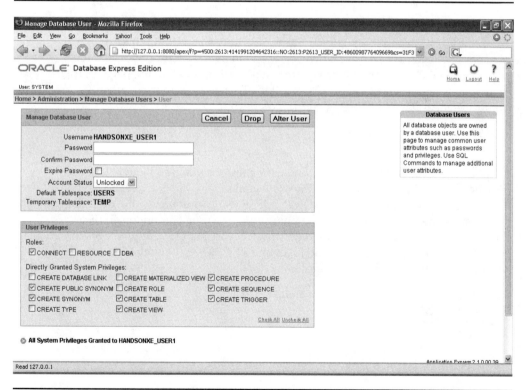

FIGURE 7-4. *Use the Manage Database User page to grant and revoke a select number of system privileges to and from a user.*

future conflicts with required database- or application-specific public synonyms. Considering this, complete the following steps to revoke the CREATE PUBLIC SYNONYM system privilege from HANDSONXE_USER1:

1. Continuing from the previous exercise, click HANDSONXE_USER1 on the Manage Database Users page.

2. Disable the CREATE PUBLIC SYNONYM option.

3. Click Alter User.

EXERCISE 7.8: Grant Object Privileges to a User

A user that owns a schema object such as a table, sequence, or procedure can grant another user corresponding object privileges with the Object Browser of the Database Home Page. For example, to grant the HANDSONXE_USER1 database user the

Revoking System Privileges with the SQL Command REVOKE

The Manage Database User page uses the SQL command REVOKE to revoke system privileges from a user. However, the Manage Database User page does not provide the ability to revoke system privileges not listed on the page, or to revoke a system privilege granted to PUBLIC. To accomplish these tasks, you must use the following abbreviated form of the SQL command REVOKE:

```
REVOKE privilege [, privilege] ...
  FROM user [, user] ...
```

For example, the GRANT statement in the previous sidebar ("Granting System Privileges with the SQL Command GRANT") grants HANDSONXE_USER1 several system privileges with the WITH ADMIN OPTION. Consequently, the user can grant the same system privileges to other users at the user's discretion. Typical application developers should not have the ability to grant system privileges to other database users. Therefore, the following REVOKE statement revokes the user's access to the system privileges:

```
REVOKE CREATE SESSION, CREATE TABLE, CREATE VIEW, CREATE ANY INDEX,
  CREATE SEQUENCE
 FROM handsonxe_user1;
```

Next, grant the necessary system privileges to the user again, but this time without the WITH ADMIN OPTION:

```
GRANT CREATE SESSION, CREATE TABLE, CREATE VIEW, CREATE ANY INDEX,
  CREATE SEQUENCE
 TO handsonxe_user1;
```

privileges to insert rows, update rows, delete rows, and retrieve rows in the
HANDSONXE07.CUSTOMERS table, complete the following steps:

1. If you are continuing from the previous exercise, your current session is
   established as SYSTEM. Click Logout to end this session and then click Login
   to present the login page for the Database Home Page.

2. Connect as the user that owns the schema objects of interest. For the
   purposes of this exercise, specify **HANDSONXE07** in the Username field,
   specify **PASSWORD** in the Password field, and then click Login.

3. Click Object Browser.

4. Select Tables in the Object Selection pane.

5. Click CUSTOMERS.

6. Click Grants.

7. Notice that there are currently no grants related to this table.

8. Click Grant.

9. Use the button adjacent to the Grantee field to display a pop-up list of users;
   then select HANDSONXE_USER1.

10. Use the Grant drop-down list to indicate which object privilege to grant: ALL
    indicates that you want to grant all object privileges for the CUSTOMERS
    table and Specific Privileges displays the Specific Privileges select list that
    you can use to grant a specific list of object privileges for the CUSTOMERS
    table. For this example, select Specific Privileges for the Grant list.

11. Use the CTRL key and your mouse to multiselect the DELETE, INSERT, UPDATE,
    and SELECT object privileges in the Specific Privileges list.

12. The With Grant Option check box indicates whether you want to allow the
    grantee to grant the selected object privileges to other users; you do not, so
    do not enable this option.

13. Confirm that the page appears as in Figure 7-5, and then click Next.

14. Click SQL and review the SQL statement that the Object Browser page builds.
    Notice that to grant an object privilege, you can use the SQL command
    GRANT. For complete information about the form of the GRANT command
    that you use to grant object privileges, refer to the *Oracle Database 10g SQL
    Reference*.

```
grant DELETE,INSERT,UPDATE,SELECT on "CUSTOMERS" to HANDSONXE_USER1
```

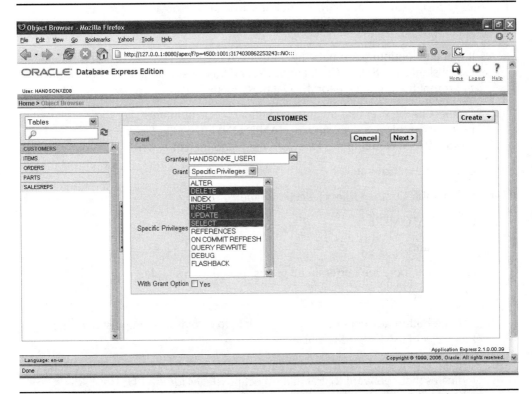

FIGURE 7-5. *The owner of a schema object can use the Grant page of the Object Browser to grant one or more object privileges for a schema object to another database user.*

15. Click Finish.

16. The Detail pane now lists the new grants for the selected CUSTOMERS table, as shown in Figure 7-6.

NOTE
This exercise teaches you how the owner of an object can grant corresponding object privileges to a user. A grantee of an object privilege with the WITH GRANT OPTION or a grantee of the GRANT ANY OBJECT PRIVILEGE system privilege can grant object privileges for another user's object by using the SQL command GRANT; the Object Browser interface of Oracle XE does not support this capability. See Exercise 7.12 for an example.

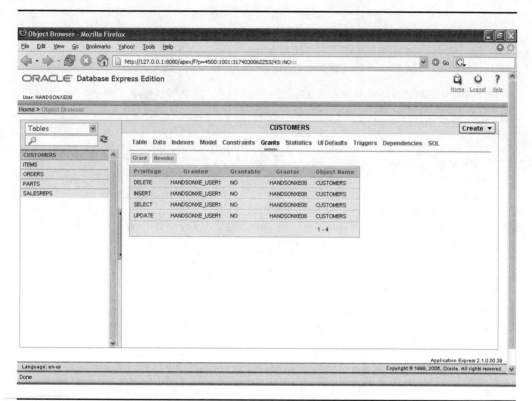

FIGURE 7-6.   *The Detail pane of the Object Browser displays grants for the selected object.*

Understanding Column-Specific Object Privileges

The object privilege grants in Exercise 7.7 implicitly encompass all columns in the corresponding table. For example, granting the basic UPDATE privilege for the HANDSONXE07.CUSTOMERS table allows HANDSONXE_USER1 to update data in any column in the table.

Oracle also supports column-specific INSERT, UPDATE, and REFERENCES object privileges for tables and views. In other words, when you grant someone the INSERT, UPDATE, or REFERENCES privilege for a table or view, you can indicate a specific list of columns in the table or view that the grantee can insert

(continued)

into, update, or reference. For example, the following GRANT statement grants column-selective INSERT and UPDATE privileges for the ORDERS table to the user HANDSONXE_USER1:

```
GRANT INSERT(id, orderdate, c_id), UPDATE(id, orderdate, c_id)
   ON handsonxe07.orders
   TO handsonxe_user1;
```

Subsequently, HANDSONXE_USER1 can insert rows into the table and update rows already in the table. However, the user's INSERT and UPDATE statements can specify values only for the columns to which the user has access. When inserting a new row, all other columns in the table or view must accept the default column values, which, unless explicitly set during or after table creation, are by default null. For example, the following statements would succeed considering the privileges granted:

```
INSERT INTO handsonxe07.orders (id, orderdate, c_id)
VALUES (1,SYSDATE,1);

UPDATE handsonxe07.orders
   SET orderdate = SYSDATE
 WHERE id = 4;
```

However, the following statement would fail considering the privileges granted:

```
INSERT INTO handsonxe07.orders (id, orderdate, c_id, status)
VALUES (1,SYSDATE,1, 'B');

UPDATE handsonxe07.orders
   SET status = 'F'
 WHERE id = 4;
```

NOTE
Although Oracle does not support column-specific SELECT object privileges for tables and views, a simple workaround for this limitation is to create a view that provides access only to the necessary columns, and then grant SELECT privileges for the view.

EXERCISE 7.9: Revoke Object Privileges from a User

You can also revoke an object privilege from a user with the Object Browser. For example, to revoke the DELETE object privilege for the HANDSONXE07.CUSTOMERS table from the HANDSONXE_USER1 database user, complete the following steps:

1. Launch the Database Home Page and connect as the user that owns the schema objects of interest; if you are continuing from the previous exercise, you should already be using a session established as **HANDSONXE07**.

2. Click Object Browser.

3. Select Tables in the Object Selection pane.

4. Click CUSTOMERS.

5. Click Grants.

6. Click Revoke.

7. Select the grantee of interest in the Revoke From select list; for this exercise, select HANDSONXE_USER1.

8. Select the privilege to revoke in the Revoke select list; for this exercise, select DELETE.

9. Click Next.

10. Click SQL and review the SQL statement that the Object Browser page builds. Notice that to revoke an object privilege, you can use the SQL command REVOKE. For complete information about the form of the REVOKE command that you use to revoke object privileges, refer to the *Oracle Database 10g SQL Reference*.

    ```
    revoke DELETE on "CUSTOMERS" from HANDSONXE_USER1
    ```

11. Click Finish.

12. Notice that the Detail pane has been updated to reflect the current object privilege grants for the CUSTOMERS table.

Privilege Management with Roles

The system and object privileges necessary to use a typical database application can be numerous. When a database application supports a large user population, privilege management can become a big job quickly if you manage each user's privileges with individual grants. To make security administration an easier task, you can use roles.

**Understanding Possible Side Effects
from Revoking Object Privileges**

Certain side effects can occur when you revoke object privileges from users. For
example, consider the following scenario:

1. You grant the SELECT object privilege for a table with the Grant option
   to a user.

2. The user in turn grants the object privilege to another user.

3. The second user creates a view that depends on the object privilege to
   function properly.

4. You revoke the object privilege from the first user.

In this case, Oracle automatically revokes the object privilege from the
second user as well, which in turn causes the second user's view to stop
functioning properly. This simple example illustrates that it is important to
investigate dependencies that exist among the user's database objects and
privileges before revoking object privileges from a user.

A *role* is a collection of related system and object privileges that you can grant to
users and other roles. For example, when you build a new database application, you
can create a new role that has the database privileges necessary to use the application.
After you grant the role to an application user, the user can start the application,
establish a connection, and accomplish work. If the privileges necessary to run the
application change, all that's necessary is a quick modification of the role's set of
privileges. All grantees of the role see the change in the role automatically and
continue to have the privileges necessary to use the application.

Predefined Database Roles

Oracle has many predefined roles that you can use to quickly grant privileges to
common types of database users. Table 7-1 is a short list of five commonly used
predefined database roles.

NOTE
*Granting the RESOURCE or DBA role to a user
also grants the UNLIMITED TABLESPACE system
privilege directly to the grantee (outside of the role).
See Exercise 7.16 for important information about
this privilege.*

Role	Description
CONNECT	A basic user role that lets the grantee connect to the database.
RESOURCE	Intended for a typical application developer, this role lets the grantee create tables, sequences, data clusters, procedures, functions, packages, triggers, object types, index types, and user-defined operators in the associated schema.
DBA	Intended for administrators, this role lets the grantee perform any database function, as it includes every system privilege. Furthermore, a grantee of the DBA role can grant any system privilege to any other database user or role.
SELECT_CATALOG_ROLE	Lets the grantee query data dictionary views.
EXECUTE_CATALOG_ROLE	Lets the grantee execute the prebuilt DBMS utility packages.

TABLE 7-1. *A Short List of Prebuilt Roles Available with Oracle XE*

Although Oracle provides predefined roles to help manage privileges for typical database users, an application that relies on these roles might not necessarily function correctly. That's because you can change a predefined role's privilege set or even drop the role altogether. In particular, the Oracle Database 10*g* documentation states that Oracle plans to no longer support the CONNECT, RESOURCE, and DBA roles in future versions of Oracle.

User-Defined Roles
You can create as many roles as you need for an Oracle database and associated applications. After creating a role, you grant privileges and other roles to the role to build the role's set of privileges. Then, you grant the role to users so that they have the privileges necessary to complete their jobs.

Enabled and Disabled Roles
A grantee of a role does not necessarily have access to the privileges of the role at all times. Oracle allows applications to selectively enable and disable a role for each individual. After an application *enables* a role for a user, the privileges of the role are available to the user. As you might expect, after an application *disables* a role for a user, the user no longer has access to the privileges of the role. Oracle's

ability to dynamically control the set of privileges available to a user allows an application to ensure that users always have the correct set of privileges when using the application.

For example, when a user starts an order-entry application, the application can enable the user's ORDER_ENTRY role so that the user can accomplish work. When the user finishes working, the application can disable the user's ORDER_ENTRY role so that the user does not use the order-entry application privileges when working with a different application.

Default Roles

Each user has a list of default roles. A *default role* is a role that Oracle enables automatically when the user establishes a new database session. Default roles make it convenient to enable roles that users always require when working with Oracle, no matter which application they use.

Role Authentication

To prevent unauthorized use of a role, you can optionally protect a role with authentication. Oracle can authenticate the use of a role using several different authentication techniques, as with database users, including password authentication. Oracle authenticates role usage when a user or application attempts to enable a role protected by authentication.

Creating, Managing, and Using Roles

In the previous exercises of this chapter, you granted several system and object privileges directly to a user account. Consider the administrative overhead if you had to repeat this process for many users in a workgroup. To make privilege management easier for fictitious application users in your system, the next few practice exercises show you how to define a new role called HANDSONXE_APPUSER that you can grant to application user accounts.

EXERCISE 7.10: Create a Role

To create a new role, you must use the SQL command CREATE ROLE; the Administration page of the Database Home Page does not support the management of roles altogether. The following is an abbreviated version of the CREATE ROLE command syntax:

```
CREATE ROLE role
  [NOT IDENTIFIED | IDENTIFIED BY password]
```

Similar to a username, the name of a role can be 1 to 30 characters long, must begin with an alphabetic character, is not case sensitive, and must conform to the same naming rules listed for usernames. Additionally, a role name must be unique among all other database users and roles—in other words, a role is not a schema object, it is a system object.

To create a role, use your SQL*Plus session left over from running this chapter's support script to establish a connection as a database administrator (for example, SYSTEM) and then enter the following command:

```
CONNECT system/...;

CREATE ROLE handsonxe_appuser
 IDENTIFIED BY yeRtw;
```

> **NOTE**
> *When you create a role, Oracle automatically grants you the role with the administrative rights to alter, drop, and grant the role to other roles and users.*

EXERCISE 7.11: Grant System Privileges and Roles to a Role

The abbreviated syntax of the SQL command GRANT for granting system privileges and other roles to a role is as follows:

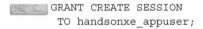

```
GRANT privilege|role [, privilege|role] ...
 TO role [, role] ...
 [WITH ADMIN OPTION]
```

For example, use SQL*Plus to execute the following statement to grant the CREATE SESSION system privilege to the new HANDSONXE_APPUSER role:

```
GRANT CREATE SESSION
 TO handsonxe_appuser;
```

> **NOTE**
> *When you grant the WITH ADMIN OPTION for a role, the grantee can grant, alter, or drop the role, and can grant the role to other users and roles. To prevent security holes in your system, it is not wise to grant system privileges and roles with administrative rights to other roles.*

EXERCISE 7.12: Grant Object Privileges to a Role

The abbreviated syntax of the SQL command GRANT for granting object privileges to a role is as follows:

```
GRANT
  privilege [, privilege] ...
 | ALL [PRIVILEGES]
 ON [schema.]object | DIRECTORY directory
 TO role [, role] ...
 [WITH GRANT OPTION]
```

For example, use SQL*Plus to enter the following statements to grant several object privileges to the new HANDSONXE_APPUSER role:

```
GRANT INSERT, UPDATE, DELETE, SELECT
  ON handsonxe07.customers
  TO handsonxe_appuser;

GRANT ALL PRIVILEGES
  ON handsonxe07.orders
  TO handsonxe_appuser;

GRANT SELECT,
  INSERT (id, lastname, firstname),
  UPDATE (lastname, firstname)
  ON handsonxe07.salesreps
  TO handsonxe_appuser;
```

NOTE
Oracle does not permit you to use the REFERENCES object privilege for a table when you receive the privilege via a role—when a user such as a developer needs this privilege, you must grant it to the user directly.

After executing the previous GRANT statements, you might be wondering why the statements executed successfully—after all, you are not currently connected as HANDSONXE07 (the owner of the objects). The grants succeed because SYSTEM is a grantee of the GRANT ANY OBJECT PRIVILEGE system privilege and can thus grant object privileges for any object in the database.

EXERCISE 7.13: Grant a Role to a User

To grant a role to a user, you use the following abbreviated syntax of the SQL command GRANT:

```
GRANT role [, role] ...
  TO user [, user] ...
  [WITH ADMIN OPTION]
```

When you grant the WITH ADMIN OPTION for a role to a user, the user can grant, alter, or drop the role, and can grant the role to other users and roles. For obvious reasons, use this option judiciously.

For example, use SQL*Plus to enter the following SQL statements to create a new database user account for a fictitious application user, and then grant the HANDSONXE_APPUSER role to the new user:

```
CREATE USER handsonxe_user2
  IDENTIFIED BY changepw123
  PASSWORD EXPIRE
  DEFAULT TABLESPACE users
  TEMPORARY TABLESPACE temp
  ACCOUNT UNLOCK;

GRANT handsonxe_appuser TO handsonxe_user2;
```

With just one GRANT statement, the new user HANDSONXE_USER2 has the necessary privileges to work as an application user in your Oracle XE database. Furthermore, if you need to change the privileges of application users, all that you need to do is grant privileges to and revoke privileges from the HANDSONXE_APPUSER role—all grantees of the HANDSONXE_APPUSER role will automatically be subject to the new privilege domain of the role.

EXERCISE 7.14: Set a User's Default Role

When you grant a role to a user, Oracle automatically adds the role to the user's list of default roles. You can explicitly set a user's list of default roles by using the following syntax of the SQL command ALTER USER:

```
ALTER USER user
  [DEFAULT ROLE
    role [,role] ...
  | ALL [EXCEPT role [,role] ...]
  | NONE  ]
```

You can specify a role as a user's default role after the user has been granted the role directly (you cannot specify roles received indirectly through other roles). Furthermore, you cannot specify a role as a user's default role if the role is authenticated by the operating system or by a security service—default roles authenticated by passwords require no passwords at connect time. Notice that you can specify individual roles, use the ALL clause to specify all or all but a list of roles, or specify no default roles for the user.

Roles and Development Privileges

While roles can simplify the management of privileges for common application users, they often prove ineffective for users such as application developers that require directly granted privileges to accomplish work. For example, consider the following scenario: an application developer is a grantee of the SELECT privilege for a table via a role, and the developer needs to create a new definer-rights stored procedure that reads the table. Even though the developer has the necessary object privileges to query the table, the developer cannot create the procedure because the privilege is available only via a role.

NOTE
If a user does not have any default roles with the CREATE SESSION system privilege, you must grant the CREATE SESSION system privilege directly to the user, or else the user will not be able to establish a database session.

Use SQL*Plus to enter the following ALTER USER statement to modify the list of default roles for the new HANDSONXE_USER2 user account:

```
ALTER USER handsonxe_user2
   DEFAULT ROLE handsonxe_appuser;
```

Subsequently, when HANDSONXE_USER2 connects to the database, Oracle XE will automatically make available the privileges granted to the HANDSONXE_APPUSER role.

EXERCISE 7.15: Enable and Disable a Role

You can explicitly enable and disable access to the privileges of a role using the SQL command SET ROLE. As discussed earlier in this section of the chapter, applications commonly use this command to make sure that application sessions have the appropriate set of privileges for using the application. The syntax of the SET ROLE command is as follows:

```
SET ROLE
   role [IDENTIFIED BY password] [,role [IDENTIFIED BY password] ... ]
 | ALL [EXCEPT role [,role] ... ]
 | NONE
```

There are several important points to understand before you use the SET ROLE command:

- Your session can use the SET ROLE command with the ALL option to enable all roles granted to your account. However, when you want to enable a role that requires a password, you must specify the role and its password using the IDENTIFIED BY parameter.

- You can disable all roles for your session by using the NONE option of the SET ROLE command.

- Oracle automatically disables any role granted to you that you do not enable with the SET ROLE command.

To display a list of the roles currently enabled by your current session as SYSTEM, use SQL*Plus to execute the following query that targets the SESSION_ROLES data dictionary view:

```
SELECT * FROM session_roles;
```

The result set should be similar to the following:

```
ROLE
------------------------------
DBA
SELECT_CATALOG_ROLE
HS_ADMIN_ROLE
EXECUTE_CATALOG_ROLE
DELETE_CATALOG_ROLE
EXP_FULL_DATABASE
IMP_FULL_DATABASE
GATHER_SYSTEM_STATISTICS
SCHEDULER_ADMIN
PLUSTRACE
XDBADMIN
XDBWEBSERVICES
AQ_ADMINISTRATOR_ROLE
```

Notice that your current session as SYSTEM has access to many roles, but not the new HANDSONXE_APPUSER role, because it is not currently enabled. To illustrate how the SET ROLE command functions, use SQL*Plus to execute the following SET ROLE statement to specifically enable the HANDSONXE_APPUSER role and disable all other roles for your current session:

```
SET ROLE handsonxe_appuser IDENTIFIED BY yeRtw;
```

Next, query the SESSION_ROLES view again and you should see the following result set:

```
ROLE
------------------
HANDSONXE_APPUSER
```

To enable the DBA, SELECT_CATALOG_ROLE, and HANDSONXE_APPUSER roles, execute the following statement:

```
SET ROLE
  DBA,
  SELECT_CATALOG_ROLE,
  handsonxe_appuser IDENTIFIED BY yeRtw;
```

Resource Limitation

In a multiuser database system, it's often necessary to limit a user's access to system resources such as disk space, shared CPU time, and disk I/O. For example, suppose that you are supporting a team of Oracle Application Express developers. One developer might have a penchant for building infinite loops in PL/SQL subprograms or establishing an excessive number of database sessions that consume an unreasonable amount of database resources at the expense of other developers trying to do their work. The following sections explain the features of Oracle XE that you can use to limit a user's access to several different system resources.

Tablespace Quotas

A user cannot create objects such as tables and indexes in a tablespace unless the user has a quota for the tablespace. A *tablespace quota* limits how much space a user's database objects can consume in the tablespace. A user can have a quota for zero, one, or all tablespaces in the database—it's entirely up to you. When you create or alter a user and give the user a tablespace quota, you set the quota as a specific number of bytes in the tablespace or as an unlimited amount of space in the tablespace.

EXERCISE 7.16: Providing Specific Tablespace Quotas for a User

To give a current user a quota for one or more tablespaces in the system, you can use the following form of the SQL command ALTER USER:

```
ALTER USER user
  [QUOTA integer [K|M]|UNLIMITED ON tablespace] ...
```

For example, use SQL*Plus to execute the following statement that provides the user HANDSONXE_USER1 with the right to use 1MB of space in the USERS tablespace:

```
ALTER USER handsonxe_user1
  QUOTA 1M ON users;
```

Now use SQL*Plus to execute the following statement that overrides HANDSONXE_USER1's specific tablespace quota for the USERS tablespace with the right to use an unlimited amount of space in the USERS tablespace:

```
ALTER USER handsonxe_user1
  QUOTA UNLIMITED ON users;
```

When a user must have an unlimited quota for every tablespace, you can grant the user the UNLIMITED TABLESPACE system privilege rather than giving the user an unlimited quota for each tablespace in the database; however, there are a few important things to understand about this system privilege:

- Oracle does not let you grant the UNLIMITED TABLESPACE system privilege to a role.

- When you grant someone the predefined RESOURCE or DBA role, Oracle automatically grants the user the UNLIMITED TABLESPACE system privilege outside of the role itself.

- Specific tablespace quotas do not bind a grantee of the UNLIMITED TABLESPACE system privilege.

NOTE
A user does not require a quota to make use of temporary space in the user's corresponding temporary tablespace.

Resource Limit Profiles

To control the consumption of several other types of system resources, you can use resource limit profiles. A *resource limit profile* is a set of specific resource limit settings that you assign to one or more database users. Using a resource limit profile, you can limit consumption of several system resources, including, but not limited to, the following:

- CPU time (in hundredths of a second), per session or per statement

- Logical disk I/Os, per session or per statement

- Concurrent database sessions per user

- The maximum amount of connect time and idle time (in minutes) per session

Profiles and Security Policies

You can use resource limit profiles to enforce security policies for database users. Using a resource limit profile, you can control the following settings for each user account that is assigned the profile:

- The number of consecutive failed connection attempts to allow before Oracle locks the account

- The lifetime of the account's password, in days, after which the password expires

- The number of days (grace period) that a user can use an expired password before locking the account

■ The number of days that must pass, or the number of times that an account's password must be changed, before the account can reuse an old password

■ Whether or not to check an account's password for sufficient complexity to prevent an account from using an obvious password

The Default Profile

Every Oracle database has a *default resource limit profile*. When you create a new database user and do not indicate a specific profile for the user, Oracle automatically assigns the user the database's default profile. By default, all resource limit settings of the database's default profile are set to unlimited; security policy settings vary.

When you create a resource limit profile, you can set specific resource limit settings or defer to the corresponding setting of the database's default profile. At any time, you can alter the settings of a database's default profile just like user-defined profiles.

Managing Resource Limit Profiles

Several steps are necessary to configure and enforce resource limitation and security policies using profiles in an Oracle database:

1. Enable resource limitation for the database instance.

2. Create one or more profiles.

3. Assign each user's profile.

The following practice exercises teach you how to complete these steps to manage resource limit profiles, password policies, and more.

EXERCISE 7.17: Enable Resource Limitation

By default, resource limitation is not enforced for an Oracle XE database. Therefore, the first step necessary to limit user access to server resources is to enable the enforcement of resource limitation at the instance level. You can enable and disable the enforcement of resource limitation without having to shut down and restart the Oracle service by using the following form of the SQL command ALTER SYSTEM:

```
ALTER SYSTEM
  SET RESOURCE_LIMIT = TRUE|FALSE
```

To enforce profile policies, with your current database administrator session as SYSTEM, use SQL*Plus to execute the following statement:

```
ALTER SYSTEM
  SET RESOURCE_LIMIT = TRUE SCOPE = MEMORY;
```

NOTE
*The example ALTER SYSTEM statement in this
exercise uses the SCOPE parameter set to MEMORY
to enable the enforcement of resource limitation
only for the life of the current database instance.
If you shut down and restart Oracle XE, the
enforcement of profile policies is subject to the
setting of the RESOURCE_LIMIT parameter in your
server's initialization parameter file.*

EXERCISE 7.18: Create a Profile

In this exercise, you create a resource limit profile that you can use with the new
application developers in your practice database. To create a new profile, you use
the SQL command CREATE PROFILE, which has the following syntax:

```
CREATE PROFILE profile LIMIT
  [SESSIONS_PER_USER integer|UNLIMITED|DEFAULT]
  [CPU_PER_SESSION integer|UNLIMITED|DEFAULT]
  [CPU_PER_CALL integer|UNLIMITED|DEFAULT]
  [CONNECT_TIME integer|UNLIMITED|DEFAULT]
  [IDLE_TIME integer|UNLIMITED|DEFAULT]
  [LOGICAL_READS_PER_SESSION integer|UNLIMITED|DEFAULT]
  [LOGICAL_READS_PER_CALL integer|UNLIMITED|DEFAULT]
  [COMPOSITE_LIMIT integer|UNLIMITED|DEFAULT]
  [PRIVATE_SGA integer [K|M]|UNLIMITED|DEFAULT]
  [FAILED_LOGIN_ATTEMPTS integer|UNLIMITED|DEFAULT]
  [PASSWORD_LIFE_TIME integer|UNLIMITED|DEFAULT]
  [PASSWORD_REUSE_TIME integer|UNLIMITED|DEFAULT]
  [PASSWORD_REUSE_MAX integer|UNLIMITED|DEFAULT]
  [PASSWORD_LOCK_TIME integer|UNLIMITED|DEFAULT]
  [PASSWORD_GRACE_TIME integer|UNLIMITED|DEFAULT]
  [PASSWORD_VERIFY_FUNCTION NULL|function|DEFAULT]
```

Use SQL*Plus to execute the following statement that creates a new resource
limit profile:

```
CREATE PROFILE handsonxe_appdev LIMIT
  SESSIONS_PER_USER 2
  CPU_PER_SESSION UNLIMITED
  CPU_PER_CALL 3000
  CONNECT_TIME UNLIMITED
  IDLE_TIME 30
  LOGICAL_READS_PER_SESSION UNLIMITED
  LOGICAL_READS_PER_CALL 1000
  PRIVATE_SGA 200K;
```

Note the following settings in the new HANDSONXE_APPDEV profile:

- A profile user can have at most two concurrent database sessions open.

- A profile user session can use an unlimited amount of CPU time, but only 30 seconds (set as 3000 hundredths of a second) of CPU time per database request. If a call reaches this CPU limit, Oracle terminates the operation to prevent further consumption of CPU time by the operation.

- A profile user session can remain connected to the instance for an unlimited amount of time without being disconnected, but can remain idle for only 30 minutes before being automatically disconnected.

- A profile user session can perform an unlimited number of logical reads (disk reads from either disk or server memory) but only 1000 logical block reads per database request. If a call reaches this limit, Oracle stops the operation to prevent further consumption of logical reads by the session.

- A profile user session that connects to the instance using a shared server can allocate and use up to 200KB of private memory for the session.

EXERCISE 7.19: Alter Profile Settings

You alter the settings of a profile by using the SQL command ALTER PROFILE:

```
ALTER PROFILE profile LIMIT
  [SESSIONS_PER_USER integer|UNLIMITED|DEFAULT]
  [CPU_PER_SESSION integer|UNLIMITED|DEFAULT]
  [CPU_PER_CALL integer|UNLIMITED|DEFAULT]
  [CONNECT_TIME integer|UNLIMITED|DEFAULT]
  [IDLE_TIME integer|UNLIMITED|DEFAULT]
  [LOGICAL_READS_PER_SESSION integer|UNLIMITED|DEFAULT]
  [LOGICAL_READS_PER_CALL integer|UNLIMITED|DEFAULT]
  [COMPOSITE_LIMIT integer|UNLIMITED|DEFAULT]
  [PRIVATE_SGA integer [K|M]|UNLIMITED|DEFAULT]
  [FAILED_LOGIN_ATTEMPTS integer|UNLIMITED|DEFAULT]
  [PASSWORD_LIFE_TIME integer|UNLIMITED|DEFAULT]
  [PASSWORD_REUSE_TIME integer|UNLIMITED|DEFAULT]
  [PASSWORD_REUSE_MAX integer|UNLIMITED|DEFAULT]
  [PASSWORD_LOCK_TIME integer|UNLIMITED|DEFAULT]
  [PASSWORD_GRACE_TIME integer|UNLIMITED|DEFAULT]
  [PASSWORD_VERIFY_FUNCTION NULL|function|DEFAULT]
```

For example, when you created the new HANDSONXE_APPDEV profile in the previous exercise, you did not specify any of the password policy settings. Use SQL*Plus to enter the following ALTER PROFILE statement that specifies the basic password management settings for the new profile:

```
ALTER PROFILE handsonxe_appdev LIMIT
    FAILED_LOGIN_ATTEMPTS 3
    PASSWORD_LOCK_TIME 1
    PASSWORD_LIFE_TIME 30
    PASSWORD_GRACE_TIME 5
    PASSWORD_REUSE_TIME UNLIMITED
    PASSWORD_REUSE_MAX UNLIMITED;
```

The previous statement sets the following password management features:

■ A profile user can attempt three consecutive logins without success, after which Oracle automatically locks the account.

■ If Oracle locks a profile user's account because of three consecutive failed login attempts, Oracle keeps the account locked for one full day and then automatically unlocks the account.

■ The lifetime of a profile user's password is 30 days, plus a grace period of 5 days, after which the user must change the password or else Oracle locks the account.

■ A profile user cannot reuse an old password.

NOTE
Oracle enforces all password management features that you set with a user's profile regardless of whether or not you enable resource limitation with the ALTER SYSTEM command or the RESOURCE_ LIMIT server parameter. Therefore, if you are not interested in restricting consumption of system resources but want to enforce security policies for passwords, don't bother enabling resource limitation as described in Exercise 7.17.

EXERCISE 7.20: Manually Force a User's Password to Expire

You can manually force a user's password to expire and require that the user change the password during his or her next session. To accomplish this task, use the following form of the SQL command ALTER USER:

```
ALTER USER user
    PASSWORD EXPIRE;
```

For example, enter the following statement to manually expire the password for HANDSXONXE_USER2:

```
ALTER USER handsonxe_user2
    PASSWORD EXPIRE;
```

EXERCISE 7.21: Use Password Complexity Checking

In the previous exercise, you specified the basic password management settings for a profile. You can also check the complexity of a profile user's password by using the PASSWORD_VERIFY_FUNCTION parameter of the SQL commands CREATE PROFILE and ALTER PROFILE. To disable password complexity checking for all profile users, set the profile's PASSWORD_VERIFY_FUNCTION parameter to NULL. To enable password complexity checking for all profile users, set the profile's PASSWORD_VERIFY_FUNCTION parameter to the name of a function that is designed to check password complexity.

For your convenience, Oracle supplies a PL/SQL function that you must create using the UTLPWDMG.SQL command script located in ORACLE_HOME/rdbms/ admin. To run this script, first start a *new* instance of SQL*Plus (leave your other SQL*Plus session intact) and connect as the user SYS; the password for SYS is the same password for SYSTEM that was assigned during Oracle XE installation. When you use SQL*Plus to connect as SYS, you must specify the special AS SYSDBA option of the CONNECT command, as the following example demonstrates:

```
CONNECT sys AS SYSDBA;
```

When you are using SQL*Plus on the same computer as Oracle XE and your current Microsoft Windows session is a member of the Microsoft Windows ORA_ DBA group, you can more simply connect SYS AS SYSDBA by using the following syntax:

```
CONNECT / AS SYSDBA;
```

Whatever method you choose, once you connect as SYS, run the UTLPWDMG .SQL command script. For example, the following command runs the UTLPWDMG.SQL script:

```
@?/rdbms/admin/utlpwdmg.sql;
```

The UTLPWDMG.SQL command script creates a PL/SQL function named SYS. VERIFY_FUNCTION and enables the password management features for the default database profile, including complexity checking with the SYS.VERIFY_FUNCTION function. SYS.VERIFY_FUNCTION includes some standard checks for password complexity, including the following:

- An account's username and password cannot match.

- A password must be at least four characters in length.

- A password cannot be one of the following common strings: "welcome", "database", "account", "user", "password", "oracle", "computer", or "abcd".

■ A password must contain at least one character, one digit, and one punctuation mark.

■ A new password must differ from the current password by at least three characters.

After you execute the UTLPWDMG.SQL script, exit this SQL*Plus session and return to your original SQL*Plus session.

Using your original SQL*Plus session (connected as SYSTEM), alter the new HANDSONXE_APPDEV profile to enable password complexity checking for all of the profile's users. The following statement alters the HANDSONXE_APPDEV profile to use the setting of the PASSWORD_VERIFY_FUNCTION parameter of the database's default profile (which is SYS.VERIFY_FUNCTION):

```
ALTER PROFILE handsonxe_appdev LIMIT
  PASSWORD_VERIFY_FUNCTION DEFAULT;
```

NOTE
*When you configure Oracle to check the complexity of user passwords, users should not use the ALTER USER command to change passwords. Instead, use the SQL*Plus command PASSWORD, as demonstrated in Exercise 7.23.*

EXERCISE 7.22: Set a User's Profile

By default, all users are assigned to use the database's default profile. To set a user's profile to another profile, you can use the following form of the SQL command ALTER USER:

```
ALTER USER user
  PROFILE profile
```

For example, using your original SQL*Plus session, enter the following ALTER USER statement to assign the user HANDSONXE_USER1 to the HANDSONXE_APPDEV profile:

```
ALTER USER handsonxe_user1
  PROFILE handsonxe_appdev;
```

EXERCISE 7.23: Experiment with Password Management Settings

At this point, all users in your practice database are subject to various password management checks because the default database profile and the new HANDSONXE_APPDEV profile have set password management options. This exercise enables you to see what happens when you try to change the password for HANDSONXE_USER1 to a very simple password. Enter the following statement, which demonstrates the use of the simple SQL*Plus command PASSWORD:

```
PASSWORD handsonxe_user1
```

When prompted, enter a new, weak password for HANDSONXE_USER1, such as **oracle**. When Oracle tries to change the user's password, it should return the following errors:

```
ORA-28003: password verification for the specified password failed
ORA-20002: Password too simple
```

Now execute the same PASSWORD statement as before and set an acceptably complex password for HANDSONXE_USER1, such as **t4R#xY32**. The dialog with SQL*Plus should resemble the following:

```
SQL> PASSWORD handsonxe_user1
Changing password for handsonxe_user1
New password:
Retype new password:
Password changed
```

EXERCISE 7.24: Alter the Default Database Profile

If you plan to use the default database profile to limit resources or enforce password management, you should pay close attention to the default limits and password management options set for this profile (see Exercise 7.28 to learn how to display information about profiles). You can adjust the default database profile's settings by using an ALTER PROFILE statement.

For example, you must disable the password management features of the default database profile so that you can run the SQL command scripts for subsequent chapters without being prompted to change the SYSTEM account's password. To disable password management for the default database profile, enter the following ALTER PROFILE statement:

```
ALTER PROFILE default LIMIT
  PASSWORD_LIFE_TIME UNLIMITED
  PASSWORD_REUSE_TIME UNLIMITED
  PASSWORD_REUSE_MAX UNLIMITED
  PASSWORD_LOCK_TIME UNLIMITED
  PASSWORD_GRACE_TIME UNLIMITED
  PASSWORD_VERIFY_FUNCTION NULL;
```

NOTE
After you enable the password management features for a profile, Oracle keeps track of when each profile user's password expires, and so on, even after you disable password management features for the profile. Consequently, in 30 days, Oracle might request that you change the password for existing database accounts such as SYS and SYSTEM.

Displaying Security Information

The following exercises demonstrate some useful queries that you can use to display information about users, roles, and profiles from your database's data dictionary.

EXERCISE 7.25: Display Information About Users

To display general information about the users in your database, including a user's username, default tablespace, temporary tablespace, and account status, the Manage Database Users page of the Database Home Page is perfectly fine. However, to report information about a user's profile setting (along with the other information), use SQL*Plus or the SQL Commands window of the Database Home Page to query the DBA_USERS data dictionary view while connected as a database administrator; when the columns returned by a query are too wide for the standard SQL*Plus display, I tend to use the SQL Commands window for the sake of convenience.

For example, establish a Database Home Page session as SYSTEM and then use the SQL Commands page to execute the following statement to reveal the account settings for the HANDSONXE_USER1 and HANDSONXE_USER2 user accounts in the practice database:

```
SELECT
   username, account_status, default_tablespace,
   temporary_tablespace, profile
 FROM dba_users
WHERE REGEXP_LIKE (username, 'user(1|2)', 'i');
```

The graphical representation of the result set should be similar to the following:

```
USERNAME          ACCOUNT_STATUS  DEFAULT_TABLESPACE  TEMPORARY_TABLESPACE  PROFILE
---------------   --------------  ------------------  --------------------  ----------------
HANDSONXE_USER1   OPEN            USERS               TEMP                  HANDSONXE_APPDEV
HANDSONXE_USER2   EXPIRED         USERS               TEMP                  DEFAULT
```

EXERCISE 7.26: Display Information About Roles

To display information about the roles in your database, you can use SQL*Plus or the SQL Commands window to query the DBA_ROLES data dictionary view. For example, use the SQL Commands window to execute the following statement to list information about the CONNECT, RESOURCE, DBA, and HANDSONXE_APPUSER roles in your database:

```
SELECT * FROM dba_roles
  WHERE role IN ('CONNECT','RESOURCE','DBA','HANDSONXE_APPUSER');
```

The result set should be similar to the following:

```
ROLE                           PASSWORD
------------------------------ --------
CONNECT                        NO
RESOURCE                       NO
DBA                            NO
HANDSONXE_APPUSER              YES
```

EXERCISE 7.27: Display Information About Tablespace Quotas

To display information about the quotas granted for each tablespace in your database, you can query the DBA_TS_QUOTAS data dictionary view. For example, use the SQL Commands window to execute the following statement:

```
SELECT tablespace_name, username, bytes, max_bytes
  FROM dba_ts_quotas;
```

The result set for this query should be similar to the following:

```
TABLESPACE_NAME USERNAME              BYTES   MAX_BYTES
--------------- ---------------- ---------- ----------
USERS           HANDSONXE04          983040     204800
USERS           HR                  1638400         -1
USERS           HANDSONXE05          786432     204800
USERS           HANDSONXE06          983040     204800
USERS           HANDSONXE07          786432     204800
USERS           HANDSONXE_USER1           0         -1
```

As highlighted in bold, the MAX_BYTES column of the DBA_TS_QUOTAS view displays the code –1 when a user has an unlimited tablespace quota.

EXERCISE 7.28: Display Information About Profiles

To display information about profiles and associated resource limit settings, you can query the DBA_PROFILES data dictionary view. For example, use the SQL Commands window to execute the following query:

```
SELECT profile, resource_name, limit
  FROM dba_profiles
 WHERE profile = 'HANDSONXE_APPDEV';
```

The expected result set is as follows:

```
PROFILE          RESOURCE_NAME             LIMIT
---------------- ------------------------- ----------
HANDSONXE_APPDEV COMPOSITE_LIMIT           DEFAULT
HANDSONXE_APPDEV SESSIONS_PER_USER         2
HANDSONXE_APPDEV CPU_PER_SESSION           UNLIMITED
```

```
HANDSONXE_APPDEV CPU_PER_CALL                   3000
HANDSONXE_APPDEV LOGICAL_READS_PER_SESSION      UNLIMITED
HANDSONXE_APPDEV LOGICAL_READS_PER_CALL         1000
HANDSONXE_APPDEV IDLE_TIME                      30
HANDSONXE_APPDEV CONNECT_TIME                   UNLIMITED
HANDSONXE_APPDEV PRIVATE_SGA                    204800
HANDSONXE_APPDEV FAILED_LOGIN_ATTEMPTS          3
HANDSONXE_APPDEV PASSWORD_LIFE_TIME             30
HANDSONXE_APPDEV PASSWORD_REUSE_TIME            UNLIMITED
HANDSONXE_APPDEV PASSWORD_REUSE_MAX             UNLIMITED
HANDSONXE_APPDEV PASSWORD_VERIFY_FUNCTION       DEFAULT
HANDSONXE_APPDEV PASSWORD_LOCK_TIME             1
HANDSONXE_APPDEV PASSWORD_GRACE_TIME            5
```

Chapter Summary

This chapter explained the security features of Oracle XE that you can use to limit and monitor access to a database:

- Only a registered database user can access a database once Oracle authenticates a connection request. You can create and manage users with the Database Home Page or the SQL commands CREATE USER and ALTER USER.

- Once connected to a database, a user can perform only those operations that the user is privileged to execute. You can grant users individual system and object privileges or use roles to group related sets of privileges and more easily manage user privileges. You create roles using the SQL command CREATE ROLE and then grant and revoke privileges to users or roles using the SQL commands GRANT and REVOKE, respectively.

- Resource limit profiles let you limit a user's access to system resources, such as CPU time, disk I/Os, and sessions. You create profiles by using the SQL command CREATE PROFILE, and then assign each user to a profile with the SQL commands CREATE USER or ALTER USER.

CHAPTER
8

Manage Database Space

onsidering that Oracle XE provides you with a maximum of 4GB of data storage, it's doubtful that managing database space is going to be the most time consuming of database administration tasks. Nonetheless, it is important to understand the principles of database storage and associated DBA tasks so that you can adequately address database storage issues when they arise. This chapter is a primer that you can use to begin learning the basics for managing the following storage structures in an Oracle database:

- Tablespaces

- Data files

- Data, index, temporary, and undo segments

- Extents

- Data blocks

Chapter Prerequisites

To practice the hands-on exercises in this chapter, you need to start SQL*Plus as instructed in Exercise 2.11 and run the following command script:

```
location\handsonxe\sql\chap08.sql
```

where *location* is the file directory where you expanded the support archive that accompanies this book. For example, after starting SQL*Plus, you can run this chapter's SQL command script using the SQL*Plus command @, as in the following example (assuming that your chap08.sql file is in C:\temp\handsonxe\sql):

```
SQL> @C:\temp\handsonxe\sql\chap08.sql;
```

Once you reply to all of the prompts and the script completes successfully, you can exit SQL*Plus by using an EXIT command.

Logical vs. Physical Storage Structures

Data independence is a primary characteristic of a relational database system such as Oracle. An Oracle database's physical structure is independent of and hidden from an end user's logical view of the data. The benefit of data independence is that typical end users and application developers can easily access data in logical structures such as tables by using simple SQL commands, without having to consider the complexities of the data's physical storage. For example, when you execute a query that targets a table, you don't have to consider where the table's data is stored on disk, because Oracle transparently maps columns and rows of the table's data to files and physical bytes on disk. And after a database administrator physically relocates the table's data for some reason, nothing changes when you want to access the table—queries that target the table continue to work unmodified.

A *logical storage structure* in an Oracle database is a storage structure that typical end users and application developers directly reference to perform their work; databases, tables, and tablespaces are examples of logical storage structures. For example, to build an application, a developer must understand what database to work with, what tablespace to create tables in, and what table to query when building a report. At no time does a typical end user or application developer even consider physical storage structures such as what file or disk stores a particular table.

A *physical storage structure* is something that usually concerns database administrators only: files, segments, extents, and data blocks. For example, before creating a new database, it is important for a database administrator to carefully plan the layout of the files that comprise each tablespace and estimate the size of each table's underlying segment to ensure that there is adequate disk space to accommodate the new database. Figure 8-1 illustrates some of the many logical and physical storage structures in an Oracle database that this chapter discusses in subsequent sections.

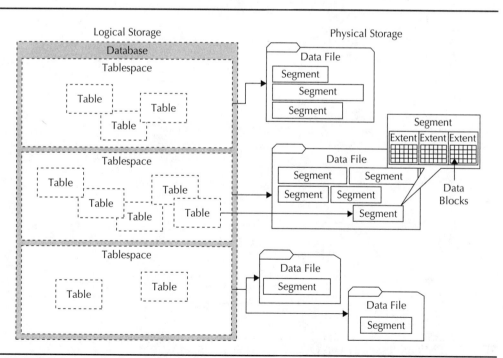

FIGURE 8-1. *Logical and physical storage structures in an Oracle database*

Tablespaces and Data Files

A *tablespace* is a logical organization of data within an Oracle database that corresponds to one or more physical *data files* on disk. Figure 8-2 illustrates the relationship between several tablespaces and their data files.

When you create a new data structure such as a table that requires space to store its data, Oracle *allocates* (reserves) space for the table from a tablespace of your choice; when you do not indicate a specific tablespace for a new table, Oracle allocates space for the table from your account's default tablespace. See Chapter 7 for more information about setting the default tablespace for a user account.

Although you can be in charge of what tablespace logically stores a data structure such as a table, Oracle transparently controls the physical storage of the table. The physical storage of data structures within a tablespace maps directly to the underlying data files of the tablespace. When a tablespace has only one data file, the tablespace must store all of an associated table's data within the one data file. When a tablespace has multiple data files, Oracle can store the data for a particular table within any file of the tablespace; in fact, Oracle might distribute the data of a single table across multiple data files of a tablespace.

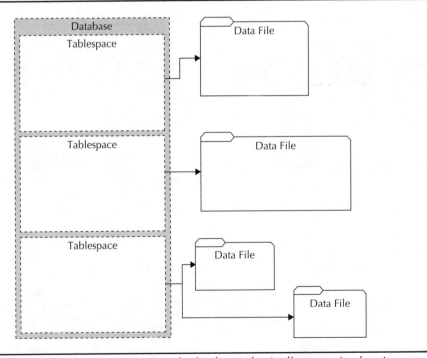

FIGURE 8-2. *Each tablespace in an Oracle database physically stores its data in one or more associated data files.*

Although it's interesting to understand specifically how Oracle stores data for structures such as tables, don't get bogged down too much by the details when you are just getting started. Remember that Oracle automatically manages physical space allocation once you lay out a database's tablespaces and data files the way that you want.

Permanent, Temporary, and Undo Tablespaces

There are three different types of tablespaces that you can create for an Oracle database; more specifically, a tablespace in an Oracle database can store one of three different types of information:

- **Permanent tablespace**   Stores user and application data (tables, indexes, etc.).

- **Temporary tablespace**   Stores temporary data used internally by Oracle to process demanding SQL statements (large sorted queries, join queries, index builds, etc.). The underlying files for a temporary tablespace are known as *temp files*.

- **Undo tablespace**   Stores undo data used internally by Oracle for transaction rollback, read consistency, and database recovery.

Permanent tablespaces are the type of tablespace most important to people such as application developers, because this is the type of tablespace that can store data for an application. Typically, database administrators are the only users who are cognizant of temporary and undo tablespaces when creating and tuning the performance of a database.

The SYSTEM Tablespace

Every Oracle database has at least one permanent tablespace: the *SYSTEM tablespace*. When you create a new Oracle database, you must indicate the names, sizes, and other characteristics of the data files that make up the physical storage for the SYSTEM tablespace.

A database's SYSTEM tablespace is essential for normal system operation because it stores the internal system tables known as the *data dictionary* or *system catalog* that Oracle uses to manage the database. Besides internal system information, the data dictionary normally stores the source and compiled code for all PL/SQL programs, such as stored procedures and functions, packages, and database triggers; databases that use PL/SQL extensively should have a sufficiently large SYSTEM tablespace. The data dictionary also maintains metadata about schema objects such as views, synonyms, and sequences, which are objects that consist simply by definition and do not store any data.

The SYSAUX Tablespace

Every Oracle database also has a tablespace named SYSAUX. The *SYSAUX tablespace* is also critical for normal database operation because it contains data for internal Oracle database features such as the Automatic Workload Repository (AWR), optimizer statistics, the job scheduler, LogMiner, and other features of Oracle that subsequent chapters of this book explain in the proper context. For now, simply understand that every Oracle database also contains a SYSAUX tablespace to store important system-related information.

Other Tablespaces

An Oracle database typically uses multiple tablespaces that logically separate the different types of data within the database. For example, immediately after installation every Oracle XE database has the following tablespaces:

- **SYSTEM and SYSAUX**   Store internal system information

- **UNDO**   Stores internal information necessary to roll back or "undo" the effects of transactions

- **TEMP**   Stores temporary data used during internal system processing such as the creation of a large index or the sorting of data for a query that uses an ORDER BY clause

- **USERS**   A default tablespace that developers can use to create tables and indexes that support applications

Tablespaces, Databases, What's the Difference?

I suspect that many readers of this book are new to Oracle, but might already be familiar with other database systems such as Microsoft SQL Server and MySQL—these database systems have no concept of a tablespace. Instead, these database systems have you create and use logical storage divisions known as databases to store data. The concept of a database in these systems is roughly analogous to the concept of a tablespace within Oracle. For example, MySQL users can think of the SYSTEM and SYSAUX tablespaces in an Oracle database as the MYSQL database in MySQL, and the USERS tablespace in an Oracle database as the TEST database in MySQL.

The important point to remember if you are new to Oracle after using Microsoft SQL Server or MySQL is that you don't want to start creating one database after another just to logically organize the storage of data. Instead, use just one Oracle database and create different tablespaces when you have logical sets of data that you want to organize separately.

Figure 8-3 demonstrates the default tablespace layout of an Oracle XE database's tablespaces.

Databases that support more than one application commonly use tablespaces to logically and physically separate each application's data, which can provide for many possible benefits. For example:

- You can easily account for and limit each application's space with operating system facilities because an application's storage relates directly to data files in a file system.

- An application's tablespaces can move in or out of a database without affecting the availability of or space available to other applications.

- You can back up and recover each application's data independently because Oracle provides tablespace-level back up and recovery features.

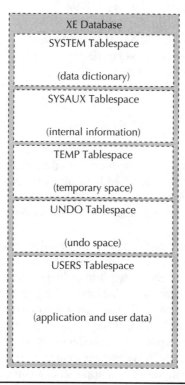

FIGURE 8-3. *Tablespaces logically and physically separate the storage of different types of database information.*

Online and Offline Tablespaces

Oracle lets you control the availability of data in a database on a tablespace-by-tablespace basis. That is, a tablespace can either be online or offline:

■ The data in an *online tablespace* is available to applications and databases. Typically, a tablespace always remains online so that the information within the tablespace is available.

■ The data in an *offline tablespace* is not available, even when the database is available. An administrator might take a tablespace offline to prevent access to an application's data, because the tablespace is experiencing a problem and requires recovery, or because the tablespace contains historical data that is typically not required by anyone.

NOTE
A database's SYSTEM tablespace must always remain online, because information in the data dictionary must be available during normal operation; if you try to take the SYSTEM tablespace offline, Oracle returns an error. In general, the SYSAUX tablespace should also remain online, but this is not mandatory.

Read-Only and Read-Write Tablespaces

Immediately after you create a new permanent tablespace, the tablespace is a *read-write tablespace*. That is, you can create, alter, and drop data structures within the tablespace, and applications can query, add, modify, and delete information from the structures contained within the tablespace. When applications must actively change data in a tablespace, the tablespace must continue to operate as a read-write tablespace.

In some cases, a tablespace stores historical data that never changes. When a tablespace's data never changes, you can make the tablespace a *read-only tablespace*. Making a tablespace read-only can protect it from inappropriate data modifications. Making a tablespace read-only can also save time when performing database backups, because it's not necessary to repeatedly back up a read-only tablespace when you back up the other tablespaces of the database.

After you create a new tablespace and add data to it, you can alter the tablespace and make it a read-only tablespace. When necessary, you can always switch a tablespace back to read-write mode so that applications can update the data within the tablespace.

A Tablespace's Data Files

A data file (or temp file) is a physical storage file, typically on disk, for a tablespace in an Oracle database. Some tablespaces store all of their data in just a single data file, whereas other tablespaces might have multiple data files that collectively store the tablespace's data.

Considering data files, a tablespace can be either a bigfile tablespace or a smallfile tablespace. The traditional type of tablespace in an Oracle database is a *smallfile tablespace*, which can have up to 1022 data files (or temp files), each of which can contain up to 4 million blocks. You typically use smallfile tablespaces when you are not working with large databases and do not require massive amounts of database storage. Because Oracle XE is not engineered to support large databases, smallfile tablespaces are the norm.

In contrast, a *bigfile tablespace* can have only one data file (or temp file), but the maximum size of the single file is 128 terabytes (TB) for a tablespace that uses 32K blocks, or 32TB for a tablespace that uses 8K blocks. You typically use bigfile tablespaces with *very large databases (VLDBs)* that rely on a logical volume manager for features such as data striping, RAID, and dynamic volume extension. You very likely would never purposely create a bigfile tablespace while using Oracle XE, but you should be aware of bigfile tablespaces just in case you graduate to using a different edition of Oracle such as Oracle Database 10g Standard or Enterprise Edition.

When you create a tablespace, all data files should comply with a standard naming convention so that they are easily recognizable when administrators work with the host operating system. It is also important to carefully consider the location of a tablespace's data files, which can dramatically affect the availability and performance of dependent applications. For example, when you place a tablespace's data files on a stand-alone disk, applications that store data in the tablespace will not be available if the disk crashes and requires recovery, and application performance might be bound by disk I/O (input/output) contention for data access. In contrast, when you place the tablespace's data files on a RAID-5 disk array that stripes and mirrors data among multiple disks, an isolated disk failure does not interrupt application availability and performance is likely to be better due to reduced disk I/O contention.

NOTE
When planning a new database or adding data files to a tablespace, Oracle Corporation recommends that you follow the guidelines described by the Oracle Optimal Flexible Architecture (OFA). *The OFA is a set of file-naming and placement guidelines that you should implement for Oracle software and databases. For more information about the OFA, please see the* Oracle Database 10g Administrator's Guide.

Use of Data File Space

When you create a new data file for a tablespace, Oracle preallocates the amount of disk space that you specify for the data file. Think of a new data file as an empty data bucket—the file contains no data, but it is a receptacle that is ready to store database information.

Any time you create a new data structure such as a table or index in a tablespace, Oracle allocates a certain amount of space from the tablespace's data files for the new object. Allocating data file space to a new data structure reduces the remaining amount of available free space in the data file. As applications insert and update data in a data structure such as a table, the preallocated space for the table can eventually become full.

If data consumes all of a data structure's available storage space, Oracle can automatically allocate additional space from the tablespace's data files for the structure. Allocating more space to extend the storage capacity of a data structure further reduces the amount of available free space in the tablespace's data files.

Data File Sizes

In general, the size of a data file remains constant. As data structures in a tablespace allocate space from the corresponding data files, the tablespace can become full if all of the data files in the tablespace become full. Applications cannot insert new data into a tablespace that's full until more storage space becomes available for the tablespace. To increase the storage capacity of a tablespace, you have a few different options:

- You can add one or more new data files to the tablespace.

- You can manually resize one or more of the existing data files in the tablespace.

- You can configure one or more of the data files in the tablespace to automatically extend when the tablespace becomes full and requires more space.

The first two options are fine if you are a watchful administrator who frequently monitors the storage capacity of your database's data files. When you notice that a tablespace is running low on free space, you can add more files to the tablespace or increase the size of one of the tablespace's data files. In contrast, the third option allows a tablespace's storage capacity to grow automatically, without manual assistance. For your convenience, all data files in an Oracle XE database will automatically extend if necessary.

Online and Offline Data Files

Oracle controls the availability of individual data files of a tablespace. A data file can be either *online* (available) or *offline* (not available). Under normal circumstances, a data file is always online. When Oracle attempts to read or write a data file and cannot do so because some type of problem prevents this from happening, Oracle automatically takes the data file offline. The encompassing tablespace remains online, because other data files of the tablespace might still be available; however, when a known disk problem occurs, you should take affected tablespaces offline so that corresponding applications do not witness unfamiliar disk I/O error conditions. Once the problem is fixed (for example, after a data file recovery), you can bring an offline data file and offline tablespace back online.

NOTE
The data files of a database's SYSTEM tablespace must always remain online, because the data dictionary must always be available during system operation. If Oracle experiences a problem reading or writing a data file in the database's SYSTEM tablespace, the system will not operate correctly until you fix the problem.

Creating and Managing Permanent Tablespaces and Data Files

Now that you have a good understanding of tablespaces and data files, the following practice exercises will teach you how to create and manage permanent tablespaces and their data files.

EXERCISE 8.1: Display Database Storage Utilization

To quickly get an overview of an Oracle XE database's storage utilization, complete the following steps:

1. Launch the Database Home Page.

2. Establish a connection as a database administrator. For example, log in using the SYSTEM account.

3. Click Administration.

4. Click Storage.

5. Notice the gauge that illustrates the total amount of storage space utilized and possible for the current Oracle XE database, as shown in Figure 8-4.

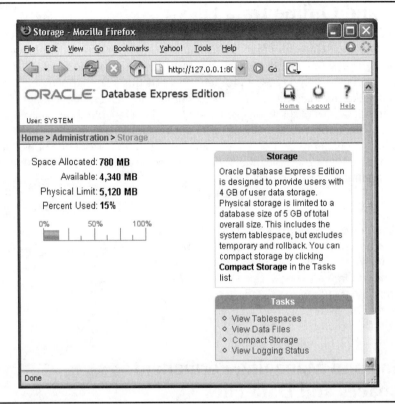

FIGURE 8-4. *The Storage page indicates the total amount of space utilized and possible for an Oracle XE database.*

Remember that Oracle XE imposes a database size upper limit of 5GB, not including the space allocated to tablespaces that support internal system operations such as temporary and undo tablespaces.

EXERCISE 8.2: Display Tablespace Information

To display information about the tablespaces in an Oracle XE database, complete the following steps:

1. Complete Steps 1 through 4 in Exercise 8.1, if necessary.

2. Click View Tablespaces (on the Tasks tab).

3. The Tablespaces page displays a storage utilization report with specific information for each tablespace, as shown in Figure 8-5.

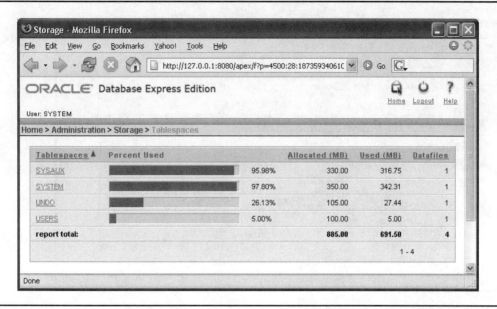

FIGURE 8-5.   *The Tablespaces page displays the storage utilization for each tablespace.*

NOTE
To avoid somewhat confusing information about storage utilization within a temporary tablespace, the Tablespaces page purposely does not display information about temporary tablespaces. See "Temporary Segments, Tablespaces, and Groups" later in this chapter for more information about temporary tablespaces and space usage within them.

EXERCISE 8.3: Display Data File Information

To display information about the data files in an Oracle XE database, complete the following steps:

1. Complete Steps 1 through 4 in Exercise 8.1, if necessary.

2. Click View Data Files (on the Tasks tab).

3. The Data Files page displays specific information for each data file, as shown in Figure 8-6.

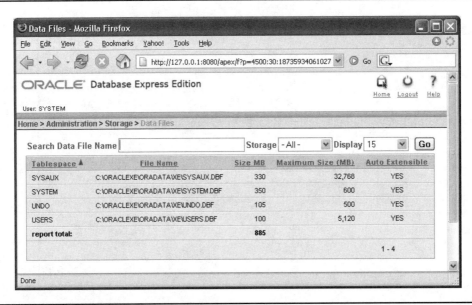

FIGURE 8-6. *The Data Files page displays the storage information about each data file.*

EXERCISE 8.4: Create a Permanent Tablespace

To create a permanent tablespace in an Oracle XE database, you must use the SQL command CREATE TABLESPACE. For the purposes of this exercise, the abbreviated syntax of the CREATE TABLESPACE command is as follows:

```
CREATE [BIGFILE|SMALLFILE] TABLESPACE tablespace
  DATAFILE
    'filename' [SIZE integer [K|M|G|T]] [REUSE]
    [ AUTOEXTEND
      { OFF
      | ON
        [NEXT integer [K|M|G|T]]
        [MAXSIZE {UNLIMITED|integer [K|M|G|T] }] } ]
  [, ... other data file specifications ... ]
  [ONLINE|OFFLINE]
```

NOTE
You must have the CREATE TABLESPACE system privilege to create a tablespace.

Notice that when you create a tablespace, you can specify one or more data file specifications for the tablespace and leave the new tablespace in an online or offline state. Assuming that Oracle XE was installed in the default location C:\oraclexe on your computer, complete the following steps to learn how to create a new tablespace called HANDSONXE:

1. Launch the Database Home Page and establish a connection as a database administrator (for example, as SYSTEM); this step should not be necessary if you are continuing from the previous exercise.

2. Navigate to the SQL Commands page (for example, choose Home | SQL | SQL Commands).

3. Execute the following SQL statement to determine whether the database's default tablespace type is smallfile or bigfile tablespaces:

```
SELECT property_value
  FROM database_properties
 WHERE property_name = 'DEFAULT_TBS_TYPE';
```

4. Notice that, by default, an Oracle database's default tablespace type is a smallfile tablespace; consequently, when you create a new tablespace and do not explicitly indicate whether the new tablespace is a smallfile or bigfile tablespace, Oracle XE creates a smallfile tablespace.

5. Execute the following SQL statement to create a new smallfile tablespace named HANDSONXE:

```
CREATE TABLESPACE handsonxe
 DATAFILE
  'c:\oraclexe\oradata\xe\handsonxe01.dbf' SIZE 100K REUSE
    AUTOEXTEND ON NEXT 100K MAXSIZE 1M,
  'c:\oraclexe\oradata\xe\handsonxe02.dbf' SIZE 100K REUSE
 ONLINE;
```

NOTE
If you installed Oracle XE in a different location, modify the file specifications in this exercise appropriately.

The previous CREATE TABLESPACE statement creates a new smallfile tablespace called HANDSONXE with two data files:

■   The handsonxe01.dbf file is initially 100K in size, and can automatically extend itself in 100K increments up to 1MB if the tablespace becomes full and an object requests more space in the tablespace.

- The handsonxe02.dbf file is 100K in size and cannot increase in size unless you manually resize the file or enable automatic extension for the file.

- The REUSE option of a data file specification instructs Oracle to reuse a data file, if it already exists; use this option in a data file specification when you want to overwrite an existing data file.

EXERCISE 8.5: Modify the Storage Properties of a Data File

You can alter the properties of a data file in a smallfile tablespace at any time by using the DATAFILE clause of the SQL command ALTER DATABASE. For the purposes of this exercise, the syntax of this clause in the ALTER DATABASE command is as follows:

```
ALTER DATABASE
  DATAFILE 'filename'
  { RESIZE integer [K|M|G|T]
  | AUTOEXTEND
    { OFF
    | ON [NEXT integer [K|M|G|T]] [MAXSIZE {UNLIMITED|integer [K|M|G|T] } ] } }
```

NOTE
You must have the ALTER DATABASE system privilege to use the ALTER DATABASE command.

For example, use the SQL Commands page to execute the following ALTER DATABASE statement to adjust the automatic extension properties of the handsonxe01. dbf data file:

```
ALTER DATABASE
    DATAFILE 'c:\oraclexe\oradata\xe\handsonxe01.dbf'
      AUTOEXTEND ON NEXT 250K MAXSIZE UNLIMITED;
```

Now execute the following ALTER DATABASE statement to manually resize the handsonxe02.dbf data file:

```
ALTER DATABASE
    DATAFILE 'c:\oraclexe\oradata\xe\handsonxe02.dbf' RESIZE 250K;
```

EXERCISE 8.6: Control Tablespace Availability

You can control the access to a tablespace using the ONLINE and OFFLINE options of the SQL command ALTER TABLESPACE:

```
ALTER TABLESPACE tablespace
  {ONLINE|OFFLINE [NORMAL|TEMPORARY|IMMEDIATE] }
```

Modifying Storage for Bigfile Tablespaces

When working with a smallfile tablespace in Exercise 8.5, notice that you must identify the name of a data file and use the ALTER DATABASE command to modify the file's storage properties. In other words, you can't just "resize the tablespace" without indicating a specific data file because Oracle wouldn't know which one of the tablespace's data files that you prefer to resize.

A subtle benefit of using a bigfile tablespace is that tablespace storage management operations are slightly easier because you never have to know about or consider the tablespace's data file after creating the tablespace; Oracle automatically maps logical storage modifications for a bigfile tablespace to the tablespace's lone data file. For example, if the HANDSONXE tablespace was a bigfile tablespace, you could more simply complete the previous Exercise 8.5 using the following statements:

```
ALTER TABLESPACE handsonxe
  AUTOEXTEND ON NEXT 250K MAXSIZE UNLIMITED;

ALTER TABLESPACE handsonxe
  RESIZE 250K;
```

Is it worth going out of your way to create bigfile tablespaces rather than smallfile tablespaces just to make infrequent storage management operations slightly easier? Probably not, but you should still understand the slight SQL syntax differences when managing smallfile versus bigfile tablespaces.

When taking an online tablespace offline, you can indicate several options:

- **NORMAL** This option, the default, indicates that you want to take the target tablespace offline under normal conditions. You can use this option only if all data files of the tablespace are currently online and available without any I/O problems.

- **TEMPORARY** This option should be your first choice if you want to take a tablespace offline under abnormal conditions. For example, you might use this option when one or more data files of the tablespace are offline due to I/O problems. In this case, a recovery operation will be necessary before you can bring the tablespace online again.

- **IMMEDIATE** This option should be your last resort when taking a tablespace offline under abnormal conditions. You can use this option only when your database operates with media recovery enabled (discussed in Chapter 9).

For example, use the SQL Commands page to execute the following query, which targets a table stored in the USERS tablespace:

```
SELECT id, description FROM handsonxe08.parts;
```

Because the PARTS table is stored in the USERS tablespace, which should be online at the moment, the result set for the query should be similar to the following:

```
ID DESCRIPTION
--------- ----------------
1 Fax Machine
2 Copy Machine
3 Laptop PC
4 Desktop PC
5 Scanner
```

Next, execute the following ALTER TABLESPACE statement to take the USERS tablespace offline:

```
ALTER TABLESPACE users
  OFFLINE NORMAL;
```

Now, re-enter the previous query, shown here:

```
SELECT id, description FROM handsonxe08.parts;
```

You should see results similar to the following:

```
ORA-00376: file 4 cannot be read at this time
ORA-01110: data file 4: 'C:\ORACLEXE\ORADATA\XE\USERS.DBF'
```

This error is an indication that the tablespace (or the tablespace's data files) that stores the PARTS table is offline. To bring the USERS tablespace back online, enter the following statement:

```
ALTER TABLESPACE users
  ONLINE;
```

Now, re-enter the previous query:

```
SELECT id, description FROM handsonxe08.parts;
```

You should again see the following results:

```
ID DESCRIPTION
--------- ----------------
1 Fax Machine
2 Copy Machine
3 Laptop PC
4 Desktop PC
5 Scanner
```

Segments, Extents, and Data Blocks

Oracle preallocates segments of data blocks as the physical storage for data structures such as tables, indexes, etc. Oracle reserves groups of logically contiguous *data blocks* from a data file for a data structure as *extents*. A *segment* is the collection of all the extents dedicated to a data structure. Figure 8-7 demonstrates the relationship between a table and its data segment, extents, and data blocks.

When you create a new data structure such as a table, you can indicate the tablespace in which you want to create the corresponding segment. Oracle then allocates data blocks from one or more of the data files in use by the target tablespace.

Types of Segments in an Oracle Database

An Oracle database can contain many different types of segments, including data segments, index segments, LOB segments, overflow segments, undo segments, and temporary segments.

- A typical table stores its data in a *table segment*, sometimes called a *data segment* by Oracle veterans.

- You can also create a table with partitions that store specific sets of table rows in physically distinct table partitions—think of a *partitioned table* as a table that has multiple table segments. You normally use a partitioned table only when working with large tables in very large databases such as data warehouses; this book does not discuss partitioned tables because partitioned tables are not likely to be useful with Oracle XE.

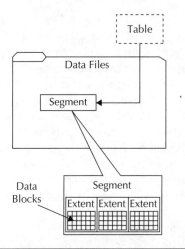

FIGURE 8-7. *A segment consists of extents; an extent is a group of logically contiguous data blocks in a data file.*

■ A typical index stores its data in an *index segment*. If the index has multiple partitions, the index stores its data in a corresponding number of index partitions (or index segments).

■ If a table has a column that uses a large object (LOB) datatype, such as a CLOB, BLOB, or NCLOB, the table can optionally store corresponding LOB values in a *LOB segment* that is separate from the table segment that holds other field values in the table.

■ An *index-organized table* is a special type of table that stores the rows of a table within an index segment. An index-organized table can also have an *overflow segment* to store rows that do not fit into the original index segment. See Chapter 10 for more information about index-organized tables.

■ An *undo segment* is a special type of segment that Oracle uses to store transaction rollback information. When a user rolls back a transaction, Oracle applies information in an undo segment to "undo" the transaction's operations.

■ Oracle creates and uses a *temporary segment* when processing certain types of SQL statements. A temporary segment is a temporary workspace on disk that Oracle can use to store intermediate data during SQL statement processing.

The preceding list is a brief introduction to the most common types of segments in an Oracle database; see the *Oracle Database 10*g *Concepts* manual for complete information about all types of segments.

Data Blocks

A *data block* is the primary unit of data I/O for an Oracle database. When you work with a database, Oracle stores and retrieves data on disk using data blocks. For example, when you query a table, Oracle might read into the instance's *buffer cache* (a memory area) all of the data blocks that contain rows in the query's result set.

When you create a database, you set the *standard* (or *default*) *block size* for the database, which you can never change for the life of the database. By default, all tablespaces that you create in the database allocate data blocks of the standard block size. The database's standard block size also determines the size of each data buffer in the corresponding default buffer caches, which you must consider when tuning an Oracle instance. Chapter 10 explains more about instance tuning.

An Oracle data block size must be equal to or a multiple of the host operating system's block size. For example, if the host operating system's block size is 512 bytes, the data block size on such a server could be 2K, 8K, 16K, and so on. An Oracle XE database's standard data block size is 8K.

Data Block Allocation

When you create a new data structure such as a table or index, Oracle allocates one or more extents for the structure's segment. An *extent* is a set of logically contiguous data blocks in a data file of the tablespace that stores the structure's segment. If all data blocks in a segment's existing extents are full, Oracle "extends" the segment by allocating a new extent (set of blocks) the next time that a transaction requires the storage of some new data.

Data Block Availability

When you insert a row into a table or update an existing row to make it larger, Oracle must find adequate space for the new data. To efficiently determine which data blocks have enough free space for new data, Oracle creates a block in each extent of a segment with a bitmap (an index) that records information about how much space is available in the data blocks of the corresponding extent. When you create a tablespace that relies on this default mechanism for controlling data block availability, known as *automatic segment space management (ASSM)*, no special storage considerations are necessary when creating data structures such as tables and indexes—Oracle automatically takes care of all the details for you.

Row Chaining and Data Block Size

When you insert a new row into a table, Oracle puts the new row into a data block that contains free space. Optimally, Oracle puts all of a row's data into one data block, assuming that the row can fit within the space of one data block. This way, when you request a row in a table, Oracle has to read only one data block from disk into memory to retrieve all of a row's data.

If a row's length is greater than the data block size, Oracle *chains* the row among two or more data blocks. Figure 8-8 illustrates row chaining.

Row chaining, while unavoidable in this situation, is not desirable, because Oracle must read multiple data blocks from disk into memory to access a single row's data. More rather than less disk I/O always slows system performance. Therefore, avoid row chaining if at all possible.

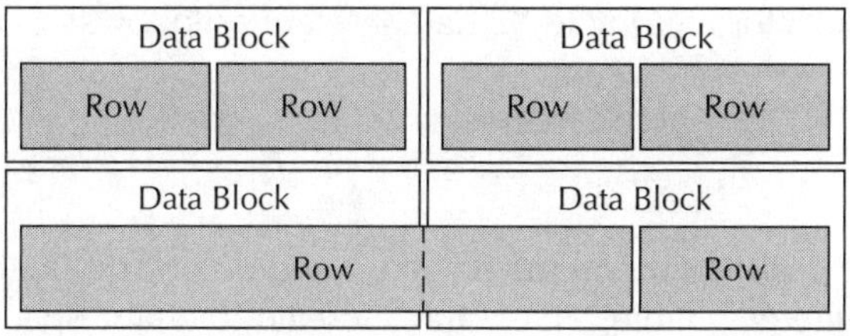

FIGURE 8-8.   *Oracle must chain a row that is too large for a single data block.*

Typically, the standard block size for an installation of Oracle XE is adequate for most databases. However, databases with certain characteristics can benefit from block sizes that are larger than the default. For example, when you plan to create a table with rows that will exceed the default block size, you can avoid row chains by creating a tablespace that uses a nonstandard, larger block size, and then use the new tablespace to store the table with long rows.

Oracle can also create a row chain when you update a row in a table. This type of row chaining only happens when you update the row so that it is longer than the original row, and the data block that holds the row does not have enough empty space to accommodate the update. When you expect that updates to the rows in a table segment will increase row sizes, you can prevent row chaining by reserving extra data block space for updates. Exercise 8.11 later in this chapter explains how to specifically control space usage within data blocks and reduce this type of row chaining.

Managing Storage for Tables and Indexes

Now that you have a general understanding of segments, extents, and data blocks, the practice exercises in this section explain some of the more common tasks related to segments and extents in an Oracle database.

NOTE
Subsequent sections of this chapter discuss specialized types of segments in an Oracle database, including undo segments, LOB segments, and temporary segments.

EXERCISE 8.7: Display the Data Block Size Information

To display the database's standard data block size, use the SQL Commands page to execute the following query:

```
SELECT name, value
  FROM v$parameter
 WHERE name = 'db_block_size';
```

The expected results for an Oracle XE database are as follows:

```
NAME                VALUE
----------------    ----------------
db_block_size       8192
```

When you create a tablespace in the database and do not explicitly specify what block size to use for the new tablespace, Oracle creates the tablespace using the database's standard block size, 8K. But what data block size do existing tablespaces use? Execute the following query to determine this information:

```
SELECT tablespace_name, block_size
  FROM dba_tablespaces;
```

The expected results for an Oracle XE database are as follows:

```
TABLESPACE_NAME   BLOCK_SIZE
----------------  ----------
SYSTEM                  8192
UNDO                    8192
SYSAUX                  8192
TEMP                    8192
USERS                   8192
HANDSONXE               8192
```

Notice that all tablespaces use the standard data block size, 8K.

EXERCISE 8.8: Display the Segments in a Schema

You can display information about all of the segments in a database by querying the DBA_SEGMENTS data dictionary view. For example, use the SQL Commands page to execute the following query that displays selected information about the segments that correspond to data structures contained in the HANDSONXE08 schema:

```
SELECT segment_name, segment_type, tablespace_name, extents, blocks
  FROM dba_segments
  WHERE owner = 'HANDSONXE08';
```

The result set should be similar to the following:

```
SEGMENT_NAME      SEGMENT_TYPE  TABLESPACE_NAME  EXTENTS  BLOCKS
----------------  ------------  ---------------  -------  ------
PARTS             TABLE         USERS                  1       8
SALESREPS         TABLE         USERS                  1       8
P_ID              INDEX         USERS                  1       8
S_ID              INDEX         USERS                  1       8
PAR_DESCRIPTION   INDEX         USERS                  1       8
```

Notice in the result set that there are several segments that correspond to the tables and indexes in the schema:

■ Each segment exists in the USERS tablespace.

■ Each segment consists of a single extent.

■ Each extent has eight blocks.

Considering that the block size for the USERS tablespace is 8K and that each segment has one extent with eight blocks, each segment's available storage space is approximately 64K (8K/block × 8 blocks/extent × 1 extent/segment).

NOTE
To display information about the segments in your current schema, you could also query the USER_SEGMENTS data dictionary view.

EXERCISE 8.9: Compact (Shrink) Segments Wasting Space

Oracle automatically allocates a new extent for the table when all available free space has been consumed and more space is necessary to store data on behalf of ongoing transactions. Alternatively, Oracle does not automatically reorganize table storage; for example, Oracle does not condense low-density data into fewer blocks nor does Oracle *deallocate* (release) extents of data blocks when the table's segment has a significant amount of unused space. Oracle assumes that new data will eventually consume the free space already allocated for the segment, and thus avoids the overhead of releasing the space just to allocate it again in the future.

While Oracle's segment space management algorithm is fine for tables that continually grow with occasional deletes, it can result in considerable amounts of unused space for other types of tables. For example, consider a table that logs information once every minute about the availability of hundreds of machines in a manufacturing plant. Every three months, a process scans for and permanently archives log records that correspond to problems, and then deletes all records from the log table. This situation results in a table that has lots of unused space for long periods of time.

Reorganizing a table's physical storage to reclaim unused space is a manual process. To shrink a table's data segment, you must use the following abbreviated form of the SQL command ALTER TABLE:

```
ALTER TABLE [schema.]table
   [ENABLE ROW MOVEMENT]
   [SHRINK SPACE] ;
```

You must first enable table segment reorganization for a table by using the ENABLE ROW MOVEMENT option of the SQL command ALTER TABLE; then you can consolidate the data in a table's segment by using the SHRINK SPACE option of the ALTER TABLE command.

To demonstrate the many concepts discussed in this exercise and practice shrinking a segment, complete the following steps:

1. Notice from the result set of the query in the previous exercise that the SALESREPS table has only one extent.

2. Use the SQL Commands page to execute the following PL/SQL block that inserts many mock rows into the SALESREPS table:

```
BEGIN
 FOR i IN 5 .. 1000
 LOOP
  INSERT INTO handsonxe08.salesreps
  (id, lastname, firstname, commission)
  VALUES (i, 'Last Name Value', 'First Name Value', 10);
 END LOOP;
 COMMIT;
END;
/
```

3. Execute the following query to see how many extents the SALESREPS table has after inserting the new rows:

```
SELECT segment_name, extents, blocks
 FROM dba_segments
 WHERE owner = 'HANDSONXE08'
   AND segment_name = 'SALESREPS';
```

4. Confirm that the result set of the query is as follows; notice that Oracle automatically allocated a new extent for the SALESREPS table because more space was necessary to hold the new rows:

```
SEGMENT_NAME      EXTENTS     BLOCKS
--------------- ---------- ----------
SALESREPS               2         16
```

5. Execute the following DELETE statement to delete the new rows from the SALESREPS table:

```
DELETE FROM handsonxe08.salesreps
 WHERE id >= 5;

COMMIT;
```

6. Repeat the query in Step 3 to see how many extents the SALESREPS table has after deleting all of the new rows; you can do this easily by reloading the previous query using the History tab of the SQL Commands page. Notice in the following expected result set that the table still has two extents—Oracle does not deallocate extents from segments.

```
SEGMENT_NAME      EXTENTS     BLOCKS
--------------- ---------- ----------
SALESREPS               2         16
```

7. At this point, the SALESREPS table has two extents, most of which consist of unused space. To shrink the table's segment, enter the following statements:

```
ALTER TABLE handsonxe08.salesreps
  ENABLE ROW MOVEMENT;

ALTER TABLE handsonxe08.salesreps
  SHRINK SPACE;
```

8. Use the History tab of the SQL Commands page to repeat the query in Step 3 to see how many extents the SALESREPS table now has after Oracle has reorganized its segment. Notice in the following expected result set that the table only has one extent.

```
SEGMENT_NAME        EXTENTS     BLOCKS
---------------- ---------- ----------
SALESREPS                 1          8
```

In the preceding example, you already knew that a significant percentage of space allocated to the SALESREPS table was unused and reclaimable. But in a real database with lots and lots of segments, it's unrealistic to expect that you are going to know just which segments are prime candidates for reorganization. To help with this common problem, Oracle automatically runs the Segment Advisor every night to identify segments with significant amounts of unused space relative to their overall size. The *Segment Advisor* is a tool based on routines in the *DBMS_ADVISOR package*. Although Oracle XE does not provide a GUI to the information captured and recommendations provided by the Segment Advisor, you can make use of Segment Advisor recommendations by completing the following steps:

1. Repeat Steps 2, 3, 4, and 5 from the preceding list.

2. Wait up to 24 hours for the Segment Advisor to run, and then notice that the SALESREPS table has a lot of unused space.

3. Navigate to the Storage page (for example, choose Home | Administration | Storage).

4. Click Compact Storage.

5. And click Compact Storage again.

6. Oracle schedules a job to compact (shrink) the storage for those segments noted by the Segment Advisor.

7. Repeat Step 8 from the preceding list and confirm the expected results.

EXERCISE 8.10: Create a Table in a Specific Tablespace

When you create a new data structure such as a table or index, you can use the TABLESPACE parameter of the corresponding CREATE command to explicitly indicate the tablespace that you want to use for the structure's segment. Provided that the owner/schema has the necessary quota in the tablespace, Oracle completes the request. If you omit a tablespace specification when creating a new table or index, Oracle creates the structure's segment in the default tablespace of the user/schema that owns the new data structure.

To practice creating a data structure in a specific tablespace, enter the following CREATE TABLE statement:

```
CREATE TABLE handsonxe08.orders (
  id INTEGER PRIMARY KEY USING INDEX TABLESPACE handsonxe,
  c_id INTEGER NOT NULL,
  orderdate DATE DEFAULT SYSDATE NOT NULL,
  shipdate DATE,
  paiddate DATE,
  status CHAR(1) DEFAULT 'F'
)
TABLESPACE handsonxe;
```

The TABLESPACE parameter for the main statement indicates the tablespace to use for the table segment, while the TABLESPACE parameter in the primary key constraint specification indicates the tablespace to use for the primary key's underlying index segment; if you omit either TABLESPACE parameter, Oracle creates the corresponding segment in the default tablespace for the HANDSONXE08 account.

EXERCISE 8.11: Reserve Space for Updates to Existing Table Rows

Figure 8-9 illustrates the basic structure of a data block. Each data block has a small header that contains internal system information; Oracle uses the bulk of the block to store user/application data.

To help avoid unnecessary row chains, Oracle reserves 10 percent of a block's available storage space for updates to existing rows. When you know that an extraordinary number of rows in a table will undergo updates that make rows longer, consider increasing the default PCTFREE storage parameter for a table. Alternatively, to avoid wasting space in tables that will not undergo updates that make rows longer, consider decreasing the default PCTFREE storage parameter for a table.

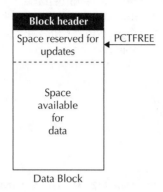

FIGURE 8-9. *The structure of a data block*

Painless Storage Management with Oracle XE

If you scan various titles in the Oracle documentation set for information pertaining to data storage, you will no doubt come across a lot of detailed excerpts explaining many different storage parameters that you can explicitly specify to control the size of segments and extents when creating data structures such as tables. With a few exceptions (such as those in Exercises 8.11 and 8.12), much of this information and related features of Oracle (such as the STORAGE clause of several SQL commands) are present for backward compatibility with previous versions of Oracle; those releases of Oracle required a lot of careful planning and configuration when allocating storage on behalf of data structures to minimize the amount of wasted space that might result in certain situations.

Fortunately, the latest releases of Oracle use tablespaces that automatically size and reuse extents in such a way that helps to minimize the amount of wasted space in a tablespace. Just in case you are curious, the relatively new type of tablespace is called a *locally managed tablespace* and the older type of tablespace is called a *dictionary-managed tablespace*. For more information about the differences between each type, please refer to the *Oracle Database 10*g *Concepts* manual and the *Oracle Database 10*g *Database Administrator's Guide*; however, realize that the older, dictionary-managed tablespace type most likely will not be supported by the next release of Oracle.

When managing Oracle XE, make your life easy—if necessary, configure additional tablespaces that you need for applications, create database user accounts for developers that have the correct default tablespace settings, and then just rely on Oracle to make good choices for you when allocating space for data structures.

For example, it's unlikely that exiting rows in the ITEMS table will require extra space; therefore, use the SQL Commands page to execute the following statement to create the HANDSONXE08.ITEMS table with nondefault PCTFREE settings for both the table's segment and the primary key index's segment:

```
CREATE TABLE handsonxe08.items (
  o_id INTEGER,
  id INTEGER,
  p_id INTEGER NOT NULL,
  quantity INTEGER DEFAULT 1 NOT NULL,
  PRIMARY KEY (o_id, id)
   USING INDEX
    TABLESPACE handsonxe
    PCTFREE 2
)
TABLESPACE handsonxe
PCTFREE 2;
```

EXERCISE 8.12: Manage Space for LOBs

Storage is normally a significant concern when working with LOBs because they are typically so big. Oracle stores and manages the data for *internal LOBs* (database-stored LOBs) such as CLOBs, NCLOBs, and BLOBs inside the database, but the host database server is responsible for managing *external files* (BFILEs).

By default, Oracle stores an internal LOB with the rest of the row's data (*inline*) when the LOB is less than approximately 4K; Oracle stores an internal LOB in a separate *LOB segment* (*out-of-line*) when the LOB is greater than approximately 4K. Oracle automatically moves an inline LOB value to a LOB segment if it grows larger than 4K.

No matter where Oracle stores the value of an internal LOB, Oracle always stores a locator for the LOB inline with its row data. A *LOB locator* is effectively a pointer to the actual location of the LOB value. A LOB column value can be null, be empty, or have a nonempty locator that references the actual LOB data.

NOTE
Whenever you create a column using a LOB datatype, Oracle automatically creates, names, and manages an index for the column to provide for efficient LOB access.

The *LOB clause* of the SQL commands CREATE TABLE and ALTER TABLE provides you with a way to explicitly control the storage of LOB data in a table. A simplified syntax listing of the LOB clause is as follows:

```
LOB
  (column [, column] ... )
  STORE AS [segment]
```

```
( [TABLESPACE tablespace]
[{ENABLE|DISABLE} STORAGE IN ROW]
[CHUNK integer]
[PCTVERSION integer]|RETENTION )
```

The following list briefly describes the parameters of the LOB clause:

- Indicate a list of one or more CLOB, BLOB, or NCLOB columns to which the LOB clause should apply. If you indicate only one column, you can name the LOB segment that Oracle creates for storing the column; however, if you list more than one column, you cannot name the LOB segment.

- Use the TABLESPACE parameter of the LOB clause to specify a tablespace for the LOB segment.

- Use the ENABLE STORAGE IN ROW option to have Oracle store a LOB value less than 4000 bytes with the other data in the same row; when a LOB value is greater than 4000 bytes, Oracle stores the LOB value in the LOB segment. Use the DISABLE STORAGE IN ROW option to always store LOB values in the LOB segment, regardless of each LOB value's length.

- Use the CHUNK parameter to specify the storage allocation unit for a LOB segment. Specify an integer for the CHUNK parameter. The storage allocation unit for a LOB segment is the result of the CHUNK parameter setting multiplied by the encompassing tablespace's data block size. For example, when a LOB segment's CHUNK parameter is 4 and the tablespace's data block size is 8K, the storage allocation unit for the LOB segment is 32K. The maximum value of a LOB segment's storage allocation unit is 32K.

- When a transaction modifies a LOB or part of a LOB, Oracle creates a new version of the LOB's data blocks and leaves the older version of the LOB intact to support queries currently reading prior versions of the LOB. Use the RETENTION option to permanently retain old versions of LOB data. Alternatively, use the PCTVERSION parameter to control the overall percentage of used LOB data blocks in a LOB segment that are available for versioning of old LOB data; PCTVERSION is a threshold of LOB segment storage space that must be reached before Oracle overwrites older versions of LOB data with newer versions. The default value for PCTVERSION is 10. When updates to LOBs are infrequent, set PCTVERSION to 5 or lower to minimize the amount of disk space required to store LOBs.

To demonstrate the use of the LOB clause in a CREATE TABLE statement, enter the following statement to create a CUSTOMERS table that can store a photograph for each customer record:

```
CREATE TABLE handsonxe08.customers (
   id  INTEGER PRIMARY KEY USING INDEX TABLESPACE handsonxe,
   lastname VARCHAR2(100) NOT NULL,
   firstname VARCHAR2(50) NOT NULL,
   companyname VARCHAR2(100),
   street VARCHAR2(100),
   city VARCHAR2(100),
   state VARCHAR2(50),
   zipcode VARCHAR2(50),
   phone VARCHAR2(30),
   fax VARCHAR2(30),
   email VARCHAR2(100),
   s_id INTEGER NOT NULL,
   photo BLOB
   )
-- storage parameters for table segment
 TABLESPACE users
-- storage parameters for LOB segment
 LOB (photo) STORE AS cust_photo (
 TABLESPACE handsonxe
  ENABLE STORAGE IN ROW
  CHUNK 4
  PCTVERSION 5 )
;
```

Notice the following points about the CREATE TABLE statement in this exercise:

■ The statement specifies a tablespace for the table's data segment using the familiar TABLESPACE parameter.

■ The statement specifies storage settings for the table's LOB segment using the LOB clause.

EXERCISE 8.13: Perform Miscellaneous Space Management Tasks

Management tasks for tablespaces may or may not affect segments in the tablespace, depending on the operation that you perform. For example, when you rename a tablespace, segments in the tablespace continue to exist and applications that access corresponding data structures continue to function without modification. However, when you drop a tablespace, Oracle also drops all segments in the tablespace; if you want to preserve the segments in a tablespace that you plan to drop, you must first move the segments to another tablespace before dropping the tablespace. This exercise introduces you to several space management topics, including renaming a tablespace, moving segments, and dropping a tablespace.

To rename a tablespace, use the following abbreviated form of the SQL command ALTER TABLESPACE:

```
ALTER TABLESPACE tablespace
 RENAME TO tablespace ;
```

For example, use the SQL Commands page to execute the following statement that renames the HANDSONXE tablespace to HANDSONXE_NEW:

```
ALTER TABLESPACE handsonxe
 RENAME TO handsonxe_new;
```

Now query the DBA_SEGMENTS data dictionary view to confirm that the segments in the previously named HANDSONXE tablespace continue to exist in the tablespace now named HANDSONXE_NEW:

```
SELECT segment_name, segment_type, tablespace_name
 FROM dba_segments
 WHERE owner = 'HANDSONXE08';
```

The results should appear similar to the following:

```
SEGMENT_NAME                      SEGMENT_TYPE  TABLESPACE_NAME
--------------------------------- ------------- ---------------
SALESREPS                         TABLE         USERS
P_ID                              INDEX         USERS
PARTS                             TABLE         USERS
S_ID                              INDEX         USERS
PAR_DESCRIPTION                   INDEX         USERS
ORDERS                            TABLE         HANDSONXE_NEW
SYS_C005450                       INDEX         HANDSONXE_NEW
ITEMS                             TABLE         HANDSONXE_NEW
SYS_C005456                       INDEX         HANDSONXE_NEW
CUSTOMERS                         TABLE         USERS
SYS_C005460                       INDEX         HANDSONXE_NEW
SYS_IL0000017053C00013$$          LOBINDEX      HANDSONXE_NEW
CUST_PHOTO                        LOBSEGMENT    HANDSONXE_NEW
```

Notice how the segments that you created for the ORDERS, ITEMS, and CUSTOMERS tables and related indexes in previous exercises now reside in the HANDSONXE_NEW tablespace.

Now suppose that you want to drop the HANDSONXE_NEW tablespace but preserve the ORDERS, ITEMS, and CUSTOMERS tables; to do this, you must first move the corresponding segments from the HANDSONXE_NEW tablespace to a different permanent tablespace.

To move a table from one tablespace to another, you can use the following abbreviated form of the SQL command ALTER TABLE:

```
ALTER TABLE [schema.]table
  MOVE TABLESPACE tablespace ;
```

For example, use the SQL Commands page to move the table segments that correspond to the HANDSONXE08.ORDERS, HANDSONXE08.ITEMS, and HANDSONXE08.CUSTOMERS tables to the USERS tablespace:

```
ALTER TABLE handsonxe08.orders
  MOVE TABLESPACE users;

ALTER TABLE handsonxe08.items
  MOVE TABLESPACE users;

ALTER TABLE handsonxe08.customers
  MOVE TABLESPACE users
   LOB (photo) STORE AS cust_photo (TABLESPACE users);
```

Notice in the last example statement that you can explicitly move a table's LOB segments; when you move a table's segment but do not explicitly move the table's LOB segments, the LOB segments continue to remain in their original location.

To move the indexes, you can use the following abbreviated form of the SQL command ALTER INDEX:

```
ALTER INDEX [schema].index
  REBUILD
  TABLESPACE tablespace;
```

For example, use the SQL Commands page to execute statements similar to the following that move the underlying indexes for the primary key constraints of the ORDERS, ITEMS, and CUSTOMERS tables—*make sure to substitute the system-generated names of the indexes in your schema*:

```
ALTER INDEX handsonxe08.sys_c005450
  REBUILD TABLESPACE users;

ALTER INDEX handsonxe08.sys_c005456
  REBUILD TABLESPACE users;

ALTER INDEX handsonxe08.sys_c005460
  REBUILD TABLESPACE users;
```

Once all of the segments that you want to preserve have been moved to a different tablespace, you can safely drop the HANDSONXE_NEW tablespace by using the SQL command DROP TABLESPACE, as the following syntax listing and list explain:

```
DROP TABLESPACE tablespace
  [INCLUDING CONTENTS [AND DATAFILES] [CASCADE CONSTRAINTS] ];
```

- You cannot drop the SYSTEM or SYSAUX tablespace.

- The INCLUDING CONTENTS option of the DROP TABLESPACE command indicates that you want to drop the tablespace, even when the tablespace currently contains data. When you drop a tablespace that contains objects, Oracle also drops the objects within the tablespace.

- The AND DATAFILES option indicates that you want Oracle to delete the data files that correspond to the target tablespace. If you omit this option, Oracle does not physically remove the tablespace's data files from disk.

- The CASCADE CONSTRAINTS option of the DROP TABLESPACE command indicates that you want to drop all referential integrity constraints that reference primary or unique keys of tables contained in the target tablespace.

For example, use the SQL Commands page to execute the following SQL statement that drops the HANDSONXE_NEW tablespace, its contents, and its data files:

```
DROP TABLESPACE handsonxe_new
   INCLUDING CONTENTS AND DATAFILES;
```

NOTE
You should never delete a data file from disk using an operating system command until after you are 100 percent sure that the tablespace that previously used the data file has been dropped from the database. If you accidentally remove a data file, you must perform a database recovery operation to make the tablespace operational once again. Chapter 9 explains more about database recovery from the loss of a data file.

Undo Tablespaces

Transactions can complete either with a commit or a rollback. A typical transaction ends with a *commit*, which permanently records the transaction's changes to the database. A rollback undoes all effects of the transaction, as though the transaction never occurred. To provide for transaction rollback, Oracle must keep track of the data that a transaction changes until the transaction commits or rolls back.

Oracle uses a special type of tablespace called an *undo tablespace* to record rollback data for all transactions. Should you choose to roll back a transaction, Oracle reads the necessary data from the database's undo tablespace to rebuild the data as it existed before the transaction changed it.

Undo Segments

To distribute the undo data generated by multiple concurrent transactions, a typical Oracle database automatically manages many undo segments in an undo tablespace as follows:

1. When a user starts a new transaction, Oracle automatically assigns the transaction to an undo segment. A user does not require a tablespace quota to use an undo segment in an undo tablespace.

2. As the user's transaction modifies data in the database with DML statements (for example, INSERT, UPDATE, and DELETE), Oracle uses the assigned undo segment to record information about changes that the transaction makes.

3. If the user should decide to roll back the current transaction, Oracle "undoes" the transaction's effects using information in the transaction's assigned undo segment.

All of the work that Oracle XE performs with undo segments is completely transparent to users and applications—absolutely no consideration of an undo tablespace's existence is necessary.

Undo Segments Are Multipurpose

Transaction rollback is just one useful feature that undo segments provide for in an Oracle database. For example, undo segments also support Oracle's unique database *multiversioning* mechanism. Using the information in undo segments rather than data locking, Oracle can generate multiple versions of the database's information to satisfy the requests of concurrent SQL statements that query and update the same set of data.

Oracle also uses undo segments during the second phase of a typical database recovery operation: after using another database structure known as the redo log to roll forward changes lost due to a failure, Oracle then uses undo segments to "undo" or roll back any uncommitted work applied during the roll-forward phase of recovery. Chapter 9 explains more about database recovery.

Managing Undo Tablespaces and Retention Times

Undo management is straightforward and automated; in fact, most installations of Oracle XE should never require any undo management whatsoever unless particular situations arise, such as the following:

■ A disk failure damages the undo tablespace.

■ The database supports an OLTP system with many concurrent, active transactions, and users report database errors indicating that there is not enough undo space (ORA-1650: Unable to extent rollback segment).

■ The database supports OLTP activity, and users running long-running queries or large data exports report database errors indicating that undo information necessary for read consistency has been overwritten (ORA-01555: Snapshot too old).

Although it is doubtful that you will encounter one of these situations while managing Oracle XE, the following exercises provide you with a basic overview of how to configure and manage a database's undo tablespace.

EXERCISE 8.14: Display and Modify Automatic Undo Management Parameters

To configure an Oracle database instance during instance startup, Oracle reads a *parameter file*, also commonly referred to as an *initialization parameter file*, a *configuration file*, or *INIT.ORA*. A database's parameter file contains initialization parameter settings that you can adjust to configure and tune the operation of an Oracle database instance.

The mechanisms that Oracle uses to automatically manage undo data for a database are known collectively as *automatic undo management*. To configure automatic undo management, you must set two initialization parameters:

■ **UNDO_MANAGEMENT** Should be set to AUTO to indicate that you want to use automatic undo management

■ **UNDO_TABLESPACE** Indicates the name of the undo tablespace used by the current instance for undo management

By default, an Oracle XE database sets UNDO_MANAGEMENT = AUTO and UNDO_TABLESPACE = UNDO. To confirm these parameter settings, complete the following steps:

1. Launch the Database Home Page and establish a connection as a database administrator (for example, as SYSTEM).

2. Click Administration.

3. Click About Database.

4. Enable the Parameters option and click Go.

5. Notice that the About Database page displays an alphabetical list of all initialization parameters, their current settings, whether each parameter's setting is the default setting, and a brief description for each parameter's purpose.

6. Scroll toward the bottom of the About Database page and confirm the expected settings for the UNDO_MANAGEMENT and UNDO_TABLESPACE parameters.

NOTE
The About Database page queries the V$PARAMETER data dictionary view (introduced in Exercise 8.7) to generate its display.

As you review the preceding parameters, notice a third initialization parameter related to undo management: the *UNDO_RETENTION parameter* indicates how long, in seconds, Oracle should attempt to maintain committed undo data before allowing it to be overwritten by new transactions. By default, an Oracle XE database uses the default parameter setting of 900 (seconds), which translates to 15 minutes.

Setting UNDO_RETENTION = 0 enables another great feature of Oracle Database 10*g* known as *automatic undo retention tuning.* With automatic undo retention tuning enabled, Oracle periodically monitors the instance for the longest-running query to date and adjusts the undo retention setting to satisfy such a query without extending the size of the undo tablespace. The minimum undo retention period possible with automatic undo retention tuning is 900 seconds.

To modify dynamic initialization parameters such as UNDO_RETENTION for the current database instance, you must use the SQL command ALTER SYSTEM. For example, use the SQL Commands page to execute the following statement that enables automatic undo retention tuning:

```
ALTER SYSTEM
   SET UNDO_RETENTION = 0;
```

Temporary Segments, Tablespaces, and Groups

SQL statements often require temporary work areas. For example, when you create an index for a large table, Oracle typically must allocate some temporary system space so that it can sort all of the index entries before building the index's segment. When processing a SQL statement that requires temporary workspace, Oracle allocates small *temporary segments* from a tablespace in the database. When the statement completes, Oracle releases the segments back to the tablespace so that other objects can use the space—thus the term "temporary segment."

To optimize the overhead associated with temporary segment allocation, the default Oracle XE database has a temporary tablespace named TEMP. A *temporary tablespace* is effectively a large temporary segment that all transactions can use for temporary workspace. A user account's temporary tablespace setting indicates the tablespace to use when temporary workspace is necessary to process a SQL statement.

When a database such as a data warehouse supports SQL statements that routinely have significant demands for temporary workspace allocation, you can create *temporary tablespace groups* that Oracle uses to automatically distribute the load of temporary space allocation across multiple temporary tablespaces.

Managing Temporary Tablespaces

Just as with undo tablespaces, you will most likely never have to manage the default temporary tablespace settings for an Oracle XE database. Nonetheless, it's good to know how to do things with temporary tablespaces just in case the need arises. The exercises in this section teach you some basic temporary tablespace management skills.

EXERCISE 8.15: Reveal a Database's Default Temporary Tablespace

When you create a new user and do not set the user's temporary tablespace, Oracle assigns the database's default temporary tablespace to the user. To display an Oracle database's default temporary tablespace setting, use the SQL Commands page to execute the following query:

```
SELECT property_value
  FROM database_properties
 WHERE property_name = 'DEFAULT_TEMP_TABLESPACE';
```

The expected results for an Oracle XE database are as follows:

```
PROPERTY_VALUE
------------------
TEMP
```

EXERCISE 8.16: Display Information About Temporary Tablespaces

As Exercise 8.2 shows, the Tablespaces page of the Database Home Page does not reveal information about an Oracle XE database's temporary tablespaces. To display this information, use the SQL Commands page to execute the following query:

```
SELECT tablespace_name
  FROM dba_tablespaces
 WHERE contents = 'TEMPORARY';
```

The expected results are as follows:

```
TABLESPACE_NAME
------------------
TEMP
```

EXERCISE 8.17: Display Information About Temp Files

A temporary tablespace uses one or more temp files for physical storage. Use the SQL Commands page to execute the following query that displays information about the TEMP tablespace's temp files:

```
SELECT file_name, bytes, autoextensible
  FROM dba_temp_files
 WHERE tablespace_name = 'TEMP';
```

The results should be similar to the following:

```
FILE_NAME                            BYTES      AUTOEXTENSIBLE
-----------------------------------  ---------- ---------------
C:\ORACLEXE\ORADATA\XE\TEMP.DBF      20971520   YES
```

Chapter Summary

This chapter has explained the logical and physical database storage structures, including databases, tablespaces, data files, segments, extents, and data blocks.

- Tablespaces are logical storage divisions within an Oracle database. You create and manage tablespaces by using the SQL commands CREATE TABLESPACE and ALTER TABLESPACE.

- Each tablespace has one or more data files to physically store its data. You can specify the names and properties of a tablespace's data files when you create the tablespace with the CREATE TABLESPACE command. You can subsequently add data files to a tablespace, or change the storage characteristics of a data file using the ALTER DATABASE and ALTER TABLESPACE commands.

- A segment is the collection of data blocks for a data structure, such as a table or index. An extent is a set of contiguous data blocks allocated to a segment. A data block is the unit of physical disk access for an Oracle database.

- When you create a data structure such as a table, you can explicitly specify storage parameters that determine where Oracle allocates extents for the corresponding segment, and specify storage parameters that determine how Oracle uses the space within the data blocks of the segment.

- Oracle uses an undo segment within an undo tablespace to record rollback data for a transaction. If you choose to roll back a transaction, Oracle reads the necessary data from an undo segment to "undo" the effects of the transaction.

- Oracle uses temporary segments in a temporary tablespace to store temporary data used internally while processing demanding SQL statements such as sorted queries, join queries, and index builds.

CHAPTER
9

Protect Your Oracle XE Database

nce you build an Oracle XE database, develop applications for it, and configure everything just the way you want, you should protect your valuable data from any type of problem—from simple system crashes that are the result of unexpected power outages, to more serious problems, such as hard disk failures. This chapter explains the sophisticated database backup and recovery mechanisms of Oracle XE that you can use to protect and repair a database. Topics in this chapter include the following:

■ Possible failures to prepare for, including system crashes and media failures

■ Database components used to protect the database, including the online and archived redo log, database backups, and the flash recovery area

■ Components used during database recovery, including a database's control file and the Recovery Manager (RMAN) utility

■ Database backup and recovery using Recovery Manager

■ Oracle's Flashback features

About This Chapter's Practice Exercises

There are several important points to consider before completing any of the practice exercises in this chapter:

■ You do not have to run a script to prepare for this chapter's exercises.

■ It is very important that you perform all of the exercises in this chapter, in the order given.

■ The first practice exercise is relatively late in this chapter, after presentations of many important and interrelated concepts.

■ You may not be able to repeat several of the exercises in this chapter that focus on database configuration. After all, once you configure the database in a certain way, it doesn't make any sense to reconfigure it the same way again!

In addition, please pay close attention to the special "Cautions" that appear throughout this chapter before several practice exercises.

An Overview of Database Problems and Solutions

Before you begin learning the specifics about Oracle XE's database protection mechanisms, you should have a general idea of the types of problems that can adversely affect a database system and the solutions that Oracle XE provides to counter such problems.

Instance Crashes and Crash Recovery

Perhaps the most common type of problem that affects the availability of computer systems is a sudden crash. A *crash* is the unanticipated failure of the system in question. Unexpected power failures, software bugs, and operating system process failures are inevitable problems that commonly cause crashes. For example, a bug in your computer's operating system might cause an Oracle background thread to suddenly fail, which, in turn, causes the entire Oracle instance to crash—this type of crash is commonly called an *instance crash*. A crash does not physically damage an Oracle database's files on disk. However, after an instance crash, all of the committed data in the instance's memory at the time of the crash that was not yet written permanently to data files has to be recovered.

While an instance crash might sound like a big problem, it generally isn't a cause for alarm. After an instance crash, during the next database startup, Oracle XE automatically recovers all of the committed work lost due to the crash and leaves the database in a transaction-consistent state. Figure 9-1 and the following bullet points explain how it works:

- Oracle XE first applies information from the database's transaction redo log to "redo" the work of committed transactions that has not yet been written to the database's data files. This phase of crash recovery is known as the *roll-forward* phase. A database's *transaction redo log*, often called just the *redo log*, is a database structure that records *redo entries* corresponding to the database changes made by committed transactions.

- To optimize the transaction logging, Oracle XE sometimes logs redo entries that correspond to ongoing transactions in anticipation of a commit. Should the database undergo crash recovery, the roll-forward phase also applies the changes in the redo log that correspond to uncommitted transactions. To remove uncommitted work and leave the database in a transaction-consistent state after crash recovery, Oracle automatically clears the uncommitted changes from the database using information contained in undo segments of the database's undo tablespace. This phase of crash recovery is known as the *rollback* phase.

Although crash recovery sounds very involved, the important thing to remember is that Oracle XE automatically does all of the work for you without requiring you to do anything but restart the database after a crash.

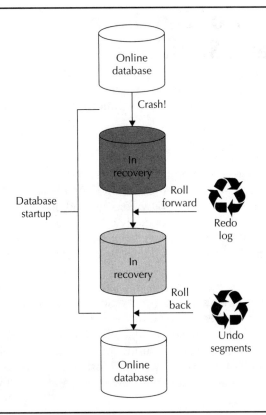

FIGURE 9-1. *The roll-forward and rollback phases of crash recovery use the redo log and undo segments, respectively.*

NOTE

Beware that many texts about Oracle sometimes refer to crash recovery as instance recovery. *Technically speaking,* instance recovery *is a process that occurs in a high-availability configuration of Oracle known as Oracle Real Application Clusters (RAC). In an Oracle RAC configuration, more than one instance of Oracle mounts and provides access to a single Oracle database. When one instance fails, other instances unaffected by the problem continue to provide access to the shared database and automatically perform instance recovery to address the failed instance. Topics related to Oracle RAC are not relevant when working with Oracle XE; see your Oracle documentation for more information.*

Media (Physical) Failures, Backups, and Recovery Manager

The physical loss of an important database file due to operator error, file corruption, or a disk failure is a serious problem that you must be prepared for, even though it might never occur. For example, let's say that one of the database's data files is accidentally deleted or becomes physically corrupt on disk through no fault of Oracle—you won't be able to recover the database from this type of a *media failure* unless you have a backup of the lost data file and have all of the redo logs necessary to roll forward the restored data file. As Figure 9-2 illustrates, media recovery is a

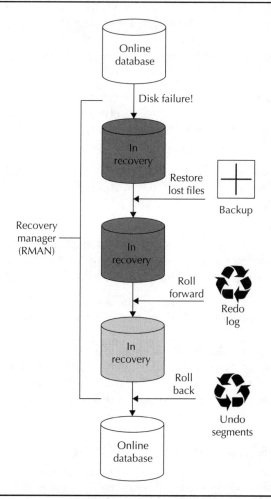

FIGURE 9-2.   *Recovery from a typical media failure requires the restoration of lost data files, roll forward, and rollback recovery.*

manual process that is not unlike crash recovery, with two primary differences: you must *restore* files from a database backup, and Oracle typically must apply more redo logs during the roll-forward phase to *recover* the committed work performed since the backup was taken.

Regular and frequent *database backups* make it possible to restore files that are lost due to user error, file corruption, or disk failures. *Recovery Manager (RMAN)* is a utility included with Oracle XE that you use to back up and recover a database's files, offering complete protection from the physical loss of data. Subsequent sections of this chapter explain how easy it is to use RMAN in your database backup and recovery strategy.

To better understand the steps that occur during media recovery and the function of database backups and the redo log, consider a brief example of how you might protect and recover an Oracle database from a disk failure:

1. Every night, you use RMAN to back up your Oracle database. Among other files, each database backup includes a backup of all the database's data files.

2. One day, something corrupts one of the database's data files. Consequently, when you try to restart the database, you receive errors indicating that a data file is unavailable. Although it is not necessary, you shut down the database so that you can recover the damaged data file.

3. You use the most recent database backup to *restore* the lost data file. However, the restored version of the data file is missing the work of transactions that committed *after* the backup was taken.

4. You use RMAN to perform database recovery. Oracle reads the redo log to "redo" (apply) the work of past committed transactions to the restored data file, which *recovers* the data file and makes it current. Oracle then rolls back the work of any uncommitted transactions using the undo tablespace.

5. After completing the recovery operation, you open the database and make it available to applications. All committed work is now available.

This concise, somewhat simplified, example gives you a general understanding of how an Oracle database's redo log and database backups all play an important role during database recovery from a media failure. Subsequent sections of this chapter explain how to configure the database's redo log in preparation for media failures and how to perform database backups and database recovery.

Logical Errors and Oracle Flashback

Logical errors are mistakes that make a database or portions of a database unusable. Logical errors generally correspond to mistakes made by either database users or applications, and result in the loss of data, data integrity, or both.

For example, consider what happens when a developer unintentionally drops an important table while maintaining an application—this is an example of a *user error* that logically corrupts a database and makes the application unavailable, even though nothing physically has happened to affect the operation of the database.

Consider another example of a logical error—an administrator applies a buggy upgrade that modifies the structure of an application's tables, and in the process, destroys the referential integrity of related tables in the application's schema. Even though none of the tables have been dropped and all of the data still exists, the application cannot function properly because the parent key/foreign key relationships among parent and child records have been jumbled.

Oracle XE has several different features that you can use to gracefully recover a database from logical failures. For example, Figure 9-3 shows how easy it is to restore a table that someone has mistakenly dropped using Oracle's *Flashback Drop* feature. The *recycle bin* is a logical structure in a permanent tablespace that holds data structures such as tables and indexes that you drop. After you drop a data structure, it remains in the encompassing tablespace's recycle bin until all available free space in the tablespace is spent and other structures in the tablespace require more space. Oracle permanently drops structures from the recycle bin to reclaim space using a first-in, first-out (FIFO) algorithm.

To display data in a table as it existed at various time points in the past, you can use Oracle XE's *Flashback Query* feature, which relies on data in the database's undo tablespace. Flashback queries are useful for reviewing modifications to specific

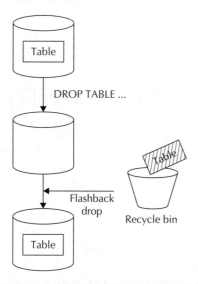

FIGURE 9-3. *To quickly restore a dropped table, use Oracle's Flashback Drop feature.*

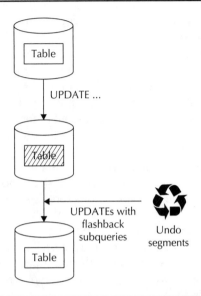

FIGURE 9-4. *You can restore the data in a table or set of related tables to a recent point in time with Oracle Flashback queries, which use undo segments in the database's undo tablespace.*

pieces of information and optionally recovering data to a previous point in time (for example, using UPDATE statements with Flashback subqueries). Figure 9-4 (above) illustrates this concept.

Subsequent sections and exercises explain how to configure and use Oracle's Flashback features to quickly recover from logical errors.

Devising a Database Protection Policy

The previous sections introduce just a few of the many problems that you may encounter and corresponding features that enable Oracle to recover a database and data. Some, all, or none of these problems may ever affect your database, and recovering from some, all, or none of them may be important to you—the only way to know with certainty is to take the time to devise a database protection policy. To do this, analyze and gather a list of requirements that are vital to your system. You can do this by answering questions such as the following:

■ After a system crash or disk failure occurs, how much time can users of the system wait for the database to undergo recovery and come back online—in other words, what is a tolerable *mean time to recover (MTTR)*? When using Oracle XE for testing, training, or application development, the MTTR may not be important; however, when using Oracle XE to support a small online business, the MTTR could be a critical consideration.

■ After a disk failure, is it necessary to recover the work of all committed transactions, or can you tolerate losing the work performed by transactions that have occurred since the most recent database backup? Is it necessary to recover any work at all? Again, the answers to these questions relate directly to how you plan to use Oracle XE.

Once you understand the requirements for your database protection policy, you can learn about and configure the features of Oracle that allow you to meet the requirements. For example, if you are using Oracle XE for training, database protection may be of little importance to you—if something affects your current system, reinstallation of Oracle XE is sufficient. On the other hand, if you are using Oracle XE to support your business's operations, protection from media failures and logical errors using database backups and Oracle Flashback features is critical to the success of your business.

Oracle Database Backup and Recovery Overview

The following sections provide detailed conceptual information about many database structures, utilities, and concepts that are all related to database recovery, including the following:

■ The flash recovery area

■ Transaction logging

■ Log archiving

■ The database control file

■ Recovery Manager

■ Database backups

Make sure that you have a good understanding of each item before you continue to the practical exercises in this chapter.

The Flash Recovery Area

The *flash recovery area* is a storage area on disk that holds all of the files necessary to recover an Oracle database from various types of failures, including such files as the most recent database backups and redo logs. The flash recovery area can be a single directory in a file system or an entire file system, depending on your particular needs. In any case, the flashback recovery area contains directories that separate the storage of different types of files.

Oracle configures a database's flash recovery area as a container that has a fixed storage capacity. Each time that you back up the database and every time that the database generates a new log file, the new files consume space in the flashback recovery area. When the flashback recovery area is completely full, Oracle reclaims space from the flashback recovery area by deleting older, obsolete files to make room for newer backups and log files. For example, Figure 9-5 illustrates how Oracle might overwrite the space used by the oldest backup in the flash recovery area for a new database backup. Oracle's automated cyclical reuse of disk space in a fixed-size flashback recovery area relieves you from the burden of having to monitor and manage the space used by Oracle's database protection mechanisms.

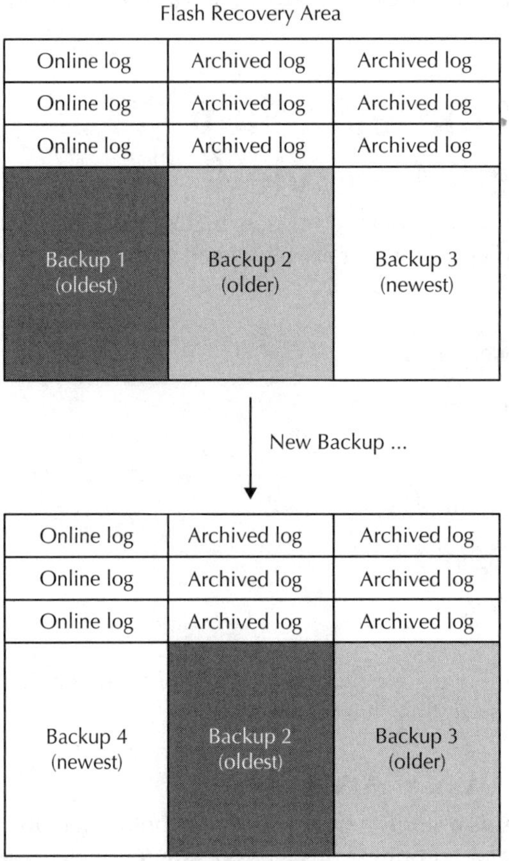

Flash Recovery Area

Online log	Archived log	Archived log
Online log	Archived log	Archived log
Online log	Archived log	Archived log
Backup 1 (oldest)	Backup 2 (older)	Backup 3 (newest)

New Backup ...

Online log	Archived log	Archived log
Online log	Archived log	Archived log
Online log	Archived log	Archived log
Backup 4 (newest)	Backup 2 (oldest)	Backup 3 (older)

FIGURE 9-5. *Oracle uses a fixed-sized flash recovery area to maintain the most recent copies of recovery-related files.*

NOTE
Although the wording is similar, do not confuse the flash recovery area as having anything to do specifically with Oracle's numerous flashback recovery features.

The Transaction Redo Log

An Oracle database's *transaction redo log* (or simply *redo log*) is an important component of the database that protects all committed work. The job of the redo log is to immediately record the changes made by committed transactions. Should the database need recovery from an instance crash, disk failure, or some other type of problem, Oracle reads the redo log during an appropriate recovery operation to "redo" the work committed by transactions that are missing from the database.

The Online Redo Log and the Log Writer

The redo log of a database is a collection of operating system files on the host computer. A database's redo log is made up of two or more *log groups*. Together, this set of log groups is called the *online transaction redo log* or *online redo log*.

Oracle uses a *log group* in the online redo log to record the log entries of committed transactions during system operation. During instance startup, the *Log Writer (LGWR) background thread* chooses one of the groups in the online log and then uses the group to begin recording log entries. The log group being written to by LGWR at any given time is the *current log group*. A log group has a static storage capacity and eventually fills with redo entries. Once LGWR fills the current log group, Oracle performs a *log switch*. During a log switch, Oracle closes the current log group, opens the next log group, and begins writing log entries to the new current log group.

NOTE
To optimize the logging of transaction redo entries, Oracle sometimes writes an open transaction's redo entries in anticipation of a commit. Therefore, at any given time, the redo log might contain a small number of changes to the database made by uncommitted transactions. However, Oracle notes these redo entries appropriately so that if database recovery is necessary, Oracle can automatically clear the uncommitted changes from the database using information in the undo tablespace.

Rather than continuously allocate more and more disk space for transaction logging, Oracle reuses (overwrites) online log groups in a cyclical fashion. For example, consider a database that has the minimum of two online log groups. Oracle writes to the first group, performs a log switch, writes to the second group, performs a log switch, overwrites the first group, performs a log switch, overwrites the second group, and continues this cycle indefinitely. By cyclically using and reusing the log groups in the database's online redo log, an Oracle database can continuously record redo entries in a relatively small, predefined amount of disk space. Figure 9-6 later in this section illustrates this concept.

The Archived Redo Log and the Archiver

To recover from a media failure, it's likely that Oracle will need to apply redo entries that are older than those currently contained in the database's online log groups—this fact is due to the nature of how log groups are overwritten and reused. To ensure that Oracle has access to all of the redo entries necessary to recover data files restored from backups, you must configure an instance to permanently archive online log groups after they fill and before they are reused—you refer to this mode of operation as either *ARCHIVELOG mode* or operating with *media recovery enabled*. While operating in ARCHIVELOG mode, after a log switch, the *Archiver (ARCH) background thread* archives each filled log group as an *archived log file* separate from the database itself. An archived log file serves as a permanent record of the log entries written to a log group. Oracle names each archived log group with a unique *log sequence number* so that it is readily identifiable. The sequence of log groups that Oracle continuously generates by archiving log groups as they fill is called the *archived transaction redo log* (*archived redo log* or *offline redo log*). To retain archived log files for long periods of time, you should immediately move or copy a database's archived log files to offline storage, such as tape. Later in this chapter, you'll learn more about how to protect a database's archived redo log.

CAUTION
When you choose to operate your database with media recovery disabled, or in NOARCHIVELOG mode (not archiving log groups), you can boost server performance a small degree and use less storage space. However, the consequences can be significant, because Oracle can no longer guarantee to protect the work of committed transactions from serious problems such as disk failures.

Figure 9-6 illustrates all of the online and archived redo log components and their relationship to one another. As ongoing transactions generate redo entries that fill log groups in the online redo log, LGWR continues to perform log switches, and

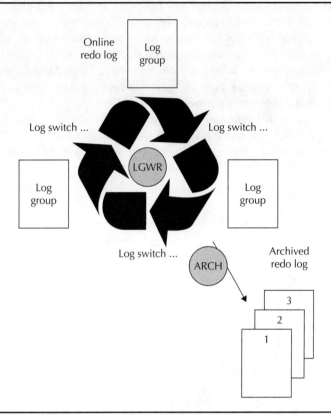

FIGURE 9-6. *An Oracle database's online redo log contains two or more log groups that are cyclically reused after being permanently archived to the archived redo log.*

ARCH archives filled log groups after each log switch, thus allowing LGWR to recycle available online log groups. When Oracle reuses an online log group to record log entries, LGWR overwrites the previous entries in the group. When you configure an instance to archive log groups after they fill, the database's archived redo log permanently preserves all redo entries.

Transaction Logging and Fault Tolerance

The redo log is a critical component in Oracle's database protection scheme. Therefore, it is wise to configure the various files that comprise a database's redo log with a level of redundancy that prevents an isolated disk failure or user error from affecting the database's availability and recoverability.

To protect a database's online redo log, you should create log groups with multiple *members* (files) that reside on different disks. Figure 9-7 shows a mirrored (multiplexed) online redo log with log groups that contain two members each.

All members of a log group are nothing more than replicas—as LGWR writes to a log group that has multiple members, LGWR writes to all members concurrently. Should one of the members in the current log group become damaged due to a disk failure or user error, LGWR can continue to write to the log group as long as one or more of the members are available. By default, an Oracle XE database has the minimum of two online log groups, and each log group has the minimum one online log member. Subsequent exercises teach you how to display information and manage your database's online log groups and members.

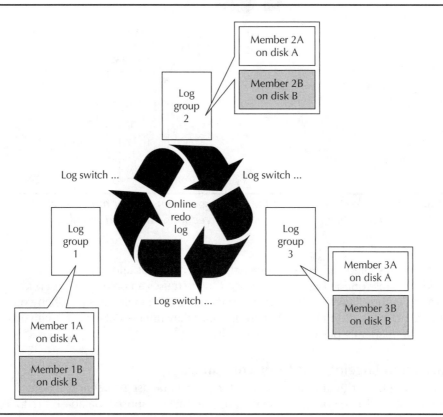

FIGURE 9-7. *To protect the online redo log from an isolated disk failure, you can create log groups with multiple members on different disks.*

NOTE
I do not recommend putting online log members on RAID-5 disk arrays to protect the physical availability of redo log components from an isolated disk failure, because RAID-5 arrays noticeably slow the process of transaction logging. If you decide to use a RAID-5 array to physically protect online log members from disk failures, it's still prudent to configure log groups with duplicate log members to provide a level of fault tolerance from logical errors, such as when an administrator mistakenly drops a log file using operating system commands.

When you operate a database instance to archive filled log groups, ARCH reads one or more of the members in a multiplexed log group to create an archived copy of the group. To protect the archived log from single points of failure, you can also mirror the archived redo log. That is, you can configure ARCH to write two or more replicas of each filled log group to distinct offline archive areas.

Checkpoints and the Database Writer

Periodically, Oracle performs a checkpoint. During a *checkpoint*, a *Database Writer (DBWR) background thread* writes all modified data blocks in the instance's buffer cache back to the data files that contain those blocks. The purpose of a checkpoint is to establish mileposts of transaction consistency on disk. After performing a checkpoint, Oracle knows that the changes made by all committed transactions have been written from memory to the database's data files. Considering this, a checkpoint indicates how many of the redo log's entries Oracle must apply if a simple server crash occurs and database crash recovery is necessary.

Oracle performs checkpoints at different times and at different levels. For example, Oracle automatically performs a *database checkpoint* during each log switch. During a database checkpoint, DBWR writes all modified data blocks in the buffer cache back to all of the database's data files. In contrast, when you take a tablespace offline, Oracle performs a *tablespace checkpoint*. During a tablespace checkpoint, DBWR writes the modified data blocks in the buffer cache that correspond to data files of that tablespace only.

Exercise 9.23 explains how to control the frequency of database checkpoints to adjust a database's MTTR after an instance crash.

The Database Control File

The information in a database's *control file* describes the physical structure of the database. Oracle also uses information in the database's control file to guide various types of database recovery operations. When using Oracle's Recovery Manager utility, Oracle also uses a database's control file to record information about administrative operations such as database backups. Because the control file has such important functions, a database cannot function properly without its control file.

To protect a database's control file and database availability from disk failures, you should always mirror the database's control file to multiple locations, just as you do with multiple members in the database's online redo log groups. When you mirror a database's control file to multiple locations, Oracle updates every copy of the control file at the same time. If one copy of the control file becomes inaccessible due to a disk I/O problem, database operation will not continue until you fix the problem; however, other copies of the control file remain intact and protect control file information.

Database Backups

Previous sections of this chapter use the term "database backup" several times to support the explanation of related topics. Although the general concept of a backup is well understood by most computer users, please read this section carefully so that you specifically understand the terms and concepts related to Oracle database backups.

Database backups are an important part of a comprehensive Oracle database protection strategy. In general, a *database backup* is a copy of the files that comprise the database. If you damage or lose a file that is part of a database, you can extract a copy of the lost file from a database backup to restore the file in the database.

Considering the abundance of tools and techniques that are available for Oracle database backup and recovery, understanding the many terms, equivalent terms, and concepts related to various types of database backups can be very confusing for a novice. To make things relatively simple, this chapter focuses on performing the most typical types of database backups using Oracle's Recovery Manager utility (discussed in the next section). Table 9-1 and the following subsections introduce the generic database backup terminology that you should understand for the purposes of this chapter.

Whole Database Backups

A *database backup*, or *whole database backup*, includes a copy of all database data files and the database's control file. A whole database backup is the most common type of backup that you perform to protect an Oracle database. With Oracle, you can make two different types of database backups: an open database backup and a closed database backup.

Open Database Backups

An *open database backup*, also called a *hot database backup*, is a database backup that you perform while the database is open and operational. Open database

Type of Backup (Synonyms)	Description
Database backup (whole database backup)	Includes all data files of all tablespaces, as well as the database's control file. This is the most common type of backup that you perform to protect a database.
Open database backup (hot, inconsistent, or fuzzy database backup)	Database backup taken while the database is open and operational (hot). Because the data in the backup does not correspond to any single transaction-consistent time point, the backup is said to be *inconsistent* or *fuzzy*.
Closed database backup (cold or consistent database backup)	Database backup taken after you shut down the database cleanly (that is, after a planned shutdown that completes normally). Because the data in the backup corresponds to a transaction-consistent time point, the backup is said to be *consistent*.
Tablespace backup	Includes all data files of a tablespace.
Online tablespace backup (hot, inconsistent, or fuzzy tablespace backup)	Tablespace backup taken while the database is open and the tablespace is online.
Offline tablespace backup (consistent tablespace backup)	Tablespace backup taken while the database is open but the tablespace is offline. If you take a tablespace offline cleanly, a subsequent offline backup of the tablespace is considered *consistent*.
Data file backup (data file copy)	Backup of a single data file.

TABLE 9-1. *General Oracle Database Backup Terms and Concepts*

backups are useful for environments in which high availability is required by one or more applications. You cannot perform an open database backup unless you *always* operate your database with media recovery enabled (that is, in ARCHIVELOG mode).

Because the data in the data files of an open database backup is being modified by transactions throughout the course of the backup, the backup is said to be *inconsistent* or *fuzzy*. That is, there is not a single transaction-consistent time point to which all data blocks correspond. Don't worry, though. After restoring a data file from an inconsistent database backup, Oracle's roll-forward/rollback recovery mechanisms regenerate missing transactions so that all data blocks in the file correspond to the same transaction-consistent time point.

Closed Database Backups

A *closed database backup* is a database backup that you perform after a planned database shutdown. A closed database backup is an option for systems in which high availability is not critical. A closed database backup is also the only option for databases that operate without media recovery enabled (that is, in NOARCHIVELOG mode). In this case, a closed database backup includes all of the database's data files, online log members, and the database's control file (note the addition of the online log members).

To perform a closed database backup, the preceding shutdown of the database should complete normally—you should not perform a closed database backup after a system crash or an abnormal shutdown. After a normal database shutdown, all of the files that constitute the database are in a transaction-consistent state with one another. Therefore, a closed database backup is often called a *consistent database backup*.

Tablespace Backups

Oracle also lets you back up individual tablespaces in a database. A *tablespace backup* is a backup of all the data files that comprise the tablespace. Tablespace backups are useful when you want to back up particular divisions of a database that applications modify more frequently than others. When you operate with media recovery enabled, you can perform two different types of tablespace backups: online tablespace backups and offline tablespace backups.

Online Tablespace Backup

An *online tablespace backup*, also called a *hot tablespace backup*, is a tablespace backup that you perform while the database is open and the tablespace is online. Because the data in the tablespace can be modified as the backup progresses, the backup is said to be inconsistent. Just as with open database backups, an online tablespace backup is useful when high availability is a must. Rather than shutting down the database or taking a tablespace offline for a backup, you simply back up the tablespace while applications are using it.

Offline Tablespace Backup

An *offline tablespace backup* is a tablespace backup that you perform while the database is open but the tablespace is offline. If you take a tablespace offline normally (that is, if Oracle can successfully perform a tablespace checkpoint and close all associated data files), the backup data generated from an offline tablespace backup is consistent.

Recovery Manager

Recovery Manager (RMAN) is the utility that Oracle Corporation recommends that you use to protect an Oracle XE database. RMAN has many features that you can use to make a database protection strategy comprehensive, automated, and relatively easy to perform. In general, you use RMAN to back up an Oracle database. If the database subsequently requires a recovery operation, you use RMAN to restore all damaged database files from a backup and then perform the necessary database recovery operation.

The following sections introduce several RMAN-specific backup terms and concepts that you need to understand before using RMAN, including RMAN commands, RMAN scripts, backup sets, backup pieces, image copies, channels, and tags.

Recovery Manager Commands

Once you start RMAN, the tool presents a simple prompt. At the RMAN command prompt, you can enter RMAN commands to back up, restore, and recover an Oracle database, as well as create, manage, and generate reports related to database backups. For example, the following simple command backs up an Oracle database:

```
RMAN> BACKUP DATABASE;
```

Many RMAN commands offer an abundance of complex parameters and options to address all possible types of environments in which you might be using RMAN. Consequently, your first impression of RMAN command syntax might lead you to believe that RMAN is too complicated to use. However, the key to getting started with RMAN is to start with some basic commands in a simple environment and then build on your knowledge as your needs demand more flexibility for various environments. With Oracle XE, you'll likely use a small subset of very basic RMAN commands.

To keep things simple and provide you with a good first impression of RMAN, the exercises in this chapter will teach you how to use the most common RMAN commands with Oracle XE. Table 9-2 provides you with a brief overview of the most commonly used RMAN commands, some of which you'll be using in this chapter. For complete information about all of RMAN's features and commands, see *Oracle Database Backup and Recovery Basics*, *Oracle Database Backup and Recovery Advanced User's Guide*, and *Oracle Backup and Recovery Reference*.

NOTE
When necessary, you can also enter SQL commands using RMAN.

Recovery Manager Scripts

You can automate the execution of repetitive RMAN commands by assembling and running scripts. In the context of RMAN, a *script* is a series of RMAN commands saved in a file that you execute to complete a task. For example, you might create and save a script of RMAN commands that you always use to back up your database. You can manually run the script when you want to perform a database backup operation, or automate the execution of the script with a job so that RMAN runs the script for

Command	Description
CONNECT	Establishes a connection to the target database
RUN	Compiles and executes a set of one or more statements as a job, delimited by opening and closing braces
ALLOCATE	Establishes a channel to use for subsequent backup, copy, restore, or recovery operations
BACKUP	Backs up a database, tablespace, data file, archived log file, or control file
COPY	Creates an image copy of a data file, archived log file, or control file
RESTORE	Restores files from backup sets
SWITCH	Switches the filenames in the database's control file from a data file to an image copy of the data file
RECOVER	Recovers a database, tablespace, or one or more data files by applying archived and online log files
LIST	Lists information about backup sets and image copies
REPORT	Reports valuable information about the current state of the database

TABLE 9-2. *Frequently Used RMAN Commands*

you. Subsequent exercises discuss several RMAN scripts supplied with Oracle XE that you can execute to back up and restore your database.

Recovery Manager and the Database Control File

RMAN simplifies and automates the process of database backup and recovery by automatically keeping track of backup-related information in an Oracle XE database's control file. RMAN uses the control file to record specific information about each database backup that you perform. When a database requires recovery, RMAN uses information in the control file to recover the damaged database with available backups and an appropriate recovery action.

An Oracle XE database's control file keeps track of a database's backup information as well as information about the physical structure of the database (data files, log members, etc.). If the database is damaged, RMAN must be able to read the control file to direct the physical restoration and recovery of the damaged database. To facilitate recovery from a media failure, it is important to mirror the database's control file to protect the current control file from an isolated disk failure. It is also important to maintain backups of the database's control file that reflect the physical makeup of the database after each structural change to the database. For example, each time that you create a new tablespace or add a data file to an existing tablespace, you should back up the tablespace as well as the database's control file. You can configure RMAN to automatically back up a database's control file.

NOTE
Catastrophic problems (fire, flood, earthquake, etc.) can potentially damage all copies of the database's control file when they are stored in the same physical proximity. When all copies of a database's control file are lost and you do not have a backup control file, database recovery can be very difficult. To further protect the availability of recovery information, you have the option to configure and use a recovery catalog. A recovery catalog is a set of tables in a remote Oracle database that RMAN can use to record the same information maintained in your database's control file. If you do not have a copy of your database's control file, you can use information in the remote recovery catalog to guide database recovery. The configuration and use of a recovery catalog is beyond the scope of this book— refer to Oracle Database Backup and Recovery Basics *for more information.*

Backup Sets and Backup Pieces

RMAN uses several techniques to perform backup operations as efficiently as possible. For example, rather than inefficiently creating a block-by-block physical copy of each database file, RMAN reads source database files that require backup and intersperses the blocks of the files together to create one large storage unit known as a *backup set*. A *data file backup set* contains blocks from one or more of a database's data files, while an *archive log backup set* contains blocks from one or more of a database's archived log groups. RMAN can also append a backup of the database's control file to a data file or archive log backup set.

By default, RMAN writes a backup set as one operating system file, which is referred to specifically as a *backup piece*. When you explicitly limit the size of a backup piece (for example, due to storage limitations of a file system or a tape drive), RMAN might have to write a single backup set using multiple backup pieces.

To reduce the total size of a data file backup set, RMAN does not write data blocks in data files that have never contained data (for example, new blocks in a new data file)—in a sense, this compresses the size of the data file backup set. To further compress the size of a database backup at the expense of extra processing requirements, RMAN can optionally use a compression algorithm to reduce the size of a backup set.

Oracle XE configures RMAN to write backup sets to the database's flash recovery area by default. You can also use RMAN to back up individual backup sets or the entire flash recovery area to permanent offline storage media such as tape. Subsequent exercises explain several of these RMAN features.

Full and Incremental Data File Backup Sets

When you back up the data files of a database or tablespace with RMAN, you can perform either a full backup or an incremental backup. A *full backup* of a data file backup set includes all used data blocks of all data files in the backup set—RMAN omits data blocks that have never been used to compress the size of the backup set. In contrast, an *incremental backup* of a data file backup set includes just the blocks of data files in the backup set that have been modified since the previous backup of the set at the same or higher level (the following paragraph explains the term *level*). The advantage of incremental backups is that it typically takes less time to back up a subset of a backup set's data rather than the entire backup set.

NOTE
Full and incremental backup sets are completely independent of one another. For example, a full backup set has no effect on previous incremental backup sets.

When you use incremental backups, you can set the *level* of the incremental backup. In general, a level-*n* backup includes the blocks of the backup set that have been modified since the most recent level-*n* backup or higher. For example, suppose you back up a data file backup set on Sunday with a level-0 backup:

- On Monday, you perform a level-2 backup of the data file backup set. The backup set includes only the blocks that have changed since the level-0 backup on Sunday.

- On Tuesday, you perform another level-2 backup of the data file backup set. The backup set includes only the blocks that have changed since the level-2 backup on Monday.

- On Wednesday, you perform a level-1 backup of the data file backup set. The backup set includes only the blocks that have changed since the level-0 backup on Sunday.

- On Thursday, you perform a level-2 backup of the data file backup set. The backup set includes only the blocks that have changed since the level-1 backup on Wednesday.

- On Friday, you perform another level-2 backup of the data file backup set. The backup set includes only the blocks that have changed since the level-2 backup on Thursday.

- On Saturday, you perform a level-1 backup of the data file backup set. The backup set includes only the blocks that have changed since the level-1 backup on Wednesday.

- On Sunday, you perform a level-0 backup of the data file backup set, and so on. The backup set includes all blocks that have changed since the level-0 backup last Sunday.

NOTE
Oracle allows you to make incremental backups of a data file backup set up to eight levels deep.

Incremental data file backup sets are primarily useful when working with large databases. Because an Oracle XE database size is limited, this chapter does not teach you how to perform incremental data file backups—see *Oracle Database Backup and Recovery Basics* if you would like more information.

Image Copies

In addition to backup sets, you can also back up parts or all of a database by using RMAN to create image copies. An *image copy* is a block-by-block, physical copy of a single data file, archived log group, or the database's control file. Image copies differ from backup sets in several ways:

- You can make an image copy of a file on a disk only—for example, you cannot make an image copy directly on a tape.

- An image copy of a file is an exact block-by-block copy of the file. RMAN does not compress an image copy of a data file by eliminating unused data blocks in the file or by compressing the file.

Because an image copy is a file that directly corresponds with a database file, you do not need to extract or restore image copies from backup sets before performing database recovery. Using RMAN, you can simply "switch" the location of the damaged file to the location of a corresponding image copy and then perform database recovery to make the file current. Because a restore operation is not necessary with an image copy, recovery is quicker—this is useful for applications that require high availability and the smallest possible MTTR.

Channels

When RMAN performs a database backup, image copy, restore, or recovery operation, it allocates at least one channel for the task. An RMAN *channel* is two things: a connection to the database that is the target of the operation, and a specification of the name and type of I/O device to be used for the operation. When you specify more than one channel for an RMAN operation, such as a backup, image copy, file restore, or recovery, RMAN automatically uses parallel processing to complete the operation more quickly.

Backup Tags

When you create a backup set or an image copy, you can assign it a *tag*, which is a logical name. RMAN automatically associates the backup set or image copy with its tag in the recovery catalog. You can use a tag when you need to perform a recovery or want to overwrite the previous version of a backup set or image copy with a new one.

Configuring Oracle XE Database Protection

Now that you have a solid understanding of some basic Oracle database protection concepts, the exercises in this section teach you how to reveal information about an Oracle XE's default database, including configuration information about the flash recovery area, the database's control files, log archiving, and online log groups and members. Then, you will learn how to make several changes to better protect your Oracle XE database.

EXERCISE 9.1: Display Information About the Flash Recovery Area

This exercise teaches you how to quickly display configuration information about a database's flashback recovery area. Oracle uses two initialization parameters to configure a database's flash recovery area:

- **DB_RECOVERY_FILE_DEST**   Set to a string that specifies the operating system location of the flash recovery area.

- **DB_RECOVERY_FILE_DEST_SIZE**   Set to an integer that determines the storage capacity of the flash recovery area. You can use the K, M, and G suffixes to more easily specify settings as kilobytes, megabytes, or gigabytes, respectively.

To display an Oracle XE's current flash recovery area parameter settings, use steps similar to those that you learned previously in Exercise 8.14:

1. Launch Oracle Application Express.

2. Connect as **SYSTEM**.

3. Click Administration.

4. Click About Database.

5. Check Parameters.

6. Click Go.

7. Scroll down the page until you see the parameter settings for the DB_
   RECOVERY_FILE_DEST and DB_RECOVERY_FILE_DEST_SIZE parameters.
   The settings for a typical Oracle XE database after installation should be
   similar to those in Figure 9-8.

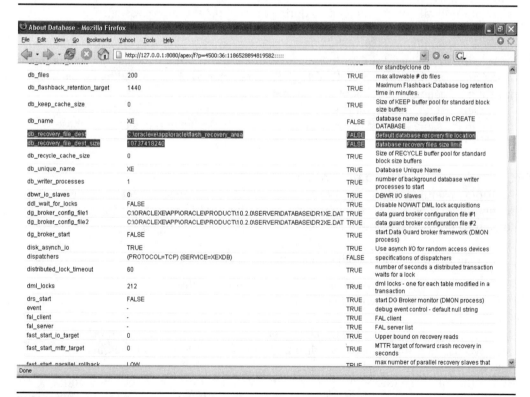

FIGURE 9-8. *You can use the About Database page of Oracle Application Express to quickly display parameter settings related to the flash recovery area.*

Notice that, by default, the storage capacity of an Oracle XE database's flash recovery area is 10GB, and that the flash recovery area resides on the same disk drive that contains the Oracle database's data files. It's very important to understand that the default location of an Oracle XE database's flash recovery area essentially makes it worthless in the event of a disk failure. Why? A disk failure that destroys the database's current files would also destroy all of the files necessary to recover the database. Later in this chapter, you will learn how to move a database's flash recovery area, but first you should explore other configuration settings as well.

EXERCISE 9.2: Display Information About the Control File

This exercise teaches you how to display information about the database's control file configuration. The *CONTROL_FILES initialization parameter* determines the names and locations of each copy of the database's control file. Oracle reads the CONTROL_FILES initialization parameter during instance startup, opens the specified control files when the instance mounts the database, and then writes control file information to all control file copies during normal database processing. The CONTROL_FILES initialization parameter is set to a comma-separated list of one or more filenames.

When continuing from the previous exercise, you can display the current setting of an Oracle XE database's CONTROL_FILES parameter by simply scrolling up the page and revealing the setting of the parameter, as shown in Figure 9-9.

Notice that the default Oracle XE database has a single control file copy that is located in the same location as the database's data files. To better protect the database, Exercise 9.11 teaches you how to add a control file copy.

EXERCISE 9.3: Display Information About the Redo Log

To display useful information about an Oracle XE database's current redo log configuration, complete the following steps with Oracle Application Express continuing from the previous exercise:

1. Click Home to display the Database Home Page.

2. In the Usage Monitor section of the page, observe the setting of Log Archiving, as shown in Figure 9-10.

By default, an Oracle XE database operates in NOARCHIVELOG mode—in other words, with media recovery disabled. If you want to protect the database from the possibility of disk failure, one of the things that you have to do is switch the database to operate permanently with media recovery enabled and then configure how to archive the log groups as they fill. Exercise 9.7 teaches you how to do this.

cluster_interconnects	-	TRUE	interconnects for RAC use
commit_point_strength	1	TRUE	Bias this node has toward not preparing in a two-phase commit
commit_write	-	TRUE	transaction commit log write behaviour
compatible	10.2.0.1.0	FALSE	Database will be completely compatible with this software version
control_file_record_keep_time	7	TRUE	control file record keep time in days
control_files	C:\ORACLEXE\ORADATA\XE\CONTROL.DBF	FALSE	control file names list
core_dump_dest	C:\ORACLEXE\APP\ORACLE\ADMIN\XE\CDUMP	FALSE	Core dump directory
cpu_count	1	TRUE	number of CPUs for this instance
create_bitmap_area_size	8388608	TRUE	size of create bitmap buffer for bitmap index
create_stored_outlines	-	TRUE	create stored outlines for DML statements
cursor_sharing	EXACT	TRUE	cursor sharing mode
cursor_space_for_time	FALSE	TRUE	use more memory in order to get faster execution
db_16k_cache_size	0	TRUE	Size of cache for 16K buffers
db_2k_cache_size	0	TRUE	Size of cache for 2K buffers
db_32k_cache_size	0	TRUE	Size of cache for 32K buffers
db_4k_cache_size	0	TRUE	Size of cache for 4K buffers
db_8k_cache_size	0	TRUE	Size of cache for 8K buffers
db_block_buffers	0	TRUE	Number of database blocks cached in memory
db_block_checking	FALSE	TRUE	header checking and data and index block checking
db_block_checksum	TRUE	TRUE	store checksum in db blocks and check during reads
db_block_size	8192	TRUE	Size of database block in bytes
db_cache_advice	ON	TRUE	Buffer cache sizing advisory
db_cache_size	0	TRUE	Size of DEFAULT buffer pool for standard block size buffers
db_create_file_dest	-	TRUE	default database location
db_create_online_log_dest_1	-	TRUE	online log/controlfile destination #1
db_create_online_log_dest_2	-	TRUE	online log/controlfile destination #2
db_create_online_log_dest_3	-	TRUE	online log/controlfile destination #3
db_create_online_log_dest_4	-	TRUE	online log/controlfile destination #4

FIGURE 9-9. *You can use the About Database page of Oracle Application Express to quickly display parameter settings related to the database's control file.*

To display information about an Oracle XE database's online log groups, click the Log Archiving link. Notice the following information displayed on the Database Logging page, as shown in Figure 9-11:

- The default Oracle XE database has two online log groups.

- Each online log group has one member.

- Each online redo log member is located in the flash recovery area.

- The log member size for each log group is 50MB.

To better protect the database, another thing that you should do is configure each log group with two or more members, placing the members of each group on a physically distinct disk drive (if possible). Exercise 9.10 teaches you how to do this (or simulate doing this).

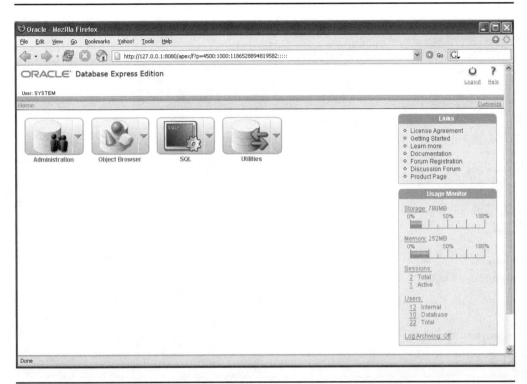

FIGURE 9-10.   *The Database Home Page reveals the current log archiving status of an Oracle XE database.*

Before continuing to the next exercise, open Windows Explorer and navigate to the flash recovery area for the Oracle XE database. Notice that the flash recovery area contains a subdirectory specifically for the database's online log members, as Figure 9-12 shows.

EXERCISE 9.4: Create a Cold Database Backup

The previous exercises identify several weaknesses of the default Oracle XE database configuration—you are going to address these weaknesses in the next few exercises. Before doing so, you would be wise to create a backup of the current database just in case you make a mistake. This exercise teaches you how to make a cold database backup of an Oracle XE database that is operating with media recovery disabled (in NOACHIVELOG mode).

To quickly back up an Oracle XE database, use the convenient Backup Database menu option on the Microsoft Windows program menu. This menu selection executes a batch file (ORACLE_HOME\BIN\Backup.bat) that determines whether the Oracle

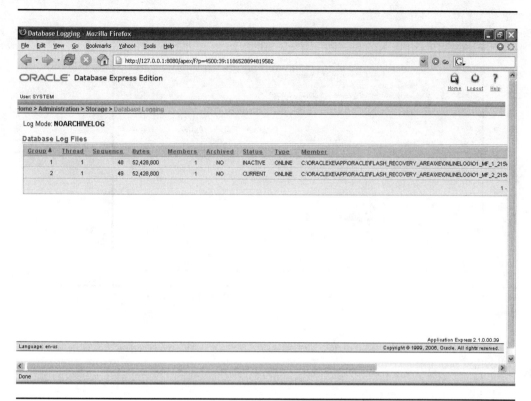

FIGURE 9-11. *The Database Logging page reveals information about an Oracle XE database's online log groups and online log members.*

XE database is currently operating with media recovery enabled or disabled. If the Oracle XE database has media recovery enabled, the batch file uses RMAN to create a hot database backup; otherwise, the batch file uses RMAN to shut down the database, create a cold database backup, and then restart the database.

To create a cold database backup of the Oracle XE database currently operating with media recovery disabled, complete the following steps:

1. Click Logout to terminate your current Oracle Application Express session.

2. Click Start.

3. Click [All] Programs.

4. Click Oracle Database 10*g* Express Edition.

5. Click Backup Database.

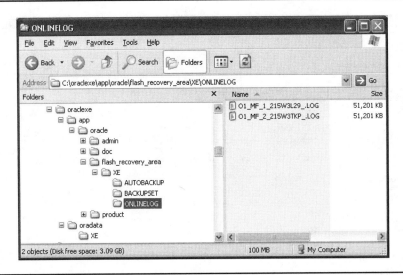

FIGURE 9-12. *The flash recovery area contains a separate subdirectory for online log members.*

At first, the batch file starts in a Command Prompt window and presents the following prompt:

Warning : Log archiving (ARCHIVELOG mode) is currently disabled. If you restore the database from this backup, any transactions that take place between this backup and the next backup will be lost. It is recommended that you enable ARCHIVELOG mode before proceeding so that all transactions can be recovered upon restore. See the section 'Enabling ARCHIVELOG Mode...' in the online help for instructions. Backup with log archiving disabled will shut down and restart the database. Are you sure [Y/N]?

This notice is expected (you should already know that the database needs to be reconfigured to operation in ARCHIVELOG mode); respond with Y to continue. The batch file then does its work to back up the database. The output from the batch file, which should be similar to the following, is quite informative and provides you with your first glimpse at several of the RMAN concepts that you learned about earlier in this chapter. To make the output more understandable, I've embedded some comments (highlighted in bold) in the sample output to explain what is happening.

Backup in progress...

Recovery Manager: Release 10.2.0.1.0 - Production on ...

Copyright I 1982, 2005, Oracle. All rights reserved.

```
connected to target database: XE (DBID=2465914590)

RMAN> set echo on;
-- SHUT DOWN THE DATABASE.
2> shutdown immediate;
-- START UP A NEW INSTANCE AND MOUNT THE DATABASE, BUT DO NOT OPEN.
3> startup mount;
-- CONFIGURE AUTOMATIC CONTROL FILE BACKUPS TO USE A DISK CHANNEL.
4> configure controlfile autobackup format for device type disk clear;
-- CONFIGURE RMAN TO RETAIN THE TWO MOST RECENT BACKUPS AND CONSIDER
-- ALL OTHERS AS OBSOLETE.
5> configure retention policy to redundancy 2;
-- ENABLE AUTOMATIC CONTROL FILE BACKUPS.
6> configure controlfile autobackup on;
-- CREATE A TEXT BACKUP OF THE DATABASE'S INITIALIZATION PARAMETER FILE.
7> sql "create pfile=''C:\ORACLEXE\APP\ORACLE\PRODUCT\10.2.0\SERVER\
DATABASE\SPFILE2INIT.ORA'' from spfile";
-- BACK UP THE CLOSED DATABASE AS A BACKUP SET, USING THE DEFAULT
-- CHANNEL THAT IS CONFIGURED TO WRITE TO THE FLASH RECOVERY AREA.
8> backup as backupset device type disk database;
-- DISABLE AUTOMATIC CONTROL FILE BACKUPS.
9> configure controlfile autobackup off;
-- REOPEN THE DATABASE.
10> alter database open;
-- DELETE ALL OBSOLETE DATABASE BACKUPS FROM THE FLASH RECOVERY AREA.
11> delete noprompt obsolete;
12>
-- THE OUTPUT BELOW CORRESPONDS TO THE COMMANDS ABOVE. YOU CAN
-- FOLLOW ALONG EASILY BECAUSE THE COMMANDS ARE ECHOED IN THE OUTPUT.
echo set on

using target database control file instead of recovery catalog
database closed
database dismounted
Oracle instance shut down

connected to target database (not started)
Oracle instance started
database mounted

Total System Global Area     230686720 bytes

Fixed Size                     1286700 bytes
Variable Size                 83889620 bytes
Database Buffers             142606336 bytes
Redo Buffers                   2904064 bytes

RMAN configuration parameters are successfully reset to default value

old RMAN configuration parameters:
```

```
CONFIGURE RETENTION POLICY TO REDUNDANCY 2;
new RMAN configuration parameters:
CONFIGURE RETENTION POLICY TO REDUNDANCY 2;
new RMAN configuration parameters are successfully stored

old RMAN configuration parameters:
CONFIGURE CONTROLFILE AUTOBACKUP OFF;
new RMAN configuration parameters:
CONFIGURE CONTROLFILE AUTOBACKUP ON;
new RMAN configuration parameters are successfully stored

sql statement: create pfile=''C:\ORACLEXE\APP\ORACLE\PRODUCT\10.2.0\
SERVER\DATABASE\SPFILE2INIT.ORA'' from spfile
-- THE DATA FILE BACKUP SET IS CREATED BELOW. NOTICE THE DATA FILES
-- THAT RMAN READS DO NOT INCLUDE TEMP FILES, WHICH ARE NOT NECESSARY
-- FOR DATABASE RECOVERY.
Starting backup at ...
allocated channel: ORA_DISK_1
channel ORA_DISK_1: sid=35 devtype=DISK
channel ORA_DISK_1: starting full datafile backupset
channel ORA_DISK_1: specifying datafile(s) in backupset
input datafile fno=00001 name=C:\ORACLEXE\ORADATA\XE\SYSTEM.DBF
input datafile fno=00003 name=C:\ORACLEXE\ORADATA\XE\SYSAUX.DBF
input datafile fno=00002 name=C:\ORACLEXE\ORADATA\XE\UNDO.DBF
input datafile fno=00004 name=C:\ORACLEXE\ORADATA\XE\USERS.DBF
channel ORA_DISK_1: starting piece 1 at ...
channel ORA_DISK_1: finished piece 1 at ...
-- NOTICE THAT THE BACKUP SET HAS ONE BACKUP PIECE, WRITTEN TO A
-- SUBDIRECTORY IN THE FLASH RECOVERY AREA. ALSO NOTICE THAT RMAN
-- AUTOMATICALLY GENERATES A UNIQUE TAG FOR THE BACKUP SET.
piece handle=C:\ORACLEXE\APP\ORACLE\FLASH_RECOVERY_AREA\XE\BACKUPSET\
2006_05_07\O1_MF_NNNDF_TAG20060507T151707_25WKXOL4_.BKP
tag=TAG20060507T151707 comment=NONE
-- IT TOOK LESS THAN 2 MINUTES FOR RMAN TO BACK UP DATA FILES THAT
-- TOTAL APPROXIMATELY 1GB.
channel ORA_DISK_1: backup set complete, elapsed time: 00:01:56
Finished backup at ...
-- THE AUTOMATIC CONTROL FILE BACKUP IS ALSO WRITTEN TO A SUBDIRECTORY
-- IN THE FLASH RECOVERY AREA.
Starting Control File and SPFILE Autobackup at ...
piece handle=C:\ORACLEXE\APP\ORACLE\FLASH_RECOVERY_AREA\XE\
AUTOBACKUP\2006_05_07\O1_MF_S_589821396_25WL1BYM_.BKP comment=NONE
Finished Control File and SPFILE Autobackup at ...

old RMAN configuration parameters:
CONFIGURE CONTROLFILE AUTOBACKUP ON;
new RMAN configuration parameters:
CONFIGURE CONTROLFILE AUTOBACKUP OFF;
```

```
new RMAN configuration parameters are successfully stored

database opened

RMAN retention policy will be applied to the command
RMAN retention policy is set to redundancy 2
using channel ORA_DISK_1
-- THIS IS THE FIRST BACKUP, SO NO OBSOLETE BACKUPS ARE FOUND.
no obsolete backups found

Recovery Manager complete.
Backup of the database succeeded.
-- RMAN LOGS ITS ACTIONS TO A FILE FOR YOUR INFORMATION.
Log file is at C:\ORACLEXE\APP\ORACLE\PRODUCT\10.2.0\SERVER\
DATABASE\OXE_BACKUP_CURRENT.LOG.
Press any key to continue ...
```

Pretty cool! With one click of a mouse and approximately two minutes later, you now have a cold database backup. Figure 9-13 shows the flash recovery area with the new backup piece for the data file backup set. Notice how RMAN was able to efficiently create a backup set/piece that is about half the total size of the database's data files combined.

With a cold database backup available, you can now feel safe moving the flash recovery area and making other database configuration changes in the next few exercises.

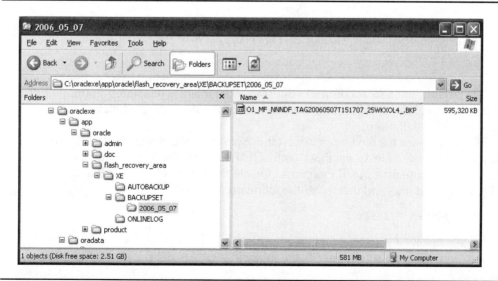

FIGURE 9-13. *By default, RMAN writes backup sets to the flash recovery area.*

EXERCISE 9.5: Establish a Privileged Administrator Session with SQL*Plus

To complete many of the following exercises in this chapter, you need to establish a privileged administrator session with SQL*Plus that allows you to perform powerful system-wide operations, such as instance startup and shutdown, database backup and recovery, and certain database configuration operations. A *privileged administrator session* is a session that has access to either or both of the following privileges:

- **SYSOPER**   Using a session with the SYSOPER privilege, you can start up and shut down an Oracle database instance; mount, open, close, back up, and recover a database; and manage a database's redo log structure.

- **SYSDBA**   Using a session with the SYSDBA privilege, you can perform any database operation and, in turn, can grant any system privilege to other database users. Therefore, it is extremely important to restrict which users have the SYSDBA system privilege.

NOTE
You control access to the SYSDBA and SYSOPER privileges using the ORAPWD utility, an administrator password file, and the SQL commands GRANT and REVOKE. This book is intended for Oracle XE users, and does not discuss how to add other administrators to the administrator password file, change the administrator password, and other operations involving the ORAPWD utility. See the Oracle Database Administrator's Guide *for more information about administrator security and the ORAPWD utility if you are curious.*

By default, the SYS account in your starter database is registered in the administrator password file, and the administrator password is whatever you set it to during installation.

To prepare for the next exercise, establish a SYSDBA privileged administrator session to your Oracle XE database with SQL*Plus using the SYS account. Start SQL*Plus (choose Start | [All] Programs | Oracle Database 10g Express Edition | Run SQL Command line) and then enter the following statement:

```
CONNECT SYS AS SYSDBA;
```

Alternatively, if your Microsoft Windows session is a member of the ORA_DBA group, you can more simply specify the following:

```
CONNECT / AS SYSDBA;
```

In either case, Oracle establishes a session with your Oracle XE instance as an administrator with all privileges, and you can complete powerful system-wide operations, such as database reconfiguration, database backup and recovery, and database startup and shutdown. Now you are ready to move the flash recovery area.

EXERCISE 9.6: Move the Flash Recovery Area and Online Redo Logs

As mentioned earlier, the default configuration of an Oracle XE database places the database's data files and flash recovery area on the same disk drive. To protect your database from a disk failure, this exercise teaches you how to move the flash recovery area, which includes the database's online log groups, to a different disk drive.

If your computer has only a single disk drive, I strongly recommend that you consider buying an inexpensive secondary disk drive so that you can safely back up all of your valuable data to a disk that is physically separate from your primary hard disk. The convenience and affordability of USB-connected external drives are perfect for this purpose.

If you do not have a second disk drive, simulate a second disk drive to practice the skills in this exercise. For example, create a directory on your hard disk that can serve as a pseudo-drive for the purposes of training. For example, you might create the directory C:\xdrive to simulate a drive with the drive label X. Following OMF guidelines, you should then create the following directory tree for the new flash recovery area:

```
C:\xdrive\oraclexe\app\oracle\flash_recovery_area
```

To create the new subdirectory hierarchy with a single command while using Microsoft Windows, start a Command Prompt and enter the following command:

```
mkdir c:\xdrive\oraclexe\app\oracle\flash_recovery_area
```

Once you decide where you are going to move the flash recovery area to, complete the following steps using the SYSDBA-privileged SQL*Plus session that you established in the previous exercise:

1. Use the SQL command ALTER SYSTEM to modify the setting of the DB_RECOVERY_FILE_DEST initialization parameter to the new location of your choice; in the following example, substitute your exact location:

    ```
    ALTER SYSTEM SET
     DB_RECOVERY_FILE_DEST =
      'C:\xdrive\oraclexe\app\oracle\flash_recovery_area';
    ```

2. Execute the ORACLE_HOME\sqlplus\admin\movelogs.sql script to move the online redo log members to the new flash recovery area location and then drop the obsolete log members from the old flash recovery area:

    ```
    @?\sqlplus\admin\movelogs.sql;
    ```

NOTE
The ? in the previous command is a shortcut for specifying the ORACLE_HOME location of the current instance.

The script then executes several ALTER DATABASE statements to create log groups in the new flash recovery area and then drops the original log groups from the original flash recovery area. You'll learn about these commands in a subsequent exercise.

CAUTION
If you have already configured a database's online log groups so that each log group has more than one member (for example, you are repeating this chapter's exercises), beware that the movelogs.sql script does not preserve multiplexed log groups and that you will have to re-create the additional log members. Exercise 9.10 explains this process.

Because you have made a significant structural change to your database, it's very important to back up the database immediately. Exit SQL*Plus and then repeat the steps in Exercise 9.4 to make a new cold database backup before continuing.

Once the cold database backup completes, use Windows Explorer to confirm the existence of the log members and the new backup set in the new flash recovery area, as shown in Figure 9-14.

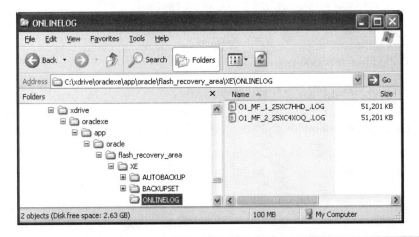

FIGURE 9-14. *Confirm the online log members and the new backup set in the new flash recovery area.*

EXERCISE 9.7: Enable Media Recovery

To switch a database so that it archives online redo log groups before reusing them, you need to complete several steps in the following order:

1. Shut down the current database instance.

2. Start a new instance and mount the database to the instance, but do not open the database.

3. Use the ARCHIVELOG option (or NOARCHIVELOG option) of the SQL command ALTER DATABASE to switch the database's log mode.

4. Reopen the database.

This exercise teaches you how to perform each of the steps in the preceding list so that you can enable media recovery for an Oracle XE database.

First, shut down the current instance of your database. Start SQL*Plus (choose Start | [All] Programs | Oracle Database 10g Express Edition | Run SQL Command line), connect as SYS with SYSDBA privileges, and then use the SQL*Plus command SHUTDOWN with the IMMEDIATE option to perform an immediate database shutdown (roll back all pending transactions, terminate all sessions, and shut down):

`SHUTDOWN IMMEDIATE;`

NOTE
The SHUTDOWN command has several options that you can use to control database shutdown. See the Oracle Database Administrator's Guide *for more information about the SQL*Plus command SHUTDOWN and its options.*

After a few seconds, you should see the following results to indicate that Oracle has shut down:

```
Database closed.
Database dismounted.
ORACLE instance shut down.
```

Now use the SQL*Plus command STARTUP with the MOUNT option to start a new instance and mount the database to the instance, but do not open the database:

`STARTUP MOUNT;`

Once this operation is complete, you should see results similar to the following:

```
ORACLE instance started.

Total System Global Area  230686720 bytes
Fixed Size                  1286700 bytes
Variable Size              83889620 bytes
Database Buffers          142606336 bytes
Redo Buffers                2904064 bytes
Database mounted.
```

Finally, you can switch your database's log mode by using the ARCHIVELOG option or NOARCHIVELOG option of the SQL command ALTER DATABASE. For example, enter the following statement to switch your starter database to ARCHIVELOG mode (media recovery enabled):

```
ALTER DATABASE ARCHIVELOG;
```

NOTE
Once you switch a database's log mode, always operate the database in this mode. It is not good practice to switch between log modes frequently.

Next, open the database to make it available using the OPEN option of the SQL command ALTER DATABASE:

```
ALTER DATABASE OPEN;
```

To confirm your changes, feel free to start Oracle Application Express and display the Database Home Page. The Log Archiving status should now indicate that the database is in ARCHIVELOG mode, as shown in Figure 9-15.

EXERCISE 9.8: Create a Hot Database Backup

As you already know, any time that you make a structural change to your database, it is very important to back up the database so that you can recover the database if a problem occurs. It is particularly important to understand that all backups made while the database operates in NOARCHIVELOG mode are not useful for recovering a database that now operates in ARCHIVELOG mode. As such, this exercise teaches you how to make a hot database backup of an Oracle XE database that is now operating with media recovery enabled (in ACHIVELOG mode).

You'll be glad to know that it is just as easy to make a hot Oracle XE database backup as it is a cold backup: just use the familiar Backup Database menu option on the Microsoft Windows program menu. When the corresponding batch file executes, it recognizes that the database is now in ARCHIVELOG mode and automatically performs a hot database backup rather than a cold backup.

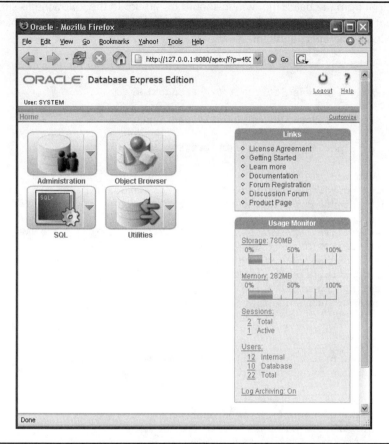

FIGURE 9-15.   *After reconfiguring an Oracle XE database to ARCHIVELOG mode, confirm the change using the Database Home Page.*

To create a hot database backup of the Oracle XE database currently operating with media recovery disabled, complete the following steps:

1. Click Start.

2. Click [All] Programs.

3. Click Oracle Database 10g Express Edition.

4. Click Backup Database.

The output from the batch file, which should be similar to the following, is similar to the output from the cold database backup, with several key differences, as noted by the embedded comments (highlighted in bold):

```
Doing online backup of the database.

Recovery Manager: Release 10.2.0.1.0 - Production on ...

Copyright (c) 1982, 2005, Oracle.  All rights reserved.

connected to target database: XE (DBID=2465914590)

RMAN> set echo on;
2> configure controlfile autobackup format for device type disk clear;
3> configure retention policy to redundancy 2;
4> configure controlfile autobackup on;
5> sql "create pfile=''C:\ORACLEXE\APP\ORACLE\PRODUCT\10.2.0\SERVER\
DATABASE\SPFILE2INIT.ORA'' from spfile";
6> backup as backupset device type disk database;
7> configure controlfile autobackup off;
8> sql 'alter system archive log current';
9> delete noprompt obsolete;
10>
echo set on

using target database control file instead of recovery catalog
RMAN configuration parameters are successfully reset to default value

old RMAN configuration parameters:
CONFIGURE RETENTION POLICY TO REDUNDANCY 2;
new RMAN configuration parameters:
CONFIGURE RETENTION POLICY TO REDUNDANCY 2;
new RMAN configuration parameters are successfully stored

old RMAN configuration parameters:
CONFIGURE CONTROLFILE AUTOBACKUP OFF;
new RMAN configuration parameters:
CONFIGURE CONTROLFILE AUTOBACKUP ON;
new RMAN configuration parameters are successfully stored

sql statement: create pfile=''C:\ORACLEXE\APP\ORACLE\PRODUCT\10.2.0\
SERVER\DATABASE\SPFILE2INIT.ORA'' from spfile

Starting backup at ...
allocated channel: ORA_DISK_1
channel ORA_DISK_1: sid=20 devtype=DISK
channel ORA_DISK_1: starting full datafile backupset
channel ORA_DISK_1: specifying datafile(s) in backupset
```

```
input datafile fno=00001 name=C:\ORACLEXE\ORADATA\XE\SYSTEM.DBF
input datafile fno=00003 name=C:\ORACLEXE\ORADATA\XE\SYSAUX.DBF
input datafile fno=00002 name=C:\ORACLEXE\ORADATA\XE\UNDO.DBF
input datafile fno=00004 name=C:\ORACLEXE\ORADATA\XE\USERS.DBF
channel ORA_DISK_1: starting piece 1 at ...
channel ORA_DISK_1: finished piece 1 at ...
piece handle=C:\XDRIVE\ORACLEXE\APP\ORACLE\FLASH_RECOVERY_AREA
\XE\BACKUPSET\2006_05_07\O1_MF_NNNDF_TAG20060507T174257_25WTH3LJ_.BKP
tag=TAG20060507T174257
comment=NONE
channel ORA_DISK_1: backup set complete, elapsed time: 00:01:46
Finished backup at ...

Starting Control File and SPFILE Autobackup at ...
piece handle=C:\XDRIVE\ORACLEXE\APP\ORACLE\FLASH_RECOVERY_AREA
\XE\AUTOBACKUP\2006_05_07\O1_MF_S_589830284_25WTLGK2_.BKP
comment=NONE
Finished Control File and SPFILE Autobackup at ...

old RMAN configuration parameters:
CONFIGURE CONTROLFILE AUTOBACKUP ON;
new RMAN configuration parameters:
CONFIGURE CONTROLFILE AUTOBACKUP OFF;
new RMAN configuration parameters are successfully stored

sql statement: alter system archive log current

RMAN retention policy will be applied to the command
RMAN retention policy is set to redundancy 2
using channel ORA_DISK_1
-- THIS NEW BACKUP SET AND NEW CONTROL FILE BACKUP WERE THE THIRD
-- BACKUPS OF THEIR KIND, WHICH MAKES THE FIRST BACKUP SET AND
-- CONTROL FILE BACKUP OBSOLETE CONSIDERING THE ABOVE RETENTION POLICY.
-- THEREFORE, RMAN DELETES THE OLDEST BACKUPS TO RECLAIM SPACE.
Deleting the following obsolete backups and copies:
Type                 Key   Completion Time    Filename/Handle
-------------------- ------ ------------------ --------------------
Backup Set           3     07-MAY-06
  Backup Piece       3     07-MAY-06           C:\ORACLEXE\APP\ORACLE\
FLASH_RECOVERY_AREA\XE\BACKUPSET\2006_05_07\
O1_MF_NNNDF_TAG20060507T151707_25WKXOL4_.BKP
Backup Set           4     07-MAY-06
  Backup Piece       4     07-MAY-06           C:\ORACLEXE\APP\ORACLE\
FLASH_RECOVERY_AREA\XE\AUTOBACKUP\2006_05_07\
O1_MF_S_589821396_25WL1BYM_.BKP
deleted backup piece
backup piece handle=C:\ORACLEXE\APP\ORACLE\FLASH_RECOVERY_AREA\XE\
BACKUPSET\2006_05_07\O1_MF_NNNDF_TAG20060507T151707_25WKXOL4_.BKP recid=3
```

```
stamp=589821429
deleted backup piece
backup piece handle=C:\ORACLEXE\APP\ORACLE\FLASH_RECOVERY_AREA\XE\
AUTOBACKUP\2006_05_07\O1_MF_S_589821396_25WL1BYM_.BKP recid=4
stamp=589821546
Deleted 2 objects


Recovery Manager complete.

Recovery Manager: Release 10.2.0.1.0 - Production on ...

Copyright (c) 1982, 2005, Oracle.  All rights reserved.

connected to target database: XE (DBID=2465914590)

RMAN> set echo on;
2> sql 'alter system archive log current';
3>
echo set on

using target database control file instead of recovery catalog
sql statement: alter system archive log current

Recovery Manager complete.
Backup of the database succeeded.
Log file is at C:\ORACLEXE\APP\ORACLE\PRODUCT\10.2.0\SERVER\DATABASE\
OXE_BACKUP_CURRENT.LOG.
Press any key to continue ...
```

NOTE
Notice that a hot database backup does not require a database shutdown; during a hot database backup, all current database sessions and applications can continue to perform work as normal.

EXERCISE 9.9: Confirm Successful Log Archiving

When you enable media recovery, Oracle XE automatically archives filled online log groups to the flash recovery area. To confirm that Oracle XE is archiving logs as expected, use Windows Explorer to display the files in the XE\ARCHIVELOG subdirectory of the flash recovery area. The previous hot backup should have forced a log switch that created one or more archived logs, as shown in Figure 9-16.

Take a moment to closely review the names of your database's archived log files; the names should be similar to the following:

O1_MF_1_**56**_25XD4P2P_.ARC

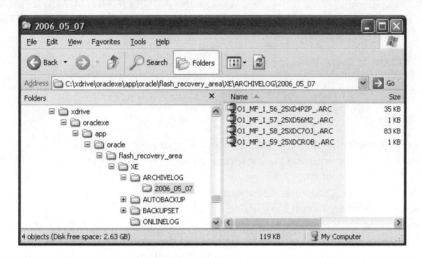

FIGURE 9-16. *After switching to ARCHIVELOG mode and making a hot database backup, confirm the successful archiving of log groups in the flash recovery area.*

Notice that the generated filename includes the sequence number (in bold) that corresponds to the online log group that was archived.

EXERCISE 9.10: Create Log Groups with Multiple Members

As you already know, the default online log groups for an Oracle XE database have only one member each. If the disk containing the log members were to crash, you might lose the data necessary to subsequently recover the database. In this exercise, you'll learn how to add members to log groups and establish a more fault-tolerant online log configuration.

For ideal fault tolerance, each log group should have two or more members, and should store the members of a log group on a mutually exclusive set of disk storage systems. For example, if a log group has two members, place each member of the log group on different disks managed by different controllers—do not place them on the same disk, or on different disks controlled by the same disk controller.

NOTE
If your starter database operates on a computer with only one disk, then you cannot fulfill the recommended log group configuration. However, you can still learn how to configure log groups with multiple members by completing this exercise—just store the log members somewhere on the same disk, but realize that this is not the optimal configuration.

To add log members to a log group, you use the ADD LOGFILE MEMBER clause of the SQL command ALTER DATABASE. A simplified syntax listing of the ADD LOGFILE MEMBER clause follows:

```
ALTER DATABASE
  ADD LOGFILE MEMBER
  ('filename' [REUSE] [,'filename' [REUSE]] ... )
  TO { GROUP integer
     | 'filename' }
```

Notice that you can specify filenames for one or more new members of a log group, and that you can indicate the log group to target by the group's unique ID or by specifying the filename of one of the existing members in the group. Also notice that you do not have to indicate a file size for the new members—Oracle automatically makes the new members match the existing member(s) in the group.

Before adding log members to your database's log groups, confirm the group numbers for your database's online log groups—when you moved the log groups earlier, it's likely that the identifying group numbers changed since their original counterparts. A database's data dictionary contains several views that you can query to display information about a database's online log groups, including the V$LOG and V$LOGFILE views. Using your current SYSDBA-privileged SQL*Plus session, enter the following query to display the names of all log members in each group of your starter database:

```
COLUMN member FORMAT a50;

SELECT group#, member FROM v$logfile
  ORDER BY group#;
```

NOTE
*The FORMAT parameter of the SQL*Plus command COLUMN, used in the previous example, lets you set the display width of a column in a query's result set.*

Your results should be similar to the following:

```
    GROUP# MEMBER
---------- --------------------------------------------------
         1 C:\XDRIVE\ORACLEXE\APP\ORACLE\FLASH_RECOVERY_AREA\
           XE\ONLINELOG\O1_MF_1_25XC7HHD_.LOG
         2 C:\XDRIVE\ORACLEXE\APP\ORACLE\FLASH_RECOVERY_AREA\
           XE\ONLINELOG\O1_MF_2_25XC4XOQ_.LOG
```

The preceding example results remind you that there are two online log groups and that the group numbers are 1 and 2. Considering the preceding results, enter the following commands to add a new member to each group, placing each new member in the old flash recovery area:

```
ALTER DATABASE
  ADD LOGFILE MEMBER
    'C:\oraclexe\app\oracle\flash_recovery_area\XE\ONLINELOG\O1_MF_1_B.log'
    REUSE
    TO GROUP 1;

ALTER DATABASE
  ADD LOGFILE MEMBER
    'C:\oraclexe\app\oracle\flash_recovery_area\XE\ONLINELOG\O1_MF_2_B.log'
    REUSE
    TO GROUP 2;
```

At this point, each log group in the starter database's online log has two members—one on the primary disk drive and one on the secondary disk drive. If one of the drives were to crash and no other part of the database were affected, Oracle could continue to log transactions using the intact members of the online log groups. You can confirm the new configuration by repeating the previous query—the results of this query should be similar to the following:

```
     GROUP# MEMBER
---------- -------------------------------------------------
         1 C:\XDRIVE\ORACLEXE\APP\ORACLE\FLASH_RECOVERY_AREA\
           XE\ONLINELOG\O1_MF_1_25XC7HHD_.LOG
         1 C:\ORACLEXE\APP\ORACLE\FLASH_RECOVERY_AREA\XE\ONLI
           NELOG\O1_MF_1_B.LOG
         2 C:\ORACLEXE\APP\ORACLE\FLASH_RECOVERY_AREA\XE\ONLI
           NELOG\O1_MF_2_B.LOG
         2 C:\XDRIVE\ORACLEXE\APP\ORACLE\FLASH_RECOVERY_AREA\
           XE\ONLINELOG\O1_MF_2_25XC4XOQ_.LOG
```

TIP
Again, any time that you make a structural or operational change to your database (such as adding a member to a log group), it is a good idea to back up the database both before and after the change so that you can recover the database if a problem occurs.

EXERCISE 9.11: Mirror the Database Control File

As you learned earlier, the default configuration of an Oracle XE database uses a lone copy of the database's control file, which resides in the same disk as the database's data files (ORACLE_BASE\oradata\XE\CONTROL.DBF). If this disk were to crash, the database's data files and current control file would be lost and database recovery could be difficult.

Considering the default database configuration's vulnerability, this exercise teaches you how to mirror the database's control file by creating a new control file copy on a different disk drive and configuring Oracle XE to concurrently maintain both copies of the control file. To accomplish this task, you need to perform the following steps:

1. Adjust the CONTROL_FILES initialization parameter in your database's parameter file.

2. Shut down the database cleanly.

3. Copy the current control file to a new location.

4. Restart the database.

First, use your existing SYSDBA-privileged SQL*Plus session to modify the setting of the CONTROL_FILES parameter in the database's parameter file. Set the parameter to a comma-separated list of fully specified filenames that includes the current control file and the new copy of the control file that you intend to create. For example, if your database's existing control file is C:\oraclexe\oradata\XE\CONTROL.DBF and you plan to make a copy of the control file as C:\xdrive\oraclexe\oradata\XE\CONTROL.DBF, enter the following ALTER SYSTEM statement:

```
ALTER SYSTEM
  SET control_files =
  'C:\oraclexe\oradata\XE\CONTROL.DBF',
  'C:\xdrive\oraclexe\oradata\XE\CONTROL.DBF'
SCOPE = SPFILE;
```

The preceding example command highlights (in bold) the use of the SCOPE parameter in the ALTER SYSTEM statement—because the CONTROL_FILES parameter is not dynamically modifiable (you cannot modify the setting of the parameter for the current instance), you must use the SCOPE parameter to limit the configuration change to the database's static parameter file.

Once you make the configuration change to the CONTROL_FILES parameter, use your SYSDBA-privileged SQL*Plus session to shut down the current database instance cleanly to continue:

```
SHUTDOWN IMMEDIATE;
```

The next step is to make a copy of the existing control file in the new location. For example, using Windows Explorer or a Command Prompt, copy the file C:\oraclexe\oradata\XE\CONTROL.DBF to C:\xdrive\oraclexe\oradata\XE\CONTROL.DBF—if these filenames and directories do not match those on your computer, make appropriate substitutions and note the new file locations.

CAUTION
Make sure that you physically copy the control file—do not create a Windows shortcut in the new location.

At this point, you can restart the instance and open the database using your current SYSDBA-privileged SQL*Plus session. Start up a new instance and mount and open the database by using the OPEN option of the SQL*Plus command STARTUP:

```
STARTUP OPEN;
```

Once the database opens, you can confirm the mirrored configuration of your control file copies by repeating the steps in Exercise 9.2 to use the Database Home Page, or you can use your SQL*Plus session to submit the following query that targets the V$PARAMETER data dictionary view:

```
COLUMN name FORMAT a13;
COLUMN value FORMAT a40;

SELECT name, value FROM v$parameter
 WHERE name = 'control_files';
```

Your results should be similar to the following:

```
NAME          VALUE
------------- ----------------------------------------
control_files C:\ORACLEXE\ORADATA\XE\CONTROL.DBF, C:\X
              DRIVE\ORACLEXE\ORADATA\XE\CONTROL.DBF
```

Backing Up Databases with Recovery Manager

The previous section includes exercises showing you how to quickly back up an Oracle XE database using a Microsoft Windows menu option that calls a batch file to execute RMAN commands. While this menu option and batch file make it easy to get started using RMAN, there's no substitute for learning how to use RMAN yourself and the basic RMAN commands for database backup.

This section's exercises teach you how to get started using RMAN with Oracle XE. You will learn how to do the following:

- Start RMAN

- Connect to the target database

- Configure RMAN settings

■ List information about backups

■ Create a compressed backup of the database

■ Report obsolete backups

■ Fine tune the standard Oracle XE backup scripts

■ Automate database backups

EXERCISE 9.12: Start Recovery Manager

To begin using RMAN, open a Microsoft Windows Command Prompt window. At the command prompt, start RMAN using the NOCATALOG run-time parameter to start RMAN without a recovery catalog:

```
RMAN NOCATALOG
```

Once RMAN starts, you should see a message similar to the following, as well as the RMAN command prompt:

```
Recovery Manager: Release 10.2.0.1.0 - Production ...

Copyright (c) 1982, 2005, Oracle.  All rights reserved.

RMAN>
```

EXERCISE 9.13: Connect to the Target Database

After you start RMAN, you need to connect to the target database—the database with which you want to work. To connect to a target database, you use the RMAN command CONNECT. For the purposes of the exercises in this chapter, the abbreviated syntax of the CONNECT command is as follows when using RMAN with the target database's control file (that is, without a recovery catalog):

```
CONNECT TARGET username[/password] [@service_name]
```

For example, enter the following command to connect to your local starter database using a SYSDBA-privileged session. Notice that no service name is necessary if you are using RMAN on the same computer that is executing only an Oracle XE database instance (in other words, no other Oracle database instances are on the same computer).

```
CONNECT TARGET sys
```

If your Microsoft Windows session is a member of the ORA_DBA group, you can more simply establish a SYSDBA-privileged session as follows:

```
CONNECT TARGET /
```

In either case, RMAN establishes a new session and displays messages similar to the following:

```
connected to target database: XE (DBID=2465914590)
using target database control file instead of recovery catalog
```

Now that you are connected to the target database, you can enter RMAN commands to work with the target database.

EXERCISE 9.14: Display and Configure Persistent Recovery Manager Settings

The routine operations that you complete with RMAN are easier to perform when you specify and rely on a consistent set of RMAN configuration settings. For example, suppose that whenever you make a routine database backup, you want to write the backup set to the flash recovery area, compress backups to conserve disk space, and automatically back up the database's control file. To set defaults for settings such as these, you can use the RMAN command CONFIGURE to specify persistent RMAN settings in the database's control file, and use the RMAN command SHOW to display these settings. For example, enter the following command to display a complete list of the current set of RMAN persistent settings:

```
SHOW ALL;
```

The results of this command should be similar to the following for an Oracle XE database:

```
RMAN configuration parameters are:
CONFIGURE RETENTION POLICY TO REDUNDANCY 2;
CONFIGURE BACKUP OPTIMIZATION OFF; # default
CONFIGURE DEFAULT DEVICE TYPE TO DISK; # default
CONFIGURE CONTROLFILE AUTOBACKUP OFF;
CONFIGURE CONTROLFILE AUTOBACKUP FORMAT FOR DEVICE TYPE DISK TO '%F';
 # default
CONFIGURE DEVICE TYPE DISK PARALLELISM 1 BACKUP TYPE TO BACKUPSET;
 # default
```

Starting RMAN and Connecting to the Target Database in One Step

You can start RMAN and connect to the target database all in one step by using the TARGET command-line parameter. For example, the following command accomplishes the same thing accomplished by the previous two exercises:

```
RMAN NOCATALOG TARGET sys
```

```
CONFIGURE DATAFILE BACKUP COPIES FOR DEVICE TYPE DISK TO 1; # default
CONFIGURE ARCHIVELOG BACKUP COPIES FOR DEVICE TYPE DISK TO 1; # default
CONFIGURE MAXSETSIZE TO UNLIMITED; # default
CONFIGURE ENCRYPTION FOR DATABASE OFF; # default
CONFIGURE ENCRYPTION ALGORITHM 'AES128'; # default
CONFIGURE ARCHIVELOG DELETION POLICY TO NONE; # default
CONFIGURE SNAPSHOT CONTROLFILE NAME TO 'C:\ORACLEXE\APP\ORACLE\PRODUCT\
   10.2.0\SERVER\DATABASE\SNCFXE.ORA'; # default
```

The SHOW command displays the text "# default" after each configuration setting that currently matches the default setting. The following list briefly explains a few RMAN configuration settings:

- **RETENTION POLICY TO**   Indicates a retention policy for data file and control file backups and image copies. For example, the default setting indicates that a data file backup is obsolete when two newer backups of the same data file already exist.

- **DEVICE TYPE**   Configures the attributes of automatic channels; RMAN relies on these settings to support operations that do not explicitly allocate one or more channels. By default, RMAN allocates one disk channel per operation (PARALLELISM 1) and creates backup sets rather than image copies or compressed backup sets (BACKUP TYPE TO BACKUPSET).

- **DEFAULT DEVICE TYPE TO**   Indicates the default device type that RMAN uses for automatic channels. As indicated in the previous output, the default device type for automatic channels is DISK (rather than TAPE). When the default device type for automatic channels is DISK, RMAN automatically writes backup sets to the flash recovery area unless you explicitly configure one or more automatic disk channels to another location. Because we want to use the flash recovery area for all database backups, the default configuration is acceptable.

- **CONTROLFILE AUTOBACKUP and CONTROLFILE AUTOBACKUP FORMAT FOR DEVICE TYPE**   Pertain to automatic control file backups. When CONTROLFILE AUTOBACKUP is set to ON, the setting of CONTROLFILE AUTOBACKUP FORMAT FOR DEVICE TYPE determines the default filename format for automatic control file backups on the specified device type (for example, DISK); when using a flash recovery area, RMAN creates automatic control file backups in the flash recovery area.

- **ARCHIVELOG DELETION POLICY TO**   Indicates the deletion policy for archived logs in the flash recovery area. The default setting NONE indicates that Oracle can delete archived logs from the flash recovery area that have been permanently backed up to another location (for example, tape) and that are obsolete based on the retention policy.

Refer to the *Oracle Database Backup and Recovery Reference* for complete information about all persistent RMAN settings.

To change the setting of a persistent RMAN setting, use the RMAN command CONFIGURE. For example, to enable automatic control file backups to the flash recovery area, execute the following command:

```
CONFIGURE CONTROLFILE AUTOBACKUP ON;
```

The expected output is as follows:

```
old RMAN configuration parameters:
CONFIGURE CONTROLFILE AUTOBACKUP OFF;
new RMAN configuration parameters:
CONFIGURE CONTROLFILE AUTOBACKUP ON;
new RMAN configuration parameters are successfully stored
```

Execute the following command to configure the default type of disk backup as compressed backup sets (rather than image copies or uncompressed backup sets):

```
CONFIGURE DEVICE TYPE DISK BACKUP TYPE TO COMPRESSED BACKUPSET;
```

The expected output is as follows:

```
new RMAN configuration parameters:
CONFIGURE DEVICE TYPE DISK BACKUP TYPE TO COMPRESSED BACKUPSET
 PARALLELISM 1;
new RMAN configuration parameters are successfully stored
```

EXERCISE 9.15: Back Up a Database

To back up a database, RMAN must perform two steps:

1. Allocate at least one channel for output. As you learned in the previous exercise, RMAN automatically allocates a single channel to the flash recovery area when you execute an operation such as a backup but do not explicitly allocate a channel yourself with an ALLOCATE command.

2. Back up the database using the allocated channel(s). To back up a database, you use the RMAN command BACKUP. For the purposes of this exercise, concentrate on the abbreviated syntax of the BACKUP command, as follows, to back up the entire database, including all data files and the database's current control file:

    ```
    BACKUP [FULL|INCREMENTAL LEVEL [=] integer] DATABASE
     [TAG [=] tag]
    ```

The following list describes the elements of the preceding command:

- **FULL option** Indicates that you want to create a full database backup set. The INCREMENTAL LEVEL parameter indicates that you want to create an incremental backup set of the specified level. By default, RMAN makes a full backup set if you specify neither the FULL option nor the INCREMENTAL LEVEL parameter.

- **DATABASE keyword** A shortcut that indicates you want to create a data file backup set containing all of the database's data files.

- **TAG parameter** Indicates a unique name that you can use to identify the backup. Carefully consider the naming convention that you use for tags. For example, a good naming convention for tags indicates whether the database is open or closed, the type of backup (database, tablespace, full, incremental, and so on), and a unique ID number.

For example, execute the following command to make a full data file backup set. The simple command defers to the persistent RMAN settings to allocate a single disk channel to the flash recovery area and create a compressed backup set.

```
BACKUP DATABASE;
```

This command will back up the database whether it is open (assuming that you completed the earlier exercises in this chapter and that the database operates with media recovery enabled) or closed. The output of this command should be similar to the following. As before, I've embedded comments (in bold) to explain things as they happen.

```
Starting backup at ...
-- ALLOCATE A SINGLE CHANNEL TO THE FLASH RECOVERY AREA.
allocated channel: ORA_DISK_1
channel ORA_DISK_1: sid=24 devtype=DISK
-- CREATE A COMPRESSED FULL DATA FILE BACKUP SET THAT INCLUDES ALL
-- DATA FILES THAT CORRESPOND TO PERMANENT TABLESPACES.
channel ORA_DISK_1: starting compressed full datafile backupset
channel ORA_DISK_1: specifying datafile(s) in backupset
input datafile fno=00001 name=C:\ORACLEXE\ORADATA\XE\SYSTEM.DBF
input datafile fno=00003 name=C:\ORACLEXE\ORADATA\XE\SYSAUX.DBF
input datafile fno=00002 name=C:\ORACLEXE\ORADATA\XE\UNDO.DBF
input datafile fno=00004 name=C:\ORACLEXE\ORADATA\XE\USERS.DBF
channel ORA_DISK_1: starting piece 1 at ...
channel ORA_DISK_1: finished piece 1 at ...
-- RMAN ASSIGNS A DEFAULT TAG NAME TO THE BACKUP SET BECAUSE THE
-- BACKUP COMMAND DID NOT SPECIFY A TAG PARAMETER.
```

```
piece handle=C:\XDRIVE\ORACLEXE\APP\ORACLE\FLASH_RECOVERY_AREA\XE\
BACKUPSET\2006_05_13\O1_MF_NNNDF_TAG20060513T170525_26DLJQOY_.BKP
tag=TAG20060513T170525 comment=NONE
-- THE COMPRESSED BACKUP TOOK SLIGHTLY LONGER TO COMPLETE THAN
-- PREVIOUS, UNCOMPRESSED BACKUPS.
channel ORA_DISK_1: backup set complete, elapsed time: 00:02:17
Finished backup at ...

-- AUTOMATICALLY BACK UP THE CONTROL FILE.
Starting Control File and SPFILE Autobackup at ...
piece handle=C:\XDRIVE\ORACLEXE\APP\ORACLE\FLASH_RECOVERY_AREA\XE\
AUTOBACKUP\2006_05_13\O1_MF_S_590346464_26DLO1SC_.BKP comment=NONE
Finished Control File and SPFILE Autobackup at ...
```

To complete this exercise, use Windows Explorer to compare the file sizes of the backup pieces that correspond to the new compressed backup set and the previous uncompressed backup sets—the compressed backup set should use considerably less disk space.

EXERCISE 9.16: Back Up an Individual Tablespace

Exercise 9.15 shows you how to back up the entire database, including all of the database's tablespaces. When a tablespace is modified more than others, you might want to back it up more frequently than others to reduce the time necessary to recover the tablespace should it become damaged.

You can use the TABLESPACE parameter of the RMAN command BACKUP to back up a specific tablespace, as the following abbreviated syntax of the BACKUP command illustrates:

```
BACKUP [FULL|INCREMENTAL LEVEL [=] integer] TABLESPACE tablespace
  [TAG [=] tag]
  [FORMAT [=] 'output_format']
```

Just as with a database backup, you can create a tablespace backup while the database is open and while the tablespace is online, if the database operates with media recovery enabled. For example, enter the following command to make a full tablespace backup set for the target database's USERS tablespace:

```
BACKUP TABLESPACE users
  TAG open_tbs_users_full_1;
```

The output of this command should be similar to the following:

```
Starting backup at ...
using channel ORA_DISK_1
channel ORA_DISK_1: starting compressed full datafile backupset
```

```
channel ORA_DISK_1: specifying datafile(s) in backupset
input datafile fno=00004 name=C:\ORACLEXE\ORADATA\XE\USERS.DBF
channel ORA_DISK_1: starting piece 1 at ...
channel ORA_DISK_1: finished piece 1 at ...
-- RMAN USES THE TAG SPECIFIED BY THE BACKUP COMMAND.
piece handle=C:\XDRIVE\ORACLEXE\APP\ORACLE\FLASH_RECOVERY_AREA\XE\
BACKUPSET\2006_05_13\O1_MF_NNNDF_OPEN_TBS_USERS_FULL__26DMBRVT_.BKP
tag=OPEN_TBS_USERS_FULL_1
comment=NONE
channel ORA_DISK_1: backup set complete, elapsed time: 00:00:07
Finished backup at ...

Starting Control File and SPFILE Autobackup at 13-MAY-06
piece handle=C:\XDRIVE\ORACLEXE\APP\ORACLE\FLASH_RECOVERY_AREA\XE\
AUTOBACKUP\2006_05_13\O1_MF_S_590347167_26DMC1NQ_.BKP comment=NONE
Finished Control File and SPFILE Autobackup at ...
```

EXERCISE 9.17: Back Up Archived Log Files

Earlier exercises in this chapter explain how to enable media recovery for your database and automatically archive online log groups as they fill. To fully protect your database's archived log files and free up disk space in the archiving destination, you should periodically use RMAN to back up the archived log files as part of an archived log backup set. You can create an archived log backup set with the following abbreviated syntax of the RMAN command BACKUP:

```
BACKUP ARCHIVELOG ALL
  [FORMAT [=] 'output_format']
  [DELETE INPUT]
```

This simple version of the BACKUP command uses the ALL option to indicate that the backup set should contain a copy of all archived log files present in the archived log destination. If the backup completes successfully and you specify the DELETE INPUT option, RMAN deletes the archived log files included in the backup set from the archive destination. Also notice that when you create an archived log backup set, you cannot specify a TAG parameter to name the backup set, nor can you specify the INCREMENTAL parameter—by default, all archived log backup sets are full backups.

To complete this exercise, use Windows Explorer to observe the archived log files stored in the various subdirectories of the XE\ARCHIVELOG directory within the flash recovery area. Then, execute the following command to back up all existing archived logs for the target database:

```
BACKUP ARCHIVELOG ALL
    DELETE INPUT;
```

The output from this command should be similar to the following (as always, my comments are embedded in bold):

```
Starting backup at ...
current log archived
-- ALLOCATE THE AUTOMATIC CHANNEL TO THE FLASH RECOVERY AREA.
using channel ORA_DISK_1
-- THE BACKUP SET IS COMPRESSED, AS CONFIGURED EARLIER.
channel ORA_DISK_1: starting compressed archive log backupset
-- DETERMINE WHAT ARCHIVED LOGS ARE IN THE ARCHIVING DESTINATION.
channel ORA_DISK_1: specifying archive log(s) in backup set
input archive log thread=1 sequence=56 recid=5 stamp=589848278
input archive log thread=1 sequence=57 recid=6 stamp=589848294
input archive log thread=1 sequence=58 recid=7 stamp=589848488
input archive log thread=1 sequence=59 recid=8 stamp=589848505
input archive log thread=1 sequence=60 recid=9 stamp=590140134
input archive log thread=1 sequence=61 recid=10 stamp=590216001
input archive log thread=1 sequence=62 recid=11 stamp=590277643
input archive log thread=1 sequence=63 recid=12 stamp=590347474
channel ORA_DISK_1: starting piece 1 at ...
channel ORA_DISK_1: finished piece 1 at ...
-- CREATE THE BACKUP PIECE IN THE FLASH RECOVERY AREA AND ASSIGN
-- A SYSTEM-GENERATED TAG NAME.
piece handle=C:\XDRIVE\ORACLEXE\APP\ORACLE\FLASH_RECOVERY_AREA\XE\
BACKUPSET\2006_05_13\O1_MF_ANNNN_TAG20060513T172434_26DMNOLB_.BKP
tag=TAG20060513T172434 comment=NONE
channel ORA_DISK_1: backup set complete, elapsed time: 00:00:57
-- NOW THAT THE BACKUP SET COMPLETED WITHOUT ERROR, RMAN CAN SAFELY
-- DELETE ALL ARCHIVED LOGS THAT HAVE BEEN BACKED UP. THIS RELEASES
-- SPACE IN THE FLASH RECOVERY AREA.
channel ORA_DISK_1: deleting archive log(s)
archive log filename=C:\XDRIVE\ORACLEXE\APP\ORACLE\FLASH_RECOVERY_AREA\
XE\ARCHIVELOG\2006_05_07\O1_MF_1_56_25XD4P2P_.ARC recid=5 stamp=589848278
archive log filename=C:\XDRIVE\ORACLEXE\APP\ORACLE\FLASH_RECOVERY_AREA\
XE\ARCHIVELOG\2006_05_07\O1_MF_1_57_25XD56M2_.ARC recid=6 stamp=589848294
archive log filename=C:\XDRIVE\ORACLEXE\APP\ORACLE\FLASH_RECOVERY_AREA\
XE\ARCHIVELOG\2006_05_07\O1_MF_1_58_25XDC7OJ_.ARC recid=7 stamp=589848488
archive log filename=C:\XDRIVE\ORACLEXE\APP\ORACLE\FLASH_RECOVERY_AREA\
XE\ARCHIVELOG\2006_05_07\O1_MF_1_59_25XDCROB_.ARC recid=8 stamp=589848505
archive log filename=C:\XDRIVE\ORACLEXE\APP\ORACLE\FLASH_RECOVERY_AREA\
XE\ARCHIVELOG\2006_05_11\O1_MF_1_60_2669542Z_.ARC recid=9 stamp=590140134
archive log filename=C:\XDRIVE\ORACLEXE\APP\ORACLE\FLASH_RECOVERY_AREA\
XE\ARCHIVELOG\2006_05_12\O1_MF_1_61_268M7L00_.ARC recid=10 stamp=590216001
archive log filename=C:\XDRIVE\ORACLEXE\APP\ORACLE\FLASH_RECOVERY_AREA\
XE\ARCHIVELOG\2006_05_12\O1_MF_1_62_26BHG03K_.ARC recid=11 stamp=590277643
```

```
archive log filename=C:\XDRIVE\ORACLEXE\APP\ORACLE\FLASH_RECOVERY_AREA\
XE\ARCHIVELOG\2006_05_13\O1_MF_1_63_26DMNC51_.ARC recid=12 stamp=590347474
Finished backup at ...

-- AUTOMATIC CONTROL FILE BACKUPS ARE ENABLED, SO BACK IT UP.
Starting Control File and SPFILE Autobackup at ...
piece handle=C:\XDRIVE\ORACLEXE\APP\ORACLE\FLASH_RECOVERY_AREA\XE\
AUTOBACKUP\2006_05_13\O1_MF_S_590347536_26DMPKQJ_.BKP comment=NONE
Finished Control File and SPFILE Autobackup at ...
```

To complete this exercise, use Windows Explorer to again check the files in the XE\ARCHIVELOG subdirectories of the flash recovery area—confirm that RMAN has deleted the archived log files after backing them up.

EXERCISE 9.18: List Information About Backup Sets

After you use RMAN to make data file and archived log backup sets, you can generate reports to display useful information about backup sets with the following abbreviated syntax of the RMAN command LIST:

```
LIST BACKUP
  [OF
  { DATABASE [SKIP TABLESPACE tablespace [, tablespace] ... ]
  | TABLESPACE tablespace [, tablespace] ...
  | DATAFILE {'filename'|integer} [,{'filename'|integer}] ...
  | ARCHIVELOG ALL }]
  [TAG [=] tag]
```

The following explains the clauses and parameters of the LIST command:

■ If you do not specify the OF parameter, the LIST command displays information about all backup sets.

■ You can specify the OF parameter to display information about backup sets that contain all data files in the database (DATABASE option), one or more data files of a tablespace (TABLESPACE parameter), a specific data file or list of data files (DATAFILE parameter), and archived log backup sets (ARCHIVELOG option).

■ You can specify the TAG parameter to display information about a specific data file backup set.

For example, enter the following LIST command to display information about the data file backup sets that contain the data file for the SYSTEM tablespace:

```
LIST BACKUP
  OF DATAFILE 'C:\ORACLEXE\ORADATA\XE\SYSTEM.DBF';
```

The output for this LIST command should appear somewhat similar to the following—for readability, some of the output has been truncated:

```
List of Backup Sets
===================

BS Key  Type LV Size        Device Type Elapsed Time Completion Time
------- ---- -- ---------- ----------- ------------ ---------------
9       Full    581.36M    DISK          00:01:42    ...
        BP Key: 9   Status: AVAILABLE  Compressed: NO  Tag: TAG2006...
        Piece Name: C:\XDRIVE\ORACLEXE\APP\ORACLE\FLASH_RECOVERY_AREA\XE\
        BACKUPSET\2006_05_07\O1_MF_NNNDF_TAG20060507T224238_25XD0ZNT_.BKP
  List of Datafiles in backup set 9
  File LV Type Ckp SCN    Ckp Time  Name
  ---- -- ---- ---------- --------- ----
  1       Full 2376872       ...       C:\ORACLEXE\ORADATA\XE\SYSTEM.DBF

BS Key  Type LV Size        Device Type Elapsed Time Completion Time
------- ---- -- ---------- ----------- ------------ ---------------
11      Full    581.36M    DISK          00:01:36    ...
        BP Key: 11   Status: AVAILABLE  Compressed: NO  Tag: TAG2006...
        Piece Name: C:\XDRIVE\ORACLEXE\APP\ORACLE\FLASH_RECOVERY_AREA\XE\
        BACKUPSET\2006_05_07\O1_MF_NNNDF_TAG20060507T224611_25XD7O8K_.BKP
  List of Datafiles in backup set 11
  File LV Type Ckp SCN    Ckp Time  Name
  ---- -- ---- ---------- --------- ----
  1       Full 2377107       ...       C:\ORACLEXE\ORADATA\XE\SYSTEM.DBF

BS Key  Type LV Size        Device Type Elapsed Time Completion Time
------- ---- -- ---------- ----------- ------------ ---------------
13      Full    107.16M    DISK          00:02:15    ...
        BP Key: 13   Status: AVAILABLE  Compressed: YES  Tag: TAG2006...
        Piece Name: C:\XDRIVE\ORACLEXE\APP\ORACLE\FLASH_RECOVERY_AREA\XE\
        BACKUPSET\2006_05_13\O1_MF_NNNDF_TAG20060513T170525_26DLJQOY_.BKP
  List of Datafiles in backup set 13
  File LV Type Ckp SCN    Ckp Time  Name
  ---- -- ---- ---------- --------- ----
  1       Full 2476336       ...       C:\ORACLEXE\ORADATA\XE\SYSTEM.DBF
```

The purpose of the columns in the report should be fairly obvious, given your current understanding of RMAN and the commands that you have used so far in this chapter's exercises. Using the syntax listing at the beginning of this exercise, experiment with some other variations of the LIST command to see what information you can display about your current data file backup sets.

TIP
The LIST command often displays information that is several screens long and wider than the default Windows Command Prompt window. In that case, use the Command Window menu to alter the layout properties for the window. Specifically, use the Layout page of the Properties property sheet to increase the window's screen buffer width and height, as well as the window's width and height. Alternatively, you can start RMAN with the LOG command-line parameter to specify a log file for RMAN output. See your Oracle documentation for more information about RMAN's command-line parameters.

EXERCISE 9.19: Report Important Status Information for a Database

The LIST command that the previous exercise introduces does nothing more than read the control file to display basic information that you might already know about available backup sets. The RMAN command REPORT is another useful tool that you can use to analyze information in the control file and generate useful reports that will help you to better protect your database. For the purposes of this introductory exercise, focus on the following abbreviated version of the REPORT command syntax:

```
REPORT
{ NEED BACKUP {INCREMENTAL|DAYS|REDUNDANCY} [=] integer
  [ { DATABASE [SKIP TABLESPACE tablespace [, tablespace] ... ]
    | TABLESPACE tablespace [, tablespace] ...
    | DATAFILE {'filename'|integer} [,{'filename'|integer}] ... } ]
| OBSOLETE REDUNDANCY [=] integer }
```

The NEED BACKUP clause indicates that you want to generate a report of all data files that need a backup. If database recovery time is a critical concern, use the INCREMENTAL parameter to report the data files that will need more than a specified number of incremental backup sets during recovery, or use the DAYS parameter to report the data files whose recovery will require more than a specified number of days' worth of archived logs. For example, when safety is your concern, use the REDUNDANCY parameter of the NEED BACKUP clause of the REPORT command to report the data files with less than a specified number of redundant backups. Assuming that your database protection policy requires that you preserve the four most recent backups of every data file in the database, enter the following command to report the data files that do not meet the policy:

```
REPORT NEED BACKUP REDUNDANCY=4;
```

If you've completed the earlier exercises in this chapter, your report should be similar to the following listing. Notice that the starter database's USERS tablespace data file is missing from the report because you created a data file backup set for just this tablespace in Exercise 9.16.

```
Report of files with less than 4 redundant backups
File #bkps Name
---- ----- ------------------------------------
1    3     C:\ORACLEXE\ORADATA\XE\SYSTEM.DBF
2    3     C:\ORACLEXE\ORADATA\XE\UNDO.DBF
3    3     C:\ORACLEXE\ORADATA\XE\SYSAUX.DBF
```

What this report tells you is that to comply with your policy, you should create another data file backup set that contains the data files in the report.

NOTE
In addition to the INCREMENTAL, DAYS, or REDUNDANCY parameter of the NEED BACKUP clause for the REPORT command, you can specify a specific object to generate a more focused report (the entire database, specific tablespaces, or specific data files).

Alternatively, you can use the abbreviated form of the OBSOLETE clause to indicate that you want to report the obsolete backup sets and image copies considering a given threshold of redundancy. For example, enter the following REPORT command to display the backup sets and data file image copies that you can consider obsolete (and thus can delete) as long as there is at least one other backup set or data file image copy available to recover the database:

```
REPORT OBSOLETE REDUNDANCY = 1;
```

If you completed the earlier exercises in this chapter, your report should be similar to the following:

```
Report of obsolete backups and copies
Type                    Key    Completion Time    Filename/Handle
-------------------     ------ -----------------  --------------------
Backup Set              9      . . .
  Backup Piece          9      . . .                  C:\XDRIVE\ORACLEXE\APP\
ORACLE\FLASH_RECOVERY_AREA\XE\BACKUPSET\2006_05_07\O1_MF_NNNDF_TAG2006...
_.BKP
Backup Set              10     . . .
  Backup Piece          10     . . .                  C:\XDRIVE\ORACLEXE\APP\
ORACLE\FLASH_RECOVERY_AREA\XE\AUTOBACKUP\2006_05_07\
```

```
O1_MF_S_589848265_25XD4C69_.BKP
Backup Set            11    ...
   Backup Piece       11    ...                  C:\XDRIVE\ORACLEXE\APP\
ORACLE\FLASH_RECOVERY_AREA\XE\BACKUPSET\2006_05_07\
O1_MF_NNNDF_TAG20060507T224611_25XD7O8K_.BKP
Backup Set            12    ...
   Backup Piece       12    ...                  C:\XDRIVE\ORACLEXE\APP\
ORACLE\FLASH_RECOVERY_AREA\XE\AUTOBACKUP\2006_05_07\
O1_MF_S_589848478_25XDC081_.BKP
Backup Set            14    ...
   Backup Piece       14    ...                  C:\XDRIVE\ORACLEXE\APP\
ORACLE\FLASH_RECOVERY_AREA\XE\AUTOBACKUP\2006_05_13\
O1_MF_S_590346464_26DLO1SC_.BKP
Backup Set            16    ...
   Backup Piece       16    ...                  C:\XDRIVE\ORACLEXE\APP\
ORACLE\FLASH_RECOVERY_AREA\XE\AUTOBACKUP\2006_05_13\
O1_MF_S_590347167_26DMC1NQ_.BKP
```

A more realistic use of the preceding REPORT command would most likely specify a higher value for the REDUNDANCY parameter. An "obsolete" report is useful as you make more and more backup sets of your database. As you create newer data file backup sets, you can usually start deleting older "obsolete" data file backup sets beyond two or three levels of redundancy to reclaim storage space.

EXERCISE 9.20: Delete Obsolete Backup Sets

The previous exercise explains that as you make newer data file backup sets, you'll eventually want to delete older, redundant backup sets to reclaim valuable storage space. To delete a backup set, you can use the following abbreviated syntax of the RMAN command DELETE:

```
DELETE [NOPROMPT] OBSOLETE [REDUNDANCY[=]integer] ;
```

The NOPROMPT option instructs RMAN to avoid prompting you to confirm the deletion of backups—this option is necessary when including a DELETE command as part of an RMAN script. Use the OBSOLETE clause to delete obsolete backup pieces, image copies, etc., as indicated by the REDUNDANCY parameter; when you omit the REDUNDANCY parameter, RMAN considers the preconfigured retention policy in the control file.

To gain some experience manually deleting obsolete backups, enter the following command. Rather than rely on the configured retention policy of two redundant backups, this example considers a backup obsolete if there are at least three other, more recent backups of all files in the backup—this is necessary to preserve some obsolete backups for the purposes of a subsequent exercise.

```
DELETE OBSOLETE REDUNDANCY 4;
```

The output of the previous RMAN command should be similar to the following:

```
allocated channel: ORA_DISK_1
channel ORA_DISK_1: sid=26 devtype=DISK
Deleting the following obsolete backups and copies:
Type                    Key     Completion Time     Filename/Handle
--------------------    ------  ------------------  --------------------
Backup Set              10      ...
  Backup Piece          10      ...                 C:\XDRIVE\ORACLEXE\APP\
ORACLE\FLASH_RECOVERY_AREA\XE\AUTOBACKUP\2006_05_07\
O1_MF_S_589848265_25XD4C69_.BKP

Do you really want to delete the above objects (enter YES or NO)? YES
deleted backup piece
backup piece handle=C:\XDRIVE\ORACLEXE\APP\ORACLE\FLASH_RECOVERY_AREA\XE\
AUTOBACKUP\2006_05_07\O1_MF_S_589848265_25XD4C69_.BKP recid=10
stamp=589848267

Deleted 1 objects
```

This exercise is a quick introduction to just one form of the RMAN command DELETE. Make sure that you read your Oracle documentation to learn more about the many other clauses, parameters, and options of the DELETE command that you can use to manage database backups.

EXERCISE 9.21: Understand Flash Recovery Area Space Usage

The previous exercise explains the procedure for manually deleting obsolete backups. While you could try to remember to manually delete obsolete backups occasionally or include DELETE OBSOLETE ... commands in an RMAN script that you use to automate backups, none of this is necessary. As explained previously in this chapter, Oracle automatically manages the reuse of space in the flash recovery area. Here's how it works:

1. According to your database protection policy, use RMAN to back up the database and archived logs in the flash recovery area.

2. As more and more backups accumulate in the flash recovery area, Oracle automatically maintains a list of obsolete backups, as determined by the preconfigured retention policy. The space occupied by obsolete backups is considered *reclaimable*.

3. When all flash recovery area space is in use and you attempt to make a new backup or when Oracle needs more space to archive a log file, Oracle automatically reuses reclaimable space.

To view information about flash recovery area space usage, query the V$RECOVERY_FILE_DEST data dictionary view. For example, use your current SQL*Plus session to execute the following query:

```
SELECT space_limit, space_used, space_reclaimable
  FROM v$recovery_file_dest;
```

The following results are representative of what you might see:

```
SPACE_LIMIT SPACE_USED SPACE_RECLAIMABLE
----------- ---------- -----------------
 1.0737E+10 1514662400         623853568
```

The unit for all space information in the V$RECOVERY_FILE_DEST view is bytes. In the preceding example output, the space limit for the flash recovery area is 10GB, the amount of space currently in use is approximately 1.5GB, and the amount of space occupied by obsolete backups (in other words, the reclaimable space) is approximately 620MB.

CAUTION
Oracle does not ever consider the space occupied by archived log files as reclaimable. To make sure that archived logs do not continue to accumulate and consume an ever-increasing amount of flash recovery area space, make sure to back up archived logs on a regular basis.

EXERCISE 9.22: Build a New Backup Script

In my opinion, the batch file provided with Oracle XE to back up the database has a few things that you can improve upon:

- The batch file does not consider archived log files. Therefore, after you enable media recovery for a database, archived log files could eventually consume all flash recovery area space and halt database operation unless you remember to manually back up archived log files regularly.

- Every time the batch file executes, it overwrites several RMAN settings that you have explicitly set in the database's control file. For example, the batch file overwrites the retention policy with a retention policy that is embedded in the script. The RMAN settings that you configure in the control file should be set once according to your needs and then always used under normal circumstances, whether someone works with RMAN interactively on the command line or via scripts. When situations arise that have special needs, you should use special options of RMAN commands rather than overwrite persistent RMAN settings. For example, if you need to specifically allocate a channel to a location outside of the flash recovery area for a backup, you can issue an ALLOCATE command before starting the backup rather than modify the standard automatic channel configuration.

■ Rather than rely on the flash recovery area's automated mechanism for reusing reclaimable space occupied by obsolete backups, the script explicitly deletes obsolete backups after making a new backup.

This exercise teaches you how to build and execute a custom RMAN backup script to address the needs of a database protection policy that includes the following requirements:

■ The database must operate with media recovery enabled (in ARCHIVELOG mode).

■ All backups and archived logs must be maintained in the flash recovery area.

■ You must retain at least the most recent two backups for every database file.

■ You must retain backups of the archived log files necessary to recover a database by using either of the most recent two data file backups.

■ You must create a control file backup each time that you create a data file or archived log backup set.

As you should already understand from previous exercises in this chapter, database configuration settings and persistent RMAN settings can address most needs for this policy. Once these are set, the backup script that you build must simply back up the database and all corresponding archived log files. To begin, open your favorite text editor such as Notepad, Wordpad, etc. Then, enter the following script:

```
CONNECT TARGET /;
BACKUP DATABASE PLUS ARCHIVELOG DELETE INPUT;
```

That's it! The first command establishes a SYSDBA-privileged connection to the local XE database, assuming the script is executed by an operating system account that is a member of the ORA_DBA group. The second command uses the PLUS ARCHIVELOG and DELETE INPUT options of the BACKUP command to complete the following steps:

1. Create an archived log data file backup set including all archived logs in the flash recovery area, and then delete all archived logs that have been backed up.

2. Create a data file backup set.

Create a new directory, **ORACLE_BASE\app\oracle\admin\XE\scripts**, and then save the text file as **rman1.rcv** in the new directory.

To test the script, complete the following steps:

1. Exit your current RMAN session by using the EXIT command:

   ```
   EXIT;
   ```

2. Restart RMAN by using the CMDFILE and LOG command-line parameters. The CMDFILE parameter specifies an RMAN script to execute, and the LOG parameter indicates a log file to which you want to redirect RMAN output. For example, execute the following command:

   ```
   RMAN CMDFILE c:\oraclexe\app\oracle\admin\XE\scripts\rman1.rcv
   LOG c:\temp\rman1.rcv.log
   ```

When you execute an RMAN script, the output is minimal and the process appears to hang because RMAN does not update your display with specific messages as it works. Eventually, the script will complete. To confirm that the script does the job you expected, view the log file specified by the LOG parameter. The log file should contain a log of RMAN's actions that appears similar to the following:

```
Recovery Manager: Release 10.2.0.1.0 - Production on ...

Copyright (c) 1982, 2005, Oracle.  All rights reserved.

RMAN> CONNECT TARGET *
2> BACKUP DATABASE PLUS ARCHIVELOG DELETE INPUT;
3>
connected to target database: XE (DBID=2465914590)


Starting backup at ...
current log archived
using target database control file instead of recovery catalog
allocated channel: ORA_DISK_1
channel ORA_DISK_1: sid=26 devtype=DISK
channel ORA_DISK_1: starting compressed archive log backupset
channel ORA_DISK_1: specifying archive log(s) in backup set
input archive log thread=1 sequence=68 recid=17 stamp=590411811
channel ORA_DISK_1: starting piece 1 at ...
channel ORA_DISK_1: finished piece 1 at ...
piece handle=C:\XDRIVE\ORACLEXE\APP\ORACLE\FLASH_RECOVERY_AREA\XE\BACKUPSET\
2006_05_14\O1_MF_ANNNN_TAG20060514T111653_26GLH7JT_.BKP
tag=TAG20060514T111653 comment=NONE
channel ORA_DISK_1: backup set complete, elapsed time: 00:00:02
channel ORA_DISK_1: deleting archive log(s)
archive log
filename=C:\XDRIVE\ORACLEXE\APP\ORACLE\FLASH_RECOVERY_AREA\XE\ARCHIVELOG\
2006_05_14\O1_MF_1_68_26GLH2XR_.ARC recid=17 stamp=590411811
Finished backup at ...
```

Automating Database Backups

Once you create an RMAN backup script, it's a trivial task to automate database backups. Simply use your operating system's native job-scheduling facility to execute the RMAN command shown in the previous exercise. For example, on Microsoft Windows, you can use the Scheduled Tasks facility to create a daily Oracle XE database backup, as shown here.

```
Starting backup at ...
using channel ORA_DISK_1
channel ORA_DISK_1: starting compressed full datafile backupset
channel ORA_DISK_1: specifying datafile(s) in backupset
input datafile fno=00001 name=C:\ORACLEXE\ORADATA\XE\SYSTEM.DBF
input datafile fno=00003 name=C:\ORACLEXE\ORADATA\XE\SYSAUX.DBF
input datafile fno=00002 name=C:\ORACLEXE\ORADATA\XE\UNDO.DBF
input datafile fno=00004 name=C:\ORACLEXE\ORADATA\XE\USERS.DBF
channel ORA_DISK_1: starting piece 1 at ...
channel ORA_DISK_1: finished piece 1 at ...
piece handle=C:\XDRIVE\ORACLEXE\APP\ORACLE\FLASH_RECOVERY_AREA\XE\BACKUPSET\
```

```
2006_05_14\O1_MF_NNNDF_TAG20060514T111657_26GLHC2M_.BKP
tag=TAG20060514T111657 comment=NONE
channel ORA_DISK_1: backup set complete, elapsed time: 00:02:09
Finished backup at ...

Starting backup at ...
current log archived
using channel ORA_DISK_1
channel ORA_DISK_1: starting compressed archive log backupset
channel ORA_DISK_1: specifying archive log(s) in backup set
input archive log thread=1 sequence=69 recid=18 stamp=590411949
channel ORA_DISK_1: starting piece 1 at ...
channel ORA_DISK_1: finished piece 1 at ...
piece handle=C:\XDRIVE\ORACLEXE\APP\ORACLE\FLASH_RECOVERY_AREA\XE\BACKUPSET\
2006_05_14\O1_MF_ANNNN_TAG20060514T111909_26GLMHP0_.BKP
tag=TAG20060514T111909 comment=NONE
channel ORA_DISK_1: backup set complete, elapsed time: 00:00:02
channel ORA_DISK_1: deleting archive log(s)
archive log
filename=C:\XDRIVE\ORACLEXE\APP\ORACLE\FLASH_RECOVERY_AREA\XE\ARCHIVELOG\
2006_05_14\O1_MF_1_69_26GLMF3R_.ARC recid=18 stamp=590411949
Finished backup at ...

Starting Control File and SPFILE Autobackup at ...
piece handle=C:\XDRIVE\ORACLEXE\APP\ORACLE\FLASH_RECOVERY_AREA\XE\AUTOBACKUP\
2006_05_14\O1_MF_S_590411953_26GLMMKJ_.BKP comment=NONE
Finished Control File and SPFILE Autobackup at ...

Recovery Manager complete.
```

Additional Database Backup Topics

Previous sections in this chapter focus on the use of RMAN to create physical database backups of a database's key operational files, including the database's data files, archived log files, control file, and parameter file. The following sections address a few additional topics related to database backups that are important to consider.

Backups of Other Database-Related Files

RMAN does not back up many other types of files related to an Oracle database that are not required for database operation, including database password files, network configuration files, custom administrative scripts, etc. You can back up all other types of files that relate to a database without performing any special procedures—simply use operating system commands or a backup utility to create backups of these files.

Logical Database Backups

To supplement the physical backups of a database's data files, archived log groups, and the control file that you make with RMAN, you can make logical backups of an Oracle database's data. A *logical backup* is a backup of database information that corresponds to the specific schemas and schema objects in the database (for example, tables). To make and use logical database backups, you use the Oracle utilities Data Pump Export and Import.

The Data Pump Export Utility

Using Oracle's *Data Pump Export* utility, you can logically back up all or a subset of data in an Oracle database. For example, Data Pump Export lets you selectively export the following:

- All objects in the database
- The objects in a specific schema
- A single table

You can export database information while the database is open and in use. Data Pump Export ensures that the export data for an individual table is consistent with itself. When you export a schema or the entire database while the database is open and being modified, Oracle uses Flashback queries to make sure that the export data is consistent in the Export file (commonly referred to as a *dump file*).

The Data Pump Import Utility

To recover lost data from a dump file, you use the companion Oracle utility, *Data Pump Import*. With Data Pump Import, you can read an Export file to restore specific database tables, schemas, or an entire database.

The Proper Use of Data Pump Export and Import

Oracle's Data Pump Export and Import utilities should never be your first or complete choice to protect an Oracle XE database, because an export of a database, schema, or table can never guarantee complete recovery from a database failure. It is very important to understand that after you import data from a dump file, there is no recovery process to complete—the work of all committed transactions that completed after you performed the export is not available. For these reasons, use database exports only as a supplement to true database backups and transaction logging.

Other Uses for Data Pump Export and Import

Besides using Data Pump Export and Import for supplemental database protection, you can use the utilities to move data from one database to another. For example, when you want to move an application schema from a development database to a production database, you can use the Data Pump Export and Import utilities to build all schema objects and transfer any initial data that might exist.

NOTE
This book does not explain the use of the Data Pump utilities. Please refer to the Oracle Utilities *documentation for more information.*

More Database Recovery Options

Hopefully, your database will never have a problem, and you will never have to use the redo log and database backups to recover lost work. However, if you do, rest assured that Oracle and RMAN have the necessary mechanisms to complete the job.

Previous introductory sections in this chapter explained some fundamental database recovery concepts, including the roll-forward and rollback stages of crash recovery, file restoration preceding media recovery, etc. The following sections explain more about database recovery options that you have to repair a damaged database. Subsequent exercises teach you how to simulate the loss of a data file and recover it using RMAN.

Complete Recovery

A *complete recovery* operation is one that recovers the work of all committed transactions. Complete recovery operations, including database recovery, tablespace recovery, and data file recovery, are the most typical types of recovery that you perform when a problem damages a database.

Database Recovery

The simplest way to recover all lost work in a database using only one operation is to use RMAN to perform a database recovery. A *database recovery* is a type of complete recovery that recovers lost work in all data files of the database. RMAN identifies damaged data files and automatically recovers them using information in the control file, available data file backup sets, and the database's redo log.

A database recovery is appropriate when many data files of the database require recovery and the database can be unavailable during the recovery operation. To perform a database recovery, the database is mounted but closed.

Tablespace Recovery

When selected portions of a database have been damaged and high availability is a requirement, consider using tablespace recovery. A *tablespace recovery* is a type of complete recovery that recovers lost work in all data files of a specific tablespace. You can use RMAN to perform a tablespace recovery while the database is open and the damaged tablespace is offline, or while the database is mounted but closed.

NOTE
If a problem damages any data file of the SYSTEM tablespace, the database cannot operate properly. Therefore, you must shut down the database after such a failure; you cannot perform tablespace recovery of the SYSTEM tablespace while the database is open.

Data File Recovery

When a single data file has been damaged, consider using a data file recovery. A data file recovery is a type of complete recovery that recovers lost work in a specific data file. You can use RMAN to perform a data file recovery while the database is open and the damaged tablespace is offline, or while the database is mounted but closed.

NOTE
You cannot recover a damaged data file of the SYSTEM tablespace while the database is open.

Incomplete Recovery

In most situations, RMAN applies all available redo log groups to perform a complete database recovery (for example, with database, tablespace, or data file recovery). In rare circumstances, you might consider performing an incomplete recovery operation. When you perform an *incomplete recovery*, Oracle recovers the work of only some of the committed transactions by applying a limited amount of the redo entries in the database's redo log.

For example, assume that on Monday at 8:06 A.M., a user accidentally drops an important database table and purges it from the recycle bin—no other damage has been done to the database. In the absence of logical backups made with Data Pump Export or other types of Oracle Flashback features, you can still recover the lost table by performing an incomplete recovery operation. For example, you might restore the entire database from the most recent backup to a different computer and then perform a point-in-time recovery up to the time 8:05 A.M. Then, you could export the table and import it back into the production database to recover from your mishap.

Oracle and RMAN support three different types of incomplete recovery: time-based recovery, change-based recovery, and cancel-based recovery.

Time-Based Recovery

A *time-based recovery*, sometimes called a *point-in-time recovery*, is a type of incomplete recovery that recovers the work of committed transactions in a database up to a specific point in time (for example, up to Monday at 8:05 A.M., just before a user dropped an important table).

Change-Based Recovery

A *change-based recovery* is a type of incomplete recovery that recovers the work of committed transactions in a database up to a specific *system change number (SCN)*. Oracle assigns a unique SCN to every transaction that commits. If you know the SCN of the last transaction that you want to include in a database recovery, you can perform change-based recovery.

Cancel-Based Recovery

A *cancel-based recovery* is a type of incomplete recovery that recovers the work of committed transactions in a database, up to the application of a specific log group. To perform cancel-based recovery, you must be able to indicate the last log sequence to apply as part of the recovery.

What About Damage to Log Groups and the Control File?

If you read the previous section closely, you noticed that there is no mention of the fact that serious failures might damage the database's online redo log groups and its control file. You might be asking yourself what type of database recovery is necessary after these types of files are damaged or lost.

If you mirror the database's online and archived redo log, as well as the database's control file, on different disks to protect them from isolated disk failures and user errors, you should not worry about recovering from the loss of these critical database files. As long as one copy of a log group or control file is always accessible, the database can continue to function properly without interruption.

In contrast, when you lose a data file and the data file is not stored on a data duplexing RAID array, database recovery is usually necessary because Oracle does not provide any facility to mirror data files. Oracle can always perform database recovery as long as you have a backup of the lost data file and at least one copy of all log groups and the database's control file.

After a disk failure, the database's redo log or control file might become unprotected (that is, unmirrored). For example, if you mirror the database's control file to two different disks and one disk fails, the control file then would be unprotected because there is no mirror copy. When such situations arise, the most urgent step that you can take is to reconfigure the database's online redo log groups and control file and protect them with at least one mirror copy. Otherwise, the database is vulnerable to an isolated disk failure.

NOTE
Even when you mirror the database's redo log groups and control file, the database theoretically still remains vulnerable to total site disasters (for example, fires, floods, and other catastrophes). With editions of Oracle other than XE, you can use Oracle's standby database feature for ultimate database protection—see your Oracle documentation for more information about these advanced features.

Recovering Databases from Problems

Now that you have a general idea of Oracle's database recovery options, the following two exercises teach you how to use RMAN to recover your starter database from a simulated system crash, and then from the simulated loss of a data file.

The exercises in this section build upon the previous exercises in this chapter. In other words, you cannot complete the following exercises unless you configure your starter database to operate with media recovery enabled (ARCHIVELOG mode) and to archive online log groups as they fill, and you have data file backup sets for all data files in the database. Additionally, the following exercises in this chapter assume that your computer is managing only the Oracle XE database (and not other Oracle databases), and that you are using RMAN with the database's control file rather than a recovery catalog.

EXERCISE 9.23: Simulate a System Crash and Perform Crash Recovery

As mentioned previously, a system crash is an unexpected or otherwise abrupt shutdown of Oracle, such that the instance does not have time to roll back current transactions, disconnect users, and leave the database's data in a clean state. To

Important Warning: Before You Start...

The following exercises show you how to purposely damage an Oracle database so that you can practice performing database recovery. Considering that you might make a mistake during the subsequent database recovery process, please do not attempt to perform the following exercises using a database that contains important data. Instead, you should use these exercises to practice your database recovery skills within the confines of an isolated test database environment, or using a database that you can afford to lose should you make a mistake.

simulate a system crash, you can use the ABORT option of the SQL*Plus command SHUTDOWN. For your convenience, RMAN supports this command as well.

To prepare a test for your simulation, use your existing SQL*Plus session to execute the following statements that create a test table and some data that you can use to confirm a successful crash recovery. Make sure to commit after inserting the first test row, but do not commit after inserting the second row.

```
CONNECT system;

CREATE TABLE system.handsonxe_recovery_test (
 id INTEGER,
 value VARCHAR2(10)
)
TABLESPACE users;

INSERT INTO system.handsonxe_recovery_test (id, value)
VALUES (1, 'Row 1');

COMMIT;

INSERT INTO system.handsonxe_recovery_test (id, value)
VALUES (2, 'Row 2');
```

Next, assuming that no one else is working with the Oracle XE database, simulate a system crash by switching to your Command Prompt window, restarting RMAN, establishing a SYSDBA-privileged connection to the XE database, and aborting the current instance:

```
CONNECT TARGET sys;

SHUTDOWN ABORT;
```

Once Oracle aborts the instance, you should see the following message:

```
Oracle instance shut down
```

At this point, pretend that a temporary power failure has just happened, causing your Microsoft Windows computer to restart. Crash recovery for your starter database automatically happens when you restart an instance and open the database. For example, using your existing SYSDBA-privileged RMAN session, enter the following command to restart the instance and open the database:

```
STARTUP;
```

The output from the command should be similar to the following:

```
connected to target database (not started)
Oracle instance started
```

```
database mounted
database opened

Total System Global Area        230686720 bytes

Fixed Size                        1286700 bytes
Variable Size                    88083924 bytes
Database Buffers                138412032 bytes
Redo Buffers                      2904064 bytes
```

Your database is now available and completely operational for users and applications. To confirm the recovery of only the committed transactions in the system, switch to your SQL*Plus session, exit and restart SQL*Plus (you must do this because the old SQL*Plus session cannot attach to the new database instance), and then query the test table:

```
CONNECT system;

SELECT * FROM system.handsonxe_recovery_test;
```

The expected results are as follows:

```
        ID VALUE
---------- ----------
         1 Row 1
```

Notice that the first row corresponding to the work of the committed transaction exists in the table, but that the second row corresponding to work of the uncommitted transaction at the time of the system crash has been rolled back.

NOTE
If you configure your Oracle database service to automatically start up when Microsoft Windows restarts (see Exercise 2.7), after an authentic crash of your Microsoft Windows computer, Oracle XE will automatically restart and perform crash recovery without any administrative intervention.

EXERCISE 9.24: Simulate a Lost Data File and a Database Recovery

If you are using Oracle XE to support a database with bona fide data, one of the worst imaginable situations would be that the database requires media recovery and you have never done it before. This exercise teaches you how to simulate the loss of a data file so that you can practice performing media recovery with RMAN. If in the future you ever need to recover the database for real, you should feel more comfortable doing so.

Controlling the Recovery Time from a System Crash

The number of redo entries in the online redo log that Oracle needs to apply during crash recovery directly affects the amount of time that it takes to complete the process and make the database available again for normal operation. More frequent checkpoints help to reduce the time necessary for crash recovery because checkpoints force Oracle to write dirty blocks in the instance's memory back to the data files, thus reducing the amount of redo that Oracle needs to apply during crash recovery. Conveniently, Oracle lets you target an MTTR from a system crash (in seconds) to suit your database protection policy with the FAST_START_MTTR_ TARGET initialization parameter. However, realize that as you lower the MTTR target, Oracle XE's performance can suffer due to the additional disk I/O necessary to complete more frequent checkpoints. See the *Oracle Database Backup and Recovery Advanced User's Guide* for more information about tuning crash recovery with the FAST_START_MTTR_TARGET initialization parameter.

NOTE
You cannot complete this exercise unless you configure your starter database to operate with media recovery enabled (ARCHIVELOG mode) and to archive online log groups as they fill, and you have data file backup sets for all data files in the database. Please do not proceed if you have not completed the previous exercises in this chapter in the published order.

This exercise takes you through the following steps:

1. Check to make sure that all data files are available in at least two data file backup sets.

2. Restore all archived log files necessary to complete the recovery.

3. Take the USERS tablespace offline in your starter database.

4. Rename the data file that corresponds to the USERS tablespace.

5. Restore the data file of the USERS tablespace.

6. Try to bring the "damaged" USERS tablespace back online.

7. Recover the damaged USERS tablespace while the remainder of the database is open and available.

8. Bring the recovered USERS tablespace back online.

The first step in this exercise is to ensure that you have at least two data file backup sets that you can use to recover your database—one for the actual recovery, and one just in case something strange happens and you need an extra safety net. You can do this by entering the following REPORT command:

```
REPORT NEED BACKUP REDUNDANCY=2;
```

The report should appear exactly as follows—no more, no less:

```
Report of files with less than 2 redundant backups
File #bkps Name
---- ----- ------------------------------------------
```

If one or more data files are listed in the report, this means that you did not complete some or all of the exercises earlier in this chapter that make data file backup sets for your database. If that's the case, *stop*—do not proceed any further with this exercise. You must complete the earlier practice exercises in this chapter so that the necessary backup sets are available for the subsequent recovery operation. On the other hand, if you have the necessary backup sets to recover your database, you can continue.

At this point, pretend that for some reason the data file that corresponds to the USERS tablespace has been lost. If this were true, the database's alert file and applications would most likely display Oracle-related error messages that indicate the name of the damaged tablespace or data file(s). When you notice this type of problem, you should immediately take the corresponding tablespace offline or shut down the database while you recover from the problem, to avoid frightening application users with all sorts of errors that they know nothing about. To continue with your simulation, shut down the database using your current RMAN session:

```
SHUTDOWN IMMEDIATE;
```

NOTE
Because you are using Microsoft Windows, which does not allow you to rename or delete a file that is in use by another process, you have to shut down the database to continue your simulation. However, please realize that in a realistic situation, you can simply take the damaged tablespace offline with the SQL command ALTER TABLESPACE ... OFFLINE IMMEDIATE and recover the damaged tablespace while the database and all other tablespaces remain online and available for normal use.

Next, you can simulate the loss of a data file by renaming the file at the operating system level with Windows Explorer. For example, the data file for the Oracle XE database's USERS tablespace is ORACLE_BASE\oradata\XE\USERS.DBF. To simulate the loss of the file, rename it to **USERS.DBF.SAV**.

The next step is to start a new instance, mount the database, and then restore the "lost" data file of the damaged USERS tablespace. To restore all data files of a specific tablespace, use the TABLESPACE parameter of the RMAN command RESTORE. For the purposes of this exercise, enter the following command to restore the data file(s) for the "damaged" USERS tablespace. The simple example of the RESTORE command automatically picks the most recent data file backup set that can satisfy the operation.

```
STARTUP MOUNT;

RESTORE TABLESPACE users;
```

The results that follow indicate the successful restoration of the lost data file from the most recent data file backup set including the data file of the USERS tablespace:

```
Starting restore at ...
allocated channel: ORA_DISK_1
channel ORA_DISK_1: sid=35 devtype=DISK

channel ORA_DISK_1: starting datafile backupset restore
channel ORA_DISK_1: specifying datafile(s) to restore from backup set
restoring datafile 00004 to C:\ORACLEXE\ORADATA\XE\USERS.DBF
channel ORA_DISK_1: reading from backup piece C:\XDRIVE\ORACLEXE\APP\
ORACLE\FLASH_RECOVERY_AREA\XE\BACKUPSET\2006_05_14\
O1_MF_NNNDF_TAG20060514T111657_26GLHC2M_.BKP
channel ORA_DISK_1: restored backup piece 1
piece handle=C:\XDRIVE\ORACLEXE\APP\ORACLE\FLASH_RECOVERY_AREA\XE\
BACKUPSET\2006_05_14\O1_MF_NNNDF_TAG20060514T111657_26GLHC2M_.BKP
tag=TAG20060514T111657
channel ORA_DISK_1: restore complete, elapsed time: 00:00:57
Finished restore at ...
```

To recover the committed work that corresponds to the restored version of the USERS tablespace, use the TABLESPACE parameter of the RMAN command RECOVER. For example, execute the following command to recover the USERS tablespace:

```
RECOVER TABLESPACE users;
```

You should see results similar to the following, which indicate a successful recovery. See my embedded comments (in bold) for more information about what happens during the tablespace recovery process.

```
Starting recover at ...
using channel ORA_DISK_1

starting media recovery

-- RMAN IDENTIFIES THE ARCHIVED LOG FILES NECESSARY TO RECOVER THE
-- RESTORED DATA FILE. RMAN RESTORES NECESSARY ARCHIVED LOGS FROM
-- BACKUP SETS WHEN THEY ARE NOT ALREADY AVAILABLE IN THE ARCHIVE
-- LOG DESTINATION.
```

```
archive log thread 1 sequence 70 is already on disk as file C:\XDRIVE\
ORACLEXE\APP\ORACLE\FLASH_RECOVERY_AREA\XE\ARCHIVELOG\2006_05_14\
O1_MF_1_70_26GRF96O_.ARC
archive log thread 1 sequence 71 is already on disk as file C:\XDRIVE\
ORACLEXE\APP\ORACLE\FLASH_RECOVERY_AREA\XE\ARCHIVELOG\2006_05_14\
O1_MF_1_71_26GS9H1L_.ARC
channel ORA_DISK_1: starting archive log restore to default destination
channel ORA_DISK_1: restoring archive log
archive log thread=1 sequence=69
channel ORA_DISK_1: reading from backup piece C:\XDRIVE\ORACLEXE\APP\
ORACLE\FLASH_RECOVERY_AREA\XE\BACKUPSET\2006_05_14\
O1_MF_ANNNN_TAG20060514T111909_26GLMHP0_.BKP
channel ORA_DISK_1: restored backup piece 1
piece handle=C:\XDRIVE\ORACLEXE\APP\ORACLE\FLASH_RECOVERY_AREA\XE\
BACKUPSET\2006_05_14\O1_MF_ANNNN_TAG20060514T111909_26GLMHP0_.BKP
tag=TAG20060514T111909
channel ORA_DISK_1: restore complete, elapsed time: 00:00:02
archive log filename=C:\XDRIVE\ORACLEXE\APP\ORACLE\FLASH_RECOVERY_AREA\
XE\ARCHIVELOG\2006_05_14\O1_MF_1_69_26GWCLZ3_.ARC thread=1 sequence=69
-- AFTER RECOVERY IS COMPLETE, RMAN AUTOMATICALLY DELETES RESTORED
-- ARCHIVED LOG FILES FROM THE FLASH RECOVERY AREA.
channel default: deleting archive log(s)
archive log filename=C:\XDRIVE\ORACLEXE\APP\ORACLE\FLASH_RECOVERY_AREA\
XE\ARCHIVELOG\2006_05_14\O1_MF_1_69_26GWCLZ3_.ARC recid=21 stamp=590421939
archive log filename=C:\XDRIVE\ORACLEXE\APP\ORACLE\FLASH_RECOVERY_AREA\XE\
ARCHIVELOG\2006_05_14\O1_MF_1_70_26GRF96O_.ARC thread=1 sequence=70
media recovery complete, elapsed time: 00:00:02
Finished recover at ...
```

Upon the successful completion of media recovery, you can reopen the database for normal use:

```
SQL "ALTER DATABASE OPEN";
```

The lack of any error messages indicates successful execution of the SQL command from within RMAN. Now restart SQL*Plus, connect as **SYSTEM**, and query the SYSTEM.HANDSONXE_RECOVERY_TEST table to make sure that the table and its committed data, created after the last database backup and before the simulated disk failure, is available as expected:

```
SQL> CONNECT system
Enter password:
Connected.
SQL> SELECT * FROM system.handsonxe_recovery_test;

        ID VALUE
---------- ----------
         1 Row 1
```

Congratulations! You just completed your first Oracle XE database recovery. You are finished using RMAN—feel free to exit and close the associated Command Prompt window.

Using Oracle Flashback Features

The final section of this chapter includes exercises that provide you with some fundamental experience using a couple of Oracle's Flashback recovery features: Flashback Drop and Flashback Table. These features are useful when you need to recover data lost due to logical data errors or corruptions rather than physical storage problems.

EXERCISE 9.25: Restore a Dropped Table Using Oracle Flashback Drop

This exercise teaches you how to recover from an all-to-common problem: someone has mistakenly dropped a table. Rather than perform a complicated database recovery operation to restore the lost table, you can use Oracle's Flashback Drop feature. As explained in the section "Logical Errors and Oracle Flashback" earlier in this chapter, the recycle bin of a permanent tablespace holds data structures such as tables and indexes that users drop. After someone drops a data structure, it remains in the tablespace's recycle bin until all available free space in the tablespace is consumed and other structures in the tablespace require more space—only then does Oracle actually drop the structure permanently. To get an idea of how easy it is to use this logical data-recovery mechanism, carry out the following steps:

1. Using your current SQL*Plus session, drop the SYSTEM.HANDSONXE_ RECOVERY_TEST table:

   ```
   DROP TABLE system.handsonxe_recovery_test;
   ```

2. Confirm that the table is no longer available by using a simple query:

   ```
   SELECT * FROM system.handsonxe_recovery_test;
   ```

3. Confirm that the table is available in the recycle bin by querying the DBA_ RECYCLEBIN data dictionary view:

   ```
   COLUMN owner FORMAT a6;
   COLUMN original_name FORMAT a25;
   COLUMN operation FORMAT A10;
   COLUMN ts_name FORMAT a10;

   SELECT owner, original_name, operation, ts_name
     FROM dba_recyclebin
    WHERE owner = 'SYSTEM';
   ```

4. Restore the dropped table by using the SQL command FLASHBACK TABLE with the TO BEFORE DROP option:

   ```
   FLASHBACK TABLE system.handsonxe_recovery_test
     TO BEFORE DROP;
   ```

The message "Flashback Complete" indicates a successful restoration of the dropped table. You can query the table as in Step 2 to confirm this fact.

Oracle XE's Flashback Drop feature is enabled by default; to disable this feature, you must set the RECYCLEBIN initialization parameter to OFF. To bypass the recycle bin when dropping a table and Flashback Drop is enabled, you must include the PURGE option of the SQL command DROP TABLE, as demonstrated in the previous exercise. To explicitly purge a recycle bin rather than wait for Oracle to reuse space occupied by recycle bin data structures, use the following form of the SQL command PURGE:

```
PURGE
{ TABLE table
| INDEX index
| RECYCLEBIN
| DBA_RECYCLEBIN
| TABLESPACE tablespace [USER user] } ;
```

The following list explains the elements in the preceding command:

- Use the TABLE parameter to purge a specific table.

- Use the INDEX parameter to purge a specific index.

- Use the RECYCLEBIN option to purge recycle bin data structures that correspond to the schema of your current session.

- While using a SYSDBA-privileged session, you can use the DBA_RECYCLEBIN option to purge all data structures for every permanent tablespace's recycle bin.

- Use the TABLESPACE parameter to purge all data structures in a specific tablespace. You use the optional USER parameter to restrict the purge operation to data structures that correspond to the schema of a particular user.

NOTE
The Database Home Page of Oracle Application Express provides an easy-to-use interface that you can employ to review, restore, and purge recycle bin data structures that correspond to your schema.

EXERCISE 9.26: Restore Lost Data Using Oracle Flashback Query

User errors or rouge application processes can occasionally corrupt the logical integrity of data in one or more related database tables. Recovering table data from such problems with Oracle's Flashback Query feature is painless, as long as you learn about the problem relatively soon after the corruption occurs, considering that Flashback Query relies on undo data in the database's undo tablespace.

To demonstrate this logical data recovery feature of Oracle, consider the following scenario:

- The child tables in a schema have referential integrity constraints that enforce the Delete Cascade referential action—in other words, when a transaction deletes a parent record with dependent child records, Oracle automatically deletes each dependent child record as well.

- A user mistakenly deletes a parent record, which also deletes corresponding dependent child records.

To prepare for this exercise, use your current SQL*Plus session to execute the support script chap09.sql that is contained in this book's support archive, similar to the way that you execute other chapters' support scripts. For example:

```
@C:\temp\handsonxe\sql\chap09.sql;
```

The script builds the HANDSONXE09 schema with the familiar HOSTS, DATABASES, and APPLICATIONS tables that you used in Chapter 6. Before you test Oracle's Flashback Query feature, take a quick look at the data in the tables beforehand by executing the following queries:

```
SELECT * FROM handsonxe09.hosts;

SELECT * FROM handsonxe09.databases;

SELECT ap_id, ap_name, db_id FROM handsonxe09.applications;
```

The expected results are as follows:

```
SQL> SELECT * FROM handsonxe09.hosts;

   HOST_ID HOST_NAME            HOST_OS HOST_OS_VERS HOST_CPUS
---------- -------------------- ------- ------------ ----------
         1 server1.mycompany.com AIX    5.2.0.0               4

SQL> SELECT * FROM handsonxe09.databases;

    DB_ID DB_NAME DB_VERSION   HOST_ID
--------- ------- ---------- ----------
        1 db1     10.2.0.1            1
        2 db2     9.2.0.7             1
        3 db3     10.2.0.1            1
```

```
          4 db4      10.2.0.1              1
          5 db5       9.2.0.7              1
          6 db6       9.2.0.7              1
          7 db7       9.2.0.7              1
          8 db8       9.2.0.7              1
```

```
8 rows selected.
```

```
SQL> SELECT ap_id, ap_name, db_id FROM handsonxe09.applications;
```

```
     AP_ID AP_NAME       DB_ID
---------- ---------- ----------
         1 owl                3
         2 finch              1
         3 robin              2
```

Now simulate a user error—look at your watch, note the time, and then execute the following DELETE command to drop the lone record in the HOSTS table and commit the encompassing transaction:

```
DELETE FROM handsonxe09.hosts
  WHERE host_id = 1;
```

```
COMMIT;
```

Because the referential integrity constraints of the tables in the schema all use the delete cascade referential action, and all rows in the schema depend on the ultimate parent record in the HOSTS table, all rows in all of the tables have silently been deleted, not just the one record in the HOSTS table. Repeat the preceding queries to confirm this fact. The expected results are as follows:

```
SQL> SELECT * FROM handsonxe09.hosts;
```

```
no rows selected
```

```
SQL> SELECT * FROM handsonxe09.databases;
```

```
no rows selected
```

```
SQL> SELECT ap_id, ap_name, db_id FROM handsonxe09.applications;
```

```
no rows selected
```

How are you ever going to recover from this mess? Flashback Query to the rescue! As long as the necessary undo data has not been overwritten in the undo tablespace, all that you have to do is query the tables as of a time point that reflects the data as it was before the logical error. For example, a typical Flashback Query scenario might go as follows:

```
SQL> SELECT * FROM handsonxe09.hosts
  2        AS OF TIMESTAMP (SYSTIMESTAMP - INTERVAL '14' MINUTE);

no rows selected

SQL> SELECT * FROM handsonxe09.hosts
  2        AS OF TIMESTAMP (SYSTIMESTAMP - INTERVAL '15' MINUTE);

no rows selected

SQL> SELECT * FROM handsonxe09.hosts
  2        AS OF TIMESTAMP (SYSTIMESTAMP - INTERVAL '16' MINUTE);

   HOST_ID HOST_NAME             HOST_OS HOST_OS_VERS  HOST_CPUS
---------- --------------------- ------- ------------ ----------
         1 server1.mycompany.com AIX     5.2.0.0               4

SQL> SELECT TO_CHAR(SYSTIMESTAMP - INTERVAL '16' MINUTE,
  2>                 'DD-MON-YYYY HH24.MI.SS.FF') AS rcv_time
  3>       FROM dual;

RCV_TIME
----------------------------
14-MAY-06 17.49.45.225000000
```

Note that the highlighted text (in bold) in the preceding example queries will vary, depending on how long ago you committed the transaction with the DELETE statement. The first two queries don't go back far enough in time to get the data before the logical error—the third query does. The final query displays an explicit timestamp derived from the relative timestamp used in the previous query—you will use this timestamp in subsequent SQL statements to recover the data.

To recover the data, execute UPDATE statements with Flashback subqueries using your own timestamp, as follows:

```
INSERT INTO handsonxe09.hosts
SELECT * FROM handsonxe09.hosts
 AS OF TIMESTAMP
   TO_TIMESTAMP('14-MAY-2006 17.49.45.225000000',
                'DD-MON-YYYY HH24.MI.SS.FF')
 WHERE host_id = 1;

COMMIT;

INSERT INTO handsonxe09.databases
SELECT * FROM handsonxe09.databases
 AS OF TIMESTAMP
```

```
     TO_TIMESTAMP('14-MAY-2006 17.49.45.225000000',
                  'DD-MON-YYYY HH24.MI.SS.FF')
  WHERE host_id = 1;

COMMIT;

INSERT INTO handsonxe09.applications
SELECT * FROM handsonxe09.applications
 AS OF TIMESTAMP
  TO_TIMESTAMP('14-MAY-2006 17.49.45.225000000',
               'DD-MON-YYYY HH24.MI.SS.FF')
 WHERE db_id IN (
    SELECT db_id FROM handsonxe09.databases
         AS OF TIMESTAMP
            TO_TIMESTAMP('14-MAY-2006 17.49.45.225000000',
                         'DD-MON-YYYY HH24.MI.SS.FF')
            WHERE host_id = 1);

COMMIT;
```

To confirm that the previously deleted rows have been restored, repeat the original three queries of this exercise. The results should be as follows:

```
SQL> SELECT * FROM handsonxe09.hosts;

   HOST_ID HOST_NAME            HOST_OS HOST_OS_VERS HOST_CPUS
---------- -------------------- ------- ------------ ----------
         1 server1.mycompany.com AIX    5.2.0.0               4

SQL> SELECT * FROM handsonxe09.databases;

    DB_ID DB_NAME DB_VERSION  HOST_ID
---------- ------- ---------- ----------
         1 db1     10.2.0.1          1
         2 db2     9.2.0.7           1
         3 db3     10.2.0.1          1
         4 db4     10.2.0.1          1
         5 db5     9.2.0.7           1
         6 db6     9.2.0.7           1
         7 db7     9.2.0.7           1
         8 db8     9.2.0.7           1

8 rows selected.

SQL> SELECT ap_id, ap_name, db_id FROM handsonxe09.applications;

    AP_ID AP_NAME        DB_ID
---------- ---------- ----------
         1 owl             3
         2 finch           1
         3 robin           2
```

Using Oracle Flashback Table

Restoring lost data for multiple tables to the same point in time, as the previous exercise demonstrates, is much simpler with Oracle's Flashback Table feature. For example, the following FLASHBACK TABLE statement would accomplish the same thing as the three INSERT and COMMIT statements in the previous exercise:

```
FLASHBACK TABLE
   handsonxe09.hosts,
   handsonxe09.databases,
   handsonxe09.applications
 TO TIMESTAMP
  TO_TIMESTAMP('14-MAY-2006 17.49.45.225000000',
               'DD-MON-YYYY HH24.MI.SS.FF');
```

Then, you may wonder, why did I show you how to do things with Flashback queries? Oracle Express Edition does not support Flashback Table or Flashback Database; only Oracle Enterprise Edition supports these features. However, as demonstrated, with a little ingenuity, you can work around this limitation.

Chapter Summary

Protecting an Oracle XE database from unforeseen problems is one of the most important jobs that you can perform if you plan to use your database to maintain important data. This chapter has explained the several features of Oracle XE that you can use to back up, restore, and recover databases when inevitable problems affect your system:

- A database's transaction redo log records the changes made by committed transactions.

- A database backup is a collection of all the files that comprise the database. If you damage or lose a file that is part of a database, you can extract a copy of the lost file from a database backup to restore the file in the database.

- A database recovery operation recovers the work lost due to some type of problem. Configured correctly, Oracle can recover a database from all types of problems, including simple system crashes and more serious disk failures.

- You use Recovery Manager (RMAN) to ease the process of backing up Oracle databases and recovering them when necessary.

- Oracle's Flashback features make it easy to recover from common user errors such as tables dropped by accident and logical data corruptions.

CHAPTER
10

Tune Application and Database Instance Performance

ecause of Oracle XE's database size and processing restrictions, applications that rely on Oracle XE will most likely not require extensive tuning to deliver acceptable performance. Nonetheless, it is good practice to develop applications and configure Oracle databases in such a way that they accomplish work efficiently, especially when you are using Oracle XE to learn how to use other editions of Oracle or using Oracle XE to prototype applications that might eventually be supported by other editions of Oracle such as Oracle Standard Edition or Oracle Enterprise Edition. This chapter provides you with a fundamental understanding of performance tuning for an Oracle database application system. Topics in this chapter include the following:

- An overview of performance-tuning concepts

- Application tuning

- Database instance tuning

Chapter Prerequisites

To practice the hands-on exercises in this chapter, you need to start SQL*Plus as instructed in Exercise 2.11 and run the following command script:

```
location\handsonxe\sql\chap10.sql
```

where *location* is the file directory where you expanded the support archive that accompanies this book. For example, after starting SQL*Plus, you can run this chapter's SQL command script using the SQL*Plus command @, as in the following example (assuming that your chap10.sql file is in C:\temp\handsonxe\sql):

```
SQL> @C:\temp\handsonxe\sql\chap10.sql;
```

Be aware that this chapter's support script generates a lot of data. Do not be alarmed while the script takes a few minutes to complete. Additionally, make a note of the time of day that you execute this chapter's support script; subsequent exercises in this chapter require that you have this knowledge to complete work.

Once you reply to all of the prompts and the script completes successfully, *leave the current SQL*Plus session open*—you'll need it later on in several of this chapter's exercises.

Oracle Tuning Concepts

Before you begin tuning an Oracle database application system, you should have a clear understanding of basic tuning concepts and some reasonable goals for performance tuning. The information in this section will help get you started.

Measures of Oracle Database Application Performance

In a broad context, the most appreciable measure of a computer application system's performance is its ability to adequately serve corresponding users so as not to detract from their productivity. To measure how well an application performs overall, ask yourself how long users of an application have to wait before they can continue doing work after they submit an operation. How long is too long, considering the work that that the system must perform to complete the operation—several seconds, minutes, hours? If users feel that an operation takes too much time to complete, perhaps you can tune the operation so that it takes less time, perhaps you cannot. In conclusion, you will generally find that you need to tune something when users feel that they are waiting too long.

In the context of small Oracle XE–based application systems, there are two specific measures of performance that you will most likely need to focus on:

- **Response time**   The amount of time that a user waits while an application handles a request and returns data or a result. For example, the response time for a SQL query is the amount of time that you must wait for Oracle XE to return a result. When the response times for an application's operations are tolerable, the application does not limit the productivity of its users.

- **Throughput**   The number of requests that the database system handles in a given time period. For example, common OLTP performance benchmarks quantify transaction throughput as the number of transactions processed per second. When Oracle XE can handle the load placed on the system by an application without hampering the productivity of its users or the performance of other applications on the same computer, the system is tuned well with respect to throughput.

Realistic and Unrealistic Performance Goals

Clear-cut performance-tuning goals are important to understand so that you focus on what is important and avoid wasting time on things of little consequence. A basic objective of computer application system tuning should be to achieve adequate response times that do not detract from user productivity and do not place on the system an unnecessary load that might otherwise detract from the performance of other system operations.

While it is admirable, your primary performance-tuning goal should *not* be to achieve the absolute best response time possible for all operations. Novice Oracle developers and administrators commonly strive to achieve such unrealistic performance goals; as a result, they waste lots of time trying to squeeze every last bit of performance out of an application when, in most cases, all noticeable performance gains are quick and easy to achieve by attending to a relatively small subset of issues.

Availability and Scalability

While typically less important with Oracle XE–based applications, availability and scalability are other considerations that can affect the productivity of its users:

- **Availability** A measure of a system's capability to provide access to a desired resource, when necessary; previous sections of this book explain many of Oracle XE's high-availability features, including dynamically modifiable instance parameters, mirrored online log groups and control file, checkpoints and MTTR settings, online database backups, and more.

- **Scalability** A measure of a system's ability to provide proportional throughput in relation to available hardware; for example, a database system scales well if with one processor it can handle 1000 transactions per second, with two processors it can handle 2000 transactions per second, and so on. While other editions of Oracle scale extremely well, the imposed processing limitations of Oracle XE restrict its ability to scale. If you find that an application system based on Oracle XE does not perform well due to these limits, consider graduating to Oracle Standard Edition One, Standard Edition, or Enterprise Edition.

Performance-tuning goals are something to consider throughout the lifecycle of an Oracle database application. You should design the system with performance in mind from the start, and then monitor the system's performance regularly to ensure that it continues to meet the needs of its users.

Tunable Components

Before you can tune something, you need to know what you can tune that will affect its performance. An Oracle application system is a complex environment that has many tunable system components. Figure 10-1 identifies many of the components that you can tune within an Oracle database application system.

In most cases, application-related problems are typically to blame when a system limits user productivity. Poorly written SQL, large tables without adequate indexes, and poor transaction design are some of the most common issues that you will routinely focus on to improve an application's performance. Subsequent sections and exercises in this chapter teach you more about application-side tuning.

Other situations require that you focus your efforts on the many components of an Oracle database server that are tunable, including the server's host operating system, data caches, redo logging mechanisms, software process architectures, and more; subsequent sections in this chapter teach you more about several topics related to database instance tuning.

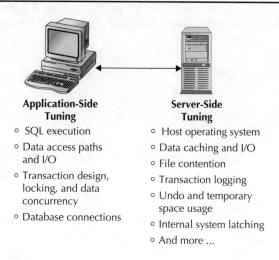

Application-Side Tuning

- SQL execution
- Data access paths and I/O
- Transaction design, locking, and data concurrency
- Database connections

Server-Side Tuning

- Host operating system
- Data caching and I/O
- File contention
- Transaction logging
- Undo and temporary space usage
- Internal system latching
- And more ...

FIGURE 10-1. *An Oracle database application system has many tunable components.*

Tuning Methodologies

Once you understand the general tuning goals and tunable components of an application system, where do you begin? This is one of the most common questions asked by novice and experienced Oracle developers and administrators alike. Although the answer varies with each system, one thing is generally true for all systems: you need a plan, or *tuning methodology*, that you can follow to achieve your goals. The following tuning methodology is a good general guideline to follow in most cases:

1. Determine your particular system's characteristics.

2. Consider known problems and issues.

3. Identify the system components that contribute most to the perceptible performance of your particular system and reported issues.

4. Tune each of these components, as necessary:

   a. Monitor and analyze the component's performance.

   b. Adjust or otherwise tune the component when it does not meet an acceptable performance level.

   c. Repeat Steps a. and b. until you achieve the desired performance.

To demonstrate, suppose that you need to tune application X. The first step is to determine what application X does. Most database applications fall into one of the following categories:

- An OLTP-type application in which users input lots of data using a standard set of transactions or batch jobs

- A decision support system (DSS)-type application that supports routine reporting operations

- A data mart– or data warehouse–type application that people use to execute ad hoc queries

Suppose you learn that application X is a DSS. You know that DSSs typically execute a standard set of read-only operations (that is, queries) to report information from operational systems. You also know that transaction logging is a feature of Oracle that records information about database modifications (that is, DML and DDL operations). Therefore, it's reasonable to assume that tuning a DSS's online redo log configuration is not a high priority. Instead, you'll most likely see the biggest performance gains from things that affect the response time of the routine queries at work in the DSS.

Taking a few moments to determine the basic characteristics of a system helps to focus your efforts on the most significant things. To further narrow your attention on things that matter most, consider specific problems that users report, if any. Suppose users of application X inform you that when hourly DSS reports were originally deployed, they ran in a matter of seconds; since then, over the past few months, hourly DSS reports have gradually required more and more time to complete, and are almost to the point of overlapping. In this case, ask yourself, why would queries that once took seconds to complete now take almost an hour to complete? You could guess as to what the problem might be, but you won't know for sure without further investigation.

At this point, you should have a short list of the system components that contribute most to the overall performance of your system and specific performance problems. To know for sure, you need to monitor and analyze the performance of suspect components. Continuing with our example, suppose that you monitor the execution of application X DSS queries and find that certain queries targeting a particular table take an extraordinarily long amount of time to complete. Further analysis reveals that a table targeted by the queries contains millions of rows, and that the table does not have any indexes other than table's primary key constraint index. Consequently, most DSS queries that target the large table are bound by full table scans that require significant amounts of physical and logical I/O.

Such focused analysis not only provides you with a greater understanding of the system components that you need to tune, but also sheds light on how the problem came to be. In our example, when the table contained only a few rows, the DSS queries executed fast despite the absence of indexes. As the table grew to contain millions of rows, full table scans gradually took more and more time to complete. Now that you know exactly what your problem is and what causes it, you should feel confident in what you need to do to fix the problem: create one or more indexes for the large table that will allow the DSS queries to execute faster, without full table scans.

Consider what might happen if you did not take the time to work through the steps in the proposed tuning methodology. For example, suppose that you now have to tune application Z, which is having performance problems. Application X works much better now that you created indexes for a large table, so you willy-nilly look for large application Z tables without indexes, and then create several indexes for columns that you think might be used to find rows in those tables. Later you find out that application Z is an OLTP system. By creating the indexes, you have actually made application Z perform worse, because now Oracle must incur the additional overhead of maintaining several indexes every time that transactions insert, update, and delete table rows. While this example is somewhat simple and overstated, it underscores an important point: *Each system that you tune will have unique characteristics—as a result, what works for one system might not work for another.* To succeed at performance tuning, spend some time up front in the process to understand the characteristics of your system, and then use this knowledge to identify, monitor, and tune the components of the system that will most likely contribute to the greatest overall effect on application performance.

The Cost of Work

To complete this introduction to basic tuning concepts, take the time to understand a set of very simple rules related to Oracle performance tuning that involve the concept of *work*:

- **Work *is not* optional** To accomplish tasks, an Oracle database application will always have to perform a certain amount of work.

- **Work = work** Work is always work, no matter what you want to call it. You might be able to shift one type of work to another type of work that is more or less expensive, but in the end, there is always a cost for doing work.

- **Less work < more work** Strive to design operations so that they complete efficiently without unnecessarily wasting resources. To achieve the biggest gains in performance, focus your tuning efforts on operations that require the most work.

- **Less work = better performance** Simply put, less work usually leads to better performance.

Remembering these simple rules will help you focus on what is important as you tune Oracle database application systems—reducing the overall load on the system to accomplish the necessary results.

Tuning Statistics

Tuning statistics are measurements that reveal useful information about system functions. You analyze tuning statistics to help you determine the issues that can benefit most from tuning. This section introduces several key concepts related to tuning statistics, including brief descriptions of several commonly referenced tuning statistics, instance efficiency ratios, the V$ data dictionary views, and Statspack.

Commonly Referenced Tuning Statistics

Oracle XE automatically collects information pertaining to many, many statistics. While each and every statistic has a purpose, some statistics are more frequently used than others. Table 10-1 identifies some of the more commonly used statistics that you will pay attention to in subsequent exercises of this chapter; for a complete list of all tuning statistics and wait events, please see the *Oracle Database Reference*.

Statistic	Description
Logical reads	A logical read happens when Oracle reads a data block from one of the database's buffer caches.
Physical reads	A physical read occurs when Oracle reads a data block from a data file because the requested data is not currently cached in one of the database's buffer caches (an in-memory cache of the most recently used data blocks). A physical read happens much slower than a logical read because disk I/O is much slower than data access from memory.
Consistent reads	A consistent read is a type of logical read that happens when Oracle reads a data block from one of the database's buffer caches on behalf of a read-consistent operation; when a data block found in the cache is too new for a query to use, Oracle may also need to apply undo information to the block to provide read consistency.
Physical writes	A physical write happens when Oracle writes a modified data block from the buffer cache to a data file.
Parses	When a user executes a SQL statement, Oracle must parse the statement before executing it. The parse phase of SQL statement execution requires several types of processing: for example, Oracle checks to ensure that the statement's syntax is valid, that all referenced data structures exist, and that the user executing the statement has the necessary data access privileges, and then determines the most efficient execution plan for the statement.

TABLE 10-1. *Some Commonly Used Oracle Performance-Tuning Statistics*

Statistic	Description
Hard parses	A hard parse happens when a user executes a SQL statement and Oracle must parse the statement from scratch, completing all of the aforementioned steps.
Soft parses	A soft parse happens when a user executes a SQL statement, but Oracle finds that the same (or similar) SQL statement is already parsed in the instance's shared pool (specifically, a cache known as the library cache); to execute the statement more efficiently, Oracle reuses the already parsed version of the SQL statement in the shared pool. This feature of Oracle is commonly referred to as *shared SQL*.
Executions	An execution happens when Oracle executes a SQL statement after parsing it. Because of shared SQL, Oracle can execute the same statement any number of times after initially parsing it and then caching it in the shared pool.
Rows processed	The rows processed is the estimated number of table rows processed by a DML SQL statement or the estimated number of rows returned for a query.
Table scans	A (full) table scan happens when Oracle must read every row in a table to process a SQL statement.
Index range scans	An index range scan happens when Oracle reads an index to find the physical ROWID(s) for a specific row or set of rows in a table. When a SQL statement targets a large table, an index range scan coupled with selective row access is much more efficient than a full table scan because far less physical and/or logical reads are necessary to process the statement.
Sorts	A sort happens when Oracle must sort the results for a SQL statement—for example, when a query uses an ORDER BY clause, or when you build a new index for a table.
Sorts (memory)	An in-memory sort happens when Oracle can process a sort operation without writing temporary information to disk.
Disk sorts	A disk sort happens when Oracle must write information to a temporary segment (also called a sort segment) to process a sort operation. Disk sorts require more work than in-memory sorts.
Wait events	A wait event is a generic term for a class of statistics. A wait event is a bottleneck that causes someone or something to wait while it finishes. Oracle's serialized data-locking mechanisms, latching mechanisms (internal system locks that are not serialized), disk I/O, synchronization events, and many more situations can produce wait events.

TABLE 10-1. *Some Commonly Used Oracle Performance-Tuning Statistics* (continued)

Now take a moment to consider the previously mentioned rules about work with respect to the specific statistics in Table 10-1. For example:

■ *Logical reads, physical reads, consistent reads, and physical writes are statistics that relate to I/O.* Oracle must always perform a certain amount of I/O work to process data. Physical reads require the most work because of slow disk I/O access, while logical reads require the least amount of work. Nonetheless, all types of I/O require work. Less I/O translates to less work, which ultimately means better performance.

■ *Oracle must always carry out a certain amount of work to execute SQL statements.* Every time you execute a SQL statement that is not in the shared pool, a hard parse is necessary. But once the parsed SQL statement is in the shared pool, subsequent executions of the same SQL statement can happen with much less work using soft parses. Coding applications and configuring database instances to take advantage of shared SQL reduces the amount of work necessary to execute a consistent set of SQL statements.

■ *Oracle must always perform a certain amount of work to access the data that a SQL statement targets.* For example, a full table scan of a large table to find just a single row requires much more work than an index scan and selective data block access. The job of Oracle's SQL statement optimizer is to determine an execution plan with data access methods that require less work rather than more work.

■ *Oracle must always perform work to sort data.* In-memory sorts require less work than disk sorts. When more memory is available for sorting, it's less likely that disk sorts will be necessary.

Instance Efficiency Ratios

The efficiency of the work that an instance performs is often measured by the instance efficiency ratios, such as the following:

■ **Buffer cache hit ratio**   Indicates how many physical reads happen relative to the sum of all physical, logical, and consistent reads. A database instance's buffer cache hit ratio is a measure of how costly the I/O work is in the system: buffer cache hit ratios approaching 100 percent for an active system indicate that the instance's buffer cache maintains the most frequently used data blocks in memory, because few physical reads happen relative to in-memory reads. Do not use an instance's buffer cache hit ratio as a measure of how little or how much I/O work the system performs, and do not make it your top priority to tune the instance's buffer cache hit ratio.

- **Library cache hit ratio**   A measure of the number of gethits (finds) for shared library cache objects (for example, shared SQL) relative to the number of total gets (lookups) for shared objects. When the library cache hit ratio is close to 100 percent in an active system, this indicates that applications are executing a consistent set of SQL statements that are taking full advantage of Oracle's shared SQL capabilities.

- **Execute to parse ratio**   A measure of how many executions happen relative to the number of parses for a system's SQL statements. When the execute to parse ratio approaches 100 percent for an active system, this is another indication that the system is taking advantage of shared SQL.

The V$ Views

By default, Oracle collects vital performance statistics such as those in Table 10-1 and makes them readily available to users via several data dictionary views. Most of these views, commonly referred to as *dynamic performance views*, are owned by SYS and begin with the prefix V$: V$SESSTAT, V$SYSSTAT, and V$STATNAME are just a few examples of such views. However, until you gain some experience tuning Oracle, querying the V$ views and making sense of the corresponding tuning statistics can be daunting.

Statspack

Oracle XE ships with a tool called *Statspack* for collecting performance statistics that you can use to help identify specific problems and tune Oracle more efficiently. Each time you execute Statspack, the tool collects statistics and stores them in your database as a *snapshot*. Subsequently, you can generate tuning reports based on snapshots.

When using Statspack, you can configure it to collect snapshot statistics with more or less detail, depending on your needs. For example, a Level 0 snapshot contains general performance statistics, including statistics related to system, wait, background, and session events; System Global Area (SGA) memory caches (including the buffer pools, dictionary cache, and library cache); and internal system latches. The default snapshot level is a Level 5 snapshot, which is a Level 0 snapshot plus statistics related to demanding SQL statements: by default, a demanding SQL statement is a statement that executes 100 times or more, a statement that performs 1000 or more disk reads, a statement that performs 1000 or more parse calls, or a statement that performs 10,000 or more buffer gets.

NOTE
Oracle XE automatically collects hourly snapshots of vital statistics related to its operation and records them in a set of database tables known collectively as the automatic workload repository (AWR). *While AWR snapshots and reports are very similar to Statspack snapshots, the AWR is not a licensed part of Oracle XE. Therefore, this chapter explains how to use Statspack rather than the AWR.*

Application Tuning

In my nearly 20 years of working with Oracle, if I had a dollar for every poorly written SQL statement, missing index, or ill-conceived transaction that I've come across, I probably would have more money than Larry Ellison. OK, that's a slight exaggeration. But seriously, here's my one-sentence theory that explains why application-side issues are typically to blame for most performance problems:

> *Application developers (and in some cases, database administrators) rarely test the performance of a new application in a realistic setting before deploying the application in a production environment.*

Believe it or not, it's that simple. The previous example in this chapter about tuning a DSS is a perfect illustration of my real-life experiences. To refresh your memory, here's a more detailed reenactment of an all-to-common scenario that takes place, I fear, every day in IT shops around the globe:

1. When developers are in the process of building the DSS application, the associated database tables contain very little data—perhaps just a few rows in each table to provide enough information to validate the functionality of the DSS application's queries.

2. Developers write the DSS queries and make sure that they return the expected results with adequate response times. No matter how complex or simple the queries are, or how much data the queries process and return, all of the queries exhibit excellent response times. Of course they do—they aren't doing much of anything considering the development data set. This type of testing provides absolutely no basis for what to expect when the application goes live.

3. Now the application is deployed in a production environment. Initially, the queries provide excellent response times because, like the test environment, the production database tables have very little data at first. Everybody is happy at this point in time.

4. As days, weeks, and months go by, more and more data is input into the operational database tables that support the DSS application queries. Queries that once returned results in seconds, now take several minutes, even hours to complete. At this point, the DBA usually gets a phone call from a developer or user that goes something like this: "The application was performing just fine a while ago. What database change *did you make* that is killing performance of the application?"

5. The DBA scratches his or her head and spends lots of time trying to determine what has changed over the past several months—after all, the application used to perform well, so the key to solving the problem must be related to something that has changed with Oracle or the host server. Have any new applications been deployed on the same computer? Could network bandwidth have increased? Maybe a disk that stores database information has become fragmented. Or perhaps there are new host operating system bottlenecks that are preventing Oracle from serving its applications well. The list of things to investigate is endless.

All of these headaches could easily have been avoided, if only that application had been tested under a realistic load using a realistic data set—it would have been obvious that certain queries perform poorly, and those queries could have been rewritten, or indexes could have been put in place to reduce the response time for the slow queries.

The next several sections explain a few of the most common application-tuning issues to be aware of as you tune an Oracle XE database application system.

Complex SQL Statements

Just because it's possible to join umpteen tables, specify SELECT list expressions for a query that call user-defined PL/SQL functions with cursors that query any number of large database tables, and use the UNION operator to combine the results of many related queries doesn't mean that you should do all these things. Nonetheless, certain people seem to think no matter what they throw at Oracle, it should be able to handle everything without any problems.

If you plan to write applications for Oracle XE, do yourself a favor: write the simplest SQL statements that you can so that they are straightforward to monitor and tune. In circumstances when you absolutely need to do something out of the ordinary, pay special attention that you code the query to execute as efficiently as possible, and spend some extra time trying to tune its performance. For example, if you have to write a query that joins ten tables, then by all means do it, but make sure that you test and analyze the query to ensure that it joins the tables as efficiently as possible.

Data Access Methods and Indexes

Unfortunately, Oracle XE databases cannot function without having to perform the work associated with physical and logical I/O. While Oracle XE cannot avoid I/O altogether, there are many ways to minimize it. For example, when a query or DML statement targets a specific row, one of two general *data access methods* are possible: Oracle can perform a full table scan looking for the target row, or Oracle can make use of some type of index to quickly identify the target row's ROWID and then read just the data block(s) that contains the target row.

The latter approach discussed in the previous paragraph might sound like it is always the best data access method, but there are many cases in which it is not. SQL statements that target large tables should typically avoid full table scans that return few rows, if possible, to avoid the work required by I/O. But with small lookup tables that utilize just a few data blocks, it might actually require more I/O to scan an index and then read a data block. Oracle determines an efficient data access method for a SQL statement during the parse phase of SQL statement execution. To compare the relative cost of one data access method versus another, Oracle's optimizer relies on statistics about the database system itself and data structures that the statement targets, including a table's available indexes. As you already know from Chapter 5, all Oracle XE databases create and schedule a nightly job that automatically and efficiently collects optimizer statistics for system and user-defined data structures so that Oracle's optimizer can do its job well. Additionally, you can manually collect other statistics that may further help the optimizer make better choices.

Indexes are important to consider for any database application schema. *Because developers are the people that best understand a database application's underlying data access routines, they are without question the best-qualified people to decide what indexes would best help minimize the physical and logical reads performed by the application.* Yet database application developers often focus only on the functionality of the application and forget to spend the any time, for example, noting which columns queries and DML statements specify in WHERE clauses. Consequently, adequate indexes are not put in place unless someone goes back and specifically considers SQL statement response times or tunes the application when it delivers poor performance. Subsequent exercises in this chapter demonstrate how to identify columns to index that would benefit application performance most.

Data Concurrency and Locking

Data concurrency is a key issue in multiuser database systems. The system must allow multiple users to concurrently share access to a database, while at the same time ensure database integrity by preventing conflicting operations. For example, consider the situation in which your transaction updates a row in a table. Other concurrent transactions should not be able to see your transaction's changes nor should they be able to update the same row until after your transaction commits.

Otherwise, users would be able to see or overwrite your work in progress, which you may or may not actually commit.

To prevent data concurrency problems such as those that the previous example intimates, Oracle automatically locks the rows and tables that a transaction modifies, and only releases the locks when the transaction commits or rolls back—this default locking behavior is a key point to consider when designing application transactions that modify data. While Oracle's locking mechanisms ensure that the updates made by many concurrent transactions cannot conflict with one another, they also have the potential to reduce data concurrency and hinder concurrent transactions from completing work. To prevent unnecessary wait times and poor OLTP application performance, strive to design DML transactions that complete a single unit of work and then commit; this type of well-designed transaction acquires the necessary locks to prevent conflicting operations, performs its work, and then releases the locks without further delay.

NOTE
Queries are read-only operations and do not normally lock any data (see the following discussion). To deliver read concurrency without locking, Oracle uses undo data to deliver its unique multiversioning mechanism, as previously explained in Chapter 8.

While Oracle's automatic locking mechanisms work fine for most applications, certain applications can benefit from or require the use of explicit locking techniques. For example, some applications let users interactively decide which rows to update or delete from a set of candidate rows. In such cases, the application can function better when it explicitly acquires row locks on all candidate rows before letting the user interactively update specific rows, rather than acquiring row locks one by one when the user identifies a target row. To explicitly acquire row locks for candidate rows, an application can use the SQL command SELECT with the FOR UPDATE clause. For example, the following query intentionally locks the rows in the CUSTOMERS table that correspond to customers in the state of Connecticut, with the intention of later updating these rows in the same transaction:

```
SELECT * FROM customers
  WHERE state = 'CT'
    FOR UPDATE OF customers.state;
```

Even though Oracle provides mechanisms for explicitly locking data, it is the developer's responsibility to ensure that transactions do not create problem situations known as deadlocks. A *deadlock* happens in a multitransaction environment when two transactions interact such that neither can proceed. For example, consider the following scenario:

1. Transaction 1 locks table T1.

2. Transaction 2 locks table T2.

3. Transaction 1 attempts to lock table T2, but ends up waiting for Transaction 2 to release its lock on the table.

4. Transaction 2 attempts to lock table T1, but ends up waiting for Transaction 1 to release its lock on the table.

5. Both transactions are waiting for each other to continue, but neither can, because of each other's table locks.

The example transactions in the preceding scenario result in a deadlock because the locking order of the transactions causes each transaction to block the other. Fortunately, Oracle automatically detects a deadlock and then resolves it by rolling back the statement that detects the deadlock. Although it might seem far-fetched, applications with long DML transactions that hold locks for extended periods of time coupled with explicit data-locking techniques (LOCK TABLE statements, SELECT ... FOR UPDATE statements) can lead to deadlock situations. When it is imperative to design transactions that explicitly lock data, it is especially important to design those transactions so that they complete as quickly as possible and release their locks, to avoid data concurrency issues.

Application-Tuning Exercises

The exercises in this section illustrate some common situations that you might experience when attempting to tune the performance of an Oracle XE database application. This chapter's support script builds a schema similar to the schema used in several previous chapters (CUSTOMERS, ORDERS, ITEMS, PARTS, and SALESREPS tables) with a couple of significant differences:

■ Each table contains a representative amount of data. The PARTS and SALESREPS lookup tables contain just a few rows each, but the CUSTOMERS table contains 50,000 rows, the ORDERS table contains 200,000 rows, and the ITEMS table contains 400,000 rows.

■ Each table has only one index, the underlying index for its primary key constraint.

TIP
See this chapter's support script for some ideas of how to quickly populate an application's tables with mock data that you can use while testing the performance of the application.

EXERCISE 10.1: Install Statspack

By default, Statspack is not available until after you install it in your Oracle XE database. When you install Statspack, the process creates a new database user account called PERFSTAT and an associated schema of tables, indexes, etc., to maintain Statspack snapshots. Before installing Statspack, realize that the PERFSTAT schema can require up to 45MB of storage, so make sure that your database has adequate free space available for the installation of Statspack.

Before installing Statspack, make sure that it is not already installed. After connecting as SYSTEM, the following simple query of the DBA_USERS data dictionary view is a quick way to check whether the database contains the PERFSTAT account—if it does, Statspack is already installed and you can skip this exercise:

```
SELECT username FROM dba_users
  WHERE username = 'PERFSTAT';
```

To install Statspack, use your current SQL*Plus session to execute the following commands:

```
CONNECT / AS SYSDBA;

@?/rdbms/admin/spcreate.sql;
```

The following example results demonstrate the prompts that you can expect to see during the installation of Statspack (example responses are highlighted in bold):

```
Choose the PERFSTAT user's password
-----------------------------------
Not specifying a password will result in the installation FAILING

Enter value for perfstat_password: azqR0200
azqR0200


Choose the Default tablespace for the PERFSTAT user
---------------------------------------------------
Below is the list of online tablespaces in this database which can
store user data.  Specifying the SYSTEM tablespace for the user's
```

default tablespace will result in the installation FAILING, as
using SYSTEM for performance data is not supported.

Choose the PERFSTAT users's default tablespace. This is the tablespace
in which the STATSPACK tables and indexes will be created.

```
TABLESPACE_NAME                 CONTENTS  STATSPACK DEFAULT TABLESPACE
------------------------------  --------- ----------------------------
SYSAUX                          PERMANENT *
USERS                           PERMANENT
```

Pressing <return> will result in STATSPACK's recommended default
tablespace (identified by *) being used.

Enter value for default_tablespace:

Using tablespace USERS as PERFSTAT default tablespace.

Choose the Temporary tablespace for the PERFSTAT user

Below is the list of online tablespaces in this database which can
store temporary data (e.g. for sort workareas). Specifying the SYSTEM
tablespace for the user's temporary tablespace will result in the
installation FAILING, as using SYSTEM for workareas is not supported.

Choose the PERFSTAT user's Temporary tablespace.

```
TABLESPACE_NAME                 CONTENTS  DB DEFAULT TEMP TABLESPACE
------------------------------  --------- -------------------------
TEMP                            TEMPORARY *
```

Pressing <return> will result in the database's default Temporary
tablespace (identified by *) being used.

Enter value for temporary_tablespace: **TEMP**

Using tablespace TEMP as PERFSTAT temporary tablespace.

```
.
... truncated for brevity ...
.
```

Creating Package STATSPACK...

Package created.

```
No errors.
Creating Package Body STATSPACK...

Package body created.

No errors.

NOTE:
SPCPKG complete. Please check spcpkg.lis for any errors.
```

After you complete the installation of Statspack, use operating system commands or a text editor to review the contents of the spcpkg.lis, spctab.lis, and spcusr.lis log files in the ORACLE_HOME/bin directory for any errors. If these log files contain evidence of errors that occurred during the installation of Statspack, correct the problem(s) and then uninstall Statspack by executing the ORACLE_HOME/rdbms/admin/spdrop.sql script before repeating this exercise.

EXERCISE 10.2: Take a Default Snapshot

A Statspack snapshot is a record of Oracle XE performance-tuning statistics, as they existed when the snapshot was taken. By comparing two snapshots, you can gain insight into what happened or what changed between when the two snapshots were taken. When diagnosing a problem with Statspack, try to choose two consecutive snapshots that bookend an occurrence of the problem; otherwise, statistics that correspond to problems tend to be less prominent as they average out over time.

For the purposes of the next several exercises, pretend that you have received complaints from users that every Friday afternoon between 4:30 P.M. and 4:45 P.M., the OLTP/DSS system performs noticeably slower. After some discussions with users, you learn that the salespeople in your organization are required to submit weekly reports including summary information about the sales that they have made during the week. You also learn that the report that each salesperson executes during this time period takes longer than they would like to complete. Other than that, you are not sure exactly what is happening.

Your plan is to create Statspack snapshots before and after the problem time period and collect statistics that will hopefully reveal more about what is happening to slow the system's performance. Pretend that it is Friday afternoon at 4:20 P.M. To manually create a new Statspack snapshot, execute the following statements with your current SQL*Plus session:

```
CONNECT perfstat;

EXECUTE statspack.snap;
```

Notice in the preceding example that making a default Statspack snapshot of current system statistics is very simple—all that you have to do is call the SNAP procedure of the PERFSTAT.STATSPACK package.

NOTE
When you call the SNAP procedure without any input parameters, as this exercise demonstrates, Oracle collects statistics for the snapshot according to the current default Statspack parameter settings. You can also call the SNAP procedure with one or more input parameters so that Oracle collects statistics for the snapshot according to the input parameter settings that you provide, or permanently modify default snapshot settings using the MODIFY_STATSPACK_PARAMETER procedure of the STATSPACK package. For complete information about Statspack, see the file ORACLE_HOME/rdbms/admin/spdoc.txt.

EXERCISE 10.3: Simulate and Investigate the Problem

To simulate the problems, use your current SQL*Plus session to establish a connection as SYSTEM and then execute the chap10_simulation1.sql support script for this book:

```
CONNECT system;

@C:\temp\handsonxe\sql\chap10_simulation1.sql;
```

The script is designed to take several minutes to run—it's supposed to simulate a situation that requires a lot of work and time to complete. Immediately after you start the script to simulate the problem situation, work through the following steps to investigate what is happening, while it is happening:

1. Launch the Database Home Page. It will most likely take more time than normal to launch, because Oracle XE is under an abnormal load.

2. Connect as **HANDSONXE10** with the password **PASSWORD**.

3. Click Administration.

4. Click Monitor.

5. Click Top SQL.

6. Enter the database credentials for **SYSTEM** to continue.

7. Notice that you can focus the report of Top SQL statements in several ways by using the form elements at the top of the web page. For the purposes of

this exercise, complete the following steps to focus the report on the SQL statements specifically of interest to you:

a. In the SQL Text field, specify **handsonxe** to limit SQL statements to those that include the string "handsonxe".

b. Select CPU Time in the Top By list.

c. Click Go.

The display of Top SQL statements given these filters should appear similar to Figure 10-2.

The top SQL statement should be a statement that has been executed hundreds of times, a query that begins with the following SQL text:

```
SELECT C.LASTNAME AS "CUSTOMER" ...
```

When you discover a problem SQL statement, you can investigate the statement's execution plan to see how Oracle executes the statement using Oracle's explain plan

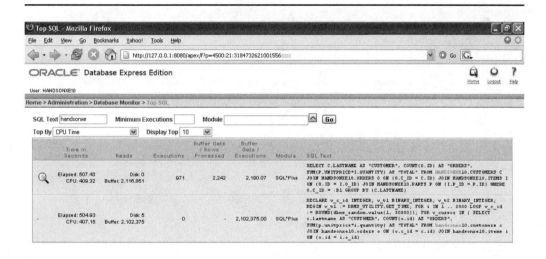

FIGURE 10-2. *The Top SQL page of Oracle Application Express provides you with information about the SQL that is performing the most work.*

feature. The SQL command EXPLAIN PLAN is the basis for this feature, but far more user-friendly interfaces to the underlying command exist in many different tools. For example, to display the execution plan that Oracle uses for the top SQL statement in the Top SQL report, click the magnifying glass icon adjacent to the statement. The execution plan for the SQL statement should appear as shown in Figure 10-3.

The execution plan for a SQL statement is an upside-down, hierarchical tree of data access methods and execution steps that Oracle uses to process the statement. Read an execution plan from the child-most bottom levels of the tree and progressively work your way up to the top of the tree to understand the order of how Oracle processes the statement. Each step in an execution plan has several attributes that are useful in diagnosing its efficiency:

- **Operation field**   Indicates what is happening for a given step in the execution plan.

- **Options field**   Indicates more information about the corresponding operation.

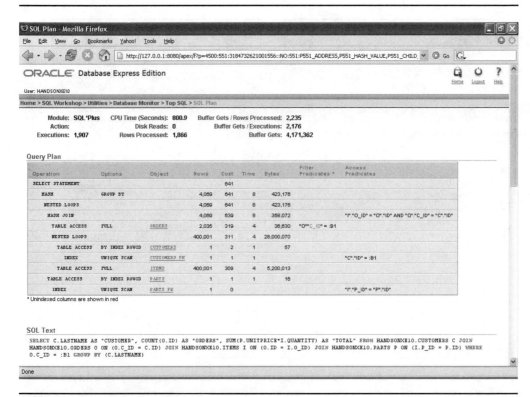

FIGURE 10-3.   *From the Top SQL report, you can drill down on problem statements to reveal their execution plan.*

- **Object field**   Indicates the data structure (table or index) that is the target of the corresponding operation.

- **Rows field**   Indicates an estimate of the number of rows returned by the operation.

- **Cost field**   Indicates a relative measurement that is the cost for the corresponding operation. The cost associated with a parent operation is an accumulation of the cost for all child operations.

- **Time field**   Indicates an estimate of the amount of time (in seconds) that the corresponding operation requires to complete. The time associated with a parent operation is an accumulation of the time for all child operations.

- **Bytes field**   Indicates an estimate of the number of bytes that the corresponding operation requires to complete.

- **Filter Predicates field**   Indicates the predicates (WHERE clause conditions) that the statement uses to limit the rows produced by the corresponding operation.

- **Access Predicates field**   Indicates the predicates that the statement uses to locate rows in data structures—for example, the join conditions used to join tables.

NOTE
The numeric value of a step's cost is a relative measurement—in other words, it does not correspond to anything tangible such as milliseconds or logical reads. Therefore, analyze costs using a comparative method rather than a quantitative method.

When looking at a problem SQL statement's execution plan, focus on what requires the most work—remember, work is what you are trying to reduce. For example, in Figure 10-3, notice the following points in the execution plan for the query:

- Oracle accesses the ITEMS table with a full table scan. This step requires 5.2MB of I/O and corresponds to an estimated 4 seconds of execution time, half the overall execution time for the statement.

- The Nested Loops join step for the CUSTOMERS and ITEMS tables processes 28MB of data.

- Oracle accesses the ORDERS table with a full table scan, and the filter predicate (WHERE clause condition) contains an unindexed column (C_ID), as highlighted in red onscreen.

Now wait until the script completes; after it does, note the elapsed time that it takes to execute the script, as displayed by the script itself. You will use this elapsed time in comparisons to elapsed times in subsequent exercises. On my slower system, it took a little more than 16 minutes for the script to complete. On my faster system, it took a little more than 4 minutes to complete. Your system may be faster or slower, but the script should give you enough time to complete the intermediate steps in this exercise.

EXERCISE 10.4: Take Another Default Snapshot

Now pretend that it is Friday afternoon at 4:55 P.M., typically after the time of the problem period. Take another Statspack snapshot by executing the following statements with your current SQL*Plus session:

```
CONNECT perfstat;

EXECUTE statspack.snap;
```

EXERCISE 10.5: Review Statspack Snapshots

You can view information about Statspack snapshots by querying the PERSTAT .STATS$SNAPSHOT view. Using your current SQL*Plus session, enter the following statements to display some information about the snapshots that you created in the previous exercises:

```
ALTER SESSION
  SET NLS_DATE_FORMAT = 'DD-MON-YYYY HH24.MI.SS';

SELECT snap_id, snap_level, snap_time
  FROM perfstat.stats$snapshot
 ORDER BY snap_time ASC;
```

The results of the preceding query will vary with each execution, but the following results are representative of what you should see:

```
   SNAP_ID SNAP_LEVEL SNAP_TIME
---------- ---------- --------------------
         1          5 06-JUN-2006 06.07.37
         2          5 06-JUN-2006 06.32.21
```

Notice that, by default, each snapshot is a Level 5 snapshot. Remember, you can change default snapshot settings such as the snapshot level by using the MODIFY_STATSPACK_PARAMETER procedure of the STATSPACK package.

EXERCISE 10.6: Create a Statspack Report

You can generate reports of Statspack information in an Oracle XE database by using the ORACLE_HOME/rdbms/admin/spreport.sql script; this script displays statistics for a range of snapshot IDs. When using the script to identify statistics that can help you reveal the source of a problem, you should pick bookend snapshots that immediately encompass the events that you are attempting to tune.

Use your current SQL*Plus session to execute the following statement:

```
@?/rdbms/admin/spreport.sql;
```

The script then prompts you for information to build the report. The dialog that you have should be similar to the following. The highlighted text (in bold) indicates representative responses to script prompts—make sure to specify your specific begin snapshot ID and end snapshot ID when prompted, as the IDs shown in the following script output are specific to my execution of the script.

```
Current Instance
~~~~~~~~~~~~~~~~~

   DB Id     DB Name      Inst Num Instance
----------- ------------ -------- ------------
 2465914590 XE                  1 xe

Instances in this Statspack schema
~~~~~~~~~~~~~~~~~~~~~~~~~~~~~~~~~~~~

   DB Id     Inst Num DB Name      Instance     Host
----------- -------- ------------ ------------ ------------
 2465914590        1 XE           xe           ...

Using 2465914590 for database Id
Using           1 for instance number

Specify the number of days of snapshots to choose from
~~~~~~~~~~~~~~~~~~~~~~~~~~~~~~~~~~~~~~~~~~~~~~~~~~~~~~~~~~~~~
Entering the number of days (n) will result in the most recent
(n) days of snapshots being listed.  Pressing <return> without
specifying a number lists all completed snapshots.

Listing all Completed Snapshots

                                                  Snap
Instance     DB Name      Snap Id   Snap Started     Level Comment
------------ ------------ --------- ----------------- ----- -------

xe           XE                 1 06 Jun 2006 06:07      5
                               2 06 Jun 2006 06:32      5

Specify the Begin and End Snapshot Ids
~~~~~~~~~~~~~~~~~~~~~~~~~~~~~~~~~~~~~~~~~~
Enter value for begin_snap: 1
Begin Snapshot Id specified: 1

Enter value for end_snap: 2
End    Snapshot Id specified: 2
```

```
Specify the Report Name
~~~~~~~~~~~~~~~~~~~~~~~~~
The default report file name is sp_1_2.  To use this name,
press <return> to continue, otherwise enter an alternative.

Enter value for report_name: c:\temp\sp_1_2.txt
```

Once you respond to the last prompt and execute the script, it outputs information to both the screen and the specified text file; you can use a text editor to view the report contents. For example, the following is an example of the first few sections in a Statspack report:

```
STATSPACK report for

Database                    DB Id
Instance                    Inst Num
Startup Time                Release
RAC
~~~~~~~~                     -----------
-----------                  --------
---------------              -----------
---
                            2465914590 xe                     1
03-Jun-06 08:21 10.2.0.1.0  NO

Host  Name:   ALIDEV2        Num CPUs:    1
Phys Memory (MB):      768
~~~~

Snapshot       Snap Id   Snap Time          Sessions Curs/Sess Comment
~~~~~~~~       --------- ------------------ -------- --------- ------------
Begin Snap:         1 06-Jun-06 06:07:37        19       4.3
  End Snap:         2 06-Jun-06 06:32:21        19       4.0
  Elapsed:            24.73 (mins)

Cache Sizes              Begin        End
~~~~~~~~~~~              --------- ----------
      Buffer Cache:       156M        152M  Std Block Size:          8K
  Shared Pool Size:        84M
      Log Buffer:                    2,792K

Load Profile                           Per Second      Per Transaction
~~~~~~~~~~~~                           ---------------  ---------------
             Redo size:                    993.56            20,766.87
         Logical reads:                  2,992.31            62,543.41
         Block changes:                      3.55                74.27
         Physical reads:                     0.90                18.76
        Physical writes:                     3.07                64.18
             User calls:                     0.14                 3.03
                 Parses:                     3.83                80.14
            Hard parses:                     0.30                 6.30
                  Sorts:                     2.00                41.85
```

```
                   Logons:                  0.00                    0.10
                 Executes:                  9.19                  192.15
             Transactions:                  0.05

   % Blocks changed per Read:      0.12    Recursive Call %:        99.83
 Rollback per transaction %:       0.00    Rows per Sort:            6.73

Instance Efficiency Percentages
~~~~~~~~~~~~~~~~~~~~~~~~~~~~~~~~~~~
              Buffer Nowait %:   100.00      Redo NoWait %:   100.00
              Buffer  Hit   %:    99.97   In-memory Sort %:   100.00
              Library Hit   %:    93.55       Soft Parse %:    92.14
           Execute to Parse %:    58.29       Latch Hit %:    100.00
 Parse CPU to Parse Elapsd %:     27.73    % Non-Parse CPU:     99.35
 .
 .
 .
```

In just a few seconds, you have created a report that provides you with an overwhelming number of statistics that you can use to help narrow your focus to system components that could benefit from tuning.

EXERCISE 10.7: Analyze a Statspack Report

Given the knowledge that you gained from earlier sections of this chapter, you should already be familiar with a number of statistics in the Statspack report. Logical reads, physical reads, total parses, hard parses, executions, instance efficiency ratios, and many more are all present in the report. When analyzing a Statspack report, your job is to find problems that correspond to the problem at hand.

Start your analysis of a Statspack report by identifying where most of the work in the system is occurring. For example, just down from the top of the report, review the statistics in the Load Profile section, which should appear similar to the following:

```
Load Profile                      Per Second        Per Transaction
~~~~~~~~~~~~~                    ---------------     ---------------
                  Redo size:           993.56            20,766.87
              Logical reads:         2,992.31            62,543.41
              Block changes:             3.55                74.27
              Physical reads:            0.90                18.76
             Physical writes:            3.07                64.18
                 User calls:             0.14                 3.03
                     Parses:             3.83                80.14
                Hard parses:             0.30                 6.30
                      Sorts:             2.00                41.85
                     Logons:             0.00                 0.10
                   Executes:             9.19               192.15
               Transactions:             0.05

   % Blocks changed per Read:      0.12    Recursive Call %:        99.83
 Rollback per transaction %:       0.00    Rows per Sort:            6.73
```

What statistic stands out from all the rest? Logical I/O! Therefore, now turn your attention to what is causing all of that logical I/O. Skip ahead to the SQL Ordered by Gets section of the report (*gets*, or *buffer gets*, is a synonym for logical reads). This section of the report should appear similar to the following:

```
SQL ordered by Gets  DB/Inst: XE/xe  Snaps: 1-2
-> Resources reported for PL/SQL code includes the resources used by all
   SQL statements called by the code.
-> End Buffer Gets Threshold:      10000 Total Buffer Gets:     4,440,582
-> Captured SQL accounts for   99.8% of Total Buffer Gets
-> SQL reported below exceeded  1.0% of Total Buffer Gets

                                              CPU      Elapsd     Old
Buffer Gets  Executions  Gets per Exec %Total Time (s) Time (s) Hash Value
-----------  ----------  ------------- ------ -------- -------- ----------
  4,382,757           1    4,382,757.0   98.7   779.14   951.06 1227126023
Module: SQL*Plus
DECLARE  v_c_id INTEGER;  v_t1 BINARY_INTEGER;  v_t2 BINARY_INTE
GER; BEGIN v_t1 := DBMS_UTILITY.GET_TIME; FOR i IN 1 .. 2000    L
OOP     v_c_id := ROUND(dbms_random.value(1,50000));     FOR v_c
ursor IN (       SELECT c.lastname AS "CUSTOMER",            C
OUNT(o.id) AS "ORDERS",           SUM(p.unitprice*i.quantity)

  4,382,509       2,000        2,191.3   98.7   777.28   950.18 1532303781
Module: SQL*Plus
SELECT C.LASTNAME AS "CUSTOMER", COUNT(O.ID) AS "ORDERS", SUM(P.
UNITPRICE*I.QUANTITY) AS "TOTAL" FROM HANDSONXE10.CUSTOMERS C JO
IN HANDSONXE10.ORDERS O ON (O.C_ID = C.ID) JOIN HANDSONXE10.ITEM
S I ON (O.ID = I.O_ID) JOIN HANDSONXE10.PARTS P ON (I.P_ID = P.I
D) WHERE O.C_ID = :B1 GROUP BY (C.LASTNAME)
```

I should note that while writing this chapter, I noticed sometimes that the SQL Ordered by Gets section of the Statspack report did not appear at all or did not show the expected SQL statement. If you look at a Statspack report and do not see SQL statements that correspond to the highest statistic in the Load Profile section, it is most likely because the default setting for a parameter of the STATSPACK.SNAP procedure is too high. In this particular case, the snapshot parameter i_buffer_gets_th is likely set too high. To address this problem, try repeating this chapter's exercises, but in Exercises 10.2 and 10.4, create the snapshots with the following call:

```
EXECUTE statspack.snap(i_buffer_gets_th=>1000);
```

Once you have a representative Statspack report in place, the statistics show that the top two statements are a PL/SQL block, executed one time, and a query, executed 2000 times, that each generate a total of 4.3 million logical reads. In reality, the chap10_simulation1.sql script is a PL/SQL block that executes the same query 2000 times, so the data in the report is a bit misleading because the PL/SQL block encompasses the query.

Next, select, copy, and paste the query's SQL text into a text editor so that you can use it later while tuning the statement. The text should appear similar to the following after you fix the interword page breaks so that the statement has valid SQL syntax:

```
SELECT C.LASTNAME AS "CUSTOMER", COUNT(O.ID) AS "ORDERS",
SUM(P.UNITPRICE*I.QUANTITY) AS "TOTAL" FROM HANDSONXE10.CUSTOMERS C
JOIN HANDSONXE10.ORDERS O ON (O.C_ID = C.ID) JOIN HANDSONXE10.ITEMS I
ON (O.ID = I.O_ID) JOIN HANDSONXE10.PARTS P ON (I.P_ID = P.ID) WHERE
O.C_ID = :B1 GROUP BY (C.LASTNAME)
```

Although its layout is different, notice that this is the same query identified by the Top SQL report in Exercise 10.3.

EXERCISE 10.8: Create Indexes for Filter Predicate Columns

The execution plan for the problem query (see Figure 10-3) highlights that the ORDERS .C_ID column used in WHERE clause condition does not have an index. Let's create an index for the column and see how it affects the execution plan for each query.

To create an index for the C_ID column of the ORDERS table using Oracle Application Express, complete the following steps:

1. Click Home.

2. Click Object Browser.

3. Click ORDERS in the list of tables.

4. Click Indexes.

5. Click Create.

6. Select Normal from the Type of Index option list.

7. Click Next.

8. Specify **ORDERS_IDX1** for the Index Name field.

9. Select Non Unique from the Uniqueness list.

10. Select C_ID(NUMBER) for the Index Column 1 list.

11. Click Next.

12. Click SQL.

13. Confirm that the Object Browser has generated the following CREATE INDEX statement:

    ```
    create index "ORDERS_IDX1"
     on "ORDERS" ("C_ID")
     /
    ```

14. Click Finish.

NOTE
*Oracle XE automatically collects statistics for each
new index that you create.*

EXERCISE 10.9: Explain the New Results

Complete the following steps to manually test the query and discover how the new index on the ORDERS.C_ID column changes the execution plan:

1. Click Home.

2. Click SQL.

3. Click SQL Commands.

4. Paste the SQL text of the problem query into the SQL Commands page.

5. Substitute a literal value for the :B1 bind variable using a number between 1 and 50,000—a subsequent exercise explains more about bind variables. For example, nicely formatted, the text in the SQL Commands page should appear similar to the following (the substituted literal value is highlighted in bold):

```
SELECT c.lastname AS "CUSTOMER",
       COUNT(o.id) AS "ORDERS",
       SUM(p.unitprice*i.quantity) AS "TOTAL"
  FROM handsonxe10.customers c
  JOIN handsonxe10.orders o
    ON (o.c_id = c.id)
  JOIN handsonxe10.items i
    ON (o.id = i.o_id)
  JOIN handsonxe10.parts p
    ON (i.p_id = p.id)
 WHERE o.c_id = 1534
 GROUP BY (c.lastname);
```

6. Click Explain.

The execution plan for the query should appear as in Figure 10-4.

Now compare the query's execution plan before and after the index was created. Notice that the plan has changed slightly—Oracle no longer needs to access the ORDERS table with a full table scan because of a new index. But there is not much overall improvement in the work performed by the query—for example, the cost of the query has only dropped from 641 to 630. That's disappointing. Now turn your attention to the columns in the query's join conditions.

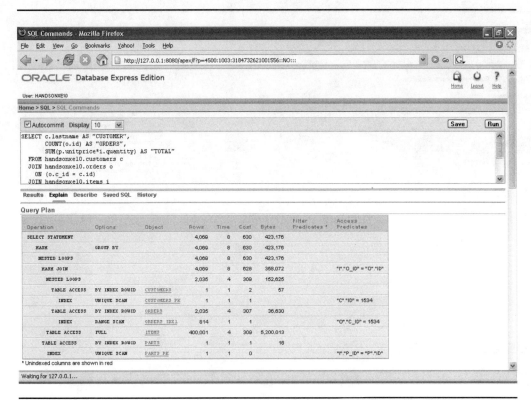

FIGURE 10-4. *The new execution plan for the problem query shows little improvement.*

EXERCISE 10.10: Discover and Display Unindexed Foreign Keys

The problem query joins four tables. The execution plans for the query list the access predicates (join conditions) for your convenience. Neglecting to index foreign key columns can result in poor join performance and lock escalation that hampers DML activity—therefore, it is common practice to index foreign keys. To see if this might be a problem, complete the following steps using Oracle Application Express:

1. Click Home.

2. Click Utilities.

3. Click Object Reports.

4. Click Tables.

5. Click Unindexed Foreign Keys.

The report should appear as in Figure 10-5.

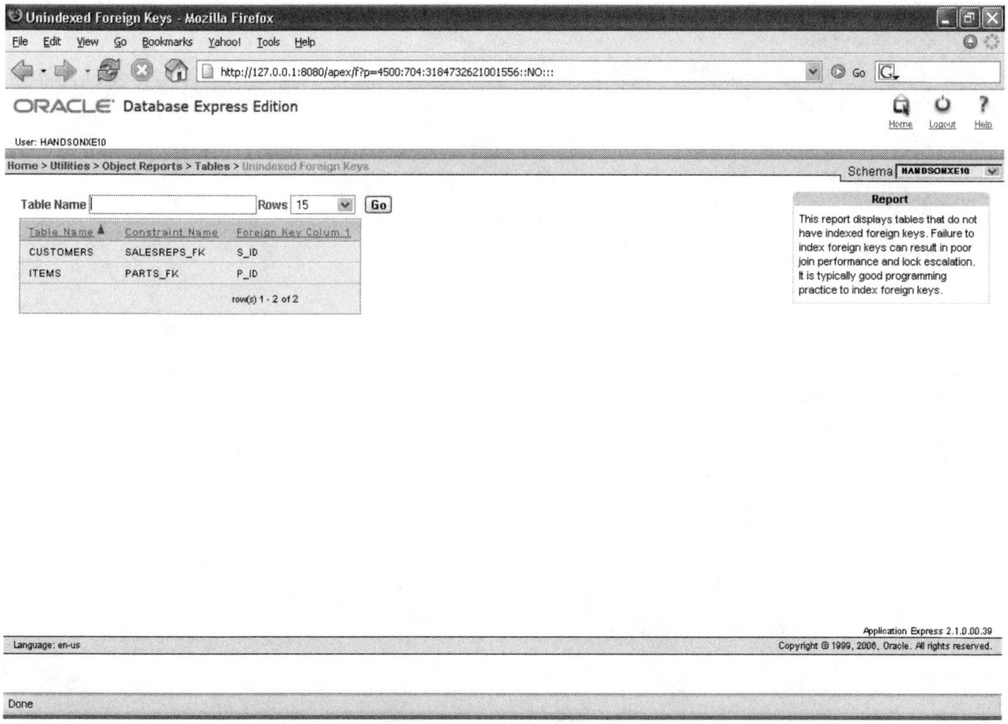

FIGURE 10-5. *Oracle Application Express makes it easy to identify foreign keys without indexes.*

Notice the foreign keys in the practice schema that do not have indexes: the S_ID column in the CUSTOMERS table and the P_ID column in the ITEMS table. The latter of the two is used in one of the join conditions for the problem query. To create an index for the P_ID column of the ITEMS table, complete the following steps:

1. Click Home.

2. Click Object Browser.

3. Select Tables from the Object Selection pane.

4. Click ITEMS.

5. Click Indexes.

6. Click Create.

7. Select Normal from the Type of Index option list.

8. Click Next.

9. Specify **ITEMS_IDX1** for the Index Name field.

10. Select Non Unique from the Uniqueness list.

11. Select P_ID(NUMBER) for the Index Column 1 list.

12. Click Next.

13. Click Finish.

NOTE
*Feel free to create an index for the S_ID column in
the CUSTOMERS table by using similar steps.*

EXERCISE 10.11: Explain the New Execution Plan

To test and display the effects of the new index, repeat the steps in Exercise 10.9.
The new execution plan for the problem query should appear as in Figure 10-6.

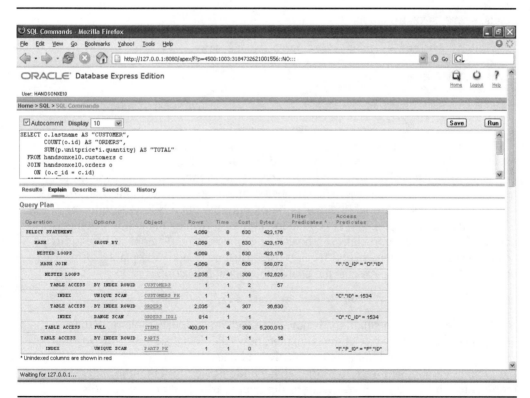

FIGURE 10-6. *The new execution plan for the problem query does not show any
improvement.*

$#%! Although it makes sense that the new index might help avoid a full scan of the ITEMS table, the new index did not change anything at all!

EXERCISE 10.12: Gather New Statistics

As you learn more and more about how Oracle executes SQL statements and you do something that makes perfect sense but Oracle's optimizer doesn't agree, you will often find that the optimizer doesn't make the correct choices because it doesn't understand the situation as well as you do. Why not? Usually it's because the optimizer does not have the statistics necessary to make the correct choices.

To make sure that the optimizer has the statistics that it needs to do its job effectively, use the SQL Commands page to execute the following PL/SQL block that refreshes the statistics for all tables in the HANDSONXE10 schema, including their indexes, and then generates some extra column statistics, known as *histograms*, for all indexed columns. A column's histogram reveals information about the distribution of data in the column, and is not normally created unless you specifically do so with procedures in the DBMS_STATS package.

```
BEGIN
  DBMS_STATS.GATHER_SCHEMA_STATS (
    OWNNAME => 'HANDSONXE10',
    ESTIMATE_PERCENT => DBMS_STATS.AUTO_SAMPLE_SIZE,
    METHOD_OPT => 'FOR ALL INDEXED COLUMNS SIZE AUTO',
    CASCADE => TRUE
  );
END;
/
```

With the new statistics in place, repeat the steps in Exercise 10.9. The new execution plan for the problem query should appear as in Figure 10-7.

That's more like it. The query no longer accesses any of the large tables using a full table scan and, as a result, the join operations are much more efficient. But wait, you are not finished yet. Although the execution plan for the query shows significant improvement, don't rely 100 percent on it. In many cases while tuning SQL statements, you will find that execution plans can be downright misleading. The only true test is to actually execute the statement and see if its response time is more acceptable. Using your SQL*Plus session, re-execute the chap10_simulate1.sql script:

```
@C:\temp\handsonxe\sql\chap10_simulation1.sql;
```

Wow! The "problem situation" is now gone. What previously took more than 16 minutes to execute on one of my computers now takes less than 5 seconds. In other testing, one time dropped from approximately 5 minutes to 3 seconds. Those are significant reductions in response time. That's undeniable proof that the statement requires much less work. If you were to dig deeper using other tuning tools (specifically, the SET AUTOTRACE command of SQL*Plus), you would find that the

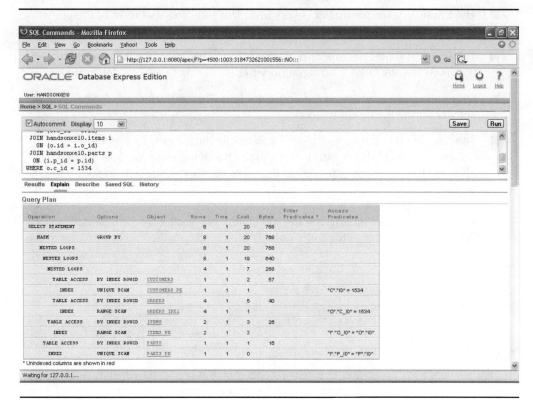

FIGURE 10-7.   *At last, the new execution plan for the query shows marked improvement.*

query once took about 2200 logical reads per execution but now takes only 36 logical reads per execution.

EXERCISE 10.13: Analyze Other Application-Related Statistics

In previous sections of this chapter, you learned about other types of application-related operations, such as parsing and sorting, that can be the source of lots of work. Even though you may feel that you have tuned the SQL statement that is the most likely culprit related to a specific problem, it's prudent to take a moment and research whether other things might be contributing to the problem. For example, take a closer look at the Load Profile section in the Statspack report:

■   The Redo size and Block changes parameters are the next highest statistics in the table. However, considering that you created a couple of new Statspack snapshots, you would expect this type of activity related to the corresponding DML operations.

- The Physical reads parameter is very low. This indicates that most of the data being used by the system is cached in memory.

- The Physical writes parameter is also very low. This indicates that very little data is written by DBWR from memory to disk during this report interval.

- User calls and Transactions are both very low. This indicates very little DML activity during the report interval.

- The ratio of Hard parses to Parses is low, while the Executes parameter is somewhat active. This means that the system is doing some work (it is not idle) and that the parsing related to the work corresponds mostly to soft parses.

Now scroll down a few lines to the Instance Efficiency section of the report, which should appear similar to the following:

```
Instance Efficiency Percentages
~~~~~~~~~~~~~~~~~~~~~~~~~~~~~~~~~~
            Buffer Nowait %:  100.00        Redo NoWait %:  100.00
            Buffer  Hit   %:   99.97    In-memory Sort %:  100.00
            Library Hit   %:   93.55        Soft Parse %:   92.14
        Execute to Parse %:   58.29        Latch Hit %:  100.00
Parse CPU to Parse Elapsd %:   27.73     % Non-Parse CPU:   99.35
```

Overall, notice that most ratios are near 100 percent. But be careful when analyzing an instance's health using these ratios—remember that these ratios are not measures of how much work the system is doing, they are measures of how efficiently the system is doing what work is happening.

For example, the buffer cache hit ratio is nearly 100 percent. This means that the ratio of physical reads to the total number of physical, logical, and consistent reads is very low. What can you conclude from this fact? One of two things: the system is doing no read I/O work at all, or the read I/O work that the system is doing is being performed as efficiently as possible (in memory). You cannot necessarily conclude that the system's I/O is well-tuned, as proven by the significant number of logical I/Os performed by the problem query in previous exercises.

Now take a look at the Soft Parse ratio. Given that the system is active and that the Soft Parse ratio is nearly 100 percent, you can conclude that the parsing happening in the system is nearly all soft parsing, which is much more efficient than hard parsing. The SQL statements at work during the report interval are coded in such a manner that Oracle XE is able to share the application's parsed SQL statements in memory. As you work more and more with Oracle XE, you will eventually notice that minor variations in SQL text can prevent the use of shared SQL. For example, the following two SQL statements are nearly identical except for the literals (highlighted in bold) in the condition of the WHERE clause:

```
SELECT c.lastname AS "CUSTOMER",
       COUNT(o.id) AS "ORDERS",
       SUM(p.unitprice*i.quantity) AS "TOTAL"
  FROM handsonxe10.customers c
  JOIN handsonxe10.orders o
    ON (o.c_id = c.id)
  JOIN handsonxe10.items i
    ON (o.id = i.o_id)
  JOIN handsonxe10.parts p
    ON (i.p_id = p.id)
 WHERE o.c_id = 24531
 GROUP BY (c.lastname);

SELECT c.lastname AS "CUSTOMER",
       COUNT(o.id) AS "ORDERS",
       SUM(p.unitprice*i.quantity) AS "TOTAL"
  FROM handsonxe10.customers c
  JOIN handsonxe10.orders o
    ON (o.c_id = c.id)
  JOIN handsonxe10.items i
    ON (o.id = i.o_id)
  JOIN handsonxe10.parts p
    ON (i.p_id = p.id)
 WHERE o.c_id = 102
 GROUP BY (c.lastname);
```

In such cases, you can code applications to use a bind variable rather than literals to supply the statement a specific value at run time. A *bind variable*, also called a *host variable*, is a variable that an application declares and uses to pass a value to an embedded SQL or PL/SQL statement at run time. By using a bind variable rather than literals in WHERE clauses and other parts of SQL statements, you can better take advantage of shared SQL. In fact, the reason that the problem query in this chapter's previous exercise generates a high Soft Parse ratio is that it uses a bind variable. To understand this better, use operating system commands or a text editor to take a closer look at the PL/SQL block inside the chap10_simulate1.sql script:

```
DECLARE
  v_c_id INTEGER;
  v_t1 BINARY_INTEGER;
  v_t2 BINARY_INTEGER;
BEGIN
v_t1 := DBMS_UTILITY.GET_TIME;
FOR i IN 1 .. 2000
  LOOP
    v_c_id := ROUND(dbms_random.value(1,50000));
    FOR v_cursor IN (
      SELECT c.lastname AS "CUSTOMER",
             COUNT(o.id) AS "ORDERS",
             SUM(p.unitprice*i.quantity) AS "TOTAL"
```

```
     FROM handsonxe10.customers c
     JOIN handsonxe10.orders o
       ON (o.c_id = c.id)
     JOIN handsonxe10.items i
       ON (o.id = i.o_id)
     JOIN handsonxe10.parts p
       ON (i.p_id = p.id)
    WHERE o.c_id = v_c_id
    GROUP BY (c.lastname) )
  LOOP
    NULL;
   END LOOP;
 END LOOP;
v_t2 := DBMS_UTILITY.GET_TIME;
DBMS_OUTPUT.PUT_LINE('');
DBMS_OUTPUT.PUT_LINE('Elapsed time(seconds): ' || (v_t2 - v_t1)/100);
END;
/
```

The basic functionality of the block is a loop that executes 2000 times. For each iteration of the loop, the block assigns a random number between 1 and 50000 to the variable v_c_id, and then executes a query (as a cursor) using the v_c_id variable in the WHERE clause of the query to target a specific row in the CUSTOMERS table. The variable's value is bound to the query at run time. Because the text of the SQL statement does not change for each execution, Oracle XE can efficiently reuse the query's parsed representation in the shared pool and avoid extra work.

In conclusion, as you develop applications for Oracle XE and know that a SQL statement is likely to execute many times, use bind variables whenever possible to eliminate the unnecessary overhead associated with hard parsing.

Database Instance Tuning

Although you will find that application-related issues normally correspond to the most substantial performance problems, it is also important to make sure that an Oracle XE database instance is properly configured to serve the expected load on the system. This section provides you with brief introductions to several important database instance tuning topics.

The System Global Area

The *System Global Area* or *Shared Global Area (SGA)* is a collective term that refers to a database instance's shared memory caches. The data in an instance's SGA is data that Oracle XE shares among processes at work in the instance. Figure 10-8 and the following list identify the most prominent memory caches that make up the SGA.

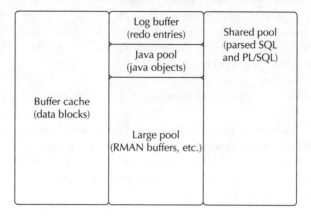

FIGURE 10-8.   *A database instance's SGA contains several memory caches, including the database buffer cache, the shared pool, and the log buffer.*

The following structures are present in every instance's SGA:

- **Buffer cache**   Stores the data blocks most recently used by applications. For example, when you update a row in a table, a process reads the data block that contains the target row from a data file into the buffer cache and then updates the block in memory. (A data block in memory is commonly referred to as a *buffer*.) Subsequently, if another user updates the same row or another row that is in the data block, Oracle avoids unnecessary physical I/O and simply updates the version of the buffer that is already in the buffer cache. Eventually, a database writer (DBWR) background process writes dirty (modified) buffers in the buffer cache back to the database's data files, either when it is most efficient to do so or when a checkpoint occurs. By default, an Oracle XE database instance has one default buffer cache; however, you can create different types of buffer caches to fine-tune the caching of different types of data.

- **Shared pool**   A collection of caches that, together, works to share the most recently and frequently used application and data dictionary access code. For example, when an application executes a query, Oracle parses the query and determines the optimal execution plan for the query. Subsequently, Oracle caches the parsed and optimized version of the query in the library cache. When another user executes the same query, Oracle notes this fact and shares the version of the query that is already in the library cache instead of processing the same statement again. Previous sections introduce and demonstrate these mechanisms as shared SQL.

■ **Redo log buffer** A relatively small SGA memory cache that the log writer (LGWR) background process uses to collect log entries. When a transaction commits, every 3 seconds, or when the log buffer becomes one-third full, LGWR writes the entire buffer to the members of the current online log group with a minimal amount of disk I/O.

Optionally, an instance's SGA can contain the following memory structures:

■ **Large pool** When an instance allocates a large pool in addition to a shared pool, Oracle allocates session memory for certain operations, such as large buffers for RMAN backup and restore operations, from the large pool rather than the shared pool. Use of a large pool can reduce otherwise unnecessary aging of shared SQL from the shared pool.

■ **Java pool** When an instance needs to support applications that take advantage of Oracle's support for Java (for example, Java stored procedures), the SGA must contain a Java pool to cache Java programs, similar to the library cache and PL/SQL programs.

Program Global Areas

Each Oracle user session has a *Program Global Area* or *Private Global Area (PGA)*. A session's PGA is a private memory area that contains data and control information for the session's user process.

A session's PGA has sections of memory that you can tune, and other sections of memory that you cannot tune. For example, you cannot tune the PGA memory that a session uses to execute and temporarily store the run-time area of a cursor or session state of a package—the size of this memory area is fixed by Oracle. Consequently, the size of each session's PGA is typically not an important tuning issue for OLTP systems because the majority of PGA memory used by an OLTP session corresponds to parts of the PGA that you cannot tune.

On the other hand, it is much more important to configure and tune the amount of PGA memory available to database sessions in a data mart, data warehouse, and DSS; in these types of environments, a database session typically executes complex and demanding queries that allocate and use work areas in the PGA to process memory-intensive operations such as sort and hash join operations. For example:

■ When a user process allocates a work area for a query in its PGA that is just large enough to fit all of the input data and auxiliary memory structures that correspond to a SQL operator (for example, GROUP BY or ORDER BY), the size of the work area is optimal.

- When a user process allocates a work area that is larger than necessary, the extra memory is wasted.

- When a user process allocates a work area that is too small, query response time suffers for two reasons: because the session's server process will likely need to generate disk I/O as it uses temporary segments in a temporary tablespace, and because the server process has to make more than one pass over the input data in the work area.

Tuning PGA memory allocation for query-related sessions can help to minimize costly operations such as sort I/O.

Database Instance Tuning Exercises

The exercises in this section demonstrate some common things that you can do to investigate the current configuration of an Oracle XE database instance's memory structures and to tune their sizes.

EXERCISE 10.14: Display Current Overall Memory Utilization

To display the current settings for an Oracle XE database instance's SGA and PGA memory allocations, complete the following steps using your current Oracle Application Express session:

1. Click Home.

2. Click Administration.

3. Click Memory.

Oracle Application Express then displays information about the instance's memory utilization, similar to Figure 10-9.

Remember that Oracle XE limits an instance's total amount of SGA and PGA memory to 1GB. The gauges in the display provide a quick look at where you stand relative to this limit.

EXERCISE 10.15: Display Information About the SGA

To display more specific information about the memory caches in the SGA, click the Configure SGA hyperlink on the Memory page of Oracle Application Express. The ensuing page should appear similar to Figure 10-10.

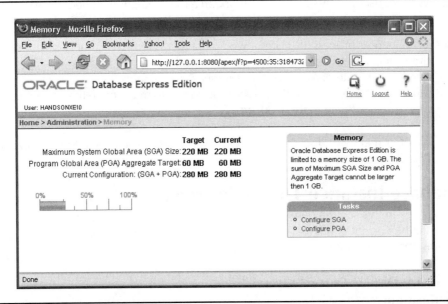

FIGURE 10-9. *The Memory page of Oracle Application Express displays how much memory the current Oracle XE instance has allocated and can allocate for the SGA and all PGAs combined.*

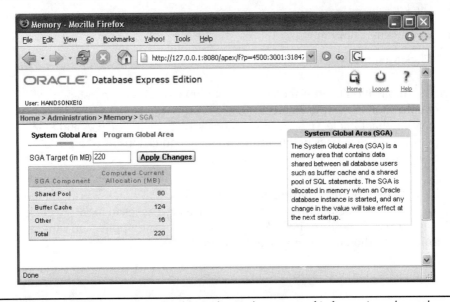

FIGURE 10-10. *The SGA page displays a limited amount of information about the memory caches in the SGA, including the buffer cache and the shared pool.*

As the display indicates, the combined size of the buffer cache, shared pool, and other optional SGA structures determines the size of an instance's SGA. You control the overall size of the SGA by using the following initialization parameters:

- **SGA_TARGET**   Set this parameter to the desired SGA size. You can set the parameter as a number of bytes, kilobytes, megabytes, or gigabytes.

- **SGA_MAX_SIZE**   Optionally, set this parameter to the maximum allowable SGA size. When you set the SGA_MAX_SIZE parameter to a number larger than SGA_TARGET, you can dynamically adjust the size of the SGA_TARGET parameter (and the current SGA) up to the setting of SGA_MAX_SIZE without having to stop and restart Oracle XE; when SGA_MAX_SIZE is set to 0, the maximum SGA size is determined by the setting of the SGA_TARGET parameter. You can set the SGA_MAX_SIZE parameter as a number of bytes, kilobytes, megabytes, or gigabytes. By default, an Oracle XE database instance's SGA_MAX_SIZE parameter defers to the setting of SGA_TARGET.

Once the size of the SGA is set, the size of individual caches in the SGA can be set either manually by you or automatically by Oracle XE. Although you can specify individual initialization parameters to control the size of individual SGA structures, Oracle Corporation recommends that you use Oracle XE's automatic SGA memory management option unless you have a specific tuning requirement. To configure automatic SGA memory management, make sure that the following initialization parameters are set as follows:

- Set STATISTICS_LEVEL to TYPICAL or ALL; doing so allows Oracle XE to automatically adjust the sizes of the default buffer cache, shared pool, large pool, Java pool, and streams pool in response to the current workload on the system.

- Set the initialization parameters that control the dynamically resizable pools mentioned in the previous item, specifically DB_CACHE_SIZE, SHARED_POOL_SIZE, LARGE_POOL_SIZE, JAVA_POOL_SIZE, and STREAMS_POOL_SIZE.

By default, an Oracle XE database instance's initialization parameters are properly configured to take advantage of automatic SGA memory management. To display the current size for the SGA's dynamic components, use your current SQL*Plus session or the SQL Commands page of Oracle Application Express to execute the following query:

```
SELECT component, current_size
  FROM v$sga_dynamic_components;
```

The results of the query should be similar to the following:

```
COMPONENT                            CURRENT_SIZE
-----------------------------------  ------------
shared pool                              83886080
large pool                                4194304
java pool                                 4194304
streams pool                                    0
DEFAULT buffer cache                    134217728
KEEP buffer cache                               0
RECYCLE buffer cache                            0
DEFAULT 2K buffer cache                         0
DEFAULT 4K buffer cache                         0
DEFAULT 8K buffer cache                         0
DEFAULT 16K buffer cache                        0
DEFAULT 32K buffer cache                        0
ASM Buffer Cache                                0
```

EXERCISE 10.16: Modify the Size of the SGA

How do you know whether the SGA is adequately sized to do its job or, conversely, is oversized and wasting memory that could be better utilized by other applications on the host computer? Before you can answer this question, you should tune the applications that are using Oracle XE so that their SQL statements execute as efficiently as you want them to—the exercises in the "Application-Tuning Exercises" section of this chapter introduce examples of this process.

Once you are happy with how the SQL executes in your system and the current instance has been operating under a representative load, use a SQL*Plus session or the SQL Commands page of Oracle Application Express to execute the following query:

```
SELECT sga_size,
       sga_size_factor AS size_factor,
       estd_physical_reads AS estimated_physical_reads
  FROM v$sga_target_advice
 ORDER BY sga_size_factor;
```

The results of the query should be similar to the following:

```
SGA_SIZE SIZE_FACTOR ESTIMATED_PHYSICAL_READS
-------- ----------- ------------------------
     165         .75                    15371
     220           1                    11305
     275        1.25                     8312
     330         1.5                     8312
     385        1.75                     8312
     440           2                     8312
```

The records in the result set indicate estimates of how many physical reads would be necessary with various SGA sizes. The preceding fictitious sample results illustrate the following points:

- For comparison purposes, the record with the SIZE_FACTOR equal to 1 indicates the current size of the SGA (220MB) and the estimated number of physical reads (11,305).

- If you were to decrease the SGA size to 165MB, the estimated number of physical reads would increase to 15,371.

- If you were to increase the SGA size to 275MB, the estimated number of physical reads would decrease to 8312.

- Further increasing the size of the SGA beyond 275MB would be a complete waste of memory because it would not reduce the estimated number of physical reads.

In my experience using Oracle XE and its companion Oracle Application Express product for a while, I've found that the instance performs better with a slightly larger SGA, as the preceding fictitious results seem to indicate. You can modify the overall size of the SGA (specifically, the SGA_TARGET parameter) from the SGA page of Oracle Application Express, as shown in Figure 10-10. Simply enter the new size, specified as a number of megabytes, in the SGA Target field and click Apply Changes. If you want to increase the SGA size, you must restart the instance for the new setting to take effect.

EXERCISE 10.17: Display Information About PGA Memory

To display more specific information about the memory used by PGA memory areas, click the Configure PGA hyperlink on the Memory page of Oracle Application Express. The page that appears should be similar to Figure 10-11.

The total, aggregate amount of the PGA memory available to sessions at work in an Oracle XE database instance is set by the PGA_AGGREGATE_TARGET initialization parameter as a number of bytes, kilobytes, megabytes, or gigabytes. You should also set the WORKAREA_SIZE_POLICY initialization parameter to AUTO, which allows Oracle to automatically tune the sizes of all internal PGA memory structures without the need for manual configuration; by default, an Oracle XE's instance is configured in this manner.

NOTE
PGA_AGGREGATE_TARGET does not limit how much memory Oracle XE devotes to PGA memory, it simply specifies the preferred target.

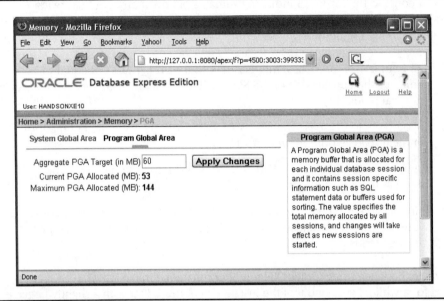

FIGURE 10-11. *The PGA page displays the aggregate total amount of PGA memory currently allocated to database sessions, as well as the overall target and maximum amount of PGA memory.*

EXERCISE 10.18: Modify the Allowable PGA Memory

Before trying to figure out whether the PGA aggregate target is properly set, again, it is good practice to tune the SQL submitted by various Oracle XE–based applications. Once you do this and the current instance has been operating under a representative load, use a SQL*Plus session or the SQL Commands page of Oracle Application Express to execute the following query:

```
SELECT pga_target_for_estimate AS pga_size,
       pga_target_factor AS size_factor,
       estd_pga_cache_hit_percentage
  FROM v$pga_target_advice;
```

This report is similar to the query in Exercise 10.16—it shows how smaller and larger PGA aggregate sizes would affect the performance of the system. The following example results indicate that the performance related to PGA memory allocations would not change, even if you were to reduce the total amount of memory available for PGAs:

PGA_SIZE	SIZE_FACTOR	ESTD_PGA_CACHE_HIT_PERCENTAGE
15728640	.25	100
31457280	.5	100
47185920	.75	100
62914560	1	100
75497472	1.2	100
88080384	1.4	100
100663296	1.6	100
113246208	1.8	100
125829120	2	100
188743680	3	100
251658240	4	100
377487360	6	100
503316480	8	100

You can modify the PGA_AGGREGATE_TARGET parameter from the PGA page of Oracle Application Express, as shown in Figure 10-11. Enter the new size, specified in megabytes, in the Aggregate PGA Target field and click Apply Changes.

Chapter Summary

This chapter has provided you with a brief introduction to Oracle performance-tuning topics, including application tuning and database instance tuning:

- The basic objective of tuning should be to achieve adequate response times that do not detract from user productivity and do not place an unnecessary load on the system that might otherwise detract from the performance of other system operations.

- In most cases, application-related problems, such as poorly written SQL, large tables without adequate indexes, and poor transaction design, are typically to blame when a system limits user productivity.

- Oracle XE database instance tuning is something to do after you are sure that application SQL executes rather efficiently. You can resize an instance's SGA and PGA memory areas to affect how much work the system must do to serve its applications.

Index

C

T

GET YOUR FREE SUBSCRIPTION
TO ORACLE MAGAZINE

Oracle Magazine is essential gear for today's information technology professionals. Stay informed and increase your productivity with every issue of *Oracle Magazine*. Inside each free bimonthly issue you'll get:

IF THERE ARE OTHER ORACLE USERS AT YOUR LOCATION WHO WOULD LIKE TO RECEIVE THEIR OWN SUBSCRIPTION TO ORACLE MAGAZINE, PLEASE PHOTOCOPY THIS FORM AND PASS IT ALONG.

- Up-to-date information on Oracle Database, Oracle Application Server, Web development, enterprise grid computing, database technology, and business trends

- Third-party vendor news and announcements

- Technical articles on Oracle and partner products, technologies, and operating environments

- Development and administration tips

- Real-world customer stories

Three easy ways to subscribe:

① Web
Visit our Web site at otn.oracle.com/oraclemagazine. You'll find a subscription form there, plus much more!

② Fax
Complete the questionnaire on the back of this card and fax the questionnaire side only to +1.847.763.9638.

③ Mail
Complete the questionnaire on the back of this card and mail it to P.O. Box 1263, Skokie, IL 60076-8263

ORACLE®

FREE SUBSCRIPTION

○ **Yes, please send me a FREE subscription to** *Oracle Magazine*.   ○ **NO**
To receive a free subscription to *Oracle Magazine*, you must fill out the entire card, sign it, and date it
(incomplete cards cannot be processed or acknowledged). You can also fax your application to +1.847.763.9638.
Or subscribe at our Web site at otn.oracle.com/oraclemagazine

○ From time to time, Oracle Publishing allows our partners exclusive access to our e-mail addresses for special promotions and announcements. To be included in this program, please check this circle.

○ Oracle Publishing allows sharing of our mailing list with selected third parties. If you prefer your mailing address not to be included in this program, please check here. If at any time you would like to be removed from this mailing list, please contact Customer Service at +1.847.647.9630 or send an e-mail to oracle@halldata.com.

signature (required)   date

X

name   title

company   e-mail address

street/p.o. box

city/state/zip or postal code   telephone

country   fax

YOU MUST ANSWER ALL TEN QUESTIONS BELOW.

① WHAT IS THE PRIMARY BUSINESS ACTIVITY OF YOUR FIRM AT THIS LOCATION? (check one only)
- ☐ 01 Aerospace and Defense Manufacturing
- ☐ 02 Application Service Provider
- ☐ 03 Automotive Manufacturing
- ☐ 04 Chemicals, Oil and Gas
- ☐ 05 Communications and Media
- ☐ 06 Construction/Engineering
- ☐ 07 Consumer Sector/Consumer Packaged Goods
- ☐ 08 Education
- ☐ 09 Financial Services/Insurance
- ☐ 10 Government (civil)
- ☐ 11 Government (military)
- ☐ 12 Healthcare
- ☐ 13 High Technology Manufacturing, OEM
- ☐ 14 Integrated Software Vendor
- ☐ 15 Life Sciences (Biotech, Pharmaceuticals)
- ☐ 16 Mining
- ☐ 17 Retail/Wholesale/Distribution
- ☐ 18 Systems Integrator, VAR/VAD
- ☐ 19 Telecommunications
- ☐ 20 Travel and Transportation
- ☐ 21 Utilities (electric, gas, sanitation, water)
- ☐ 98 Other Business and Services

② WHICH OF THE FOLLOWING BEST DESCRIBES YOUR PRIMARY JOB FUNCTION? (check one only)
Corporate Management/Staff
- ☐ 01 Executive Management (President, Chair, CEO, CFO, Owner, Partner, Principal)
- ☐ 02 Finance/Administrative Management (VP/Director/ Manager/Controller, Purchasing, Administration)
- ☐ 03 Sales/Marketing Management (VP/Director/Manager)
- ☐ 04 Computer Systems/Operations Management (CIO/VP/Director/ Manager MIS, Operations)
IS/IT Staff
- ☐ 05 Systems Development/ Programming Management
- ☐ 06 Systems Development/ Programming Staff
- ☐ 07 Consulting
- ☐ 08 DBA/Systems Administrator
- ☐ 09 Education/Training
- ☐ 10 Technical Support Director/Manager
- ☐ 11 Other Technical Management/Staff
- ☐ 98 Other

③ WHAT IS YOUR CURRENT PRIMARY OPERATING PLATFORM? (select all that apply)
- ☐ 01 Digital Equipment UNIX
- ☐ 02 Digital Equipment VAX VMS
- ☐ 03 HP UNIX
- ☐ 04 IBM AIX
- ☐ 05 IBM UNIX
- ☐ 06 Java
- ☐ 07 Linux
- ☐ 08 Macintosh
- ☐ 09 MS-DOS
- ☐ 10 MVS
- ☐ 11 NetWare
- ☐ 12 Network Computing
- ☐ 13 OpenVMS
- ☐ 14 SCO UNIX
- ☐ 15 Sequent DYNIX/ptx
- ☐ 16 Sun Solaris/SunOS
- ☐ 17 SVR4
- ☐ 18 UnixWare
- ☐ 19 Windows
- ☐ 20 Windows NT
- ☐ 21 Other UNIX
- ☐ 98 Other
- 99 ☐ None of the above

④ DO YOU EVALUATE, SPECIFY, RECOMMEND, OR AUTHORIZE THE PURCHASE OF ANY OF THE FOLLOWING? (check all that apply)
- ☐ 01 Hardware
- ☐ 02 Software
- ☐ 03 Application Development Tools
- ☐ 04 Database Products
- ☐ 05 Internet or Intranet Products
- 99 ☐ None of the above

⑤ IN YOUR JOB, DO YOU USE OR PLAN TO PURCHASE ANY OF THE FOLLOWING PRODUCTS? (check all that apply)
Software
- ☐ 01 Business Graphics
- ☐ 02 CAD/CAE/CAM
- ☐ 03 CASE
- ☐ 04 Communications
- ☐ 05 Database Management
- ☐ 06 File Management
- ☐ 07 Finance
- ☐ 08 Java
- ☐ 09 Materials Resource Planning
- ☐ 10 Multimedia Authoring
- ☐ 11 Networking
- ☐ 12 Office Automation
- ☐ 13 Order Entry/Inventory Control
- ☐ 14 Programming
- ☐ 15 Project Management
- ☐ 16 Scientific and Engineering
- ☐ 17 Spreadsheets
- ☐ 18 Systems Management
- ☐ 19 Workflow

Hardware
- ☐ 20 Macintosh
- ☐ 21 Mainframe
- ☐ 22 Massively Parallel Processing
- ☐ 23 Minicomputer
- ☐ 24 PC
- ☐ 25 Network Computer
- ☐ 26 Symmetric Multiprocessing
- ☐ 27 Workstation
Peripherals
- ☐ 28 Bridges/Routers/Hubs/Gateways
- ☐ 29 CD-ROM Drives
- ☐ 30 Disk Drives/Subsystems
- ☐ 31 Modems
- ☐ 32 Tape Drives/Subsystems
- ☐ 33 Video Boards/Multimedia
Services
- ☐ 34 Application Service Provider
- ☐ 35 Consulting
- ☐ 36 Education/Training
- ☐ 37 Maintenance
- ☐ 38 Online Database Services
- ☐ 39 Support
- ☐ 40 Technology-Based Training
- ☐ 98 Other
- 99 ☐ None of the above

⑥ WHAT ORACLE PRODUCTS ARE IN USE AT YOUR SITE? (check all that apply)
Oracle E-Business Suite
- ☐ 01 Oracle Marketing
- ☐ 02 Oracle Sales
- ☐ 03 Oracle Order Fulfillment
- ☐ 04 Oracle Supply Chain Management
- ☐ 05 Oracle Procurement
- ☐ 06 Oracle Manufacturing
- ☐ 07 Oracle Maintenance Management
- ☐ 08 Oracle Service
- ☐ 09 Oracle Contracts
- ☐ 10 Oracle Projects
- ☐ 11 Oracle Financials
- ☐ 12 Oracle Human Resources
- ☐ 13 Oracle Interaction Center
- ☐ 14 Oracle Communications/Utilities (modules)
- ☐ 15 Oracle Public Sector/University (modules)
- ☐ 16 Oracle Financial Services (modules)
Server/Software
- ☐ 17 Oracle9i
- ☐ 18 Oracle9i Lite
- ☐ 19 Oracle8i
- ☐ 20 Other Oracle database
- ☐ 21 Oracle9i Application Server
- ☐ 22 Oracle9i Application Server Wireless
- ☐ 23 Oracle Small Business Suite

Tools
- ☐ 24 Oracle Developer Suite
- ☐ 25 Oracle Discoverer
- ☐ 26 Oracle JDeveloper
- ☐ 27 Oracle Migration Workbench
- ☐ 28 Oracle9i AS Portal
- ☐ 29 Oracle Warehouse Builder
Oracle Services
- ☐ 30 Oracle Outsourcing
- ☐ 31 Oracle Consulting
- ☐ 32 Oracle Education
- ☐ 33 Oracle Support
- ☐ 98 Other
- 99 ☐ None of the above

⑦ WHAT OTHER DATABASE PRODUCTS ARE IN USE AT YOUR SITE? (check all that apply)
- ☐ 01 Access
- ☐ 02 Baan
- ☐ 03 dbase
- ☐ 04 Gupta
- ☐ 05 IBM DB2
- ☐ 06 Informix
- ☐ 07 Ingres
- ☐ 08 Microsoft Access
- ☐ 09 Microsoft SQL Server
- ☐ 10 PeopleSoft
- ☐ 11 Progress
- ☐ 12 SAP
- ☐ 13 Sybase
- ☐ 14 VSAM
- ☐ 98 Other
- 99 ☐ None of the above

⑧ WHAT OTHER APPLICATION SERVER PRODUCTS ARE IN USE AT YOUR SITE? (check all that apply)
- ☐ 01 BEA
- ☐ 02 IBM
- ☐ 03 Sybase
- ☐ 04 Sun
- ☐ 05 Other

⑨ DURING THE NEXT 12 MONTHS, HOW MUCH DO YOU ANTICIPATE YOUR ORGANIZATION WILL SPEND ON COMPUTER HARDWARE, SOFTWARE, PERIPHERALS, AND SERVICES FOR YOUR LOCATION? (check only one)
- ☐ 01 Less than $10,000
- ☐ 02 $10,000 to $49,999
- ☐ 03 $50,000 to $99,999
- ☐ 04 $100,000 to $499,999
- ☐ 05 $500,000 to $999,999
- ☐ 06 $1,000,000 and over

⑩ WHAT IS YOUR COMPANY'S YEARLY SALES REVENUE? (please choose one)
- ☐ 01 $500,000,000 and above
- ☐ 02 $100,000,000 to $500,000,000
- ☐ 03 $50,000,000 to $100,000,000
- ☐ 04 $5,000,000 to $50,000,000
- ☐ 05 $1,000,000 to $5,000,000

100103

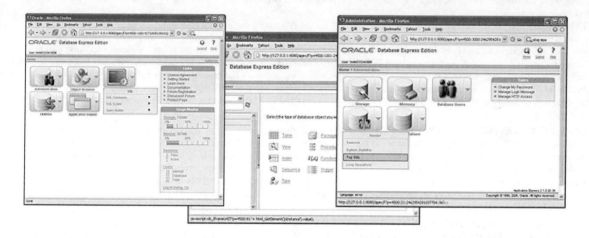